CITIZEN TRUDEAU

CITIZEN TRUDEAU

AN INTELLECTUAL BIOGRAPHY | 1944–1965

ALLEN MILLS

OXFORD
UNIVERSITY PRESS

OXFORD
UNIVERSITY PRESS

Oxford University Press is a department of the University of Oxford.
It furthers the University's objective of excellence in research, scholarship,
and education by publishing worldwide. Oxford is a registered trade mark of
Oxford University Press in the UK and in certain other countries.

Published in Canada by
Oxford University Press
8 Sampson Mews, Suite 204,
Don Mills, Ontario M3C 0H5 Canada

www.oupcanada.com

Library and Archives Canada Cataloguing in Publication

Mills, Allen George, 1945-, author
Citizen Trudeau : an intellectual biography, 1944-1965 / Allen Mills.

Includes index.
ISBN 978-0-19-900596-3 (bound)

1. Trudeau, Pierre Elliott, 1919-2000—Philosophy.
2. Trudeau, Pierre Elliott, 1919-2000—Political and social views.
3. Trudeau, Pierre Elliott, 1919-2000—Knowledge and learning.
4. Prime ministers—Canada—Intellectual life. 5. Prime ministers—
Canada—Biography. I. Title.

FC626.T7M54 2016   971.064092   C2015-906976-9

Cover image: TheTrudeau Papers, LAC MG 26-02, box and file 8.22

1 2 3 4 — 19 18 17 16

Since in all sorts of ways a modern State is a State which governs a great deal, it is important above all for citizens to seek ways by which they will be governed well.
Pierre Elliott Trudeau, 1954.

For Yana

Contents

PREFACE

————— • ◆ • —————

I am grateful to Marc Lalonde and the literary executors of the Trudeau Estate for giving me access to Trudeau's Papers in Library and Archives Canada, in Ottawa. Christian Rioux and Sophie Tellier were helpful guides to these papers. To Alexandre Trudeau I am especially grateful for letting me examine his father's library in his house on Pine Avenue in Montreal. The experience was more than obviously remarkable: it was the only occasion ever when I actually put my life at risk in the cause of scholarship as I perched atop a twenty-foot ladder to reach some of the highest shelves. Carol Harvey has been a loyal accomplice and has helped me immensely with translations of Trudeau's French. Others who offered counsel on translation were Belle Jarniewski, Anna Borisenkova, and Adina Balint-Babos. Of course I remain responsible for any infelicities of translation. Sid Noel, master scholar, has been a constant supporter as has Ramsay Cook whose vast knowledge and sharp mind challenged many of my assumptions. Charlie Peters and Mildred Gutkin taught me much about English grammar and style and there have been other indispensible intellectual companions along the way: Peter Ferris, Joanne Boucher, Lloyd Axworthy, Paul Vogt, Donn Hanna, Jeffrey Anderson, Andrew Valko, and Bill Blaikie. Then there are all the lads in the coffee shop, Richard, Tony, Barry, Gord, and Bill: "Up United." Ed Broadbent set me thinking about Trudeau early on and he instructed me a great deal in the meaning of social democracy. He shares a lot in common with Trudeau. Jen Rubio at Oxford University Press gave me constant editorial encouragement and guidance and there was the indispensable help there of Michelle Welsh and Heather Macdougall. Thanks are also due to Petr and Alena Červenych in whose house much of this book was written. And, finally, I dedicate this work to someone who entered my life almost exactly at the same time as I started writing it. May she flourish in Pierre Trudeau's Canada.

INTRODUCTION

Even many years after his death, Pierre Elliott Trudeau (1919–2000) remains a controversial figure. The signposts that might over time have pointed to more definite conclusions about his life and politics have, as it turns out, produced only confusion because so many of them, sometimes wilfully, have been made to point in different directions. Perhaps Trudeau was partially to blame. He was blessed—some would say cursed—with an unbending inclination to say impolitic and disagreeable things, often about those in positions of power, and this unwavering contrariness inevitably landed him in trouble. Consequently, many of his critics, especially in Quebec, have felt little compunction in responding to him in kind, and adding something extra, just for him. They have not quite realized the extent to which they have been unhinged by him. With Trudeau the debate is never lukewarm; discussion quickly comes to a boiling point. In one bizarre, "public" survey, in 2007, Trudeau was judged to have been the "worst Canadian in history," no less.[1] In the estimation of the respondents in that survey, at least, he places slightly behind the country's most notorious serial-killers and child-molesters. Getting to the truth about Trudeau involves swimming in perilous waters where there lurk fish with razor-sharp teeth.

Yet while there are those who will wish to destroy him, others have come to praise him. Some have even raised him to the empyrean of statesmanship. Trudeau's tenacious hold on prime ministerial office for the better part of sixteen years between 1968 and 1984 is surely one measure of his singular prowess. Others cite his resolve during the October Crisis of 1970 and his defeat of the sovereigntists in the referendum ten years later. In most reckonings the Charter of Rights and Freedoms, entrenched in the Canadian constitution in 1982, is mentioned. The Charter, which has had such huge consequence, would not have come about if Trudeau had not championed it, a rare instance of a single politician making a world of difference. From Guy Laforest, often a critic of Trudeau, has come an almost panegyrical estimate of his political effectiveness:

> Trudeau was the last of our founders. He was the equivalent of Lincoln for twentieth-century Canada. He was the last political leader who was able substantially to modify the thought and the idea of the foundation of Confederation. What Trudeau almost single-handedly achieved in the early 1980s is incredible; whether you like it or not, you have to be awed by the achievements of the man. He changed the political culture of Canada from a culture enshrined in the traditions of British parliamentarianism to a political culture much closer to eighteenth-century republicanism, much closer to American influence.[2]

James Madison, then, moved among us, along with Alexander Hamilton and Abraham Lincoln.[3]

Alan Cairns, another noted Canadian political scientist, has also been very complimentary:

> The Charter . . . clearly was designed with two purposes in mind by its chief architect, Trudeau. The prime one . . . is . . . a way of protecting citizen rights against the state. From Trudeau's perspective, however, the much more important goal was the attempt to generate a national identity, and this really meant an attack on provincialism. It was a way of trying to get Canadians to think of themselves as possessors of a common body of rights independent of geographical location, which would constitute a lens through which they would then view what all governments were doing. So it was really a de-provincializing strategy, primarily aimed at Quebec nationalism, but also at the general centrifugal pressures that were developing across the federal system. Trudeau's thought on this goes well back to before he entered politics.[4]

Some have claimed that, not only did Trudeau perform prodigious feats of political initiative but he did so in fulfillment of
some kind of grand intellectual design. For Trudeau's renown also
includes a reputation as a political thinker. Sometimes dismissively
and at other times approvingly, he has been called a philosopher-
king. Mackenzie King he did not wish to be, degrading politics and
debasing its idealistic coinage through cynical manoeuvres and
obfuscating accommodations. Trudeau aspired to think clearly and
systematically about all matters political. He was, it has been said, a
man of cold Cartesian logic and implacable reason. In office, he was
an intellectual at work, coolly serving the common good. By this
measure his life was not just a practical one but a theoretical one as
well. Trudeau himself believed that his thought and action were of
one piece. His period in government, he said in his *Memoirs*, was an
exercise in applying an already established philosophy, one he had
established in his mind by the time he had left the London School
of Economics (LSE) in 1948:

> When I left that institution, my fundamental choices had been
> made. I was to acquire more knowledge and to encounter count-
> less options throughout my life. But my basic philosophy was
> established from that time on, and it was on these premises that I
> based all my future political decisions; it was that philosophy that
> underlay all my writings.[5]

Although it is tempting to write about the extent to which Trudeau
while in political office after 1965 was true to his early beliefs, it is
one that I will mainly resist. My principal purpose is not to deal
with Trudeau the parliamentary politician and prime minister but
rather to explore a less well-known side of him, namely his role as
a public intellectual in Quebec in the 1950s and early 1960s. What
I am seeking to do is to map those theoretical structures which,
he said, he had acquired by 1948 and which he developed in the
next seventeen years. My aim, then, stealing the terminology of

Trudeau's English mentor Harold Laski, is to establish the grammar of his politics and to delineate how his early political theory emerged, and how it was structured and cohered. Inevitably the later parliamentary period will come into the picture. Regardless of what his critics believe, it cannot be seriously maintained that he ceased to think after he became an elected politician and inevitably his thought moved in new directions later on. But his eventual political career is not my principal focus.

My subject is not someone of whom I think ill or whom I disdain. Indeed for the most part I think well of Trudeau, although it has not always been so and even now it cannot be completely so. I was a young immigrant to Canada in September 1967, fresh off the plane from Ireland and with newly minted labourist ideals in the pocket of my well-worn Harris Tweed jacket. I cut my teeth in Canadian politics less than a year later, knocking on doors for Doug Fisher, the federal New Democratic Party (NDP) candidate in York Centre, in Toronto. This was the famous election in which "Trudeaumania" swept the land and flowers and hosannas were showered upon this strange and accidental eminence. For a while Trudeau was adored and he won a majority government, the first such victory for the Liberals since 1953. In Toronto, especially, it was not a good time to be an NDPer, or a Progressive Conservative (PC) for that matter. Estimable Tories like Dalton Camp went down to defeat, along with equally impressive social democrats like Fisher.

The election taught me two sharp lessons. The first was that a tweed jacket was definitely not suitable attire for steamy summer days in airless, fluorescent-lit, apartment corridors in Downsview. The other had to do with the futility of door-step discussion with voters who had already made up their minds and definitely not in favour of one's own candidate. They stared at me incredulously when they learned I was representing some other party than the Liberals. Campaigning, door-to-door, against Trudeau, certainly in that riding, in that election, was like conducting a conversation in the midst of a cyclone. While the exchanges were pleasant enough they were seemingly pointless. My next "brush" with Trudeau was two years later, during the infamous October Crisis. By now living in hippie-like simplicity in a farmhouse in Maple, just north of Toronto, I thought that Trudeau's response to the kidnappings by the Front de libération du Québec (FLQ) of James Cross, the British trade commissioner, and Pierre Laporte, the provincial cabinet minister, was excessive and needlessly destructive of civil liberties. I was part of a small platoon of Canadians—in my case a soon-to-be Canadian—who thought that Trudeau had taken a sledgehammer to crush a peanut, to use the apposite phrase of Tommy Douglas, the NDP leader. Soon afterwards, I was approached, I thought, to serve on an Independent Citizens' Commission of Inquiry into the War Measures Act. I have always supposed that because there was literally no one in rural Ontario who was opposed to Trudeau's actions except myself, I was considered mainly in order to secure some sort of regional balance on the Commission. To my knowledge it never met or, at least, I was never informed of its meetings. Perhaps I had misunderstood the invitation. After participating in the Waffle group, the left-wing, nationalist ginger-group in the NDP in the late 1960s and early 1970s, and after disagreeing with what I regarded as its quasi-separatist stance on Quebec, I decamped and worked for Ed Broadbent's campaign for the NDP leadership in 1971.

In 1967 Ed Broadbent had been one of my first teachers at York University. It was he—though a social democrat to his core—who introduced me to the ideas of Michael Oakeshott, the English conservative philosopher, something for which I have always been grateful. I still enjoy reciting to my freshmen classes at the University of Winnipeg Oakeshott's oracular observations about how politics is unsuitable for the young and inexperienced.[6] Perhaps I am a sadist. I also acquired from Broadbent deep misgivings about Trudeau. I helped him research his own indictment of Trudeau's politics, which in the counter-cultural argot of the times he called *The Liberal Rip-Off*.[7] In the next fourteen years I never once voted for Trudeau's Liberals and by 1984 it was, I thought, time for him to go. Who can forget that awful list of patronage appointments as he departed the federal scene? Since then I have had second thoughts, though not about that list. Perhaps it is my sense of what is politically possible that has been adjusted, something about how experience teaches us about feeling the balance of a thing in our hands, as Oakeshott put it.[8] The obduracy of the established order in Canada and the difficulty of undertaking transformative policies in a country that is so diverse and fractious have led me to conclude that, all things considered, Trudeau was among the most accomplished of our prime ministers. He achieved reforms in many areas; he was a Churchillian rock in the referendum in Quebec on sovereignty-association in 1980; his governments were in many respects progressive; and there can be no disputing his personal and intellectual brilliance. And of course there was the Charter of Rights and Freedoms. By the measure of the Charter alone a case can be made for regarding him as the maker of the modern Canadian political identity, doing for Canada today what Sir John A. Macdonald achieved in post-Confederation times.

But even with a profound regard for him—some will no doubt see it as more—the task of the biographer cannot be to write a partial account of his subject and, of course, whatever *is* claimed about him cannot be woven out of thin air. Though not a fashionable view, my judgment is that there must be a factual basis to claims about the past, even if the project of a pure historical objectivity is of course misconceived and ultimately impossible. We will never know exactly how it was and so there will never cease to be alternative interpretations of Trudeau. But whatever views are held of him, these should at least be based on the "facts." Leszek Kołakowski put it well when he talked of his work on Marxism as offering a "handbook" that included "the principal facts that are likely to be of use to anyone seeking an introduction to the subject."[9] I would like to think that I have done the same for Trudeau. There may be no "objective" or "final" version of history but some versions are more objective than others. What is apparent about the historiography of the life of Trudeau, in this case the development of his political thought between 1944 and 1965, is the degree to which much of it has been written either in conscious dismissal of the "facts" or, in some cases, without any knowledge of them at all.

This book is, then, an exercise in a sort of inductive history. What follows examines Trudeau's thought empirically, analytically, and thematically under several categories: early influences, Quebec and French Canada, religion, the state and economics, international affairs, federalism and the constitution, and, finally, party politics. As I proceeded what became clearer and clearer to me was that, contrary to the received opinion of him as some kind of *philosophe* and Enlightenment rationalist, what he was gestating was a theory, to be sure, but one that was more about political action in the real world than about abstractions in an ideal one. He was always thinking about what constituted valid, effective political action. Out of this has emerged what might be called my "pragmatic" version of Trudeau. But action was not his only concern. Action must be wedded to intelligence so that thinking clearly about political questions was essential too. While he believed that there was a limit to the application of theory to reality, this did not lead to a denial of the relevance of theory and principle altogether. Trudeau advanced the project of what I will call "intelligent realism" and in so doing he asserted not just the importance of an intellectual understanding of politics but also a profound belief in the power and relevance of human ingenuity and agency. Trudeau knew of the extent to which politics existed in a world of determinisms: classes rising and falling, the intransigence of vested interests, and the cruelty of collective violence. While only too well aware of these he insisted on independence of personal thought and action. Above all, he held that politics required individuals of conscience, persons unafraid to speak and act publicly and frankly about what they believed. Such a perspective is surely timeless. But Trudeau offered more.

A Portrait of the Activist as a Young Man

———— ⸱✦⸱ ————

For in a young man the yearning for "action" is at times stronger than that for "knowledge"; and the very number of deeds still undone is an entreaty to prefer the World to the University. But the first to act is not always the wisest; and what is needlessly premature is useless. Besides there may be some truth in the aphorism that "avant 30 ans un homme n'est pas intelligent." With such thoughts in mind, I easily refrain from accomplishing such little things as may be of some utility to-day, in the hope that reflexion [sic] and study may make my work fitter to-morrow.

Pierre Elliott Trudeau

"My friend," said he, leading me back past the old pear tree still in healthy bloom, "to please the fashionable wits, you speak rather lightly of your early philosophy. I pity any man who in his youth did not have a passion either for or against liberty."

Charles Péguy

I

Much that has been written about Trudeau's early life has been turned topsy-turvy by the opening up of his private papers, the Trudeau Papers (TP), in the National Archives in Ottawa, after his death in September 2000. These papers have helped John English, Max Nemni, and Monique Nemni to provide not just new, unexpected perspectives on the young Trudeau but, sometimes, unsettling and shocking ones too.[1] In contrast the first generation of biographies—notably those by Stephen Clarkson and Christina McCall, Michel Vastel and Richard Gwyn—must now be seen as having been fatally compromised by psychological conjecture and factual gaps and errors.[2] One early biographer did have the singular advantage of extensive interviews with Trudeau but, without access to his private papers, George Radwanski too had little opportunity to measure how accurate Trudeau's memory was.[3] We now know that Trudeau could be selective in his recollections of his earliest political activities and beliefs. Nevertheless he did have the integrity to preserve his papers and to allow early access to them after his death.

Second-generation biographers, such as English and the Nemnis, confirm that the young Trudeau was indeed a precocious intellectual-in-the-making, perhaps even more gifted than had been thought. He possessed an uncommonly curious mind. And he was a perfectionist in what he wanted to say. Many of his letters and essays went through several drafts and many of these he kept. Indeed he retained a great deal of the records and paraphernalia of his life: tickets to the theatre and dance performances and piano recitals, and maps and mementos from far-away places. He even kept his traffic tickets.[4] To his questing mind he added an unshakeable passion for ethical and theoretical inquiry and exactitude. These characteristics never left him. Trudeau was, from an early age, a morally self-conscious and deeply serious individual. Paradoxical as it may seem, this might have originated in his privileged background. Trudeau grew up in a family of great wealth. His father, Charles, had made the passage from a small family farm in St-Michel de Napierville, near Montreal, to urban lawyer and successful businessman. After the purchase by Imperial Oil of his gas stations and Automobile Owners' Association for $1.2 million in 1931, he became one of the first Canadians to be made fabulously wealthy by the new petroleum economy. He was a thoroughly self-made man and suddenly very rich.

Charles and his wife, Grace, were well able to afford a privileged education for their son, Pierre-Phillipe, who, with the sudden death of Charles in 1935, came to manage and to benefit from the family's large fortune. A lifetime of financial security was afforded him. In the forty-six years of Trudeau's life before he entered federal politics, he only belonged to the conventional world of the wage-salariat for two short periods: first, between 1949 and 1951, when he was in the Privy Council Office (PCO) as a "functionnaire, classe 1" with an annual salary of $2,880; and then between 1961 and 1965, when he was a professor.[5] Even his life as a lawyer was unusual. In the 1950s he ran a small, one-man legal practice out of his mother's home, where he lived for much of the time, but such legal work as he did perform was intermittent, sometimes provided pro bono and, when it was remunerated, often insignificantly so. His income from print, radio, and television journalism and public speaking was hardly munificent either.[6] While his independent means eventually allowed him such personal indulgences as made-to-measure suits and European sports cars, he mainly used his wealth to underwrite a life of intellectual inquiry and legal and political activism: paying for his university education in the 1940s and, thereafter, financing foreign travel, subsidizing the publishing costs of *Cité Libre*, engaging in extra-parliamentary politics, representing individuals in human rights cases and trade unions in arbitrations, and, altogether, pursuing the life of a public intellectual. It was a full life and a hard-working one too. Nothing is farther from the truth than the allegation that Trudeau was a lazy man. Also conspicuously evident early on were his phenomenal gifts of memory, perspicuity, and articulate expressiveness, all rolled into one extraordinary bundle of dramatic energy and personal ambition. And so intelligence, education, and inherited wealth begat in him a near-aristocratic demeanour of political independence, outspokenness, and an unquenchable inquisitiveness about the meaning of things.

His education by Jesuit priests at Brébeuf College in Outremont contributed greatly to his emerging character. John English and Max and Monique Nemni argue convincingly that the young Trudeau was very much an obedient son of the Church. He saw his life as following the path of Catholic piety and discipline, not so much as Christian in *The Pilgrim's Progress*, for that would have been much too Protestant an example (although sections of the Church came to accuse him of that too) but as a St. Francis Xavier or a St. Ignatius of Loyola, following the latter's "Spiritual Exercises."[7] In time Trudeau would become a more independent-minded Catholic layman, a personalist, and a socialist. But he remained, throughout his life, a believer in God, and, as the journalist Norman DePoe once put it, "an unostentatiously dutiful Roman Catholic."[8] It is said that his faith was sorely tested after the death of his son Michel in an avalanche in British Columbia in 1998, two years before his own passing.[9] But in his youth, certainly, Trudeau operated readily within the assumptions of conventional Catholic theology and practice: obedience to authority, exercises of denial and mortification, receiving the sacraments, and attending retreats. Later he became a radical Catholic and some suggested that he held heretical views.[10] On metaphysical matters Trudeau always evinced a deep curiosity about human freedom, the role of conscience, and the mysteries of divine grace. If it is not correct to represent Trudeau as a mystic, a hair-shirted anchorite or a saint-in-waiting, or even as an orthodox Catholic, nevertheless he was more like these than the popular conceptions of him as a playboy, a hedonist, and a skeptic. His was a deeply ascetic and contemplative disposition. Throughout his life Trudeau regularly attended retreats with the Dominican fathers and meditations with Benedictines.[11] Michael Higgins, an authority on Canadian Catholicism, recalls:

Trudeau frequently chose Saint Benôit-du-Lac—a community of the Solesmes [Benedictine] tradition—for his retreats, as well as meditating and attending the Hours and the Eucharist at Montreal's Benedictine community with some regularity. I saw him there once at the Office of Sext, seated on the floor, meditating, emptying his mind, his personal mantra methodically recited, his visage serene, posture perfect, surrounded by young McGill students and fellow intellectuals such as Charles Taylor.[12]

Trudeau especially expressed his sense of the transcendent in his love and respect for nature and of human striving within it, as well as in his exacting and often courageous pursuit of abstract questions and especially the meaning of the good. One of the earliest revelations of his sense of the mystery of nature was his essay, "Ascetic in a Canoe," published in 1944 in *Journal JÉC* in Montreal. B.W. Powe, who has written extensively about the spiritual side of Trudeau, sees him as having a fundamentally religious temperament. If his comments are a trifle hyperbolic, they are nonetheless apposite: "Yet we also see in his actions and in his notes the hunger for breadth, and for breath, the broadening of being. We feel momentum in his soul's urgings. And we sense the looming contests. His mysticism will help to make him charismatic. It will lead him into fiery engagements, raging disputes. He was writing scripts for the self."[13] Michael Higgins puts it less dramatically but no less pointedly: "His spirituality, although undoubtedly intellectualist in part, was a genuine spirituality of resistance, grounded in love both for justice and for the contemplative dimension."[14]

Until he entered the House of Commons, Trudeau's principal means of expressing his high seriousness were his essays and commentaries in newspapers and reviews and on radio and television. Measured against the most accomplished Canadian political essayists and pamphleteers of his time—Abbé Groulx, André Laurendeau, Léon Dion, Frank Scott, Charles Taylor, Frank Underhill, Barry Callaghan, George Grant, Mordecai Richler, Ramsay Cook, Pierre Vadeboncoeur, Pierre Vallières, Hubert Aquin—Trudeau holds his own very well. His essays were intensively researched and strike the reader as tautly coherent and morally bold. In style, they are lively and concise, elegantly written, unusually provocative, sometimes impertinent and incendiary; they engaged (and still do) a real world of pressing political concerns, in Canada and abroad. Trudeau was a political writer and moralist of powerful apologetic and literary ability and, of course, of immense historical and political consequence. Above all his essays are never boring. They can still be read with pleasure. More, they can be read in order to discern the intellectual suppositions of the one person in modern Canadian politics who, on matters of democracy, human rights, and the contentious issue of nationalism, dragged his country kicking and screaming towards a new political imaginary—or, at least, towards the major revision of an existing one. His political and intellectual significance was and is immense. As more than one commentator has said, the fate of Trudeau's ideas may likely be the fate of Canada, a claim whose poignancy, even with the passage of time and even after his death, has little diminished.[15]

II

Trudeau was famously guarded about discussing his inner self. However, in 1977 he gave eight hour-long interviews to George Radwanski, whose 1978 biography, *Trudeau*, helped consolidate an early interpretation of him as almost preternaturally liberal and rebellious, someone who had emerged—almost from his mother's womb it seems—as a dissident and transgressor of received opinions. Trudeau talked about his early tendencies at Brébeuf to challenge authority. It was a liberating moment, he explained, when he discovered St. Thomas Aquinas's distinction between the morality of the slave and that of the free man:

> I found I could be a free man and yet accept certain moral codes and certain precepts. Hence . . . my love of saying that if I was disciplined it was self-discipline. . . . I guess I was trying . . . to prove a point: "I was I, I was me."[16]

In his early years, he claimed, he had rebelled against well nigh everything, including the influence of his father. A few years later, in the "Foreword" to *Against the Current: Selected Writings 1939– 1996*, Trudeau explained that his behaviour in early childhood was conformist but that later he became "contrarian":

> It was during my teens that I began to change. I still had a thirst for knowledge, but I was looking for consistency too: things had to make sense. The word of an authority was not proof enough: I became argumentative. Fortunately for me, the "authorities" understood, as did my father: if I could justify my disagreement or my disobedience, I would be let off easily.[17]

Trudeau mischievously challenged the dominant nationalist ethos of his classroom:

> Since they were nearly all nationalists, I would say I wasn't. And, when during the history class, they used to applaud the victories of the French armies, I, on the contrary, would applaud the victories of the English armies.[18]

He was "thoroughly disinterested [*sic*] in politics at that stage," including the events of the Second World War. It was only in the 1960s, he said, that he became ambitious for political action. In the early 1940s his interest was in "abstractions" rather than "contingencies." He claimed that he "[had] missed the big war—not by thoughtlessness as much as by inadvertence." The one exception he admitted to his self-imposed political quietism was the federal by-election in Outremont in November 1942 when he spoke on behalf of the anti-conscription candidate, Jean Drapeau. Looking back on that event, thirty-five years later, Trudeau confessed that his intentions had hardly been honourable: "I fear my motives were not the most noble. I think it was sort of to bug the government."[19]

In his *Memoirs*, Trudeau reiterated much of what he had told Radwanski. He emphasized that in his adolescence he was mainly a

contrarian, "opposing conventional wisdoms and challenging prevailing opinions."[20] Particularly he mentioned his indebtedness to
two teachers at Brébeuf, Father Robert Bernier and François Hertel,
the latter the *nom de plume* of Father Rodolphe Dubé. Hertel became
a life-long friend and for Trudeau the paragon of the rebel-priest,
although they would have a falling-out in the 1960s.[21] He introduced Trudeau to new literature, art, and music but, apparently,
not to politics. Indeed in his *Memoirs* Trudeau emphasized that,
with the onset of the war, he had "not [had] the slightest interest in
either the news in general or political developments in particular."
At that moment, he "intellectualized" everything: "Was the war in
Europe important? Sure, I told myself, but ancient campaigns like
the Trojan Wars also deserved to be learned about."[22] He conceded
that, of course, he had known that the war was going on but "the
instinct that has always made me go against prevailing opinion
caused me to affect a certain air of indifference." His interest in
the war, such as it was, he had devoted to the conscription issue.
French Canadians of his generation, he went on, thought of the
war as an affair of the "superpowers." Many of them believed that to
introduce conscription was a breach of the promise made by Prime
Minister Mackenzie King in 1939 that no one would be coerced into
military service. It was not a just war, Trudeau said. Remembering
the by-election in Outremont, his recollection was brief to a fault:
"Drapeau mounted a vigorous campaign, and I participated in it by
speaking at one of his rallies. That was, I believe, my only participation in the politics of that era."[23]

Only after he had entered Harvard in 1944, he said, did he begin
to appreciate the significance of the war, which by then was coming
to an end. It was also there that his early contrarianism was given
a more consistently liberal direction, although he insisted that his
journey towards a fundamental belief in freedom had actually begun
earlier. He had carried with him to Harvard, he said, his growing
fascination with the fundamental questions of political and legal
theory: the nature of the state, the status of individual freedom and
the use of law for social change. These questions, he stated, had

begun to stir at law school at the University of Montreal after 1940. But Trudeau was at pains to point out that his early liberalism, no matter when or where it was conceived, was always anchored under agreeably communitarian skies. His year in Paris in 1946–47 consolidated the influence of two personalists, Jacques Maritain and Emmanuel Mounier, he said, and so his world view was never one of "absolute liberalism": "The person according to these two teachers, is the individual enriched with a social conscience, integrated into the life of the communities around him and the economic context of his time, both of which must in turn give persons the means to exercise their freedom of choice. It was thus that the fundamental notion of justice came to stand alongside that of freedom in my political thought."[24] Later, in 1998, Trudeau made a similar point: "I found personalism a good way to distinguish my thinking from the self-centred individualism of laissez-faire liberalism (or modern-day neo-conservatism, for that matter) by bestowing it with a sense of duty to the community in which one is living."[25]

It was also at Harvard that Trudeau first encountered the ideas of Harold Laski, another formative influence. He would meet Laski face-to-face when he attended the LSE in 1948. In his *Memoirs* Trudeau spoke of how impressed he had been by Laski's *A Grammar of Politics*.[26] Another revelation about his time in London, concerned someone—he did not identify him except to say that he was a Marxist—who introduced him to the writings of John Henry Newman, the nineteenth-century Catholic divine and cardinal, who became another important inspiration to him.[27] Trudeau also mentioned the positive impressions there of other, less well-known academics. Glanville Williams, a specialist in public law, pointed him towards the work of Knut Olivecrona, a Swedish legal theorist:

At the time, I was particularly interested in authors who developed a general theory of the state. I wanted to know the roots of power. I wanted to know how governments work and why people obey. Does the ultimate authority lie in the state or in the human individual? . . . I learned the philosophy of T.H. Green, whose liberalism preceded the personalism of Maritain and Mounier in saying that the focal point was not the state but the individual—the individual integrated into society, which is to say, endowed with fundamental rights and essential liberties, but also with responsibilities.[28]

And finally Trudeau recalled the impetus given to his accelerating leftward tendencies at the LSE by radical students, in that blissful dawn when Clement Attlee's Labour government was in office and its fiery Minister of Health, the Welsh socialist Aneurin Bevan, was launching the National Health Service.[29]

III

By his own account, Trudeau implied that it was only after he had entered Harvard that political affairs first significantly swam into his consciousness. The Trudeau Papers have diametrically challenged this view.[30] Already in his high-school days, Trudeau had begun to grapple with public questions and to imagine an eventual political career.[31] At the time politics in French-speaking Catholic Quebec was mainly about nationalism and religion. But far from being inordinately anti-nationalistic and jauntily non-conformist—as a good contrarian might have been—the young Trudeau enthusiastically fell in with the clericalist and nationalist ethos around him and an extreme version of it at that. He was at times anti-English and moderately anti-Semitic and avidly supported an independent, Francophone, Catholic, corporatist state of "Laurentie." It is an astonishing story, sometimes an "appalling" one, as John English puts it, and it was capped off by his membership in a clandestine revolutionary cell that plotted—how seriously it is not clear—some kind of *coup d'état* in 1942.[32]

These political inclinations had germinated at Brébeuf.[33] The priests who taught him emphasized intellectual striving, clear thinking, good works, and personal religious obedience and observance. Only approved books could be read and disobedience might bring expulsion. Trudeau sometimes objected to the number of religious exercises he was required to participate in but he was, for the most part, a willing believer and sometimes an enthusiastic one.[34] Predictably, the school's curriculum emphasized religious knowledge and the philosophy of St. Thomas Aquinas, commonly called Thomism, and, of course, the study of Greek and Latin. Mathematics and science were less exactingly studied. The non-religious part of the curriculum dwelt on the classical period of late seventeenth-century French literature and the great dramatists of the time, Molière and Corneille. Sports were important too since the mastery of the body was part of the Jesuit ideal. Trudeau participated in lacrosse, hockey, and skiing but it was as a budding intellectual that he shone the most. He was a brilliant student, exceeding all his contemporaries, except Jean de Grandpré, his great rival for school prizes and honours and later chief executive officer of Bell Canada. Trudeau's early academic precociousness, combined with his often religiously inspired quest for "truth," conspired to intensify his reading habits, which sometimes ventured into the unorthodox. However he did not run afoul of the school's rules about forbidden books; his teachers seemed to display more than a little flexibility in their definition of what was forbidden. And so Trudeau was introduced to Machiavelli, Cervantes, Schiller, Goethe, Nietzsche, Dostoevsky, Tolstoy, and Ibsen, many of whose works were on the Index of Forbidden Books. Whenever his interest ran towards the unorthodox, he diligently sought permission to read them from his bishop, something he continued to do until as late as 1950. No matter how heterodox was his proposed reading he always received permission.[35]

Political ideas were not absent at Brébeuf either, especially those of Abbé Lionel Groulx, and these helped establish an ethos there of strong nationalism. In 1940, at the University of Montreal, Trudeau would attend Groulx's lectures. Also in the air at Brébeuf were the ideas of such authors as Charles Maurras, Maurice Barrès, Jacques Bainville, Robert Brasillach, and Alexis Carrel, all of them adepts of the interwar conservative movement in France and especially of Action française. Their mentality was anti-liberal, anti-democratic, anti-republican, usually strongly Catholic and monarchist, and often anti-Semitic, sometimes rabidly so. Later, at the LSE, Trudeau would take lectures from Dorothy Pickles who would describe the likes of Barrès and Maurras as "new authoritarians."[36]

The Nemnis in particular make much of the education of the young Trudeau and the books he read. In 1937 he read Alexis Carrel's famous book, *L'homme, cet inconnu.* Carrel, a Nobel laureate (though for medicine and not for literature) railed against the degeneracy of bourgeois civilization, capitalism, and democracy. He was also the advocate of a particularly nasty version of eugenic theory. He fulminated against the influence of the Jews, modern life, and the emptiness of mass society. Disdainful of popular sovereignty he accorded a redemptive role to a hereditary, biologically superior elite. Trudeau commented approvingly on some of Carrel's ideas: "The democratic principle has contributed to the undermining of civilization by impeding the development of the elite," he said.[37] Trudeau did not explicitly align with some of his more extreme opinions but he did not express disagreement with them either. In the same year, in a student debate, he articulated several Groulx-like ideas, such as the need to protect the French language from American and Anglophone influences; the advantages of the so-called revenge of the cradle—the higher birthrate of the Québécois—which would allow them eventually to overcome their linguistic foes; the priority of discouraging immigration to Canada, which mainly added numbers to the Anglophone side; and the importance of fostering Francophones' divine calling to spread French and Catholic ideas in the New World.[38] There was also the tepid anti-Semitism of Trudeau's play, *Dupés,* written in 1938, about the commercial threat to Francophone small businesses from Jewish shop-keepers. Trudeau was eighteen years old when he expressed these last views. They are clear evidence of an already highly politicized mind and an illiberal one too. However, John English is right to point out the contradictions in his thinking. For, as well as his clericalism and nationalism, and his religious conformity, there were opposing inclinations: his celebration of the Queen's birthday; his contacts with students at Fordham University in New York; his attraction to New York City; his passion for American films and theatre; his first love, Camille Corriveau, an American of a French-Canadian background; his rejection of French unilingualism; and, at various times, the special pride he took in his Anglophone background and Scottish "blood."[39]

While he clearly held political views at the beginning of the war, Trudeau was cautious in publicly expressing them. However, as the anti-conscription agitation intensified, he not only privately embraced more radically clericalist, nationalist, and anti-democratic positions but he became less guarded in publicizing them. English claims that "the war made [him] into a Quebec nationalist,"[40] and the Nemnis conclude that, by 1942, he was more or less a disciple of Charles Maurras.[41] Indeed Trudeau's right-wing political inclinations had already been in evidence in the 1930s, not just in his reading and writing but in public action as well. In 1937 he became a member of a shadowy, secret society, Les Frères Chausseurs, or LX as it was also called.[42] And he likely took part in public demonstrations in the late 1930s against the visits of André Malraux and other supporters of the Republican cause in the Spanish Civil War. In March 1942, he was probably involved in riots in Montreal that ended in attacks on Jewish property. His role in these riots is not known but he was called as a defence witness in the trial of one of the rioters. Later in 1942 he was involved in a suddenly revived cell of LX. The group produced a manifesto but it seems to have hesitated about actually mounting a *coup d'état*. The manifesto, however, did talk dramatically about the idea of strong leadership and of political authority descending from above. It condemned parliamentary democracy, was explicitly corporatist in its view of the state, and defined the Quebec nation as "a community of faith, of mentality, of blood, [and] of language."[43]

Trudeau's reading at the time gave intellectual succour to such views. There were two works by Maurras, *La seule France* and *Enquête sur la monarchie*, and Jacques Bainville's *Les conséquences politiques de la paix.* Theories about *coups d'état* and insurgencies were provided by Curzio Malaparte's *Technique du coup d'état* and by books about Leon Trotsky. He read Georges Sorel's *Réflexions sur la violence* and Plato's *Republic*. He criticized the latter's views on the family, common property, and the arts but there was no mistaking his appreciation of his search for truth and his ideal of a morally uplifting elite:

> I have rarely come across . . . a man with so constant a concern for the triumph of the good. There is truly a just man who feared God. . . . He is outstandingly sincere and his pre-eminent characteristic, surely, was his magnificent virtue of justice. His purpose was to discover and teach what would lead men to perfection and please the gods.[44]

Clearly Trudeau subscribed to the notion that a well-ordered society depended on the health of its ruling class. If the masses were degenerate, this was because of their leaders, a theme that was endemic to interwar French thought. It was a theme of Georges Sorel's too, who preached the need for a dramatic popular myth that would mobilize the masses for revolution. Of course, it was Plato who had expounded the necessity of a "noble lie" that would legitimize the rule of the philosopher-ruler. Such ideas dovetailed with Henri Bergson's conception of the crucial role of "mystics" as provocateurs of a universal brotherhood in his *Les deux sources de la morale et de la religion* (1932), which was another book that Trudeau read at this time.[45] Again, care must be taken not to overlook the full range of his reading. For as well as Bergson, he read Maritain's *Humanisme intégral* (True Humanism), a work that was profoundly critical of contemporary nationalism and political authoritarianism, although Trudeau's response to this work—at least at the outset—was not overtly enthusiastic.

In any account of Trudeau's wartime extremism his famous intervention in the Outremont by-election of November 1942 is usually emphasized. The draft of the speech in his personal papers confirms that political vanguardism and insurgent elitism continued to permeate his thinking. Without strong leadership, Trudeau proclaimed, the people perish. He castigated the politicians and the Catholic Church for not being sufficiently opposed to conscription:

> If Outremont is so infamous that it elects La Flêche [the pro-conscription candidate], and if because of Outremont conscription for overseas service comes into effect . . . I beg of you to eviscerate all the damned bourgeois of Outremont who voted for La Flêche just to serve their own interests.[46]

The constituency contained a large number of Anglophones, many of them Jewish. Even so Trudeau was provocatively exact about which ethnic group had the right to determine the outcome:

> A people is a being that like a man, has its own intrinsic value, and no one has the right to debase it into a tool, like a slave in the service of another people, even if it be the immortal Anglo-Saxons. . . . [The] French Canadian people understands the meaning of war. It has never for one single instant since its birth been free of a struggle, at first against the Iroquois, and since then against other savages. Citizens of Quebec, the election of Jean Drapeau must mark the close of an era when the French Canadians were the suckers and the beginning of the era when the dishonest outsider starts to take a tumble. . . . [E]nough of the tragedy; enough of the big shots, enough of the traitors. Enough of the arrow of the conquerors, long live the flag of freedom! We've had more than enough of band-aids [*cataplasmes*]; now let's move on to the cataclysm.[47]

The Outremont speech showed the measure of his alienation and extremism. A little earlier, in March 1941 writing to Camille Corriveau, Trudeau had talked of his feelings of isolation and disaffection from the law school he was attending:

These different circumstances cause me to envelope myself in a world apart, where I crazily read and wrote, and dreamt about music and beauty and revolutions and blood and dynamite.[48]

Such a comment and his Outremont intervention offer telling evidence of Trudeau as a young *enragé*, a sort of gilded counter-revolutionary. The moral and spiritual rhetoric was unforgiving and absolute, and he projected a brooding violence, a sort of furious, white-heat of youthful authenticity. The shape of his world was unambiguous and there were no limits, it seems, to his desire to be true to his political imaginings. On the other hand there is a sense in which his rhetoric with its heady ideas and preposterous punning may not have been altogether as extravagant and threatening as it sounded but more theatrical and bombastic. Confirmation of this can be found in the other pranks and antics he indulged in at the time: his membership in the Club of the Dying—a joke among his friends, who would suddenly keel over and appear to be dead in front of unsuspecting strangers—his conspiracy with friends to fire blanks from a revolver during public debates; and his habit of wearing a military helmet during his rides around the Quebec countryside on his motorbike. Yet there can be no mistaking Trudeau's overall political inclinations at the time: he was a virulent critic of the federal government's wartime policies. While he was not an apologist for Hitler and the Nazis, he *was* uncritical of Pétain and the Vichy regime and he showed little if any sympathy for those who had stood in the breach against Hitler and his expanding Reich, which after 1940 included France. Esther Delisle mentions how, after the Second World War, French-speaking intellectuals in Quebec—and she specifically includes Trudeau—used conscription to create a memory that allowed them to forget their support of near-fascist dictatorships and their antipathy towards Britain, Canada, and the Free French:

Conscription is the face-saving event around which forgetfulness has been structured. Anti-Semitism, fascism, Pétainism, attraction for an array of European dictatorships are the sounds buried beneath the wall of silence that the architects of collective memory have carefully constructed around World War II in Quebec.[49]

Trudeau was less than forthright about his wartime views and activities. Indeed he used opposition to conscription as a pretext or a camouflage for his indifference towards the European conflict; and his clericalist nationalism did incline him towards the Catholic dictators, Salazar, Franco, and Pétain. This was the agenda he advanced while Canada was at war.

But then he began to rethink things. The change did not come at once but new convictions and a more cosmopolitan sensibility began to infiltrate his consciousness. His attending foreign universities and his world travels greatly contributed to this outcome. While at Harvard, Trudeau read *Behemoth*, by the German émigré Franz Neumann, and realized "what horrors Hitler had wrought."[50] And in his *Memoirs*, he claimed that it was during this time that he began to

appreciate fully the historic importance of the war that was ending. . . . I realized then that I had, as it were, missed one of the major events of the century in which I was living.[51]

Trudeau Agonistes

---◦◆◦---

In the midst of this hullabaloo appeared a perfectly serene and remarkably intelligent book on Canadian federalism. Naturally, our fantastic élite lost no time in impressing upon the author that he had been unbearably pretentious to mention ideas in an argument about race. Condemned, before it had even been written, by the man who remains (in spite of all) our most lucid journalist, disowned by the then rector of Laval University, misunderstood yet opposed by a professor of history at the University of Montreal, this work received the only fate it could expect at the hands of our official intelligentsia.
Pierre Elliott Trudeau

In this age, the mere example of nonconformity, the mere refusal to bend the knee to custom, is itself a service. Precisely because the tyranny of opinion is such as to make eccentricity a reproach, it is desirable, in order to break through that tyranny, that people should be eccentric. Eccentricity has always abounded when and where strength of character has abounded; and the amount of eccentricity in a society has generally been proportional to the amount of genius, mental vigour, and moral courage which it contained. That so few dare to be eccentric, marks the chief danger of the time.
John Stuart Mill

Heretics are given us so that we might not remain in infancy. They question, there is discussion, and definitions are arrived at to make an organized faith.
Augustine of Hippo

I

What have academic commentators said about Trudeau's political world view after 1944? A great deal and much of it highly critical. No doubt this is to be expected, given Trudeau's tendency to engender antagonistic reaction. Thesis generated anti-thesis and so there emerged around him an endless farrago of mutually reinforcing invective. René Lévesque once said of Trudeau that he had an "inborn talent for making you want to slap his face."[1] Slightly adjusting the metaphor, Trudeau became for many a sort of grand punching-bag. If, in response to such criticism, the open hand was not quite Trudeau's style, the fist enclosed in a boxing glove certainly was. His consolation lay in knowing that in his many bouts he gave as good as he got, usually better, and more frequently. He later admitted that he sometimes went too far and exhibited too much "aggressivity," and that, on some occasions, he had instigated such behaviour just for the hell of it.[2] For Trudeau was an extraordinary controversialist and provocateur. To his extreme candour was joined a delectable aptitude for the counter-punches of disdain, sarcasm, and satire. The ruthless, peremptory deductiveness of his mind, honed by his Jesuit teachers, had something to do with this. Trudeau was irascible and contentious, and impious and impudent too. Preternaturally oppositional, he was also instinctively courageous and self-assertive. There was a quiet rage in Trudeau.[3] He was not captive to discretion; he was unusually intelligent; and he believed that to keep silent was to commit a sin. He was, it may be said, a great, questing, and roaring lion seeking monsters to devour. Especially he wished to consume those who were politically ambiguous and opportunistic.[4] Madeleine Albright considers Václav Havel as "one of the most important intellectual-troublemaking statesmen of his time."[5] Something similar could be said of Trudeau.

Devotees of Trudeau have pointed to these qualities as proof of his innate boldness and integrity. His detractors think otherwise. Bob Rae says of him that "he needed an enemy, and [that] he was never stronger or clearer or more effective than when eviscerating an opponent."[6] Even a sympathetic interpreter, John English, takes note of Gérard Pelletier's concern over Trudeau's "bitter sarcasm and unexpected cruelty in debate,"[7] and English himself refers to Trudeau's tendency in later years to be "downright contemptuous and dismissive" of the press and members of the House of Commons.[8] Trudeau reserved a special disdain for those with power. And in the 1950s he was especially unrelenting towards Jesuit priests who were, it seems, particularly determined to correct their wayward child.

Ramsay Cook views Trudeau differently. According to him, he was essentially shy, polite, and courteous, someone who listened intently in conversation and was genuinely interested in the opinions of others:

> His arrogance, if that is what it was, was saved for those whose questions and comments arose not from interest in his answers but from a desire to score points.[9]

Ron Graham observes something similar. He had been the producer of a Canadian Broadcasting Corporation (CBC) television series about Trudeau in the early 1990s and he came to understand that his subject would be extremely open if he was approached sympathetically:

> He would tell me anything—this legendary privacy was not really there if you just asked the question in a way that made him believe that you sincerely wanted an answer and were not just looking for a fight. When I asked questions that way they revealed an extremely tender, polite, vulnerable, decent, kind, patient gentleman.[10]

Cook also emphasizes Trudeau's intellectual openness: "When he asked your opinion, he seemed genuinely to want to hear it."[11] Otto Lang, who was in Trudeau's cabinets from 1968 to 1979, agrees: "he never spoke to you without speaking totally to *you*."[12]

Such views are apposite when they are seen to be about the private Trudeau in one-on-one conversations or in small groups. But there was also a public persona who was provocative and bold in debate and seized by the claims of truth. He was in a sense a perfect Platonist, at least in his identification with the sweeping nature of Plato's declamations. He quoted him often and, like him, aspired after a sense of truth that was clear and definite.[13] Of course Trudeau was not strictly a Platonist. He did not believe in the theory of eternal Forms and Ideas beyond the world of empirical sense and in some epistemological matters he was quite consciously anti-Platonic. But there was with Trudeau a constant audaciousness and assertiveness.[14] At its best his public rhetoric had the oracular, spacious, and crystalline quality of someone who above all reached after universal and fundamental things, the kind of declaratory language often found in preambles to bills of rights and declarations of independence. The risk, however, was that his ambitious and reaching language could at times sound bombastic and pretentious, not to mention rather depressing in its unremitting indictment of everyone in high office as somehow wretchedly corrupt or, at the very least, incompetent. Another risk was that his dismissive, clever rhetoric about his opponents could become a cartoonish over-simplification that undermined the more objectively inclined tendencies of his analytic endeavours.

Certainly, the utter disdain in which Trudeau held many of his contemporaries did not lead to an easy acceptance either of his ideas or his person. Usually Trudeau was not disturbed by this because he believed that an important vindication of the critic was precisely his social separateness. He was in thrall to the Millian ideal of the sovereign individual who cared little about social acceptance and etiquette, and who knowingly—even joyfully—trod unexplored paths to truth. By this account those who subscribed to widely held views were likely wrong and their ideas smug and reactionary. The politician should worry when he became too popular and he should definitely be concerned when he was adored:

It is unnecessary to look further for any other constant in my thought than that of opposition to received ideas. . . . A regular feature of history is that sooner or later the greatest reformers are betrayed by their too loyal disciples. When a reform enjoys too complete popularity there is a good chance that it has passed over into a state of reaction, and it is the duty of the free man to contest it.[15]

Although he was critical of all politicians in the 1950s and early 1960s, Trudeau was especially dismissive of those in Quebec, particularly Duplessis. It is sometimes hard to know which speech or essay by Trudeau was the zenith of his denunciations, but here are a couple of instances of Trudeau in full discursive flight. This was written in 1958:

We live the absurdity of a craven people that makes itself the servant of the state, which is the very definition of totalitarianism. I am not thinking so much of the multitude of buffoons and good-for-nothings who are the flunkeys of politics and who sponge off the state. People like that are not direct threats to freedom because usually they are more inclined to give up their own freedom without envying that of others. At the same time it must be said that granting favors as a means of political "protection" is an obnoxious habit for the body politic. Still, it is not the rogues that are to blame but the politicians—though the two terms are not exactly mutually exclusive. For this system—in addition to helping to spread a slave mentality throughout a population that is already strongly affected by it—is in reality very costly. If access to the civil service, the provincial police and the range of public positions were based on competence rather than "protection," the state would gain much more in efficiency than it would cost to make all the incompetents retire or go to a home or a school and send all the crooks to jail. But the truly guilty ones are those in authority who in different sectors provide the example of political enslavement. . . . It is also noticeable that the leaders of trade unions who are most opposed to political action by unions are the very ones who most practise a particular form of politics that one can only call grovelling, in the hope of strengthening their position or obtaining personal favors.[16]

Then there were his comments in 1962 about Quebec as a

veritable charnel-house where the better half of our rights has been lost through decay and decrepitude, while the other half was devoured by the maggot of civic immorality and the microbe of corruption.[17]

Such philippics, and there were many others, set off a brittle, complicated dialectic between Trudeau and his audiences. Some reacted angrily to what they saw as his aggression. Yet anger did not always serve his critics well. In the matter of Trudeau's political thinking many so completely disliked both his person and, later, his statecraft that they ridiculed and dismissed his ideas. It is as if they did indeed take Trudeau at his word and assumed that his thought, his politics, and his personality were one whole piece. Many within Quebec's sovereigntist intelligentsia, for example, rejected his abstract ideas or interpreted them to suit themselves not because they were convinced they were philosophically invalid but simply because Trudeau, the Great Satan, was the originator of them. When contempt was not based upon ad hominem arguments, often it sprang from some sort of methodological objection: no good theory could ever have undergirded such bad political practice as the War Measures Act in 1970, his trouncing of Lévesque in the referendum of 1980, and the "imposition" of his constitution in 1982. Nor have Anglophone intellectuals been strangers to such a perspective. Consider the secular rejection of Trudeau, the man and his intellect, by two important opinion leaders of the time, Denis Smith and Abraham Rotstein, noted editors of the *Canadian Forum*, mainly because of his actions during the October Crisis and his putative inaction on foreign ownership of the Canadian economy.[18] As we shall see, Reg Whitaker's account of Trudeau is also very much based on an elision of real-life concerns about his politics—in this case the economic dislocations of the late 1970s—with Trudeau's thinking. Whether Trudeau was more abusing than abused is not easy to determine. Yet amidst the welter of controversy swirling around him the unacknowledged—in some cases the acknowledged—hands of bias and hatred have sometimes been present.[19] R.F. Foster, the Irish historian, has coined a wonderful word for this: he calls it "begrudgery." That said, beyond apoplexy and antipathy—and begrudgery too—there *is* an academically credible literature on Trudeau's political thought, albeit one that is, to repeat, generally critical of him.

II

Marçel Rioux was, at one time, very close to Trudeau. They first met in Paris in 1946 and when they found themselves both working in Ottawa—Trudeau in the PCO, and Rioux at the National Museum of Canada—they frequently had lunch together.[20] Later, back in Montreal, they talked about articles each had submitted to *Cité Libre*. However, by the time Rioux published *La question du québec*, in 1969, they were at daggers drawn.

In his book Rioux situates Trudeau within a Marxist and postcolonial problematic. For Rioux, French Canadians, and especially Québécois, have been colonized by the British from without and by the English-Canadian political and commercial classes from within. And so the liberation struggle continued on two fronts: a class struggle against Anglo-British and American capital, and a cultural one for national independence and the protection of the French language and culture. Rioux accuses English Canada of unceasing "cultural genocide." The majority's urge to power was to establish one, undifferentiated English-speaking people, to "create a people, if not a nation, with the Other."[21] In a stinging coda he castigated the role of French-speaking, federalist leaders in collaborating with the assimilative project of English Canada. Sir Wilfrid Laurier and Louis St. Laurent were the main betrayers but so also was Trudeau whose comprador role, he said, was prefigured in his early writings. Everything becomes clear, Rioux claims, if one understands, first, Trudeau's account of the state, reason, and checks-and-balances; and, secondly, his theory of functionalism:

> Trudeau's intentions, like those of his master Lord Acton, theoretician of checks and balances, are good. He does not want social classes or nations to be ruled and exploited in the name of some irrational principle like class struggle or national sentiment; he wants them to obey the voice of reason. What could be more praiseworthy? In his words, "The rise of reason in politics is an advance of law; for is not law an attempt to regulate the conduct of men in society rationally rather than emotionally."[22]

But the objectivity and fair-mindedness of this rule of law—what is generally called the *Rechtsstaat*—are a chimera, an abstraction. Trudeau, he said, was oblivious to such injustices as the exploitation of workers and the suppression of the organic identities of nations like the Québécois: "The universality so prized by Trudeau is the old abstract universality of the bourgeois State."[23]

Ministering to the same execrable outcome was Trudeau's version of functionalism. Rioux linked this to the family of structural-functional theories that were popular in the immediate postwar years, especially in the United States. The idea here is that an institution's "function" is to maintain the equilibrium of the prevailing socio-economic order. Predictably Rioux deduced from this decidedly conservative implications:

> Opting for the system which incarnates the theory of checks and balances and equilibrium, he [Trudeau] has no use for social and human realities. His utterances are so spare, so abstract that his system is suited to a nonexistent country.[24]

Trudeau, by this account, had no understanding of the "real" forces of class struggle and national liberation, no sensitivity whatever

to the actual injuries of class exploitation and cultural subordina-
tion; in a word no sense of distributive justice. Rioux regards him as
little more than an apologist for a reactionary politics and a class-
based state, all of which he had somehow wrapped in a self-serving
metaphysics. Once in power, Trudeau became the oppressor and
breaker of the Quebec nation. Trudeau's intention in invoking the
War Measures Act, Rioux says, was "to destroy the possibility of
independence in the egg."[25] Trudeau, the supposed anti-nationalist,
gave vent to a pan-Canadian nationalism dedicated to expunging
Quebec's own nationalism. He imposed a "State nationalism."[26]

Kenneth McRoberts, a substantial Anglophone critic, views
Trudeau through the framework of "dualism" as the *sine qua non* of
Canada's survival.[27] With him, the story of Trudeau can be brought
forward from Rioux's time of writing—the founding of the Parti
Québécois (PQ) and the October Crisis—to the coming to power of
the PQ in 1976, the 1980 referendum, the new constitution in 1982,
the Meech Lake Accord in 1987, the Charlottetown Agreement in
1992, and the narrow defeat of the second referendum on sovereignty in 1995. McRoberts's claim is that Trudeau's hand in all these
matters was decisive and perverse. Trudeau was a sort of political
deus ex machina who rejected the normal practices and theories of
federal–provincial relations and brought both risk and potential
disaster to the unity of Canada. At the root of his destructive federalism, McRoberts says, was his Canadian nationalism, which went
against the grain of the country's history and constitutional conventions. Trudeau, in a word, "misconceived" Canada.

A dualistic accommodation, McRoberts claims, has held
Canada together from its beginnings in the late eighteenth century.
Canada is a community of two peoples rather than a community of
individuals who speak two languages. Confederation, he concedes,
was not established on a consistently dualistic basis and was a compromise. Quebec was given control over its culture and education
but a strong central government was established over other jurisdictional spheres, thus meeting English Canada's concerns. But the
provincial rights movement of the 1880s and 1890s mitigated and

"dualised" this arrangement, and, by the early twentieth century, opinion leaders such as Henri Bourassa had successfully established a version of Canada that was a double dualism: a compact between the French and the English, and another one between Quebec and the rest of Canada. The model accords a special standing to Quebec as the primary territorial state of French Canada and the Quebec government as its main protector. Trudeau's constitution of 1982, McRoberts continues, destroyed one of these dualisms: that of Quebec and its relationship to the rest of Canada. Even the English–French dualism Trudeau reinterpreted in an individualist manner: there were for him two linguistic groups but they were made up of French and English-speaking individuals and these individuals were dispersed throughout the country, not coterminous with any province or provinces. It is the individual who is the bearer of linguistic rights rather than the Quebec government and territory or the Francophone collectivity.

McRoberts observes that these ideas characterized Trudeau's thinking long before he entered federal politics. He recognizes that his individualism, rooted in Catholic personalism, did however stress personal responsibility. And he also concedes that his constitutionalism emphasized human rights, but the problem was that these rights he conceived only in limited, traditional terms: the right to vote, the right of free association, and the right to habeas corpus, for example. Trudeau did not embrace "new" rights such as economic and social ones. He opposed nationalism and advocated a type of federalism grounded in "rationality," although McRoberts does not quite explain what Trudeau meant by this. The idea of functionalism, too, was crucial in Trudeau's early thinking, McRoberts says, and this was mainly to do with "the technocratic notions of systems management and planning that were making the rounds in the 1960s."[28]

McRoberts published his work just two years after the near-successful sovereignty referendum of 1995 and for this too he found Trudeau greatly responsible, even though he was mainly a bystander to the event.[29] McRoberts admits that before 1965

Trudeau did indeed hold to a balanced conception of Canadians' constitutional identities: they must hold dual loyalties, to the region and to the centre, and that the balance between them must be constantly adjusted. However, this changed after 1982, when Trudeau came to regard the national level as the predominant one. Quebec nationalism was to be vanquished by a pan-Canadian one. The latter was to be a nationalism of common values, in support of a non-ethnic identity. This, according to McRoberts, was Trudeau's "new Canadian messianism."[30]

With Claude Couture the focus is slightly different. His main concern is with the version of Quebec's history that lay at the back of Trudeau's thinking.[31] This went as follows: New France was based on feudal, pre-capitalist arrangements; the Conquest severed New France from its metropolis and French Canada turned inwards in order to preserve an identity that became more and more at odds with that of the motherland, especially after the French revolution in 1789; the Constitutional Act of 1791 gave Lower Canada a legislative assembly and French Canadians political rights, but local habitant nationalism pressed for greater powers and precipitated the rebellions of 1837 and 1838; French Canadians continued to be removed from trade and commerce; they fell increasingly under the control of a rigid, ultramontane Catholic hierarchy and, with the support of the Church, the idea of French-Canadian *survivance* came to predominate; French Canadians set their face against liberalism, capitalism, democracy, urbanization, and industrialism and—especially emphasized by Trudeau—they came to develop the black arts of manipulating "democratic" institutions in order to secure their interests; these "Dark Ages" were at their darkest under Duplessis and his passing in 1959 became the "moment of salvation and purification," the coming of the Quiet Revolution.[32] Trudeau's account, Couture concedes, is widely held by French-Canadian historians, nationalists among them. But for Couture it is an over-simplification. Other historical realities were at work: French-Canadian agriculture after 1760 did in fact develop markets; some French Canadians participated in the commercial world; a significant liberalism existed throughout the nineteenth century. In Couture's view Quebec society from 1850 to 1950 was complex and pluralistic, and vastly different from the tradition-bound, homogeneous, authoritarian "folk" stereotype posited by Trudeau.

Couture's own schematic might be said to fit into a type of Quebec historiography recently called "revisionist" by Ronald Rudin.[33] This school, which emerged in the 1960s and 1970s, broke away from the conventional preoccupation with New France and the Conquest and emphasized the idea of Quebec as a "modern," urban, secular, and capitalist society, more or less like other societies in North America. It places less emphasis on Quebec's supposed uniqueness and its status as a "victim," and more on its "normalcy." However Couture departs from this paradigm when it claims that Quebec's destiny was to become part of a universal and modern order-of-things. This was an emphasis of Trudeau, who, he says, gave it an anglophilic twist in his belief that the coming of industrialism and capitalism, with all their supposedly liberating and modernizing benefits, was an English achievement, an offshoot of general Anglo-American success in politics and economics in the nineteenth century. According to Couture, Trudeau's position was that it was the English who had been the vanguard of progress in Canada. They dominated commerce, were more zealous for responsible and representative government, and, in their hamfisted and self-serving way, were more eager for liberal rights and social advancement. In contrast Quebec was authoritarian, backward, anti-modern, priest-ridden, and profoundly immoral, duped by its leaders and believing in democracy only when it suited it.

Couture points to a huge irony in all this. Trudeau was a self-declared individualist and a liberal and, presumably, sensitive to the existence of difference and diversity. His very methodology should have made him aware of the multiple ways in which the passages of Quebec's history had been traversed. In all this there is more than ample evidence of Couture's indebtedness to post-modernist thinkers such as Michel Foucault, Richard Rorty, and Edward Said.[34] He concludes that Trudeau offered a view of Quebec that was unrelentingly monolithic, homogeneous, holistic; in a word, collectivist. He, apparently, believed that he had discovered the essence of Quebec.[35] He committed what is for post-modernists the cardinal sin of essentialism in his failure to notice Quebec's internal diversity. Trudeau was, literally, narrow-minded. As Trudeau saw it all pre-modern societies were destined to progress beyond a folkish, rural, traditional, hierarchical, religious stage into one that was resoundingly secular, urban, democratic, egalitarian, capitalist, innovative, and liberal. And so, according to Couture, Trudeau saw Quebec as a case of incomplete or arrested development. He shared the evolutionary, linear, progressivist views of the Chicago school with which other Quebec sociologists such as Hubert Guindon, Jean-Charles Falardeau, and Marcel Rioux were identified.[36] In Trudeau's version, according to Couture, the bridging of the gap between the way things are and the way they should become was to be attained through a "pragmatic functionalism," a public discourse that combined realism with a non-ideological, disinterested rationalism, not so much a Rioux-like belief in system-maintenance but more like McRoberts's idea of a cool technocracy.[37]

While prime minister, Trudeau acquired the means to implement his vision. And so the complicated tension within him between individualism and collectivism persisted, says Couture. Trudeau believed fundamentally in individual rights. Yet in office he brought in the Official Languages Act, multiculturalism, and, later, the Charter of Rights and Freedoms, Section 15 of which prohibits discrimination while sanctioning affirmative action as well. Other sections provide enlarged linguistic and educational rights for Francophones and Anglophones and for Aboriginal people as well. All of these provisions presuppose some conception of "collective" rights, Couture claims. The Charter was not perfect however and he believes that the Meech Lake and Charlottetown Accords, if implemented, would have improved it. Consequently he is deeply resentful of Trudeau's resistance to both of them. In both cases, he says, Trudeau argued that Quebec did not need distinctive constitutional rights and that according such rights would be destructive of individual rights. Thus in Couture's view, Trudeau's end-games revealed his true colours as an "ethnic liberal" and "Anglo-Canadian nationalist."[38]

Couture's theory has affinities with that of James Tully whose argument in *Strange Multiplicity* (1995) is that Trudeau espoused a "liberal" view of citizenship, one that—particularly in its influence on the Charter—imposed a uniformly individualist political/ constitutional doctrine upon the reality of the varied and hybrid identities of Canada's many peoples, especially its indigenous peoples and Québécois.[39] Tully also emphasizes that Trudeau embraced "modern" constitutionalism in his account of law as the command of an identifiable, all-powerful sovereign who had either obliterated or subsumed older forms of sovereignty. Trudeau's view stood in opposition to an "ancient" one that saw law as deriving informally, contingently, and organically from an "assemblage" of common law, custom, tradition, and convention and in which there is an ongoing continuity of previously exercised sovereignty unless the latter is consensually extinguished. There are echoes here, as we shall see, of what Trudeau would have heard in lectures from Charles McIlwain at Harvard in 1944. If Tully is right then he had evidently not been persuaded by McIlwain. What Tully fundamentally rejects is Trudeau's procrustean view of the constitution as one in which the state must somehow be culturally neutral, society composed only of equal, rights-bearing citizen-individuals, and the provinces held to identical powers. This, says Tully, was a uniform, unvarying, and monistic conception with no regard for the cultural uniqueness of French-speaking and indigenous peoples.

Reg Whitaker's essay, "Reason, Passion and Interest: Pierre Trudeau's Eternal Liberal Triangle," remains the most accomplished single account of Trudeau's political thought.[40] Whitaker primarily places him within a set of theoretical concerns that were burning issues at the time of his writing in the late 1970s: stagflation and the rise of separatism and, overall, a legitimation crisis of the capitalist state. Whitaker's claim is that Trudeau's ideas and practice lay at the back of all of them. Whitaker was one of the first to recognize the religious dimension of Trudeau's life and thought. A personalism derived from Emmanuel Mounier, he observes, gave a theological basis to Trudeau's view that a liberal order rested upon respect for the conscience of each citizen. Whitaker especially made use of a series of articles that Trudeau wrote in 1958 in *Vrai* in which he explained the presuppositions of democratic politics: humans needed to participate in a social life yet society existed basically to allow each citizen to pursue his self-interest; government's decisions were ultimately sanctioned by the consent of the individual citizen who was justified in rebelling if his rights were abrogated; popular consent required universal democracy but it did not require direct democracy for, in a complex technological age, there were limits to the ability of the average citizen to understand public issues; and a democratic order, of course, presumed the existence of such rights as freedom of speech, the right to vote, and free elections. The ideal situation was one in which a majority of the citizens supported the government but where the government respected the rights of minorities. So the hallmark of a legitimate government was its embodiment of the "common good" or the "general will." The ruler must not govern on the basis of his own point-of-view but must take account of the wishes of every citizen.

Whitaker acknowledges that there were elements in Trudeau's early thought that suggested a socialist perspective, citing the article "Economic Rights" (1962) specifically. But, after weighing everything, he concludes that Trudeau was an insubstantial democrat and, at best, an ersatz socialist. He was a conventional liberal who took as given the existence of the market, a strong (even authoritarian) state, and a non-participatory politics. Although he makes much of Trudeau as a Lockean with democratic frills, it is through treating him as a disciple of Hobbes, Whitaker believes, that there lies the greatest insight into Trudeau's thought. Here Whitaker is indebted to C.B. Macpherson, another Canadian Marxist, whose important claim was that Hobbes's state of nature was not a pre-political, asocial abstraction but a description of an actually emerging capitalist economy in mid-seventeenth-century England. The fissiparous, brittle antagonisms of such a society made necessary a strong state, even an authoritarian one. Whitaker reads this version of Hobbes into Trudeau. Humans, he sees Trudeau saying, were moved by their passions, which established their sense of what is good; each person's reason was subordinate to his passions and functioned solely as a calculating device to allow him to estimate how best to get what he wanted; the world was a place of scarcity and uncertainty; and, to ensure the peace, a strong government was necessary. If Hobbes's civil society was in any way about the common good it was so only in an inconsequential fashion. What mainly constituted the good of individuals in Trudeau's philosophy was something that each of them subjectively defined. In Hobbes's world—and in Trudeau's—justice was neither an overarching standard of community well-being, nor a transcendental measure of right behaviour, but simply a procedure for the peaceful resolution of the competing claims of individuals. Trudeau evinced the characteristic deportment of liberalism: the combining of a super-structural idealism with a realistic, cynical acceptance of capitalism and a strong state.

Trudeau, then, allowed no room for the idea of the good because all he considered as the common good, in step with Hobbes, was a narrowly focused social contract of mutual advantage and self-interest. And what of Trudeau's many invocations of the general will and the common good? So many footling abstractions and misconceptions, Whitaker seems to contend. Trudeau did not have any sense of the actualities of the state's relation to civil society under capitalism. Trudeau lacked a conception of the class-relations of late capitalism that generated inequality and gave control over the state to the corporate class. And what of Trudeau, the reputed socialist, who in the 1950s and early 1960s was a powerful advocate for Quebec workers, who articulated socialist beliefs and belonged to the Co-operative Commonwealth Federation (CCF)? Simply, Whitaker sees little significance in such facts:

> Trudeau read the struggles of labour and capital in a thoroughly Hobbesian way, especially when he praised the workers'

escalating demands as a part of the motor of economic progress, while at the same time noting that the conflict was never solved on more than a temporary basis.[41]

Leo Huberman, the founder and famous postwar editor of the *Monthly Review*—the Bible of American Marxism—was one Marxist who seemed to believe that Trudeau belonged to the socialist family.[42] However, what was lacking in Trudeau, according to Whitaker, was any real belief in the historic resolution of the class struggle; he had no sense of the predetermined end of history. Trudeau, then, was neither an orthodox Marxist, nor a true socialist.

Continuing the Hobbesian interpretation, Whitaker contends that Trudeau saw the role of the political leader as amoral or morally neutral: the leader was to be a technician or manager. In civil society citizens pursued their particular inclinations and as long as these were peaceably and legally expressed, all will be well. Sometimes, though, there was conflict, at which point the leader's usefulness lay not in overcoming conflict by applying a transcendent ideal of justice, but in maintaining the whole competitive system in peaceful equilibrium and balance. "Justice" was procedural justice, as it is commonly called. Whitaker goes on to claim that Trudeau's account of federalism fitted neatly into this interpretation: the law-maker's job was to blunt the passions of citizens and ensure an enlightened, "rational" self-interest prevailed. One of these passions was nationalism, an irrational idea that over-stimulated the emotions. It was a collective feeling of belonging and a collective aversion towards those who did not belong. It was a danger to civil order and had the potential to become genocidal. Consequently federalism became the great "rational" architecture of any multinational society, an endless system of counterweights and counterbalances. This emphasis in Trudeau's thought, Whitaker alleges, came not from Montesquieu or de Tocqueville as has usually been supposed but, again, from Hobbes. Whitaker's reading of Trudeau's federalism is that Trudeau was not opposed to nationalism in principle, only insisting that it be contained. And so Trudeau can be seen as advocating the nurturing of nationalism at one level of government if it can counter-balance nationalism at another level.

Whitaker also posits a crucial continuity within Trudeau's thought between the so-called practical rationality of the law-maker and the art of *realpolitik* with its priority of grounding policy in actual circumstances. If politics is all about balancing and fine-tuning the civil order, the ruler needed only to take account of what is called effective demand. But, in that case, lacking any "valid" sense of justice, the Hobbesian/Trudeauian ruler had no sense of the "just" causes of groups that were voiceless and powerless. To act only on what had been explicitly expressed made governing an exercise in studied apathy. Whitaker applies a similar assessment to Trudeau's argument: the existence of rights lay in demographic numbers. It was the size and power of a group and its ability to destabilize things that were the crucial considerations. Thus, in Canada, the political leader did not need to take account of the lin-guistic rights of any other groups than the French and the English because only they had the wherewithal to break up the country. Without a conception of justice, what Whitaker calls Trudeau's *realpolitik* becomes conservative and, worse still, deeply cynical. For Whitaker the theory that was closely connected with this in Trudeau's thought was his functionalism. This he summarizes as a scientific technique systematically applied to the organization of society: politics was about problem-solving and the offsetting of conflict; politics was merely about administration. Functionalism maintained the system roughly as it was and presumed the ben-eficial uses of technology, particularly as a means of expanding human freedom.

In "The Universalist Liberalism of Pierre Trudeau," James Bickerton, Stephen Brooks, and Alain-G. Gagnon provide a startling contrast to Whitaker.[43] Although they too have mined the pre-1965 writings, they come to very different conclusions. What they dis-cern in Trudeau's thought is a sophisticated and compelling set of moral claims to do with human dignity, autonomy, and enlightened liberty and with an emphasis on the common good, which gave his thought a very Kantian aspect.[44] Trudeau's account of the common good, they say, was broadly imagined and constituted an overarching conception of justice. By the common good, Trudeau understood something more than the Hobbesian social contract. Rather, he saw a complex range of other normative priorities: individual rights, economic planning, the welfare state, equality of opportunity, and the protection of culture. Trudeau's argument was that to be free and virtuous was possible only within society. In other words, freedom takes place only within a real community under a common good. Freedom was not its own reward nor was it its own justification. Such an account, they believe, places Trudeau outside the "primacy of rights" school of liberal individualism of such theorists as Robert Nozick. Bickerton et al. see the origin of Trudeau's notion of human dignity in his reading of the Russian religious existentialist, Nicolas Berdyaev.[45] Berdyaev influenced Mounier and other personalists who concluded that "the sources of human dignity and the meaningfulness of one's life [are located] in the individual's own experiences."[46] This emphasis on individuality and enlightened choice makes it clear that Trudeau's view was that the free and enlightened individual was beyond the claims and constraints of tradition, community, and ethnicity, unless the individual freely and rationally chose such associations. Enlightened freedom challenged hierarchy as it also sought to "overcome the ascriptive ties of community."[47] Trudeau's liberalism is not communitarian in the way that Charles Taylor's is, for example.

However the largest individual intellectual influence the authors say was that of Jacques Maritain.[48] In *Man and the State* (1952), they contend, Maritain provided Trudeau with a crucial distinction between "community" and "society." The former was organic and traditional; it was produced through natural cultural forces and had much to do with human instinct and feeling. Community shaped human identity: humans instinctively felt that they belonged to family, church, or nation. But, especially with the rise of liberal democracy, there had come into existence the sphere of society, which was about the creation of a moral order over and above the community. Society was the site of consent and law that established a universal standard of inclusion and citizenship. It was also the sphere of reason, and required the recognition of conscience and free will. Society provided dignity to all; men and women were free and equal within it. The mistake of nationalism, according to Maritain, was to base the state upon community. The state—which ideally existed to take account of the interests of every citizen—became under nationalism exclusively the voice of those with particular *community* characteristics: religion, race, language, nation, and such. But, if society included a plurality of national groups, government must then take account of the rights and identities of everyone. Maritain, they say, was also crucial in delineating another dimension of Trudeau's thought, namely his development later on of a version of nationalism for Canada founded on the civic values of the universal rights of all citizens.

III

Finally, there is the important perspective of Charles Taylor to consider. He and Trudeau were, in many personal respects, alike. Although Taylor was twelve years younger, both were born in Montreal and brought up in privileged, conservative, Catholic, and bilingual households. As John Hellman puts it, they were two Catholic boys from Outremont.[49] Taylor's mother was from an old Quebec family, Beaubien, and his father, a businessman and industrialist, from Toronto. Taylor has recounted how in his youth he puzzled over where he belonged between the two solitudes of French and English.[50] He was raised in his maternal grandfather's home and in Anglophone private schools, Selwyn House in Montreal and Trinity College School in Port Hope, Ontario.[51] He studied history at McGill University and while there developed strong political interests, first becoming a Liberal and then a supporter of the CCF.[52] He won a Rhodes scholarship to Oxford University in 1952 where he was introduced to the English analytic tradition of philosophy. However, more important for Taylor's future philosophical development was his unlikely exposure to Maurice Merleau-Ponty's *Phénoménologie de la perception*, whose special character, according to Taylor, was its account of human life as lived within the body and the world and of human consciousness as a kind of "novelistic flow" in the manner of Marcel Proust's *Á la recherche du temps perdu*. Part of Merleau-Ponty's influence was the idea of society preceding the individual. All in all he gave Taylor the wherewithal to challenge the prevailing philosophical orthodoxies: that natural science was the primary, definitive way of knowing the world; that the human being was a mechanism; and that true knowledge required the stance of the disengaged observer standing outside the natural and social worlds. Taylor's first book, *The Explanation of Behaviour* (1964) predictably disputed the primacy of natural science and behaviourism and argued instead for the then unfashionable view that human agency was purposive and intentional.

Similarly non-conformist, too, were his early views on politics. Part of the ferment of new ideas on the Left after the twin crises of late 1956—the Suez Crisis and the Hungarian uprising—Taylor in 1957 was one of the four founders of the *Universities and Left Review* and a strong supporter of the Campaign for Nuclear Disarmament (CND). Taylor's early political journalism criticized both major British parties. Nor was he impressed by Soviet Communism. He was a man of the Left, certainly, but, although a member of the Labour Party, he was drawn to more original ways of conceiving socialism, what came to be called the New Left and which included such notable British intellectuals as Stuart Hall, Raymond Williams, and E.P. Thompson. In 1960, in two articles in the *New Left Review*, "What's Wrong with Capitalism?" and "Changes of Quality," Taylor wrote of the need for a socialism of "qualitative change," one that would be less concerned about traditional parliamentary electioneering and statist governance and more about stimulating popular, local "institutions" and "movements" as nodes of change that would transform society from within. It was a version of participatory politics as socio-cultural transformation.[53]

Taylor returned to Canada in 1961 to an appointment in Political Science at McGill. He quickly became a contributor to *Cité Libre* and one of its editors. He had known Trudeau in the 1950s—Trudeau had visited him in England in 1957—but especially through his involvement in *Cité Libre* in the early 1960s they were brought very close together. He also joined the newly established NDP, standing as a federal candidate not once but four times: in 1962, 1963, and 1965 in Mount Royal riding, and then, in 1968, in Dollard. In the second of these elections, Trudeau campaigned on his behalf, driving him around the riding in his Mercedes sports car. Then in September 1965, Trudeau stunned Taylor and many others with his decision to run for the Liberals. Taylor was one of four members of the editorial board of *Cité Libre* who offered a semi-official critique of his decision.[54] Trudeau eventually found a seat in Mount Royal, where, as it happened, Taylor was preparing to run for the third time. Taylor has said that at the time he "felt a little bit angry" at having his friend run against him. He also believes that "the Liberal machine," which did not want to recruit Trudeau but only wanted Jean Marchand, went out of its way to punish Trudeau by so arranging things that Trudeau was left with little choice but to run against him in Mount Royal.[55] Indeed it was a quandary for Trudeau. A few weeks into the campaign Gérard Pelletier describes receiving a phone call from an anguished Trudeau seeking advice about what he called his "*mauvaise action.*"[56] He was thinking of resigning his candidacy and leaving the Liberal Party altogether. In the end his confidence was bolstered after Pelletier, with Marchand's help, convinced him that Taylor was pursuing a lost cause and was certain to be defeated, no matter who ran for the Liberals. They also assured him that they too would have run against a friend in such circumstances. Reassured, Trudeau resumed normal partisan warfare.

On the hustings Trudeau attacked the NDP as a marginal political force, doctrinaire in its socialism and wrong-headed in its policy of special status for Quebec, while Taylor accused the Liberals of speaking with a forked tongue, uttering one message in French and another in English. Specifically he accused Trudeau of misrepresenting the NDP's "two-nations" policy, which, he said, was essentially about minority French-English language rights in different parts of the country, something, he said, Trudeau himself believed in.[57] In the event Trudeau won the election handily, outpolling Taylor by a margin of two to one.[58] Even after yet another defeat, this time in 1968 in Dollard riding, Taylor remained undaunted and persisted in his political activism, serving as vice-president of the federal party. Taylor eventually returned to Oxford as Chichele Professor of Political and Social Theory.

The rivalries and solidarities of Trudeau and Taylor can easily be thought of as the stuff of legend: two giants whose paths intersected and diverged and who in the end dramatically fell out with each other. Both went on to remarkable careers, Taylor becoming an accomplished philosopher engaging the most eminent thinkers of the age, among them Isaiah Berlin, Maurice Merleau-Ponty, J.L. Austin, Hans-Georg Gadamer, Michel Foucault, John Rawls, Jürgen Habermas, Leszek Kołakowski, and Bernard Williams. At the same time, Trudeau developed into a political eminence who reshaped Canada's constitutional order and rubbed shoulders with Mao Zedong and Fidel Castro. Trudeau was not as philosophically creative or informed as Taylor. He certainly knew more about public law, federalism, and the Canadian constitution but Taylor was paramount in the range and subtlety of his theoretical reach. Both yearned for political involvement; both spiced their academic prose with the chatty idiom of the street; and both would now and then demonstrate a sartorial panache for wearing a cape. *Le style, c'est l'homme même*, as Buffon put it. Their arguments, mainly expressed on the respectful terrain of academic article and public lecture—though sometimes fought along the sharp edge of electoral and political combat—have enlightened and shaped many of the important debates among liberals, social democrats, socialists, and nationalists in Canada in the last fifty years.

Taylor was a natural critic of Trudeau. They had stood against each other for a seat in parliament and their partisan differences were significant. Taylor's fully formed critique came in 1970, in his book *The Pattern of Politics* (*The Pattern*).[59] By then Trudeau was well into his first prime ministership and Taylor was still involved with the NDP (he remains involved to this day). In *The Pattern*, to make the case for socialism, he made a case against Trudeau, the unsocialist apparently. He categorized him as a believer in what he called the "consensus" model of politics.[60] Against this Taylor prescribed the politics of "polarization," by which he understood a perspective that sought to overcome through widespread, popular participation the structured power of society. The consensus view accepted things as they were and delivered, at best, "rough justice," Taylor said. It saw the existing "system" as not being stacked against any class or group. Historic social antagonisms such as the struggle between classes were presumed to have been superseded:

> Within this vision of politics, the ideal maturity of a society comes with the "end of ideology" when all politics revolve around nego-tiable differences of interests rather than confrontation between deeply held principles.[61]

The consensus model, though, was not averse to change and it anticipated a future in which technology and the modern corpo-ration, presided over by a technocracy of managers and scientists, would deliver beguiling possibilities and benevolent effects.

In debt to John Kenneth Galbraith—as was Trudeau—and espe-cially his recent work, *The New Industrial State* (1967), Taylor rec-ognized that the contemporary corporation was an improvement over the nineteenth-century capitalist firm.[62] With its huge scale, its power of advertising, large profits, and retained earnings the contemporary corporation had moved beyond risk and competi-tion; it made possible higher real wages and extensive research and development. The modern firm was a source of immense economic stability. Much of this was positive, Taylor conceded, and socialists must revise their thinking accordingly. (In his political journalism, in the late 1950s, Taylor noted that postwar growth and the com-ing of newly affluent workers had radically altered the conventional idea of the working class.)[63] But, Taylor continued, for all its benefits the private corporation represented a system of unacceptable values: it was a system of "power" and with the structural priority it accorded to profit-seeking it was fundamentally incapable of meeting such social needs as universal education, affordable housing, and liveable cities. The contemporary firm privileged private consumption and conspired with a broad trend in contemporary culture to favour the individuated, privatized self.[64]

Other important influences on Taylor at the time were the nationalist economic views of Kari Levitt of McGill and Mel Watkins of the University of Toronto.[65] With their help Taylor emphasized the ways in which foreign, mainly American corporations had distorted investment patterns and research-and-development priorities in Canada. Foreign investment concentrated industrial development in particular regions and its creation of a branch-plant corporate structure discouraged innovation. There was, as well, the constant drain on the country's financial resources of profits being patriated abroad, mainly to the United States. Taylor's main point was that the modern corporation, whether foreign or domestically owned, was perfectly compatible with consensus politics and vice versa. Trudeau's fondness for technocratic governance and his capacity for compromise aligned him nicely with the "soulful," multi-national corporation.

There was also an extensive though implicit cultural critique in *The Pattern*.[66] Taylor's view was that Canada was undergoing a seismic shift of values along with the whole Western world. This "civilizational" upheaval he later explored in depth in his *Sources of the Self: The Making of the Modern Identity* (1989), *Modern Social Imaginaries* (2004), and *A Secular Age* (2007). In *The Pattern*, Taylor expounded upon the loss of collective, coherent meanings that the rise of capitalism and liberalism and the decline of religion had brought about. Canadians' lives were becoming "desacralized": individuals and groups were losing their place within what once was seen as a religiously conceived cosmic order such as the Great Chain of Being or the idea of a Christian society. Contemporary society was being "fragmented" and individualized, and the human subject "set free" to fend for him- or herself.

In *The Pattern* Taylor explored another aspect of modernity, this one of particular application to Trudeau, namely the phenomenon of charismatic leadership. During the election of 1968, Trudeau provided the first significant instance in Canada of a type of politics in which mass participation was somehow mobilized by and refracted through the image of the hallowed, extraordinary leader. Charismatic leadership had arrived. Taylor mocked this as the cult of the "New Young Leader," or the "NYL."[67] He explained its etiology in the collapse of shared, public meanings in modern society. Yet, in spite of this, people continued to seek identification with a significant public reality. For Taylor participation in such a reality was something more fundamental than the satisfying of a need; it "constituted" humans as persons. If this priority was not properly met, or if "authentic" involvement was denied, false prophets would arise to lead us down false paths. In his later work Taylor applied the term "pathology" to human behaviour that diverged from the coherence and authenticity of a "significant reality." In *The Pattern*, he used language about "spurious" and "surrogate" types of social participation. Involvements in totalitarian movements and in certain kinds of nationalism were flagrant examples of modern individuals' failure to properly "connect." So was "the cult of the New Young Leader." Taylor could not hide his disdain:

> The striking thing about the contemporary cult of the NYL is its dream-like nature; everything crucial happens inside the head of the participant. For the image of youth and renewal is left quite indeterminate as to content; it is an invitation to each and all to project their own hopes and dreams into it and see them as ratified by it. No-one will contradict you, for the image itself has no inherent shape, offers no resistance. And just as what one receives is one's own dream, so one's participation is without real substance.[68]

The final bone Taylor picked with Trudeau was over the issue of French Canada.[69] During the 1968 campaign Trudeau had boldly advocated an improved policy of bilingualism to remedy the alienation of French Canada. But he also spoke out uncompromisingly against the two-nations theory and special status for Quebec, the positions of the Conservatives and the NDP, and Taylor too. For Taylor French Canadians—he preferred that term to "Quebeckers," at least at that time—had a complicated identity, strongly identifying with their "heartland" of Quebec but also possessing a sense of belonging to Canada. They typically defended Quebec's provincial powers but they also saw virtue in identifying with Canada's "national purposes." The *nation canadienne-française* was neither separatist nor federalist. It was a plural and contradictory entity whose character could not readily be captured in the words and formulae of conventional constitutional doctrine. Only something like special status did justice to Quebec's complexity, and so Canada's federalism must be an "asymmetrical" kind. Relations between individual governments and levels of government must be ad hoc, indeterminate, and accommodationist. For Taylor the "projective" virtue of Canada and the standard of its possible national identity lay in celebrating its deep cultural particularities within a loose unity; uniformities were to be banished. Consequently Taylor has been a constant critic of the constitutional principles of the equal powers of the provinces and of the federal government's uniform treatment of all of the provinces, principles markedly favoured by Trudeau.

Another dimension of Taylor's thinking—and in his estimation explicitly juxtaposed to Trudeau's views—had to do with his communitarianism. In *The Pattern*, Taylor wrote at length about the ways in which human life and identity were embedded in webs of social contexts, in what he later called "interlocutory communities" and "human life-forms." It was these ideas that informed the importance he gave to a "dialogue society."[70] Dialogical relations were about the many ways human beings' subjectivity was built up through engagements with Others and with alternative realities. Humans were not atomized individualists but were constituted by their belonging to larger sodalities and groups. Language, of course, was integral to this for it was within and through a language community that one "expressed" one's self. Language rights were not just about being allowed to use one's own language—to speak freely one's mother tongue as it were or to speak the language of one's choice—but presupposed an ability as well to be linked to and to be part of an identifiable historic language community that would continue to exist and survive. In *The Pattern* Taylor contended that Trudeau's insistence on a bilingualism of *individual* rights could not adequately capture the communal, ongoing dimension of linguistic identity.[71]

Events took their course, and by 1982 Taylor's companionable antagonist had achieved his long-held ambition to entrench a bill of rights in the Canadian constitution. For Taylor, Trudeau's Charter disregarded collective goals—Couture believes otherwise—and did not recognize Quebec's distinctive identity. It privileged individual rights which, according to Taylor, were one of the two arches of Trudeau's "revolution"—the other, of course, being bilingualism. (The principle of the equality of the provinces might be said to have been the third.) In Canada, outside of Quebec, Taylor continued, "Charter patriotism" had swept the land. The historic dualism of Canada, which had gone unrecognized in 1982, was revived in 1987 with the Meech Lake Accord. The latter, for Taylor, offered some hope of solving the Canadian dilemma of two nations, each of which required distinctive recognition. But it was defeated, and Trudeau, he thought, had played a large part in its demise.

In an article written in 1992 in the aftermath of the defeat of the Accord, Taylor explained his dismay.[72] What had helped sink the Accord, he said, was the subtle influence of procedural liberalism. He uses Ronald Dworkin, the American jurist and liberal, as the epitome of this view. According to Taylor procedural liberalism drew a distinction between the ends of life, or substantive values as the possible objects of a government's concern, and procedural ones to do with government's treating each citizen with fairness and equal respect. The liberal state avoided the former and adhered strongly to the latter. Under liberalism, the purpose of government was to ensure individuals the enjoyment of their rights. As such it must avoid legislating particular definitions of what was good or valuable, especially values sanctioned by religion or nationalism. Instead, in a liberal society, government should respect each citizen's autonomy. The individual must be thought of as "primarily a subject of self-determining or self-expressive choice."[73]

Taylor's consideration of Dworkin brought him inevitably to the central question of the vaunted neutrality of the liberal state. For Taylor, the liberal state is inconceivable without some account of a good, even if it has only to do with rights, freedom, equality of opportunity, fairness, and so on. This is part of Taylor's more general conviction that moral reasoning of whatever kind presupposes "strong evaluation," that is, judgment within some larger moral horizons or frameworks. Thus liberalism's account of what is morally valuable is incoherent without a sense of a constitutive good that explains what it is or why it is that human beings are deserving of respect, freedom, and opportunity. This is an angle of consideration on Trudeau that Whitaker also discussed.

Taylor refers to the liberal theory of the neutral state and procedural justice as the rights model. This, he says, has come down to us from Hobbes and Locke and integral to it is the theory of atomism in which the individual is seen as, somehow, preceding or pre-existing society, and separate and independent from it—what Taylor has called the stance of the disengaged self. This is in contrast to the communitarian emphasis on the dialogical idea of the self and its knowledge of the world. In Taylor's view atomism has generated a politics of unconditional rights in which the rhetoric of rights has became the sole or primary language of moral debate, rights being seen as self-evident and in need of little if any justification. But the denial of the inherently social nature of human life means that, while the citizen enjoys rights and expects them to be secured, her obligations are the ones she assumes only through her consent.

Atomism offers, at best, what Taylor has called a "thin" conception of social belonging.

Yet Taylor is not opposed to the idea of rights as such and of people enjoying them. In his view, a rights-based polity does not presuppose an atomistic account of the person. His criticism of the rights model derives from its inadequate justification of rights. As he put it in his essay, "Atomism," human beings may be said to possess rights because "[humans] exhibit a capacity which commands respect" and rights are therefore integral to what it means to treat human beings respectfully and in a manner consistent with their capacities.[74] Claiming a right is more than asserting a claim not to be interfered with; it is about avowing the worthiness of the activities that the right permits and encourages. Thus a right of free speech affirmed the importance of a life based on personal conviction and a willingness to follow rationality.[75] With the triumph of the rights model in Western political theory, Taylor contends, there has predominated an instrumentalist view of politics. Political activity is regarded as devoid of intrinsic value and simply a means to protect rights and keep the civil and economic order tidy and ship-shape. Politics has come to be about particular, limited concerns, single issues and sectional perspectives. It has also become "judicialized" as more and more matters have come to depend on the decisions of courts and judges and their interpretations of bills of rights. Legislatures and their politics have been relegated to secondary importance. In denying the very validity of the communal, the rights model undermined the importance of institutions as the embodiment of collective values.

In Taylor's estimation, by the late 1980s the alliance of procedural liberalism and the rights model had come to represent grave danger to the collective values of French Canada. In a mood of post-Meech gloom he doubted that Canada could avoid the separation of Quebec. Expressing himself less in the language of socialism and more in that of a communitarian liberalism, Taylor asserted that Quebec stood for an alternative liberalism, different from Trudeau's. Rights were important but so were collective goods. A society can give itself over to a common interest *and* a respect for minorities as long as the "fundamental" liberal rights are guaranteed to all:

> One has to distinguish the fundamental liberties, those which should never at any time be infringed and which therefore ought to be unassailably entrenched, on the one hand, from privileges and immunities which are important, but which can be revoked or restricted for reasons of public policy—although one needs a strong reason to do so—on the other. A society with strong collective goals can be liberal on this view, provided it is also capable of respecting diversity, especially concerning those who do not share its goals, and provided it can offer adequate safeguards for fundamental rights.[76]

One final suggestive idea in Taylor is his republican thesis in which he summed up an alternative account of politics and brought together themes to do with patriotism, social solidarity, collective action, and participation. In the republican model Taylor posited the importance of a prior, implicit dimension in democratic politics, a dimension that gave a sociable framework to the tenuous "unity" of a political order of endlessly clashing sectionalisms and enervating self-strivings. For democratic action to be properly conceived and engaged in, says Taylor, there needs to be a prior loyalty to the common values and traditions that undergird democratic politics itself, what he has referred to in *Modern Social Imaginaries* as the "common purposes and reference points" that sustain a self-governing people.[77] Again, freedom cannot stand alone. It requires reference to some more fundamental good or ontology—for example mutual respect, the dignity of the person and of deliberation as the basis of political decisions. Taylor's republican thesis he has referred to elsewhere as the de Tocquevillian model of "civic humanism."[78]

> This makes us look at society as a participatory community in which the common institutions, the common rules and laws that

give structure to the forms of this participatory life, are seen as the common repository of the human dignity of all the participants.[79]

Here is another depth against which to measure Trudeau.

IV

The critics provide several, often contradictory, accounts of Trudeau as a political thinker. He is seen as the reactionary breaker of the Quebec nation and the simple-minded stigmatizer of his people; yet he is the father of modern Canada and the architect of a more realized individualist and atomist account of his country. He was the master prestidigitator who, though avowedly a socialist, a libertarian, and a Christian, was an apologist for capitalism, an authoritarian state, and an amoral secularism, as well as being the rationalist modernizer seized by an unbending constitutional centralism and uniformitarianism. Trudeau has generally been regarded as irremediably anti-nationalist and so a common irritation among his critics has been over his own pan-Canadian nationalism. There is criticism that his functionalism rendered him a political conservative. There is too much of Hobbes and Locke in him, it is said, and not enough of Rousseau and Marx. And then there is the sophistication of Taylor's critique of Trudeau's rights model of society, his possibly "unrepublican" view of politics, and, if one agrees with Couture, the universalizing of his account of modernity. Finally, Bickerton and his colleagues, demonstrating that not all Trudeau's commentators have been detractors, argue that there was more substance and coherence in Trudeau than has generally been admitted. Regarding the intellectual influences upon him, they suggest that those of Kant, Maritain, and Berdyaev should also be considered. Trudeau's critics are not always in agreement among themselves and in the eyes of some of them he is guilty of serious political and theoretical transgressions.

Mounier, Maritain, and Laski: Getting an Education

———— • ◆ • ————

The first priority, when we choose a political system, is the importance of the human person. Not the person as an abstract notion; what is of prime importance is concrete human beings, you, me, the farmers, the workers, the businessmen . . . the workers of Windsor and the fishermen of Gaspésie or Newfoundland.
Pierre Elliott Trudeau

Le pire n'est pas toujours sûr.
Charles Péguy

I

Trudeau was unusually well-educated. Perhaps no prime minister of Canada read as widely and voluminously as he did. On a boat trip up the River Nile early in 1952 he read a book a day.[1] And in his retirement he revealed to a visitor that he had recently been reading poetry by Rainer Maria Rilke and William Butler Yeats.[2] Trudeau also had the advantage of an extensive formal education. It is not surprising, then, that he approached politics philosophically.

By his own admission, and with the general consent of most commentators, three thinkers were especially important to Trudeau's intellectual development: Jacques Maritain, Emmanuel Mounier, and Harold Laski. While it can be fairly accurately established which of these individuals' works Trudeau read and when he read them— he also had the benefit of extensive face-to-face encounters with Laski—unfortunately such straightforward details do not themselves establish equally straightforward proofs of intellectual influence. It does not follow that a book once read would have left an indelible impression. Nonetheless to clarify the genealogy of Trudeau's ideas and to measure the possible impact of these three thinkers we need a detailed map of their intellectual universe. Only then can we begin to discern the extent to which Trudeau undertook his intellectual journey along pathways pioneered by them.

II

In April 1944 the federal government granted Trudeau a student postponement of his military training and permission to leave the country. He was now free to pursue further education abroad. He considered a number of universities: Georgetown in Washington, Columbia in New York City, and Cambridge, England, but he settled on Harvard in Cambridge, Massachusetts. A little later permission of another sort arrived, from the secretary to the Archbishop:

> The Right Reverend Vicar General, Monsignor Hickey, directs me to say that, in view of the circumstances outlined in your letter, he hereby grants you permission to read (and keep) whatever books or pamphlets may be necessary in the pursuit of your studies in Political Sciences and Economy at Harvard.[3]

Trudeau's studies began in November 1944 and he was to pursue a PhD. It was his first extensive experience of living and working in a non-Francophone and non-Catholic environment. Trudeau took twelve half-courses: seven in economics and five in government. Passing all of them was necessary to staying in the program. Generally he did very well, especially in economics, and overall he received four As and four A minuses. The closest to an unsatisfactory grade was the B he received in W.Y. Elliott's course on Contemporary Political Theory and a "satisfactory" in Herman Finer's course on Comparative Government.

Harvard University was a socially exclusive and conservative place at the time, and far from the meritocratic and liberal paragon it apparently has become. Nor were all of Harvard's professors necessarily models of scintillating inquisitiveness and intellectuality. The economist, Joseph Schumpeter, for one was unimpressed by some members of the Economics Department, at least in the late 1930s.[4] But the professors who taught Trudeau were almost without exception a formidable collection of scholars, either already well-known in their fields or soon to become so. Several of them had emigrated from interwar Europe essentially as refugees from that troubled continent. Two of them—Wassily Leontief and Gottfried von Haberler—would become Nobel laureates in economics. Leontief, born in Czarist Russia though educated at the University of Leningrad, introduced Trudeau to John Maynard Keynes and his famous work, *The General Theory of Employment, Interest and Money*, published in 1936. Haberler, born in 1900 in what was then Austro-Hungary, was a disciple of the Austrian school of economics and partial to Friedrich Hayek's theories of laissez-faire and the "catallaxy" of the spontaneous order of markets and society. Haberler was critical of Keynes.

Schumpeter, also a native of Habsburg Austro-Hungary, taught Trudeau in a course on central banking. Generally he favoured free markets and was "suspicious of broad public intervention" but he was not a market fundamentalist and believed that there were important functions for the state at crucial stages in the evolution of capitalism.[5] He was, however, critical of Keynes too. Schumpeter's own reputation derived from his ideas about the roles of entrepreneurship, creativity, risk, and credit as indispensable elements in capitalism's development. He saw the latter as an inherently unstable and protean process of "creative destruction," as he put it in his famous work *Capitalism, Socialism and Democracy* in 1942. Trudeau regarded Schumpeter's book as a paragon of considered and balanced analysis:

> Schumpeter predicts that capitalism is gradually decomposing—though not for marxian reasons of class war, but [for] reasons of the inherent nearness of fully developed capitalism to socialism—loss of sense of property (stocks, bonds . . .), mechanization or bureaucratization of the capitalistic process, neglect to form a political class etc. Socialism is bound to arise from the ashes, though it will not probably be the classical or marxian type, but something nearer to fascism.[6]

Trudeau concluded that his book was "great" because of its inquiring spirit and unorthodox stance towards "the apparent commonplaces of truth."[7] Trudeau also took courses from Carl Friedrich, a native of Germany, and from Charles McIlwain, who was almost unique among Trudeau's professors in being American-born. These last two in particular built upon the interest he had developed at the University of Montreal in theories of the state and public law.

Although Harvard's faculty contained its share of conservative thinkers, particularly J.H. Williams (who taught a course on money and banking) and W.Y. Elliott, the preponderance of the influences upon Trudeau were nonconforming ones. Classical economics and market theory were basic to the curriculum but consideration was also given to newer paradigms that addressed the asymmetries and breakdowns of Western economies. That was why Keynes's work was so extensively embraced and why it was that a belief in economic planning and regulation was so prominent. Paul Sweezy—in the 1930s a student and teacher at Harvard and later a famous Marxist economic theoretician and co-founder of *Monthly Review*—concluded that Keynesians had gained the ascendancy at Harvard after 1936.[8] D.E. Moggridge claimed that Alvin

Hansen, another of Trudeau's teachers, was "Keynes's major senior American disciple and interpreter."[9] And there were other sources of unorthodoxy. After his coursework at Harvard, especially Merle Fainsod's Dictatorship and Bureaucracy, Trudeau probably knew as much about the economy of the USSR and its renowned constitution of 1936 as he did about almost anything else.

In his economics courses the discussion of the nature of capitalism was nonetheless a given. There were, however, many varieties of it, including historical, Austrian, Marshallian, and mathematical, to name just a few. Yet Marxist and social democratic perspectives were canvassed also: works by Marx himself and by Joan Robinson, the British, left-wing Cambridge economist, who would be a delegate with Trudeau at the conference on economic co-operation in Moscow in 1952. The British government's White Paper on Employment (1944) also figured in the curriculum along with a very early work by the Swedish social democrat Gunnar Myrdal. But these were more than offset by readings from classically liberal authors such as Irving Fisher, Ludwig von Mises, Friedrich Hayek, and Arthur Pigou. There was also Oskar Lange's famous book that attempted to bridge the ideological divide by arguing for socialist markets, On the Economic Theory of Socialism (1936). Trudeau's copy of Lange's classic text remains in his library where there are well-used copies of Hayek's The Road to Serfdom and Keynes's The General Theory of Employment, Interest and Money.[10]

However, it was Keynes who mainly embodied Harvard's affinity for alternative economics so that with the ideas of Hayek available as well it might be said that Trudeau had a front-row seat at the great debate between these two titans about the fundamental structures of modern capitalism. Trudeau wrote in his lecture notes J.H. Williams's version of Keynes's basic lesson:

We should prevent saving from equalling investment at a low level of employment. To get the equality at a high level, we must fill the gap between saving and investment two ways 1) Deficit spending, to increase incomes of poorer people 2) Progressive taxation, which by redistributing income would absorb the excess savings in the higher incomes.[11]

Trudeau later recalled that it was through Williams, an adviser at the Bretton Woods Conference, that he learned about the emerging order of the World Bank and the International Monetary Fund.[12] In another course Trudeau took note of Professor Herman Finer's opinion of the "limits" of laissez-faire:

> some economic activities no capitalist is prepared to take up; [there] is often [a] clash between "profits" and "public service"; laissez-faire can lead to monopoly.[13]

In the same course, Trudeau pondered a Hayek-inspired essay question, "A totalitarian dictatorship is the necessary result of a planned and controlled economy. Do you agree?" He offered a tantalizing non-Hayekean reply: "[It] depends on the depth of planning."[14]

In his more political courses Herman Finer, author of *Theory and Practice of Modern Government* (1932) and *Mussolini's Italy* (1935), provided a dizzying commentary on the undulations of recent Western history. Marx's class analysis was too simplistic, he said; there were many divisions in society and not just two; Russia in 1917 might have experienced a successful liberal revolution but events had fallen Lenin's way because of his superior organizational ability; the war had dislocated Russia; and Alexander Kerensky, the social democratic leader, had been an ineffective political leader. In Finer's words:

> The great bonanza for the revolution was the winning over of the garrison of St Petersburg. So it was the revolution of a minority (in the interests of all.) . . . The upshot is that the people were not asked. The party replaced the people, [and] the peasants were overruled.[15]

Finer also had decided views on the failure of the 1919 Weimar constitution in Germany. The revolutions there in 1918 had been due more to war weariness than anything else, he said, and the constitutional settlement that had emerged had failed to dislodge the old order of the Kaiser, the great landowners, the military and big business:

> Judiciary, civil service and army were all made from these controlling groups: no Jews, no Catholics, no socialists. In that context democratic elements were not strong enough (a democrat can't be liberal where democracy is questioned).

Trudeau added in his notes his own interpolation: "a democrat shouldn't be liberal where democracy is questioned."[16]

If Trudeau was becoming more open to left-wing views it did not follow that he was starry-eyed about the Soviet Union and fellow-travellers who advertised its successes. About Sidney and Beatrice Webb's controversial work, *Soviet Communism: A New Civilisation?* (1935) he offered the acerbic comment:

> The more you read of this seemingly thorough and detailed analysis the more you realize that respectable political scientists can also indulge in pseudo-science. And into inspiring cadres [*sic*] man as a citizen, as a consumer, as a producer, in the vocation of leadership—are poured an incredible number of insignificant facts, of naïve or unwarranted judgments, by gullible and often idiotic minds. . . . Take for example the note p. 435 where it is claimed that criticism is easy in the USSR yet where the same breath [*sic*] admits that [it] is not easy to get hold of the surreptitious pamphlets expressing it.[17]

Later, in 1952, Trudeau himself would be accused of harbouring fellow-traveller tendencies.

In his course Modern Political Thought, Carl J. Friedrich presented the canonical tradition in Western political thought, in this case from Luther and Machiavelli to Marx and ending with Jacob Burkhardt and Wilhelm Dilthey. Surviving among Trudeau's books are well-read copies of Friedrich's *Constitutional Government and Democracy* (1937) and *The New Belief in the Common Man* (1942). The former was Friedrich's grand text about the evolution of liberal-democratic government, especially in the United States and Britain, and the importance of constitutions, federalism, the separation of powers, judicial review, parliaments, political parties, and interest groups, while the other work grappled with the significance of the rise of mass democracy, popular sovereignty, majority rule, and rights and freedoms. Yet Trudeau never easily submitted to the arguments of an author and he was in two minds about the latter work: "This book is not much of a contribution," he said. It provided no new knowledge and was very superficial:

> However it does succeed in its main point: bringing to the public's attention the common man, as opposed to the elite, and showing that if reasonable goals are expected of him he will attain them.[18]

Friedrich gave Trudeau an important introduction to liberal constitutionalism. He also introduced him to Thomas Hobbes, about whom he had so far learned very little. From the evidence of the underlining in his own copy of *Leviathan* Trudeau read him very closely. According to Friedrich, at least as recorded in Trudeau's notes, Hobbes sought a sort of scientific method; he was "concerned with instrumental rather than a normative reason." For Hobbes, natural laws were theorems only, not commands of God. Friedrich also discussed the legal positivism of Hans Kelsen and the views of Roscoe Pound about law as an instrument of social engineering. Friedrich also made much of Immanuel Kant's essay on universal peace and was likely the first person to introduce Trudeau to the ideas of Harold Laski. A guarded optimism characterized Friedrich's account of the struggle within Western civilization:

But within the century (Abbé Sieyès, Rousseau, Kant) men would have come to the realization that there had to be a universal ordering of the world. Today we realize it even more. The stumbling block is; who is right as [to] how it should be done: bourgeois federated constitutionalisms (Kant) or the centralized united proletariat of Marx? Friedrich's conviction is that this conflict can be democratically resolved, i.e. without war. Though not inevitably so.[19]

The crucial premise of McIlwain's lectures had to do with the difference between medieval and modern forms of legality and law-making; in other words, it was concerned with the difference between medieval and modern constitutionalism.[20] The pre-modern kind, for McIlwain, did not consider sovereignty as law made by a sovereign but as something that was already made and found in custom or common law. Sovereignty in the Middle Ages was fragmented and diverse; it was shared and overlapping, and frequently contested between king, lord, and bishop. This changed with the collapse of feudalism and the rise of aggrandizing, absolutist kings such as Henry VIII in England. The new type of monarch defined sovereignty as the will of one person, usually himself. The divine-right-of-kings principle gave further lustre to the doctrine. But the emergence of religious pluralism brought new challenges to centralizing, single-minded monarchies. For McIlwain, the seminal thinker of early modern times was Jean Bodin, the sixteenth-century French *politique* who, while modern in his view of sovereignty—that sovereignty was the will of an identifiable sovereign—also believed in religious toleration and the need for checks and limits upon the sovereign. Bodin, for McIlwain, launched the modern doctrine of constitutional monarchy. Trudeau wrote:

> [His] innovation over all predecessors was to add the word "legislative" to the one "sovereignty." He discovered that governments in his time had arrived at the point where they were not only the power who applied law but the one who made law.[21]

Bodin held that the King was

> absolute in the sense that he ruled alone, and had no equal in government. But he was not absolutist in our present sense; that is, he was not above all laws. He was not arbitrary.[22]

According to Trudeau, McIlwain further claimed that Bodin had in effect been the great tutor of John Locke and, later, the fathers of the American constitution. Locke, for McIlwain under Bodin's influence, emerged as a sort of conservative medievalist who placed limits in law upon the sovereign. By implication the American founding fathers were "medieval" too in their constitutionalism.

Constitutional government suffered a significant intellectual challenge, according to McIlwain, with the coming of Thomas Hobbes and Jean-Jacques Rousseau and, in the nineteenth century, John Austin. Hobbes held that the sovereign's will was not only law but that his sovereign power was arbitrary and absolute, and somehow the people had consented to this arrangement.[23] In the nineteenth century, Austin would reinvigorate this account of unlimited sovereignty. But the greatest danger, said McIlwain, occurred when Hobbes's view was joined to the idea of the will of the people and became the doctrine of absolute *popular* sovereignty, in effect majority tyranny. This was Rousseau's baleful contribution. In his idea of the General Will the people were never wrong and, if the General Will was in effect embodied in the majority and/or represented in legislatures, then there was no limit to government's power to oppress individuals and minorities.[24] For McIlwain the solution was to limit sovereignty along the lines of the American Bill of Rights. Trudeau, prophetically perhaps, recorded McIlwain's advice about overbearing legislatures:

> [He] thinks that if the danger ever arises that Parliament should override the fundamentals, then the fundamentals will be put into a Bill of Rights, beyond the power of parliament.[25]

The voices of McIlwain and Friedrich were strong ones on behalf of liberal constitutionalism.

In the Trudeau Papers there is evidence of some of Trudeau's own opinions while at Harvard. After reading J.W. Allen's *A History of Political Thought in the Sixteenth Century* (1925), Trudeau made a very Catholic comment:

> Note the origins of protestantism [*sic*]. The impartial history of these origins seems to be the strongest proof against the divinity of such a religion.[26]

He was critical of the newly founded United Nations and the provision in its Charter to give the Great Powers permanent standing on the Security Council and a veto over its decisions. This was inconsistent with the principle of "sovereign equality," he said: "Let the government of nations be elective—if we believe in democracy, and accept [the] results of pressure groups—or even chosen by lot."[27] About the Nuremberg Trials, which had begun in November 1945, and perhaps registering an early influence of legal positivism and pragmatism, Trudeau took issue with the idea of war crimes tribunals. Individuals should be tried for specific, existing crimes like murder and brought before national courts. International crimes, such as initiating or making war, could only be judged by history and not by courts, he concluded.[28]

III

If the Trudeau Papers, with their extensive collection of his lecture notes, tell us more about the views of his professors, the great exception was his own long essay, "A Theory of Political Violence."[29] The fifty-six pages of its text and three pages of bibliography bristle with his ideas and opinions. However the essay was not well received and was only given a grade of B from his tutor, W.Y. Elliott, who wrote that "it misses the systematic analysis and application of concepts."[30] Probably some kind of personality conflict between Trudeau and Elliott was a factor, as John English alleges. Elliott had gone from Tennessee to Oxford on a Rhodes scholarship and was an anglophile. He was skeptical of both pragmatism and the pluralist theory of the state, especially the ideas of Harold Laski. Trudeau was already developing an interest in pragmatism; and he would soon become a disciple of Laski; and, in spite of what his critics have said, he was never an undiscriminating admirer of all things British.[31] Further evidence of Elliott's lack of sympathy is evident in a tetchy comment he made on the essay. At one point Trudeau claimed that Charles Maurras had given a new impetus to nationalism at the beginning of the twentieth century, to which Elliott pencilled in the comment: "Alone and unaided? What a man." Never one to resist responding to a provocation, Trudeau offered an addendum: "A better one than you." And after Trudeau had discussed "para-political societies" in Canada, mentioning the "Chevaliers de Jacques-Cartier . . . [and] our Masons and Orangemen," Elliott had added "and Fascists?" to which Trudeau added the petulant comment: "poor, stupid Elliott." Clearly it was not an amicable relationship. Elliott seemed especially interested in Trudeau's ethnic roots. On the title page of the essay he commented on Trudeau's name and wondered if he belonged to the Elliott clan. Later, in a copy of his *The Pragmatic Revolt in Politics: Syndicalism, Fascism and the Constitutional State*, he inscribed: "For Pierre Elliott Trudeau with the best wishes for his continued scholarly success, from another Elliott—William Yandell—and the honor of the clan!"

The essay did have weaknesses however. Trudeau did not yet write well in English and his elaboration of concepts was sometimes unclear and woolly. Its greatest weakness perhaps was that it was a sort of damp squib. After elaborating a rather complex and dramatic line of reasoning, in the final pages Trudeau actually reversed his argument. At the same time, the piece had very evident strengths. Trudeau was already impressive in the range and depth of his historical knowledge and the prodigious ambition and daring of his theorizing. His goal was indeed to write the definitive account of political violence and in slightly less than sixty pages. Overall the essay provides evidence of his ongoing though still incomplete turn from the anti-democratic, clericalist nationalism of his early years towards, in this case, such liberal ideas as the primacy of skepticism and the conscience-centred, self-determining individual. Yet such views he held with a strong sense of a moral order transcending individual choice. It was just that in his view this moral order was to an important extent opaque and indeterminable. The essay also gives evidence of Trudeau persisting in some of his previous political preoccupations. While there were indications of new reading—works by J.W. Allen, Charles McIlwain, Alfred Cobban, and John Dewey—his bibliography was stocked heavily with authors from his pre-liberal past: Henri Bergson, Curzio Malaparte, Charles Maurras, Georges Sorel, Vladimir Lenin, and Leon Trotsky. The only books he recycled from the old days that did not quite fit the non-liberal mould were *Humanisme intégral* by Jacques Maritain and Charles Péguy's *Notre jeunesse*.[32] The essay reverberates with Trudeau's youthful excitement over political *terribilità* and extremisms: insurrection, assassination, terrorism, *coups d'état*, *coups de force*, and such. Proof perhaps of this was Trudeau's disconcerting tendency to sprinkle his argument with examples drawn from the world of dynamite and ordnance.

One of the features the essay disclosed was a move towards the pragmatism of John Dewey (1859–1952), in particular his eight-page article, "Force and Coercion," published in the *International Journal of Ethics* in 1916. In his lifetime Dewey was considered the epitome of the American liberal and progressive and his reputation remains so to this day. His liberalism was of course not of the laissez-faire type and he is more accurately described as a socialist, although not of the communist type. In the essay Dewey drew a distinction between power, coercion, and violence. His claim was that all politics was about the application of power and force. "Power," or what he also called "energy," was the institutionalized rule of a regime over its subjects or of a movement over its followers; it was more like an intimidating psychological hegemony that ensured that leaders' decisions would be complied with. But the threat to use force and coercion was implied in it. For Dewey the fundamental challenge to the practitioner of politics was to match ends and means. Politics was essentially about practical matters requiring practical solutions. Context counted for a lot but his overall claim was that a particular political activity presupposed a given end or goal and so the pre-eminent task of the political leader was to select an effective means to attain whatever end had been chosen. When there was failure to provide effective, successful methods, "violence" occurred. Failed power and misdirected force were what caused violence.

From Dewey's perspective there was no a priori, abstract under-standing of what might be effective in a given situation. Judgment was situational and the political leader must be open to doing what-ever worked in the circumstances. Power and force must necessar-ily be deployed. In some contexts "sophisticated, legal methods" might work better than "primitive methods of force." But some-times legality will not work:

> There is always a possibility that what passes as a legitimate use of force may be as wasteful as to be really a use of violence; and *per contra* that measures condemned as recourse to mere violence may, under the given circumstances, represent an intelligent uti-lization of energy [power]. In no case, can antecedent or *a priori* principles be appealed to as more than presumptive; the point at issue is concrete utilization of means for ends.[33]

These ideas Trudeau embraced in his essay. He would do so in later life too.

Another important methodological innovation in the essay, also influenced by Dewey, was Trudeau's application of concepts drawn from physics to political phenomena. He hoped it would have a decidedly heuristic value. Physics' terms, Trudeau observed, were "concrete" and "visual" and "unpassioned too," and they would render the study of history and politics objective.[34] He was posit-ing something like a mechanistic account of society and politics. For Trudeau, elites—political leaders primarily—were the dynamic

forces or "vectors" of history and the non-elites were generally passive. Let us suppose, said Trudeau, that society can be thought of as
a mass of atoms, molecules, or particles that are set in motion when
an impetus is brought to bear on them. Without "power" or "force,"
human beings remain "inert" and unmoved. Consequently his essay
became to a large extent a taxonomy of the various ways in which the
actions of the few acted on the mass and produced a variety of political forms and effects. If power and force were used by all kinds of
governments, equally they were utilized by a variety of popular and
insurgent movements: revolutions, rebellions, insurrections, campaigns of civil disobedience and terrorism, *coups d'état*, and *coups de
force*. Nevertheless it can be said of all of them, Trudeau went on, that
they pursued some kind of moral goal—justice and peace were two
he mentioned rather generally—so that all forms of political action
could be said to use power and force to realize preconceived moral
ends. Thus for Trudeau, following the lead of Dewey, the pre-eminent consideration in politics must be efficiency and effectiveness in
carrying out the goal that each particular political group fashioned
for itself. His interest for now was not to distinguish between the
moral purposes of different kinds of political projects but rather to
assess whether there could be a kind of successful calculus of political
effectiveness consistent with whatever goals the groups happened to
chose: "All we ask of a method is that it work well";[35] and

> the only question before any political initiative should be is it
> absolutely efficient; and is it absolutely necessary to attain the
> right ends of the political society?[36]

His theory was tilted towards the idea of politics as an instrumental activity: given the goals in mind, there was little point in holding them if they were inadequately or unsuccessfully pursued. But
of course his conception of politics was not altogether devoid of a
sense of ends. But ends were not worth imagining, however, if they
could not be realized.

Central to power and force, in Trudeau's argument, then, were the elements of "coercion" and "compulsion." There was no hint of pacifism or voluntarism. At one point Trudeau disparaged those he called

> chicken-livered sentimentalists . . . who would preach a complete divorce of societies from power, simply because power too often degenerates into violence. . . . [W]ithout political force or power masses would be doomed to complete inertia.[37]

There is a sinister tone in this, although probably all that Trudeau was saying was that the basic techniques available to any government or political movement were necessarily founded on the use of power and force, or certainly the *threat* to use them. At the same time he did allow for the possibility of effective power being based on consent. But democratic government was not exempt from the requirement that it be effectively practised.

The subject of his essay was specifically "political violence," which, he said, resulted from an ineffective use of power, force, and coercion:

> Many of our conclusions could be stated as physical laws: the greater the mass that must be moved, the greater must be the power or force to succeed. And the greater the method of applying force or power, the greater the degree of violence that may result from its ill-use. . . . Unfortunately we have not the time to do this more thoroughly, so we will have to be content with laying down three general rules, which might be of help in avoiding violence.
>
> 1. That method shall be chosen which is the best apportioned to the desired end;
> 2. That method shall be applied implacably; and
> 3. That method shall be subject to perfect control.[38]

Trudeau elaborated these rules:

> The first rule may appear self-evident on paper; but it certainly is not followed by all political leaders, many of whom think they can prevent communist infiltration by strengthening the police force. And at the other extreme, we have those who are always clamoring for revolution, when all that is needed is a good political machine and a few thugs on election day. In my opinion, the best trick of all is to succeed in licking the opponent at his own game: for cheating is not wicked when the game is to cheat. A little more thought should be given to the taking of power by insidious infiltration or by indirect means. The French-Canadians, for instance, could work miracles if they had a little less faith in politics, and more in economics and technical ability; surely, revolution is a handy tool to show through one's pocket, but a tool like the cooperative movement can be used even out in the open. It seems to me that the Premier of Portugal, Mr. Salazar, proved a lot of things when he made his "Revolution through Peace." . . .
>
> The second rule calls for the utmost determination in employing the method. If a fight is unavoidable, strike hard and first. If a course has been singled out as the only plausible one in the circumstances, it is sheer stupidity to begin belly-aching over its illegality. Laws are made to sponsor the progress of societies; when they block it, they should be changed. I must add, however, that a bad law, if it is constitutional, is not violence; so that if violence is to be avoided in resisting it, much care must be taken.[39]

An all-prevailing instrumentalism, then, gave forth a worldly-wise and cold realism. Often the worst can only be prevented, Trudeau said, by extreme actions. Trudeau seems to be amoral, worldly, even cynical and Machiavellian, certainly unsentimental. He apparently took pride in thinking through the implacable logic of action based on reality, including accepting the necessary exigencies, hypocrisies, and ironies of political existence. Yet in his youthful, inconsistent fumblings—co-operativism as a substitute for revolution and Salazar as a paragon of peaceful change—he also seemed somehow naive and perhaps a little idealistic, because for Trudeau, politics was not always about extremism and sang-froid. He went on to say that effectiveness pre-supposed "wisdom" in juxtaposing ends and means. Everything depended on context. Moderate means were sometimes the efficient ones although the examples he cited became more and more extreme and incendiary as the essay wore on.

Trudeau set himself the goal of prescribing a political tech-nique and calculus for every context and situation and so he could not but eventually recommend extreme and questionable methods for extreme and questionable situations. The casual reader might be led to believe that the small voices of moderation and decency located in more everyday contexts become insignificant in his mind although they did not completely disappear. A more certain judg-ment about his claims is that for him politics was such a changeable activity that everyday peaceable contingencies governed by moder-ate methods might need to be replaced by extreme ones and so the politician must be prepared to get his hands dirty:

> The last [third] rule calls for perfect control. For since the chosen method is to be applied ruthlessly it would soon cause violence if it got out of hand. It is because of instinctive application of this rule that the so-called wise men always resort to moderate means. And in a way they are right; for when a digger doesn't know the art of sapping he is wise to prefer the pick to dynamite. Moderate means generally being a sum of many non-physical political instruments, such as propaganda, bribery and corruption, they are under almost perfect control, since when the desired effect is obtained, they can simply and surely be discontinued. Whilst a revolution is apt to behave like some of these "perpetual-motion" machines: once touched off they revolve faster and faster until they fly right through the roof of the pseudo inventor's barn. But that is not to say, of course, that physical methods should never be used. . . .

Consequently, it is not superfluous to point out that the wise-men are not so wise in refusing to consider any means that are not "moderate." For their wisdom in observing the third rule makes them ridiculous by violating the first: what is the use of estimating well the strength of one's tool, if the size of the work is grossly under-estimated? First, see what must be done; second, learn (as Trotsky did) how to manipulate the tool that can do it; third, work relentlessly.[40]

But, after such sweeping judgments, finally what bathos! Having put out a great effort to establish a detailed calibration of the joining of ends and means, Trudeau ended on a note of doubt and uncertainty. He admitted that his argument smacked of moral relativism. But this was only true of him, he wrote, if "politics" was considered separately from "ethics." In fact, he declared, politics was bound to include ethical considerations. He also admitted to radical doubts about the possibility of perfect knowledge of the relations of means and ends and so in effect he doubted the existence of a successful calculus of means and ends. There was a shape to human affairs, to be sure, he said, but humans cannot discern it well and no one can perfectly predict the ideal trajectory of mankind in any given situation. He also gave another reason for skepticism, and this was that politics dealt with peoples' fears and uncertainties, so there was a never-ending tendency among politicians to seek ever more power in order to control every imaginable situation and it created a tendency on their part to exaggerate what was necessary in most situations.

In effect, Trudeau concluded his essay by admitting that it was based on premises in which he did not quite believe or which were implausible. It was as if he had inflated a colourful balloon only in the end to burst it. As the air hissed out he offered an alternative view:

Since life won't wait for final solutions, however, but must be acted upon *hic et nunc*. What must "A" do? . . . A must hierarchize [*sic*] values according to certain fundamentals inherent in human nature; and when confronted with a concrete political gesture, he can judge it accordingly to its place in the hierarchy. Firstly then, A must inquire whether his political ends are compatible with his "heaviest values." Then, he must seek those means to the ends which are admissible to him, considering again the heavier values. Finally, he will choose one of the admissible means and apply it, by following the three rules of avoiding political violence. . . . After that, A can be as sure as is humanly possible to him that his acts will be absolutely non-violent."[41]

Here Trudeau asserted that both means and ends have to be subject to moral considerations. His claim was not that there can be no knowledge of the shape or curvature of civilization and of particular trends within it but rather that we can only know *some* of these things but unfortunately never enough to guide our actions perfectly. In principle the ideal curvature of history—what he called history's "sinusoid"—must be consistent with "human fundamentals" but, if we cannot know its outline, we cannot be guided by it. Equally, Trudeau continued, these very "fundamentals" were uncertain and a matter of deep dispute. History was not transparent and human judgments within it were fallible and contested. We can only know in part. All that we can do is to offer our best judgment of what should be done and we should not be surprised if others disagree because they too were situated behind a veil of partial ignorance.

Yet for Trudeau there was no escape from both responsibility and choice. Skepticism about the extent of our social knowledge led him neither to disengagement nor to a vulpine amorality but to involvement in the worldly fray *and* an emphasis upon the importance of a moral compass. All one can do is to be true to one's conscience. Nevertheless living in a world of uncertainty the politician moved in a constant half-light and he may, at times, be called on to do unsavoury things. That said, the emphasis of his final position seems to have been that there was in fact virtue in the moderate politics of a peaceable, predictable society, a politics that in turn would nurture the maintenance of such a society: a regime of modest ambitions in which leaders made limited, unextreme decisions was preferable to one in which the risks of wrong decisions were enormous given the heightened consequences of being wrong. But whatever considerations were entered into they could not be a prelude to doing nothing.

Trudeau concluded with an allusive but unelaborated comment about how "reality" was the ultimate testing-ground for discovering these moral "fundamentals." Presumably he meant by this that the course of human events educated the individual in what was valuable and in the necessary methods to attain results that were of value. Human knowledge, because it was always partial, had need of testing and revision through action and engagement. The other point of considerable interest in the essay is the importance Trudeau placed on pursuing a life of moral curiosity and endeavour. Trudeau's was a skeptical, realistic, and potentially tragic world view but still it was a moral one. Politics was more than technique, he said, but it was imperative that it not overlook the importance of practice. Political life must embrace a realism of method while never losing sight of the truth that politics must be about the good.

IV

In the autumn of 1946 Trudeau's educational odyssey took him to the Sciences Po in Paris. He arrived in a city still suffering from wartime depredations with many of the buildings needing a fresh coat of paint and antagonisms still festering between those who had sided with the Resistance and those who had been complicit with the Nazis and the comprador Vichy regime. There had been many spontaneous acts of violence and revenge. Towards some retribution had been meted out more formally and definitively. Charles Maurras and Robert Brasillach, both of whom Trudeau had read approvingly during his rightist youth, had been found guilty of collaboration, the former condemned to life in prison and the other to death before a firing squad.[42] By 1946, however, Trudeau was travelling along a different highway. With his scholarship from the French government and his own money to spend—he had brought his Harley-Davidson motorbike too—Paris represented not so much previous, regrettable dalliances but new possibilities: uncongested boulevards and the ideas of Jean-Paul Sartre, André Siegfried, André Malraux, Jacques Maritain, Raymond Aron, Henri Daniel-Rops, Étienne Gilson, Gabriel Marcel, Pierre Teilhard de Chardin, and Louis Aragon.[43] He attended many of their lectures and read many of their books. Among those who impressed him was Emmanuel Mounier, a personalist and a socialist.

Trudeau remembered his discovery of personalism as a kind of epiphany:

> It involved coming to the realization that he was "a whole person . . . my own judge and my own master." He called this a recognition and acceptance of "the concept of incarnation . . . as the personalists put it."[44]

His exposure to personalist ideas had begun at Brébeuf through his friendship with François Hertel. He also knew about personalism through his reading of Jacques Maritain. In 1942, Hertel had published *Pour un ordre personnaliste*, a personal copy of which Trudeau received from his friend although this particular copy remains uncut in Trudeau's library. He did however include the title in the bibliography of his essay on political violence. In any event it is not clear that Hertel would have introduced him to Mounier specifically for in his book he did not mention Mounier at all.

When Trudeau first met him face-to-face, likely in late 1946, Mounier was at the height of his renown.[45] In 1970 in a brief interview with John Hellman, a biographer of Mounier, Trudeau revealed that he had been particularly impressed by Mounier's short book, *L'affrontement chrétien*, first published in April 1945, in Switzerland.[46] He acquired the work in Paris in October 1946 and from the evidence of the markings in his copy he read it closely. He attended lectures by Mounier and in his record of his dreams for his Paris psychoanalyst, Georges Parcheminey, Trudeau claimed to have dreamt of attending a gathering at Mounier's house![47] Jacques Monet believes that, while in Paris, Trudeau often talked with Mounier's colleague, Henri Marrou. By then Hertel was also in the city so that "through Marrou and Hertel, he was also in touch with such liberal theologians as Marie-Dominique Chenu, Yves Congar, Jean Danielou, and Henri du Lubac."[48] Hellman speculates that Trudeau might have had some contact in Paris with Mounier's *Esprit* group's experiment in communal living, perhaps that house from his dreams.[49] In Trudeau's Papers there is the program of a conference by the Personalist Group on "Existentialism and Personalism," in High Leigh, Hoddesdon, outside London in January 1948, a conference which, presumably, Trudeau either attended or was interested in attending.[50] Listed were lectures by Gabriel Marcel and George Catlin, and one by Mounier on "The ambiguities of personalism." Trudeau, then, knew of personalism during the war but his exposure specifically to Mounier likely only began in earnest in Paris.[51] Later on, Gérard Pelletier, his close friend, whose thinking was massively shaped by personalism and who himself was likely introduced to it in Paris by Trudeau and Hertel, would have been an ongoing conduit for personalist ideas and those of Mounier in particular.[52] So also would have been the other members of the editorial board of *Cité Libre*.[53] After the war Trudeau subscribed to Mounier's review, *Esprit*,[54] while several of Mounier's colleagues from Paris and from *Esprit*—Henri Marrou, Paul Vigneau, and Albert Béguin—regularly visited Montreal in the early 1950s.[55] Béguin succeeded Mounier as editor of the review and it was Trudeau who, in June 1957, wrote his obituary in *Cité Libre*.[56]

Pelletier and Trudeau had first met in 1941 in Montreal although it was not until they were in Paris that they forged a close friendship.[57] After going their different ways their lives converged during the Asbestos strike of 1949 and then a year later with the founding of *Cité Libre*. It is easily forgotten how much that review was in its inception a project of members of Jeunesse étudiante catholique (JÉC) who were followers of personalism, especially of Mounier and

Esprit. Particularly important was Pelletier who was a leader of the JÉC in the province.[58] The group's personalism would in time come to represent an important modernizing force within the Catholic Church in Quebec, shifting it away from being a conservative and clerically dominated institution towards one that would be laity-oriented, reformist, and even a little socialist. The JÉC, and *Cité Libre* came to see many of their aspirations realized in Vatican II, the great reforming Council called by Pope John XXIII in 1962. As E. Martin Meunier and Jean-Phillipe Warren put it, personalism in Quebec was a sort of "religious exiting from religion," and "an anti-clericalism from within."[59]

In 1950 Trudeau was neither a member of the JÉC nor of any other Catholic Action organization, nor did he have a close association with the group involved in launching *Cité Libre*. Yet he had had some association with Catholic Action through his early friendship with Claude Ryan who was its national secretary after 1945 and while on his world trek in 1948–9, Trudeau met many members of the movement, who were serving in missions.[60] In fact Trudeau's own religious views were not far removed from those of the JÉCers in *Cité Libre* and in late 1949 he was invited to address a summer school of the Jeunesse indépendante catholique, "Où va le Monde."[61] Consequently if there was initial resistance to bringing Trudeau onto the board of *Cité Libre* this was not so much because of his theological views but because of his reputation for being distant, imperious, and rich. In the end, Pelletier's influence prevailed, convincing the skeptics to include him.[62] Coincidentally the very first issue of *Cité Libre* included a report on the death of Mounier written by Pelletier.

Personalism emerged in the late eighteenth century in reaction to some of the more determinist tendencies of Enlightenment thought. Friedrich Jacobi and Friedrich Schelling were early devotees and they launched a tradition of discourse that would eventually take in elements from Søren Kierkegaard, Friedrich Nietzsche, Nicolas Berdyaev, Henri Bergson, Karl Jaspers, Gabriel Marcel, Martin Heidegger, Albert Camus, Jean-Paul Sartre, Maurice Blondel,

and, of course, Mounier. The idea of an immersion in a presuppositionless, pre-interpretive consciousness that was the person-in-the-
world underlined personalism's debt to phenomenologists like Max
Scheler and Edmund Husserl. Early influences on Mounier included
Henri Bergson, Charles Péguy, Jacques Chevalier, and Scheler,
and, in regards to his political views, Pierre-Joseph Proudhon.[63]
Personalism's later disciples would include an obscure theologian,
Father Karol Wojtyła, of the Catholic University in Lublin, Poland,
who would go on to become Pope John Paul II in 1978.[64] What all
personalisms shared—and there were several types including non-
religious ones—was a belief in the "centrality of the person as the
primary locus of investigation for philosophical, theological and
humanistic studies."[65] The human person was of fundamental worth
and possessed "an inviolable dignity that merit[ed] unconditional
respect."[66] Personalism was profoundly anti-authoritarian and, in
many instances, gave rise to a radical socialism. This was the case
with Mounier who expressed, with many on the radical Left at the
time, an unrelenting antagonism towards parliamentary democracy
and capitalism.[67]

Mounier's imaginary was an intriguing mixture of individualism and communitarianism. He was a communitarian who nonetheless placed the rights of the "individual" person in high regard.
The individual he set within a Christian theological framework.
Freedom was God's gift to humanity and proof of His love for His
creation. Such love was the precondition of what he called the "intimacy" (*intimité*) possible between the individual person and God
Himself, and between the person and other persons. Early in his
life Mounier studied the Spanish mystic, John of the Angels, and
mysticism lay behind his partiality for the doctrine of the Mystical
Body of Christ and the mystical unity of the self with God and the
Church.[68] Similar suppositions undergirded his view of the common personhood of all and of the existence of a shared "person,"
that was to be a transformed society.[69] The self, in Mounier's formulation, was not so much a literal, psychological locus within
the human body or brain as it was the nodal point of a moral and

spiritual creativity that was bound to reach out to others.[70] It was a "spiritual" presence in a human being, neither "psychologically isolable" nor "localized in space," and it constituted a "moral absolute," an "ontological ultimate," for at the core of the person was her conscience.[71] There was with him a sense of the radical equality of all individuals and peoples in their common personhood and in their universal capacity for moral choice. He was strongly anti-imperialist and an early supporter of feminism.

Mounier was born in 1905 in France, the son of "a humble Grenoble pharmacist, ... [he] took a romantic pride in his four peasant grandparents."[72] He attended the local university and later the Sorbonne. At Grenoble he was influenced by Jacques Chevalier who was a follower of Bergson and his belief that interiority and intuition rather than rational thought were the foundations of spirituality and religious insight.[73] For Mounier too, personalism was not so much a system of thought as it was an orientation towards the world. It did not provide certain, general knowledge; it was pluralistic in its sensibilities, and it was open to others' intuitions especially those of other denominations and religions and indeed those of non-believers too. Hence his life-long dialogue with Marxism and existentialism.[74] Yet he was always convinced of the fundamental presence of the Holy Spirit. He named the review that he founded in 1932 *Esprit*. If Mounier did not quite place politics above spirituality, it was still an important part of his overall outlook. He stressed the need for a revolution that would be both spiritual and moral—a kind of religious, cultural revolution—and which would supersede parliamentary democracy, capitalism, and communism.[75] In the 1930s he was an advocate of a "third-way" mentality, beyond liberal democracy and Marxism.[76]

The political convictions of Mounier and *Esprit* were complicated, for the review encouraged a diversity of opinion. Mounier himself was impressed by Marx and the Soviet Union but, before the war, he believed that Marxism constituted a materialist system devoid of spirituality.[77] He changed later on. Some of his views, especially his anti-capitalism and anti-parliamentarianism, might have inclined him to the clericalist nationalism of the French Right, especially *Action française* and thinkers like Charles Maurras. However Mounier himself—though not always his colleagues—scrupulously avoided such an association.[78] Nor was he impressed by conventional French Christian Democratic politics.[79] That he was not an automatic supporter of the Catholic Church was demonstrated during the Spanish Civil War when, although mainly neutralist in outlook, he expressed horror at the Franco regime's violence on behalf of the Catholic cause.[80] Continuing his anti-Francoism, in June 1937 he publicly condemned the infamous Nazi bombing of Guernica.[81]

Nevertheless, according to John Hellman, Mounier's and *Esprit*'s views on Nazi Germany were complex and controversial.[82] Mounier was a constant critic of the Versailles settlement and what he saw as its humiliation of Germany. It was French foreign policy that was largely responsible for the unfortunate course of German politics in the interwar period. For Mounier Nazi Germany was a sort of flawed yet genuine version of an organic society, awkwardly rebalancing and respiritualizing itself in difficult times. Later he became more critical of Hitler but he never regarded the Nazi regime as an extreme aberration.[83] As Hellman puts it, "Mounier thought that there was something universally human in German National Socialism."[84] These views played a major part in his disagreements and eventual falling-out with Jacques Maritain. Even after the Munich Agreement in 1938 and the dismemberment of Czechoslovakia, Mounier continued to counsel pacifism and what others called appeasement.[85]

Further controversies arose with the onset of the war and the German invasion of France in 1940.[86] Mounier was in two minds about the Vichy regime, as was the *Esprit* group in general. Positively disposed at the beginning, they saw in its establishment a moment of possible French regeneration. Mounier was well connected. His early mentor, Jacques Chevalier, became a minister and adviser to Pétain. However in January 1941 Mounier broke with the regime over its treatment of French Jews. He doubted that he

could be of much use to the Resistance but, in the end, he probably was involved in it in some way.[87] Certainly the government
believed so and he was arrested in January 1942 and imprisoned.
He went on a hunger strike. Eventually put on trial he was released
for want of evidence. Mounier repaired to the small community of
Dieulefit, in the Drôme, in the southeast of France, where he wrote
L'affrontement chrétien in the winter of 1943–4.[88]

In his book Mounier invoked the authority of Friedrich
Nietzsche, usually thought of as an apostate from and an antagonist
of Christianity. Clearly his purpose was to offer a searing critique
of French Catholicism for its lack of vitality and its fear of the passions. Mounier noted that Nietzsche had referred to Christianity
as a "castration."[89] In this he felt that Nietzsche had made a misplaced identification for it did not apply to Christianity in general
but rather to Catholicism in its late-bourgeois phase. In Mounier's
view what ailed the contemporary French Church was its isolation
from the vitality of working class culture. The Catholic Church had
become "a religion of women, old men and the petit-bourgeois."[90]
Here was Mounier functioning as both sociologist and prophet
articulating a sense of the Church as becalmed within a particular social order, overwhelmed by sin and corruption and awaiting
redemption by the grace of God. But the failings of the Church must
be confronted, particularly its conformity and timidity; its repression of the body, and its obsession with money and the bourse.[91]

Nor did Mounier necessarily agree with Nietzsche in other
respects. In particular he criticized him for the despair and mean-
inglessness of his world view. However if for Mounier the Christian
world view was not quite one of despair, it was one that was well
acquainted with tragedy. The world was a broken place but it was
also a place of hope and love and the presence of God. But God's
purposes were never completely knowable and the world the
Christian passed through was an uncertain one. At the heart of
the Christian tragedy lay the indeterminacy and ambiguity of existence. The implications of Mounier's views were anti-utopian, anti-
idealistic, and skeptical of systems of thought.[92]

According to Mounier, in preaching its unadventurous gospel the petit-bourgeois Church had embraced a religion beyond tragedy. Its other defect had been a flight from the real and the earthly into the other-world of the mystical and the ascetic. The devout Catholic housewife and the other-worldly nun were two sides of the same coin. Mounier's point was that without a sense of the tragic there can be no sense of Christian intensity, anger, and engagement. A Christian vitality must be returned to the Church. Crucial in this regard was the obligation of the Church to embrace the working class and to revive the buried traditions of earlier authentic Catholic experiences, for example the spiritualizing of the passions in the late medieval church.[93] The established Church was obsessed with sex and its insistence on repressing it had bred psychoses in the lives of the faithful so that the bourgeoisie hated the body and its instincts. The education of the young in sexual matters was usually an exercise in ignorance and denial. The Church had over-idealized love and womanhood, especially through its worship of the Virgin Mary.[94]

In a word what the bourgeois Church lacked was "virility," perhaps better translated as "manliness." It was a religion of the feminine, characterized by passivity, humility, dependence, and conformity. For Mounier the body and its passions must be accepted and transformed by faith and Christian spirituality. Christians too were embodied, manly creatures. There was an authentic Christian passion, aggression, and adventurousness and, if there was not quite a Christian reason to kill, there was certainly a duty to be courageous, especially in the face of death.[95] L'affrontement chrétien was a provocative work: angry, denunciatory, and dismissive. Though Mounier's message was ultimately one of hope and transcendence, it was a dark, intense work suffused with the nightmares and tribulations of existence.

At the end of the Second World War, Mounier was well positioned to play an important role in French politics. His Resistance credentials were burnished enough to allow him to move in the mainstream of a postwar order dominated by Socialists,

Communists, and the Christian Democrats of the Mouvement républicain populaire. He now shifted even more emphatically to the Left. Mounier had always admired the bracing nature of Marxism's socio-economic analysis but felt that its world view was irreligious. After 1945 he became especially interested in a Marxist humanism and the theme of alienation in Marx's early writings.[96] He was highly critical of what he saw as the emerging American-dominated global order with its Atlantic Charter and the North Atlantic Treaty Organization (NATO) in 1949.[97] He disliked the idea of Europe becoming some kind of "buffer zone" between the two Great Powers.[98] Part of his neutralism was a more accommodative attitude towards the Soviet Union and more openness towards French Communists and Marxists.[99] But events conspired against him. In May 1947 the Communists were dismissed from the French government; and throughout the world the Cold War began to take hold. There was the show-trial in September 1947 of Nikolai Petkov, the Bulgarian non-Communist political leader, and in February 1948 the Communist coup in Prague, as well as ongoing reports of Stalin's concentration camps. Mounier now put some distance between himself and communism though he remained a socialist. In 1950 he died of a heart attack, at the early age of 44.

In 1949 Mounier produced what would become the final account of his thought, *Le personnalisme*. Its argument has many echoes in Trudeau's thought, such as his realism and theory of engagement, as well as his liberalism-by-default and social democracy. Mounier's phenomenological realism emphasized that humans were embodied creatures, inhabiting not just actual bodies but a particular time and place. Engagement with the world was not just one's duty; it was how one's being was constituted. One was both in and of the world which, when it was not a daunting place, was also a place of courageous adventure, where values were shaped and the Other engaged. Mounier's epistemology and ontology focused on the particular and the unique and were averse to the idea of truth as a system of unvarying universal and rational truths. Above all, ideas did not derive from beyond our world, in utopia for example.[100] Truth and knowledge were discovered within the world and discerned dialectically, through action with and in association with others. Mounier's existential communitarianism became the bedrock of what he called his "objective" account of truth. Humans must be free to choose the good but they were not free to make it up for themselves. For Mounier the uplifting message of personalism was of freedom as a divine gift that brought enlightenment and self-discovery, and a self-consciousness that disposed the person to identify with others in mutually affirming discoveries.[101] He explicitly rejected Greek thought and what he viewed as its tendency to abstract generalizing. Plato was a primary object of his criticism though Aristotle was problematical as well.[102] Here was a major philosophical difference with Jacques Maritain.

Mounier set out five ways-of-being in the world: contemplative, political, technical, moral, and prophetic. All were necessary in a good society. A large part of life was necessarily devoted to economic tasks and ensuring human survival. But economic life devoid of moral principles was merely utilitarian and efficiency-oriented. Politics was the crucial site where economic action was subject to morality and the prophetic impulse. What Mounier alleged, in so many words, was that politics must be an exercise in principled realism.[103] He was in no doubt about the strange uncertainties of politics-in-the-world and the perplexities and agonies of immersion in it:

> We understand that the cause of the good and the cause of evil are only rarely juxtaposed as black and white, [and] that sometimes the cause of truth is distinguished from that of error by a hair's breadth.[104]

From the evidence of his essay on political violence Trudeau was already well disposed towards a Christian realism though it might not yet then have registered the effects of Mounier's specific ideas.

Another important emphasis in *Le personnalisme* was Mounier's critique of liberal democracy, the essential deficiency of which, he thought, had to do with its misconceived individualism. Its mistaken senses of inwardness and self-determination were, he felt, oblivious to the claims of social solidarity. Yet his world view did presuppose some kind of individuated self within a sphere of liberty. He recognized that each person must be free to listen to his conscience and to choose the good in order to reach out in love to others. It followed that the good could not be imposed, either by the state or by others. For Mounier freedom to choose meant that political change had to be through persuasion and education. The consensual socialism he preached was a pluralist one, open to different cultural forms and to experimentation and gradual change. While in Mounier's mind there existed a difference between liberal democracy and what he called "personalist democracy," the pursuit of the latter presupposed the existence of many of the rights, liberties, and institutions of the former.[105] However if traditional rights and freedoms were important, newer social liberties and schemes of personal empowerment were too:

> Before proclaiming freedom in our constitutions or exalting it in our conversations, we should guarantee the *common* conditions of biological, economic, social and political freedom which permit to average folk the chance to participate in the highest longings of humanity.[106]

Mounier also talked of the importance of moving beyond the machine-based party and parliamentary politics of the time towards a transfigured and public-spirited electorate and transformed economy, a true democracy. Yet his thinking on a future socialist state presupposed some kind of *Rechtsstaat* or rights-based rule of law.

Trudeau's admiration for Mounier popped up in the most unlikely of places. In November 1970, in the aftermath of the October Crisis, at a Liberal Party conference, few of whose delegates would have even heard of his name and fewer have known anything about his ideas, Trudeau invoked his early mentor although in the cause of a protective state:

This conception of our responsibility to the individual and to society is in keeping with the vision of the state and its role held by Emmanuel Mounier, a thinker who has had a profound influence on so many men of my generation. "The role of the state," he said, "is limited to guaranteeing the fundamental rights of the individual, and placing no obstacle in the path of free competition between schools of thought. The state is nonetheless obligated to guarantee these fundamental rights of the person. The performance of this service justifies compulsion in specific circumstances."[107]

V

Trudeau cited Jacques Maritain, also a personalist, as another important influence on him.[108] As early as 1936, he was aware of his work and during the war he attended lectures given by him in Montreal.[109] One of Maritain's most important political books was *Humanisme intégral* (*True Humanism*), published in 1936, which, from the evidence of the inscription in his copy, Trudeau acquired in 1941. He read and commented on it a year later, in August 1942.[110] Trudeau recognized the author's Thomism, his advocacy of a new, revolutionary Christianity, and his defence of the person's rights against corporatist groups. Trudeau's comments were percipient and, if he was indeed persuaded of them, it would have put him at odds with the Maurrasian orthodoxy that he had hitherto absorbed. But to what extent did they represent his actual convictions at the time? The Nemnis argue that they did not, although they seem to have arrived at their conclusion more by what Trudeau did not say rather than what he did.[111] Nevertheless, they are probably right. It is likely that only after Trudeau's change of political direction two years later did he become truly receptive to Maritain. In Paris he read Maritain's *Les droits de l'homme et la loi naturelle* (*The Rights of Man and Natural Law*) which he had acquired in the autumn of 1946. The work had first appeared in 1940 and it enjoyed a wide circulation in both English and French.

Maritain was from a generation slightly older than Mounier's. Born in Paris in 1882, the son of a Protestant lawyer, he was a Catholic through conversion. He studied at the Sorbonne and after developing an early interest in Baruch Spinoza and Henri Bergson, he settled on what became his life's work, elaborating the philosophy of Aquinas and his ancient teacher, Aristotle. After 1914 Maritain held an academic position at the Catholic Institute in Paris and this he combined after 1932 with regular sabbaticals at the Institute of Medieval Studies in Toronto. The Institute had been founded by another well-known modern Thomist, Étienne Gilson, with whom Trudeau would also became familiar. Maritain was in Canada when the war broke out in 1939 and he stayed in North America for its duration, holding professorships at Princeton in 1941–2 and at Columbia between 1941 and 1944. From 1945 to 1948 he was France's ambassador to the Vatican.[112] Maritain's turn towards political questions came in the late 1920s. He was close to Mounier and other personalists such as Nicolas Berdyaev, Gabriel Marcel, and the *Esprit* group. However in the 1930s, his relations with Mounier and *Esprit* became strained. Maritain was a devout Catholic and he never quite shared with Mounier his contention that the root of the Catholicism's problems lay in its being an emanation of the petite bourgeoisie.[113] For Maritain, Mounier and *Esprit* were not sufficiently Catholic and Christian.[114] But their main disagreement was over politics. Maritain was categorical in denouncing what he called "the totalitarian spirit."[115] And so in 1935 he parted ways with Mounier and *Esprit* mainly over Nazism.[116] He saw the Second World War as a war for civilization and after the fall of France he was a critic of the Vichy regime and a publicist for General de Gaulle and the Free French.[117] Maritain and Mounier also disagreed over fundamental philosophical questions. Maritain with his scholasticism was partial to what Mounier considered the errors of abstract metaphysics and universal conceptions of the good.

The two books by Maritain that Trudeau did read at this time, *True Humanism* and *The Rights of Man and Natural Law*, had much in common. In the first Maritain sought to refute what he saw as the two dominant humanisms of the time: liberal individualism— he called it "bourgeois liberalism"[118]—and Soviet Communism. He offered in their place a "true" one. Part of his argument, particularly in *True Humanism*, had to do with a conception of a new Christian temporal order. In an era when much of Catholic thought still hankered after the lost Christian unity and ecclesiastical privileges of the Middle Ages, Maritain believed that history had moved far beyond these. Protestantism had emerged along with extensive technological progress, and also the rise of the state and a grow- ing regard for human equality and rights. Maritain emphasized the "universalizing of human conscience" and how the political unity of traditional societies was being replaced by a consensual order founded on law, justice, rights, civic friendship, and political par- ticipation. There was an increasing acceptance of the pluralistic nature of society, in religious and ethnic affairs and in civic associa- tions and trade unions. Sprinkled as well throughout the two books were references to the Aristotelian and Thomist idea of the natural- ness of society and government and of the inherently valuable char- acter of social and civic life. Non-Christians and unbelievers, said Maritain, were capable of understanding universal social truths and even "pagan" states could exercise legitimate authority. To these insights Maritain added a social democratic insistence upon life on earth being more than a vale of tears to be endured until the return of Christ.[119] Christians were called to make the world a better place and to make available to all the material and spiritual means to personal fulfillment. He believed that the groundwork for this had been laid in the encyclicals of Leo XIII and Pius XI, *Rerum Novarum* and *Quadragesimo Anno*.[120] Trudeau referred to these in similar terms in his essay on the Asbestos strike in 1956.

Maritain inevitably confronted the ancient riddle of the pow- ers of church and state and who had primacy over the other. His conclusion was that since the unity of Christendom had now been shattered and since all human beings were worthy of respect and human rights, there must be a commitment to a liberal democratic order and the Church must subordinate itself to this new order. As a community of the faithful in a free society, the Church was certainly entitled to religious rights and tolerance but no more than any other religious association or civic group. What the Church could not claim were privileges from the state; nor could it look to the state to enforce its specific doctrines and beliefs. The Church was the beneficiary of civic tolerance but it must accord the same tolerance to other religions. Even so, Maritain's message was not on behalf of a wholly secular state. His ideal was of a *Christian* society and, although government was to be consensually sustained, somehow the state should not be neutral, uninterested in, nor dismissive of religion. The state must not privilege any religion or any confessional community, but not because religion was a private matter and of no concern to government. Rather it was because any privilege accorded to one religious group would be discriminatory towards others and thus an elevated status for one violated the consciences and rights of others.

It was through his version of personalism that Maritain brought together the many strands of his thought. Here was the closest affinity between himself and Mounier:

> A person is a unity of a spiritual nature endowed with freedom of choice and so forming a whole which is independent of the world, for neither nature nor the State may invade this unity without permission. God himself [*sic*], who is and who acts from within, acts there in a particular way and with a supremely exquisite delicacy, a delicacy which shows the value He sets on it: He respects this freedom, in the heart of which nevertheless He lives; He solicits it, but He never compels.[121]

This was Maritain's account of the Incarnation—of God among us—and of humans made in the image of God. At the core of the person were conscience, creativity, and freedom, all of them created by God. The state had no right to control conscience and conscience retained a right to err in its freedom.[122] Maritain shared with

Mounier the central idea that personalism, although a libertarian doctrine, was also a communitarian one. Society was more than an aggregate of individual parts; it possessed a "common good" above the individual. There were occasions when the state must enforce conformity, for example in instances of violence and theft. This was law as punishment. But there was a role for law as an educative instrument and as the "pedagogue of liberty" and this presumed a role for the state as instructor of the citizen in the precepts of natural law and the common good: the integrity of the person, mutual respect, and the building of a society of universal concern.[123]

Maritain offered what he referred to as a "theocentric humanism," whose distinctive features allowed him to differentiate himself from the other dominant political idioms of his time. The first of these, bourgeois individualism/liberalism, which he believed was founded on the error of nominalism. This liberalism, atomist liberalism in other words, did not hold to an objective reality but based itself on ideas that were deemed to represent reality. Liberalism was about a notional individual, disengaged and self-sufficient, a consciousness unto himself, and so it rejected a common good. In effect its conception of society was about individuals exploiting weaker citizens. Capitalism was its dreadful economic consequence.[124] Then there was Marxism and the Soviet Union. Maritain was sympathetic to the socialist and Marxist critique of individualism and capitalism. But Marxism had failed to provide a valid alternative. It had no respect for the "person" and it had collectivized the spirit and freedom of the individual. In essence it was totalitarian. In *True Humanism*, Maritain estimated that seven million religious believers in the Soviet Union had been the victims of state "terror" and imprisonment in camps.[125] Finally, in his taxonomy of invalid humanisms, Maritain dismissed Nazism with its "Germanic" character and its "totalitarian-racist conception." It was, he said, a spurious form of social communion, a "nostalgic longing to be together," a surrogate for "loneliness and distress," and a substitute for "religious energies."[126] The German aptitude for "marching together" (*zusammenmarschieren*) had led inexorably to its need to posit an enemy against which to measure itself.[127] In light of what Trudeau would consider the xenophobic and genocidal tendencies of nationalism, Maritain's views establish substantial continuities between them.

A view of history informed Maritain's personalism. His evolutionary account owed a great deal to Pierre Teilhard de Chardin. History had no predetermined logic, but it did have a direction, mainly provided by the spirit and creativity of human beings. But history was a struggle, replete with suffering and human error. It was not cyclical and so once a civilization had passed away, it could not be revived, a view that informed his conviction about the need for a *new* Christendom, not one that returned to the Middle Ages. But his main point was that history was the context of human action, the place where humanity sought to realize moral ideals. Maritain worked within Aquinas's idea of analogical reasoning in which history was the context of the interaction of "existence" and "essence." The essence of life in society was the pursuit of the common good, but the application of the ideal could take many forms. Two theoretical errors had to be avoided, those of "univocity" and "equivocity." The former argued that for any given ideal there must be only one form of its realization. Equivocity was a contrary falsehood which had it that since there were so many ways and means whereby "truth and right" were sought, there could be no such thing as an immutable principle. The solution, according to Maritain, was to be found in the philosophy of analogy:

> The principles do not vary, neither do the supreme practical laws of human life: but they are applied in ways which were essentially diverse, corresponding to one and the same concept only by a similitude of proportion. [128]

According to this principle the common good could be achieved in different ways. A society that was democratic was as much the embodiment of the common good as late medieval theocracy. Clearly much depended on time and circumstance.

Connected to this Maritain expressed a kind of calculus of practicality. If leaders were capable of making bad decisions, how could they be brought to make good ones? Maritain proposed what he called a "concrete historical ideal," which used history to instruct leaders in an understanding of the roles of actual contexts and real possibilities in good decision making. Assuming that the leader was morally serious—as Maritain saw it, there was always the possibility of an amoral Machiavellianism—then the concrete historical ideal would be a practice based on an understanding of the necessary interplay of essence and existence, ideal and reality. That understood, Maritain nonetheless stipulated that a moral politics must be more practical than theoretical. It must not be an exercise in pure theory as, for example, geometry. Equally it must not be an exercise in pure existentialism, so to speak, in which the leader only took account of contingencies and eventualities, a politics devoid of principle, an "empirical" politics of "opportunism." Instead Maritain called for a politics of "prudence," a summons to leaders to bring to decision making a regard for the good while recognizing that what may be abstractly true was of no worldly consequence and in its actual implementation might be "inhuman."[129] In the matter of the international order, Maritain advocated just war theory. At times, force and violence had to be applied but only as a last resort. The wise politician should always try to improve the integrity of the means employed and the means should be proportional to the end in view. Before force was used "edification" should be attempted; there must be patience and even voluntary suffering. Nevertheless Christians should avoid the sin of "Pharisaical purism" and its misplaced belief that virtue resided in avoiding soiling oneself through contact with history and real events.

Maritain's political thinking came to its apogee in the importance he gave to human rights. There were three kinds: rights of the human person, civic or political rights, and, finally, the rights of workers. With regards the first, he argued for broad intellectual freedoms: religious freedom and freedom of conscience. The rights of the family were included under this first type as were the rights of individuals to choose to marry whomever they wished. He predicated such rights on the existence of a space of privacy, beyond the intrusions of government. Regarding political and civic rights, Maritain specifically invoked Aristotle's claim about humans being political animals so that the person "naturally asks to lead a political life and to participate actively in the life of the political community."[130] On this principle, he said, rested other important *political* rights: a right to vote and a right of political association. Other rights of the civic person were rights to equal citizenship, equal treatment before the law, and a right of non-discrimination. Of course none of these rights were absolute in Maritain's mind: persons were free to choose the good but they were not free to do whatever they wanted; an association of evil-doers did not have a right of free association; a right of free speech did not establish a right to propagate lies and calumnies.

Maritain's conception of workers' rights suggests a description of him as a cross between a liberal, a social democrat, and a Proudhonian syndicalist. He was not impressed by capitalism and its "cult of earthly riches."[131] He believed that there was a right to property but not to unlimited amounts and he sought above all to move beyond the dominance of property holders and the wage system's tendencies to exploit the worker. Yet he did not favour socialism, understood as the wholesale nationalization of the means of production. He preferred a middle position in which associations of workers, co-operatives, and unions would enter into experiments in co-ownership and co-management with private owners. He rejected central planning but thought there was a need for some regulation of the economy, what he called an "adjusted economy."[132] Maritain was a strong proponent of workers' rights to form trade unions, to obtain a just wage, and to find work. As well he supported a cluster of provisions central to the modern welfare state: unemployment insurance, social security, and sickness benefits. Above all he favoured a kind of economic voluntarism since it was the system most consistent with the principle that economic matters were not the proper concern of the state.[133] It was a liberal insight, though expressed on behalf of a Proudhon-like voluntarism and group pluralism.

Altogether Maritain offered a libertarian, rights-based politics, touched by communitarianism but undergirded by a tough-mindedness:

> A democratic society is not necessarily an unarmed society, which the enemies of liberty may calmly lead to the slaughterhouse in the name of liberty. Precisely because it is a commonwealth of free men, it must defend itself with particular energy.[134]

Trudeau expressed similar sentiments at Harvard in 1945 and certainly he was aggressive in defending a free commonwealth in the face of terrorists during the October Crisis in 1970.

VI

Harold Laski was an unlikely mentor to Trudeau. He was Jewish by birth, and if he was not a complete atheist, he was certainly an agnostic. He was also a committed socialist and at different points in his life heavily indebted to the insights of anarcho-syndicalism and Marxism. Some considered his stance towards the Soviet Union as that of a fellow-traveller and apologist. When Trudeau first became aware of Laski's ideas in Carl Friedrich's class at Harvard the encounter was not necessarily one of immediate amity. Trudeau reviewed his book, *A Grammar of Politics* and took pains to point out its weaknesses and inconsistencies. Yet he thought enough of Laski to give a book by him to Thérèse Gouin in the summer of 1946.[135] Trudeau met Laski for the first time at the LSE a year later when he registered as a "research student." He seems to have been intent on pursuing a PhD there although the documentary evidence about this is unclear.[136] Roughly half of the courses he took were with Laski: the British Constitution, Political and Social Theory, American Political Theory Since 1914, and a course on the Nature and Causes of Social Revolution.[137]

Laski was born in Manchester in 1893, the son of a cotton trader whose family had originally emigrated from Poland. He studied at Oxford University. Deemed medically unfit for service in the First World War, he worked for a short time at the *Daily Herald* in London and in 1914 obtained a lectureship in history at McGill University. Later he taught at Harvard and Yale. Already politically active, while in Canada Laski travelled as far afield as Winnipeg speaking to labour groups. He first attained public notoriety by supporting the Boston police strike in 1919, thus acquiring a life-long reputation as a dangerous radical and "Red." He returned to the LSE in 1920 to teach political science and remained there until his death thirty years later. Laski was one of the foremost public intellectuals of his generation. As a lecturer he was compelling and full of ideas. As for his radical politics, Laski started out a "socialist pluralist," in F.M. Barnard's apt phrase, and ended up as a sort of democratic-liberal Marxist.[138] At the outset he drew on the ideas of Pierre-Joseph Proudhon, G.D.H. Cole, J.N. Figgis, Ernest Barker, and A.R. Orage, and even Catholic conservatives like G.K. Chesterton and Hilaire Belloc; he was also influenced by American pragmatists, like John Dewey and William James. Most of these were anarcho-syndicalists of some kind although two of them were Tory localists. In their manifold ways, however, they celebrated the virtues of decentralization, self-sustaining communities, federalism, and the limited state.

In his earliest works, *Studies in the Problem of Sovereignty* (1917) and *Authority in the Modern State* (1919), Laski challenged what he believed were the two dominant views of the state and sovereignty. The idealist one, he said, saw the state as the expression of the rational and "real" interests of its citizens. This was what he called the "mystical," "monistic" theory of the state.[139] Georg Wilhelm Friedrich Hegel had given birth to it, he said, with some prior assistance from Rousseau and later encouragement from two English thinkers, Bernard Bosanquet and T.H. Green. The second dominant tradition was the legal theory of sovereignty going back to Hobbes and refined in the nineteenth century by John Austin and A.V. Dicey. According to this theory the state was a sovereign dictator whose will was backed by its monopoly of force, whose rule was determinate and uniform, and whose commands brooked no query or exception; sovereignty was hierarchical and civil society subordinate and dependent. Early Laski argued instead for a socialist pluralism in which civil society was self-sustaining and able to furnish its own spontaneous coordination of the plural goods of society's many groups.[140]

In the mid-1920s Laski came to see a larger role for the state as a coordinator and balancer of the many interests of a complex society and as a provider of such "identical" universal public goods as material equality, education, opportunity, publicly owned industries, as well as order and security. Here was the statist part of the eventual balance Laski struck; it informed his writing of *A Grammar of Politics* in 1925. But his revised theory of the state nonetheless emphasized that government must embrace popular consent and must regard its fundamental duty as seeking the common good and serving all its citizens. Under the new formulation Laski was much more acceptant of "political," parliamentary processes whereas his early pluralism had tended to prioritize the economic and the voluntaristic.

This synthesis survived until the 1930s when, with the Depression taking hold and fascism and Nazism in the ascendant, Laski embraced a more emphatically Marxist analysis. He became more convinced that socialism must be transformative of society and economy and no longer beholden to what he saw as the Fabian incrementalism of the Labour Party. Socialism would be achieved by an invigorated democratic majority led by a truly socialist Labour Party. But, since such initiatives would likely be resisted by the dominant class, Laski believed a socialist government must be prepared to employ emergency powers. Later Laski came to believe that the analysis contained in *A Grammar of Politics* was naive in its conception of the state as a benevolent aggregator of everyone's interests. Reiterating Marx's and Engels's famous dictum about the state under capitalism being the executive committee of the bourgeoisie, Laski affirmed the need for a "revolution through consent." This was the gist of his books, *The State in Theory and Practice* in 1935 and *Parliamentary Government in England* in 1938 and the theme of an introductory chapter, "The Crisis in the Theory of the State," which he wrote for the fourth edition of *A Grammar of Politics*, also in 1938. In 1936 he had published *The Rise of European Liberalism*, which took a thoroughly Marxist view of how the celebrated liberal ideas of rights and freedoms had in effect been the blinkered, self-serving ideology of a rising middle class of traders and entrepreneurs whose political triumph had been at the expense of the workers. The bourgeois state, in the grip of laissez-faire and in some cases resorting to political authoritarianism in moments of economic crisis, needed to be overthrown.

Laski now tacked even more in the direction of the Soviet Union as the ideal of socialism and indeed of civilization. He had never been less than well disposed towards the Soviet Union but, with the apparent failure of capitalism and the onset of Stalin's five-year plans, he saw tangible proof of communism's accomplishments: state planning and fairness for all, science applied to industry, progressive jurisprudence and penology, social mobility, and so on. He was never unheeding of what he felt were the failings of the Soviet Union—the absence of competing political parties, its political repressiveness, its denial of basic rights and the imprisonment of dissidents—but Laski either felt these deficiencies were outweighed by its achievements or he doubted that rapid, transformative change could ever be attained without extreme practices. As he put it in 1944:

> No doubt as the revolutionary idea has established itself, it has involved in those whom it has influenced cruelty, cowardice, dishonesty and disorder. These are part of the price a society is bound to pay which attempts the transvaluation of values.[141]

Laski's world view produced a predictable set of second-order positions on the politics of his time. He was a supporter of the

Spanish Republic and markedly anti-imperialist. Originally a devotee of the League of Nations, later he saw it as a club of imperialist powers. This went together with a newly kindled view of
imperialism as a necessary, later stage of capitalism, leading to war,
a theory developed in the early twentieth century by the economist J.A. Hobson. Laski was an undying critic of Italian Fascism
and German Nazism but he opposed rearmament by Britain in the
1930s although he did reverse his view after the Munich Agreement
in 1938. In general, Laski called for a more accommodative attitude
towards the Soviet Union, one that sought neither to harass it nor
to isolate it. After the war began in 1939 he supported the eventual
Churchill-Attlee coalition and later exulted in Britain's alliance with
the Soviet Union. Laski was not convinced that Clement Attlee was
the best leader of the Labour Party and he plotted to replace him.
But he celebrated the coming of the Labour government in 1945,
provided it pursued a truly socialist agenda.

In postwar international affairs Laski continued to be partial
to the Soviet cause and was critical of the United States's "folly"
and its "messianic" anti-communism, as well as its pursuit of an
expanding sphere of influence in a polarized world. Trudeau would
later advocate similar views. Laski called for the Americans to share
their nuclear information and to place their nuclear bomb under
international control. In 1947 he was invited by the United Nations
Educational, Scientific and Cultural Organization (UNESCO)
to participate in the drafting of the United Nations' Universal
Declaration of Human Rights (1949). He pressed for the inclusion
of not just traditional liberal rights but also women's rights and
social rights to do with equal opportunity and material equality. In
the end, disappointment overtook him. Laski was "heartbroken" by
the Communist coup in Czechoslovakia in February 1948 and its
repression of a multi-party democratic state.[142] However, he never
rejected Marxism or the Soviet experiment outright.

When Trudeau expressed his deep regard for Laski, it was his
work, *A Grammar of Politics*, which figured centrally in his judgment. The work itself was a big, ungainly thing—over six hundred

pages—but at its core was its author's pragmatism. The book was an argument against metaphysics. Laski's claim was that humans learn through experience. History, he said, had convinced the present generation that democracy, freedom, and equality were literally "common sense." Integral to this was the idea of the individual as necessarily dependent on society for his fulfillment and "sharing in the benefits of a moral order made by him in cooperation with his fellows."[143] Yet the individual person, Laski believed, was an "unassimilable" entity, possessed of will, each different in his own way—"the inexpungible variety of human wills," as Laski put it—and moved by a capacity to experiment and to be creative.[144] Crucial to the development of the self were human rights and freedoms as well as equality. Part of freedom was the right to participate in politics. Universal adult suffrage was a fundamental good, and upon this Laski built his sense of an ideal political system that was in fact not that far removed from existing British parliamentary practice: two dominant but competing political parties, parliamentary debate, cabinet government, and independent judges and courts. Some reforms were necessary: for example he favoured the abolition of the House of Lords, but other political proposals such as proportional representation should be resisted. Yet, while citizens were ultimately the agents of their own "creativity" and "self-expression," they had duties towards the whole society.

This moral framework merged agreeably with what Laski meant by "functionalism," an idea to which Trudeau was very partial and about which there has been much misunderstanding among the latter's critics. Laski's contribution here was to notice that the idea of the common good constituted a standard against which existing institutions could be measured.[145] Human beings created structures and institutions in order to embody their moral ideals, though these were always specific to the historical moment and context. And so critics could always ask about existing institutions: to what extent did they function in a manner consistent with current ideals? The emphasis was placed upon the performance and the "doing" of these institutions, another dimension of Laski's pragmatism. Were they performing their proper functions, that is, their "moral" functions? Parliament's "function" in a democratic age was to represent all the people and to legislate on the basis of the consent of everyone. In light of this should it be reformed—or indeed replaced—in order to improve its compliance with prevailing ideals?

Another theme in *A Grammar*, and of huge consequence in Trudeau's world view, was Laski's pluralism and his view of modern society as inherently federal in nature.[146] Here again Laski approached things from a pragmatic point of view. As a matter of "fact," and because of given "realities," society was becoming increasingly diverse and heterogeneous, in a word "federal." The Reformation had brought religious pluralism, and to religious diversity had been added the later particularities wrought by industrialism and technology: the coming of cities, the working class, trade unions, political parties, self-help groups and learned societies, and so on. Internationally, innovations in communication and transportation had brought the telephone and airplane and had reduced geographic and social distance so that the world was a place where intensifying differences and conflicts were increasingly in need of resolution.

If one added to the equation, as Laski did, the importance of the principle of a territorial state respecting social differences in a democratic and egalitarian way, then the logical conclusion was that the state in the exercise of its sovereignty was responsible to the whole civil society and bound to consult and listen to its rich and dense multiplicity. The modern state could not be a national state because it must govern on behalf of everyone and not just some dominant national group.[147] Nor could it govern in the manner prescribed by Hobbes and Hegel whereby the state neither consulted its publics nor mobilized popular consent but proceeded by command and legal prescription. At its best the modern state should govern on the basis of a "compromise" between itself and society. The true test of the authority of law was not a legal one but a moral one.[148]

What of Trudeau's early responses to Laski's overall political mentality? A fifteen-page book review of *A Grammar* written while at Harvard survives in his papers.[149] While it tells us little about his sense of the *validity* of the book's argument, it does reveal enough to establish that Trudeau was, at least at this time, hardly an uncritical follower of Laski. Intriguingly what piqued Trudeau's interest in Laski's views at this time was the issue of personalism. He worried that Laski did not make sufficiently clear whether he was an individualist, a personalist, a collectivist, or a communitarian. He suspected that Laski might be an individualist. This was, presumably, in his mind a defect. Trudeau's anxiety, using the later terminology of Charles Taylor, was over whether Laski had a "thin" sense of society and perhaps an atomized—Laski elsewhere called it an "atomic"—conception of the person. Also it might have been that what disturbed Trudeau was the lack of religious foundations in Laski's thought. In other comments he criticized Laski's penchant for advocating elections, as many as one a day in "Laskiville," as he put it. Confronting Laski's description of the many consultatative committees at the many levels of state-owned industries in his ideal order, Trudeau sighed again: "More and more elections." When Laski favoured a policy of birth control, Trudeau—not always a consistent progressive—commented: "Some freedom."

For the most part though, the book review was marked by Trudeau's assiduous and careful analysis and ability of summarization, especially of what he felt was Laski's version of sovereignty as moral and federal in nature and what this entailed for individual consent and obedience. Trudeau's account also tells us much about Laski's pragmatism, and his view of the limits of direct democracy:

> Authority [for Laski] is a function of relations; and it derives its validity from the way in which those relations are organised. Authority co-ordinates the experiences of men into relations that harmonise the needs they infer from those experiences.
>
> The experience of citizens is the true maker of law. What they find true to that experience will have authority for them.
>
> The state must discover the legality of law, by compounding it from the experience of its citizens.

If this be true, it follows that what there is of unity is not a priori these [thesis?] . . . The attachments of each piece of our experience guide our personalities into a system of loyalties. . . . The co-operation I discover myself to need is federal and not imperial in character.

Important implication for political philosophy. The centre of significance is no longer the search for unity but what that unity makes. And what it makes must, if it is to win my allegiance, include results I recognise as expressions of my needs.

The structure of social organisations must be federal if it is to be adequate: all the interrelationships between myself, groups and State must be involved. The solution does not, as in the classical theory of politics, begin by postulating the necessary unity of society and continue by insisting on the supremacy of the state as the organ of that unity.

It agrees that unity is not there but has to be made. And argues that obedience is only creative when it arises from a self imposed discipline. My will cannot be represented at all, and my experience is essentially private to myself. But I can recognise, in any average legislature, men whose actions reveal a purpose sufficiently akin to my own to enlist my support. The problem of representation is to enable me to have contact with those men. Yet the rush of business can't allow the representative to refer back constantly to the constituents; all the direct power of the citizen must consist in periodic re-elections, and in the intervals actions through his pressure group. We need permanent and continuous organs to be consulted before decisions are made.

Yet since no association includes the whole of myself, no association can legislate successfully for the whole of myself. The case for the territorial State is that it moves beyond the partial glimpse to the wholeness. Because society is federal, authority must be federal also: making decisions out of the interests which will be affected by them.

It means the abandonment of the sovereign State in the sense which equates the latter with Society, giving it the right to dictate to associations in Society. [Laski] admits that the organisation he desired is immensely more complex than what we have at present.

Law to be adequate must be built upon an induction from the widest possible experience it can know. Our present capitalist system forces the voice of many to remain unheard: so equality is a condition of liberty. The consequence of so defining law is that he denies that submission is ever a moral obligation unless, as an act, it carries with it the individual conviction of rightness which makes it moral.

The only State to which I owe allegiance is the State in which *I* discover moral adequacy; and if a given State fails to satisfy that condition I must attempt experiment. (As with T.H. Green, he says that rebellion is a contingent duty; but he doesn't as Green, restrict resistance to cases where many others share the same view.) We so act at our peril; but the peril induced in obedience may in the end be greater than the penalty of rebellion.[150]

Trudeau went on: "Finally [Laski] answers the argument that we must give govt. to the best by saying that the best are all over, not in one class."[151] Trudeau seems grudgingly to have agreed.

A shorter piece by Trudeau, also written at Harvard, offered a clear criticism of Laski's *The State in Theory and Practice*, a work of his later Marxist period.[152] Trudeau again provided a perceptive summary of its argument: under capitalism the State was biased in favour of those who owned the means of production; in harsh economic times, the governing class was prepared to overthrow democracy, which hitherto it had tactically supported, and resort to fascism. As Trudeau rightly perceived, Laski's conclusion was that only some kind of revolution could overthrow such an entrenched and self-interested class whose phenomenal power was reinforced by its control of the army. Trudeau, in his best dialectical style, however, thought that Laski had failed to convince. Instead he made a case for social democracy:

> It should be noted however that [Laski's argument] is based on several unproven postulates: e.g. the fundamental one, that socialism is able to produce as much and satisfy more people than capitalism; also that capitalism is incapable of any further expansion whereby profits for one class *and* concessions to the other would be desirable; and that a mixed system of socialism and capitalism (private ownership of *some* means of production) is not durable or even desirable.[153]

There was another allusive comment he made in a review of another book by Laski, *Liberty in the Modern State*, where Trudeau argued that Laski had not sufficiently advanced the argument of *A Grammar*.[154] He had not done enough to develop the idea of personalism and continued to advocate individualism:

> Only the basis of this position is not the person defined by a Final Cause, but on the "reconnaissance pragmatique" that in the last analysis there is only the individual conscience, the individual's experiences which can produce action.

Was it that Trudeau felt Laski's pragmatism and individualism had trumped ideas about the final good and the theological assumptions that should inform personalism?

During his year at the LSE Trudeau took extensive notes of the lectures he attended. The notes contain little of his own opinions but they do reinforce the sense of the rich, suggestive theorizing to which Laski in particular exposed him. Laski and Trudeau were kindred spirits. In one of his lectures Laski declared that "the central problem of political science is why people obey some authority." A Cartesian appetite for indubitable first principles was something that preoccupied Trudeau too.[155] There were similarities between them not just over everyday politics but "extraordinary" politics as well; Laski's thoughts on revolution and counter-revolution had obvious continuities with Trudeau's early fascination with the political exotica of violence, coups, and rebellions.

In Trudeau's lecture notes there is Laski's final word on the question of Marxism and the Soviet Union.[156] He elaborated his established line about the capitalist state being dominated by a particular class, "a small number of people [who] shape the society to preserve their authority." He used language about the "effective demand" of this particular group and how it constituted the structural bias of the liberal-democratic state. But, said Laski, churning away below was the great materialistic dialectic of the forces of production and the relations of production. A crisis will emerge when the two will come into contradiction and the property-owning class will stand in the way of the productive potential of a new industrial order. Laski's view saw revolution as a drawn-out socio-economic process. In its final moments political revolution will break out and the workers will seize power and launch the dictatorship of the proletariat.

Yet Laski qualified this view with a display of characteristic skepticism. He observed that Marx and Engels were "not specific" about what would happen after the revolution, as power passed from class to class. But certainly it would not be without some rules and directions. On one matter, Laski said, the rules *were* clear and they precluded Blanquism. This was the idea of Marx's contemporary, Louis Auguste Blanqui—Trudeau mentioned him in his essay on political violence—to do with a small revolutionary group seizing power and bringing revolution from above. The Marxist revolution, according to Laski, would occur in two stages: a consolidation of the proletariat's victory and the eventual withering away of the state. About the latter, Laski noted Marx's and Engels's point that the process might take as long as fifty years. Laski was convinced that what had occurred in the Soviet Union contradicted these postulates. Lenin had, in actual fact, practised Blanquism and a faux Marxism:

Laski's difficulty: when power is given to men to maintain a new order, there is no a priori reason why these men shouldn't regard power as any other men: there is no anxiety to part with power. All biographies show this. Marxism is a method, not a body of dogmatic principles. Today Laski thinks that in Russia the dictatorship of the proletariat is not of but over the proletariat. [It is] like any police state, inability to criticise even harmlessly. Lenin has made Marxism nearer to Blanquism. There is in the early Marx an affinity for a more anarchic form of state, though opposed to anarchy for anarchy's sake which was more Bakunin's position. Laski has faith that ultimately Russia will become a democracy more real than any we know. In the real Marxian state, there may still be strikes, managers will be ill tempered, workers lazy.[157]

Another significant subject to which Laski's lectures exposed Trudeau was the announcement of his change of mind regarding the ontological status of the group. In his early, pluralist years Laski had insisted that the group was "real" and that it had an identity that was more than the sum of its individual parts. Now his claim was that the group was no more than a metaphor for an aggregate of individual persons. The confession launched Laski on a train of discourse that had at its foundation a more or less liberal, though by no means atomistic, understanding of the relationship of the individual to society and the state:

Laski denies the reality of corporate personality. (Laski in Harvard Law Review in teens [of the twentieth century] wrote the contrary.)

Only individuals are real. Their linkage to common purposes doesn't make their purposes a reality different from the whole of the individuals.

To talk of England as a personality is to argue by metaphor. A community is an aggregate of persons, not an organism.

So we don't exist for the sake of the state power. It exists for us. It may be right to obey this power. But it may also be wrong. The source of judgement of an order given (law) is within the individual. We supply the legality of the law. Legality is made by its impact on individual human beings.

But this doesn't mean that we can be Robinson Crusoes. We only know of men in society. (Bergson's "*choses données*.") So what is assumed by the state is not necessarily subtraction from the individual's freedom; it may well be the conditions of his fulfillment.

Individuals in a community are defined by their relation to the state power.

Laski denies that the state power is the highest form of power in any except a legal sense; e.g. duty of a Roman catholic [sic] under the Kulturkampf is not to do what Bismarck or Pope orders; it is to follow his own conscience.[158]

Trudeau recorded Laski's thoughts on the nature of citizenship under a democratic scheme of sovereignty and how this affected popular consent and obedience:

1. How to make the ultimate unified authority [to] command willing allegiance, to maximize consent as opposed to coercion.
2. Finding ways and means of making the citizen effectively able to present the results of his experience for consideration.
    The making of conditions in which one's profession is exercised. Laski favours producer sovereignty permeating consumer sovereignty.
3. The state authority must never a priori [be] taken as preeminent over all other authorities simply because it creates the framework where we operate. . . .

Don't approach "the state with fear and trembling." (Green)
    Against Hobbes who imposes order as the highest good.
    It depends what the order is for.
    British liberties were not obtained without violence. Barons to John (Magna Carta), Pym, Hampton [presumably John Hampden] to Ch[arles] First.

[He is] [a]lso against Rousseau's General Will: there is an individual will which has more value to me.

Order is good if it is coincident with certain general qualities.

Further it is the duty of authority to embody multiplicity of experience and law is only successful in so far as it does.

So in any society there is always a contingency of disobedience, anarchy, where frontiers of law are capable of challenge. Authority is valid because of what it does.

[Laski] [d]enies that obedience is the supreme good. A man is not an effective person in a society if he is merely the recipient of orders. Hence need for the maximum association of citizens with the law-making power.

By excluding my experience, the state evades me as a reality and I cease to be an end.[159]

Laski, Mounier, and Léon Blum, the former French socialist prime minister, died within eight days of each other in March 1950. In his homage to Laski in *Cité Libre* Trudeau expressed a profound regard for his genius and moral importance.[160] He described him as a man of action, a Marxist but not a Stalinist, and as someone who stood outside of the polarities of the atomic age and the "totalitarianisms" of East and West. Trudeau viewed him—and Blum—as men of independence, beholden to neither side: "Socialists, they nevertheless rejected the pre-eminence of Stalinism. And as democrats they similarly denounced the liberal State." Trudeau's other comments—more than a little florid and extravagant—reveal the degree to which he placed Laski within the framework of Mounier's and Maritain's accounts of "the free society" and its instantiation as a work of "love":

His vast body of work, both written and spoken, has been but a continuous search for the free city in which people might live in tolerance and possibly in love. It is because of this that both capitalists and Stalinists were his sworn enemies.[161]

Trudeau was never uncritical of Laski but in him he found a mentor.

VII

Although they seem to have inhabited different philosophical worlds, Mounier, Maritain, and Laski were not a discrepant group. Mounier was an existentialist of sorts, Maritain a Thomist, and Laski a pragmatist. Yet all three spoke the language of the common good and community. All three emphasized engagement and a conception of political action grounded in realism. Two of them were committed socialists and positively disposed towards Marxism. Maritain has often been represented as a liberal but he was critical of capitalism and he can properly be thought of as a social democrat. All three were pluralists, who had in various ways been influenced by the syndicalist anarchism of Proudhon. All of them were deeply anti-nationalist, especially Laski and Maritain but Mounier as well. All were strong advocates of a federal understanding of society and what this entailed for the shape of the state. All three had a deep commitment to equality and the importance of rights. Maritain himself had once noticed that there could be "practical agreement among men whose theories were opposed one to another."[162] Yet on the political questions of their times their positions tended to disagreement. Laski and Mounier, especially, struggled with the extremisms of the age—as Trudeau would in his own time—their personal predicaments made more difficult because of their attraction to one of the extremes, namely Soviet Communism. Mounier was ambiguously disposed towards Nazism and the Vichy regime. Not so Maritain who rejected all totalitarianisms. He was much less critical of the United States in the postwar world than either Laski or Mounier, both of whom feared American dominance and aggression towards the Soviet Union. Consequently both strongly endorsed the idea of a Europe that would stand outside the polarizing logic of the Cold War.

As for recommending political models, the three were more at odds than in concert. Mounier was the most radical in his rejection of conventional parliamentary democracy and in his predilection for a new kind of politics, even if its specific shape was not always clear. That he rejected Christian Democracy and parliamentarism was clear however. (Mounier's inchoate yearning for something wholly new in politics comes to mind when considering Trudeau's own experiments with the non-party, collaborative models of the Rassemblement and the Union des forces démocratiques later in the 1950s.) In contrast Laski was in many ways a partisan of the traditional British parliamentary model—as Trudeau was too, most of the time—but this was greatly adjusted after 1930 by his insistence that the Labour Party endorse a democratic revolution, a revolution requiring special powers and possible state coercion. Maritain was if anything the most conventional of the three on political matters. He did not wish to give up on traditional electoral and party democracy and he rejected Marxist analysis altogether.

Finally, all three shared a view of the importance of freedom, not just in the sense of the priority of rights but in believing that individual conscience must be pre-eminent in the relation of the individual to the state, especially in matters of personal and religious choices. For Maritain and Mounier this emphasis derived from personalism and the idea of the divinely founded dignity of the person. Laski came to similar conclusions about conscience and human dignity but without invoking any evident theological premises. For all his criticism of liberalism and his apologia for Soviet Communism Laski remained loyal to the ideals of individual freedom and a consensually based state. Although a critic of European liberalism he was at least a *political* liberal. Socialism for him was inconceivable without primary political rights and freedoms. In effect all three were political liberals, although both Mounier and Laski were constant in their exposure of the deficiencies of liberal democracy.

Trudeau's Profound Moralism: The Matter of Quebec

———— • ◆ • ————

Living comes first, and philosophy comes later.
Pierre Elliott Trudeau

The world we live in is not static; either we move forward
with the human caravan, or we die in the sands of time.
Present technical and political developments point to a future
industrial and social revolution compared to which the
previous revolution will have been mere child's play.
And it is more important than ever that we ourselves decide
what place we human beings will hold in that future.
Pierre Elliott Trudeau

I

In the years immediately after the Second World War there is little documentary evidence of the cast of Trudeau's thinking on Quebec and French Canada.[1] The general opinion is that he was moving away from clericalist and nationalist points of view and putting distance between himself and the anti-conscription agitation of 1942 and his membership of the Bloc populaire canadien in 1944. However in 1947 and early 1948 he wrote a number of essays and articles that provide a reading on his thinking. Two of these are of particular importance: "La promesse du Québec" and "La politique Canadienne." Neither was ever published. Both were originally given as lectures in Paris in 1947, the first in April and the second in December.[2]

In "La politique Canadienne," Trudeau showed himself to be modestly patriotic about Canada though not without a warm affection for Quebec. Even if, as John English has noticed, there lingered a "Laurentisme" even as he embraced more liberal-democratic ideas, Trudeau gave no hint at all of separatism.[3] He took Canada as a given. He may not have been deliriously patriotic but he went to great lengths to emphasize that Canada was an independent country and he downplayed the constitutional significance of vestiges of British colonialism. He saw Canada's politics as non-ideological, aggregative, and accommodationist, the epitome of what is now referred to as either the brokerage or elite accommodation model, although Trudeau did not explicitly use these terms. Much of this political analysis Trudeau might have acquired from André Siegfried, the French political anthropologist who wrote two books about Canada, *Le Canada, les deux races: problèmes politiques contemporains*, published in 1906, and *Canada: An International Power* in 1937.[4] Siegfried helped establish a way of thinking about Canada's politics that has become almost an iron law. Although he favoured an ideologically divided two-party system along British lines, Siegfried emphasized how Canada's ethnic, religious, and regional heterogeneity had produced a party politics devoid of principle and ideology and based on such practical imperatives as survival, winning elections, holding power, and maintaining national unity.[5] Trudeau was familiar with Siegfried's ideas because he attended lectures by him in Paris in 1946–7.[6] But in his own essay he did not disclose his sources and he presented his observations as a matter of simple fact, without either judgment or emotion, a sort of laconic academic coolness, although, as we shall see, he did state that alternative possibilities were being hatched amidst the unhelpful fissures and compromises of Canada's political landscape.

Trudeau began his lecture with some observations on history, specifically addressing those in his audience who were "Marxists and behaviorists." He was, he said, not a determinist but he believed that there was some truth in Marx's claim that history was made by more than ideas alone. Action took place in a "given context" and men's—his language was pre-feminist—freedom to act was greatly circumscribed. He argued that the main "context" of Canadian history had been its multi-form diversity. Canada was a "federated country." What he was referring to was not so much Canada's constitutional structure as its sociological configuration, "its ethnic and geographic facts." It was a country of several peoples and many far-flung regions. He went on: Canada did not have a history of absolutism nor had it experienced conflicts like a War of the Roses, which might have produced a centralizing tendency as it had in England. Yet, at its moment of unification in 1867, it had created a strong central government as a bulwark particularly against American expansionism.

A claim Trudeau went to great lengths to emphasize was that Canada was a sovereign, independent country. It had its own monarchy and its own powers to appoint ambassadors and to make its own declarations of war. If it ever sought to amend its constitution, the British Parliament was obliged to follow Canada's instructions and, if it still submitted judicial appeals to the Privy Council in London, this could be changed in a trice, if Canada chose to do so. Its constitution, he said, was a mixture of British parliamentary democracy and American federalism; the powers of the crown were largely symbolic; it followed the British tradition of prime ministerial and cabinet government, a form in which the executive was held accountable to Parliament; and so on. But Trudeau did find one branch of the Canadian political establishment especially repugnant: the Senate. This, he said, combined the worst features of the American and British upper houses and was "perfectly useless." In a federation the justification of an upper house was to protect the interests of the federated parts; he called them "*les pays fédérées*." Canada's founding fathers feared autonomist tendencies and invented a system that sought somehow to "globally" represent the regions rather than the provinces. The Senate's democratic standing was hardly improved by having senators appointed by the central government. Trudeau concluded dismissively:

> the Senate. . . was intended to serve as a bulwark against the rising waves of popular democracy. In reality the bulwark above all ensures that ninety-six old big-wigs will sleep peacefully and lucratively.[7]

All of this was essentially presented in the manner of a civics lesson, which to some extent is what it was. The more intriguing part was what Trudeau said about Canada's party system. The country's heterogeneity, he said, had caused national political parties to appeal to a broad range of " interests" and their platforms and policies were consequently vague: "The ideology of the party must be extremely imprecise [he used the world 'floue,' meaning 'blurred' or 'fluffy'] and as neutral as possible." Canada's two main political parties were conservative but they had been flexible too and had adapted their message to their circumstances. After Confederation, he said, they had developed within a centre-region dynamic with one party favouring a strong central state and the other asserting greater provincial autonomy. The Conservatives under John A. Macdonald had pursued economic development based on the St Lawrence valley: tariff protection for infant industry and the opening up of domestic markets in western Canada. Conservatism was supported by the financial and industrial interests of Ontario, the merchant classes of the Maritimes and the old conservative French and English families of Quebec. In trying to cobble together an alternative coalition, the Liberals initially had had little to work with. Industrial workers were few in number and ill-organized, and farmers and farm labourers were widely dispersed. Together they hardly constituted a natural political bloc. The Liberals had found it hard to rally the Québécois to their cause, for they radiated too much the anticlericalism of the Rouges and were only popular in intellectual circles. The Church supported the so-called Bleus (who were Gallicans) and the Castors (the ultramontanes), and this had been to the electoral advantage of the Conservatives. Three events, he said, had changed this: the execution of Louis Riel, the death of Sir John A. Macdonald, and the popularity of Wilfrid Laurier. In 1896 Laurier successfully put together an electoral alliance of French Canadians and westerners. This endured until his defeat in 1911.

Fundamental to Trudeau's analysis was his view of the party system as an endless merry-go-round where the two dominant parties vied for advantage and worried little about consistent and precise principles. Trudeau pointed out the contradictions of the Liberals coming to depend on the two "most traditionally conservative" constituencies in the country—Catholics in Quebec and farmers—while the Conservatives, the party of imperialism, were the ones who under Borden were instrumental in establishing greater political independence from Britain and who under Bennett in the early 1930s went on to become the first to introduce a left-wing economic agenda, the so-called New Deal. Trudeau spoke at length about third parties but not with any great expectation of their likely success in Canada's environment of multiple cleavages. Third parties of principle, he said, were likely to fail because they had too narrow a focus and they found it hard to make interprovincial alliances. This had changed somewhat with the founding of the CCF in 1932 under J.S. Woodsworth who had been astute enough to build on farmer resentments and create a broader party of the Left. Perhaps the CCF nationally was treading water, awaiting a mature working-class consciousness, a slow though inevitable process in Canada. And so in the future the CCF might threaten the oligopoly of the two old parties. If so, Trudeau thought the Conservatives were especially vulnerable. Trudeau went on: for now the two main parties were more than adept at fending off new challenges and absorbing left-wing priorities. The Conservatives under John Bracken had come to call themselves "Progressive" and the Liberals had a left wing too:

I would not like to leave the impression that the Marxist class struggle has already been engaged. Liberalism in Canada has not exhausted its historic role: the self-confidence of the middle classes has not yet been broken on the proletarian wall.[8]

Later, sometime in 1948–9, Trudeau confided to his notebook:

In Canada a party like the Liberal Party which moves slowly to the left can in the abstract become the vehicle leading the nation towards this popular future [of socialism]. But its laudable impulse to embrace the better elements of socialism clashes with those who represent the interests of money. I believe a great deal in the wisdom of the middle classes who are erroneously represented under the name of the bourgeoisie. . . . Nevertheless it is necessary for the proletariat to raise itself to the level of the middle class. It is never better to rely on others for your own good.[9]

Trudeau was not preaching Marxist class warfare but he was aligning himself with a possible Canadian socialism.

After immersing his audience in the realities of Canada's politics, it might be wondered if Trudeau held out any hope that its politics could be altered. Recent European history and the tragic conflicts of the Old World, he admitted, offered a bleak perspective but a westward look revealed a brighter prospect.

Canada is perhaps one of the last countries where one can still examine in the light of faith and reason the challenges that confront us, to choose without passion the best of all the camps and make a synthesis based on peace and justice.[10]

In Quebec too, in spite of its "legendary immobility" and "reactionary politics" there were signs of change. Last year, he said, provincial spending on education had doubled, and a Ministry of Welfare and Youth and several technical schools had been established:

Mainly we have need of charity which alone can prevent political struggles being transformed into civil wars. We need to create the mystique of the modern city. This ought to be possible in a new country like Canada which does not carry the heavy burden of being embittered by regimes based on caste and privilege and where the intrinsic dignity of the adversary has not been forgotten amidst deep conflicts.

But time is running out and the common denominator has been found which can reduce regionalism and even Canadian federalism: it's the proletariat. Scarcely two months ago, we witnessed something unheard of: French Canadian workers responding to the proletarian appeal rather than to that of nationalism.

The crucial hour has come when new alliances are forming and new loyalties are sought. If our social system were to disintegrate from the bottom up; if the masses were to turn away in disgust from the "ruling" classes still completely entangled in their super-ego, I wouldn't give much for the *"quelques arpents de neige"* on which our ancestors based so much of their hopes.[11]

Already in 1947 Trudeau subscribed to the view that the working class had a redemptive role to play, breaking apart the unintellectual stasis of traditional Canadian politics.

"La promesse du Québec," dealt with many of the same themes.[12] He contrasted European experience with that of North America; Europe was not the measure of all things, he reiterated. But neither was the United States, which was sterile in artistic things, he said, nor did it appreciate the intrinsic value of work; it was uncultured and vulgar and lacking in humility:

Such facts as these give us cause to think that the great people of America has not cultivated within itself the personality that expresses the refinements of the soul.[13]

The basic problem of the United States was that it was too big. The citizen was a cipher and there was a lack of a human scale:

> In the small homeland [*la petite patrie*] . . . the love of oneself and
> one's neighbors can become a foundation from which to reach
> out to all humanity . . . This must be borne in mind in under-
> standing the unique promise made to the world by my country
> [*pays*], called Canada, and above all by my small homeland [*petite
> patrie*], Quebec.

Canada was increasing as an industrial power and its territory and
resources were immense but, unlike the United States, it had maintained an appreciation of "the inner virtues." Quebec had contributed a great deal to this happy outcome and the federal system too,
for French Canadians had always insisted on preserving their "spiritual and intellectual autonomy." And, again because of federalism,
Canada respected "the big and the small, the one and the several;
it is bureaucratized but still vital." What Trudeau was delineating
was a view of Canada as a union of small homelands. Canadians
approached the higher values through the local and the particular,
he said.

Trudeau probed deeper into what he called this "ambivalence"
of strong French-Canadian assertiveness on the one hand and the
claims of a federal Canada on the other. Canada was an independent country, he said, whose people were mainly made up of English
and French speakers. Every Canadian was proud of his country no
matter where he considered himself at home. Trudeau imagined a
prickly interrogator:

> But are you first and foremost Canadians or French Canadians?
> That's the question that the problem-solvers pose with all their
> cunning and which they hope allows them to announce once
> and for all whether we are generous or narrow in spirit. Oh, well;
> we are at once Canadians and French Canadians, just as we are
> Americans because we live in America. Who is so narrow-minded
> that he cannot envisage several horizons? The important thing
> is not to give a reply to such questions; so let us rather aim to
> put the problem in the sphere where truth is to be found. It was

French Canadians who forced respect for their faith, their language and their law in the thirty years after the conquest. But it was the *Canadians* who repelled the arrogant invaders from the United States in 1812. And, it was neither the one nor the other but quite simply *the man* in us who protested against Canada's participation in the iniquitous war against the Boers in 1900.[14]

Here was an early, bold affirmation by Trudeau of the virtue of multiple identities and multicultural belonging. Part of this was a deep identification with Quebec:

But if it is necessary to specify what constitutes for the French Canadian his homeland [*patrie*] in the present state of affairs, it is proper to say that it is Quebec. Our ancestors still haunt the soil of this province which they won from the forest, and defended in turns against Redskins and red uniforms. Our customs were formed there, the language we speak was transformed there, and so too the songs and dances we love. There our crafts and then our arts took on their distinctive forms and shapes. And the far flung reaches of our land are still the well-spring of myths and legends.[15]

A folkish account, then, of Quebec was something to which Trudeau adhered. He also can be seen to be making an argument for communitarian traditions as inherently valuable and crucial to the identity of the individual. He illustrated this with some comments on Quebec's own version of law, the Civil Code. The ancient French law, mainly the Coutume de Paris, he said, had been preserved in the Quebec Act in 1774 and carried forward in subsequent provincial legislation:

This may not be the time to compare French law with foreign law, ancient law with the new. But one risks nothing in affirming that ancient French law, which contributed a significant civil regime within our national character, was more significant than anything else in establishing the durability of our spirit.[16]

Trudeau gave instances of how in Quebec matrimonial law had presumed a community of goods and incorporated religiously based prohibitions on marriage. He saw this as generally a positive thing. Even if Quebec's legal traditions, he said, were not deemed to be much better than those of others, they nonetheless possessed the merit of "being our own. . . . Consequently it forces us to be ourselves and it's easy to understand how this strengthens our personality."[17] The role of the Church in shaping Quebec's identity, Trudeau said, had been significant:

> It is thanks to the clergy that French Canada has survived to the present. But it is without the clergy that French Canada survives at the present time. After the surrender of Canada to Protestant England in 1763 the priests and the religious orders were at the same time our spiritual fathers, our intellectual elite, our political thinkers, our teachers, our nurses and the indefatigable defenders of our national heritage. For a long time they were the only ones to see to what extent our language and faith were indispensable to each other; thus the apostle doubles as the patriot; and in their eyes the survival of Quebec was also the survival of Catholicism in the North of America. Under their tutelage, our people got used to thinking of "Protestant" when they said "English" and these two words evoked the double-headed danger of assimilation. One gains nothing in hiding the fact that such an education leads to certain unfortunate consequences: a conservatism hostile to all forms of change, a religiosity verging on Jansenism, and a certain narrowness which leads to xenophobia. Moreover it turns out today that the clergy is slow to perceive how much these characteristics damage the flourishing of our people. . . . [I]t is why, in the matter of education, and social education above all, the guardianship of the clergy weighs heavily on us and engenders the tragic necessity of looking for the forces of emancipation outside the Church of Quebec. . . . The rough-hewn reform movement outside the Church is not ranged against Her; because the best of our elite,

which includes a number of priests, is as deeply Catholic as it is anti-clerical.[18]

Trudeau continued: Quebec's constitutional standing as a province was fundamental to the survival of French culture in Canada. It was the one province where French was an official language, where ancient French jurisprudence had the force of law, and where the Catholic Church was universally established and respected. French-speaking communities outside the province may be strong but they needed to "commune with the source" of their ongoing strength.

Trudeau did not overlook English Canada. He believed it too had contributed immensely to the "rich inheritance" of the Canadian state:

> Doubtless British institutions are not perfect in comparison with the ideal; but if one considers what exists elsewhere I think we should rejoice that here we have a political credo based on respect for the individual. This respect—which is hard to achieve—brings with it civil liberty (for example habeas corpus, the presumption of innocence in criminal cases) and political liberty (a democracy founded on the famous "agreement to disagree.") Moreover, since history has imposed the British parliamentary regime on us, it is important to be grateful to English Canadians for communicating to the rest of the population those virtues that are indispensable to its functioning: I speak of a certain spirit of moderation in the appreciation of principles, and of a respectable realism which has preserved for us a lame multi-partyism.
>
> Out of the encounter at the federal level of two such different national characters there has emerged a quite felicitous mix. The French Canadian has a solid philosophy of life which gives him direction and hope; while the English Canadian is more pragmatic. The one is generous; but it is the other who will channel this virtue in the direction of socialism. The first is very assiduous; the second will organize his efforts better. Both of them are more complicated than the American from the United States;

but they are also less pretentious, as happens to people who have
known defeats.[19]

Trudeau saw Canada as a compelling example of successful
intercultural exchange. He was offering a complimentary account
of British influences and a positive view of Anglo-French cultural
hybridity. But at the same time he was not being naively guilty
of anglophilia because while, he said, the "two nations" had
exchanged qualities between themselves, they had also traded
hard blows. Addressing relations in the present day Trudeau went
on: leaders in both nations have fallen for the mistaken idea of
a crude national sovereignism in which each group deemed the
fundamental purpose of the state as providing the means to control things to its own advantage and to dominate the other: "We
[are] deceived by the fallacy made by legal minds the world over
whereby the State is defined as the juridical personification of one
Nation."[20]

Out of this fallacy, said Trudeau, there have emerged three possible scenarios for the future, all of them "equally disastrous." The
first, the "separatist" one, concluded that if Canada was "two ethnic
entities," each of which possessed some kind of collective will, then
out of this dualism two sovereign states must be made. This might
have an amicable outcome, said Trudeau, but it overlooked issues
of territorial partition and, of course, at the heart of each of the
successor states would immediately arise new minority problems.
The second scenario—Trudeau referred to as the "Imperialist"
one—was mainly voiced by English Canadians, although French
Canadians who adhered to the strategy of the revenge-of-the-
cradle held similar views. This one happily anticipated "assimilat-
ing" or "annihilating" the minority through the power of numbers.
It was, he believed, an increasingly unpopular option, the obsession
of an extremist minority of "megalomaniacs, paranoids and mal-
contents." And finally, there was the option that offered Canada
what he called a "bastard union." It placed such an emphasis upon
the idea of a homogeneous, unitary state that it was prepared to

trade away "language, faith, culture, patriotism, honor, and identity" in exchange for national unity:

> National unity was a *sine qua non* for them, a first principle that must be achieved immediately, at any cost. All these fine folk were leading us toward the shameful barter of trading, one by one, our language, faith, culture, patriotism, honor and personality in exchange for that famous "unity."[21]

What he seemed to be describing—his language was sometimes ambiguous—was a point-of-view that placed so much emphasis upon a centrifugal dynamic and the unity of the country that Canada's cultural and political diversity would be completely obliterated, a sort of melting-pot philosophy. Later in the essay he called this position "pan-Americanism." Whoever they were that favoured this bastard union—and Trudeau intimated some of them were French Canadians—he had no tolerance for them, calling them "toadying foot-soldiers, bounty hunters, not to mention spineless collaborators, too naïve to prevent one concession leading to a thousand more."[22] Clearly Trudeau had not lost his capacity for the verbal excesses of his Outremont speech.

The rest of the essay was an impressive, indirect meditation on Laski and to a lesser extent on Mounier and Maritain: a pragmatic view of political truth, the federal nature of society, the nature of sovereignty, the perils of nationalism, and critical insights derived from a functionalist way of thinking. Trudeau reasoned that the problems now confronting Canada derived in some ways from its failure to properly join together legal logic with the actualities of history. For over four hundred years, he said, theories of sovereignty had peddled the false idea of the identification of the state with the nation. This was redolent of Laski's critique of nationalism. If there was to be a theory of the state it must be founded on "facts" and "reality." The present age, he said, was the era of the World Bank, international cartels, economic imperialism, international communism, inter-state commissions and the atomic bomb. The state must cease its obsession with nationalism and assume its proper role as the representative of all of the people living in its territory. The separate but overlapping realities of the local, the national, and the international could better be captured, he claimed, by a dynamic and flexible federalism. Nations must cease to be rivals; ethnic groups should pursue their particularist goals while, of course, co-operating with each other to establish larger unities.

So what was to be Quebec's place in such a world? Quebec, Trudeau said, encompassed a small people, with a strong sense of its communal identity. It was a place where

> hearts listen and beat in unison. . . . But our homeland is also an integral part of an immense country where we are apprentices of the supra-national at the same time as we are attempting adventures commensurate with our energies.[23]

Trudeau made clear that this would require moving beyond the rickety 1867 pact of Confederation and the British North America Act. In its time, he said, this had represented a happy political compromise between two nationalities seeking to live together without abandoning their separate identity. The Act's division of powers along economic and social lines rather than ethnic ones was a judicious arrangement. But its precepts had been subverted by conflicts between the two nationalist groups in Canada. At the same time constitutional theory had been taken over by the idea of an "indivisible and inalienable sovereignty," the very legal fallacy that Trudeau saw embodied in the three "disastrous" options that he had just adumbrated. Something different was needed:

> A new distribution of powers is necessary, between sovereign entities that have become multiform and changing: the Canadian Nations will not deprive themselves of anything that they judge indispensable to their fulfillment. As for the Canadian State, it will coordinate economic activities; it will know the

material needs; it will establish the administrative mechanisms required to satisfy these needs; and in general it will exercise the functions which relate to the country as a whole. Many other functions will be beyond its competence such as organizing for world peace and in this regard nations will enter into other federations. This multi-form organization of society will always be at the service of the improvement of mankind. In this way those who are at the bottom will find themselves at the top but enlarged by love for one's fellow man and enriched by all the exchanges that follow.[24]

Laski's influence was also evident in Trudeau's comments about the importance of a "functionalist politics." Trudeau employed the term in a two-fold way. First, there was the simple idea that political problems should be approached from an attitude of unprejudiced innovativeness, in the manner of the new school of architecture that had dispensed with traditional ornamentation and embellishment in the name of unadorned simplicity and purpose. Secondly, Trudeau understood the term as a type of critical analysis that gave direction to the design of political institutions by first establishing what their "good" might be and thus what "function" they were intended to meet. In Trudeau's hands—as in Laski's—functionalism was an ethical theory, and a radical one at that.[25] *Pace* Marcel Rioux, Kenneth McRoberts and Reg Whitaker, functionalism for him had nothing to do with the maintenance of systems, the management of conflict, or the espousing of some kind of presuppositionless technocracy. It was about a refreshingly radical critique of the existing institutional order in the name of both justice and uncomplicatedness.

An ethical functionalism must as well embrace a pluralism of values. Here Trudeau seems to have been saying that there was no single ideology that made moral sense of the world but rather there were several, each true within its specific context or institution of applicability. Truth was multiple, just as the world itself was pluralistically constituted:

A politics of functionalism will not be captive to the thousand prejudices of the past which encumber the present, but will wish to build for mankind. Now, there is no single human measure of man; there are several. For every one of our activities in society we will discover an appropriate social measure. Our institutions will be judged according to the function they are meant to fulfill: municipal councils are not governed the way one governs penitentiaries! And so, in different matters we will consent to be well served by collectivism, liberalism, totalitarianism and anarchy all at the same time. So why just ask for the moon when you can also have the sun, the stars and the ocean.[26]

The presence of totalitarianism in the list is puzzling but perhaps Trudeau was thinking of how penitentiaries were to be governed! And surely as he penned that final sentence he must have cracked a smile, noticing perhaps that his rhetoric sometimes carried him away. Anyway, Trudeau swept on to his dramatic conclusion. Quebec had entered a new age; its young people understood the implications of their multiform world:

[They] are getting ready to teach the synthesis of a warm-hearted patriotism and a broadly based humanism. Their struggle will not be long for if they do not succeed soon Quebec will quickly have become a reactionary obstacle in the path of America. But their struggle will be all the harder because they will have to lead in the attack a people which owes its survival to being on the defensive. They will have to change this people from being conservative to revolutionary.[27]

French Canadians must exhibit a radical, transformative insurgency. But it must be expressed democratically.

In an article published in *Notre Temps* in February 1948, "Réflexions sur une démocratie et sa variante," Trudeau offered further powerful evidence of the far-reaching postulates informing his world view.[28] The spur to this piece was the news that Adrien

Arcand, a noted Quebec fascist, who had been interned during the Second World War, was suing the federal government. Trudeau's concern was not so much to defend Arcand but to remind his readers about what he regarded as the thoroughly undemocratic conduct of the wartime Ottawa government. When it came to democracy, he observed, French Canadians have displayed an ambivalent mentality. In most respects they "hold a grudge" against democracy and one day, he said, he hoped to explain why this was so. Yet, paradoxically, they cherished values that could only be fulfilled if they lived within a truly democratic country. For Trudeau personalism, for that was what informed his comments, presumed a liberal-democratic order:

> [French Canadians] believe in the immeasurable dignity of the human person and in the inalienable right of everyone to freely pursue the complete flourishing of their personality. To this end each follows his vocation and conceives it according to his own lights: some will take reason as their guide, others faith, and yet others will defer to the commands of some authority or other. But the experience of life is for each of us unique and "every man should bear his own burden" (Saint Paul); in the last analysis each man justifies his actions by obeying his own conscience.
>
> It is the glory of democracy that it strives to apply these principles to the political city. The conscience of the citizen is its constant reference point; it is referred to periodically at the ballot box and in the meantime one seeks by every means to discover and follow its dictates: from it flow freedom of the press, of assembly, of speech, religious tolerance and equality before the law.[29]

In the late 1940s, then, Trudeau was of the view that Quebec was still ill-disposed towards liberal democracy. It would become a commonplace of his thinking in the 1950s. But he was concerned to expose English Canadians' disdain for democratic precepts too. And so he tore strips off an Anglophone-dominated federal government for its oppressive conduct during the war: the internment of Arcand and Camillien Houde, the prosecution of René Chaloult who opposed conscription, the farce of bilingualism in the army, the "trickery" of the conscription issue, the "gag of censorship," the Drew letter, the scandal of Canadian troops overrun in Hong Kong, and so on. In a democracy, he claimed, the government by itself could not know what was best for the people because invariably government fashioned its own separate interest from that of the people; civil liberties were not to be suspended even in time of war, and, if they were, this could only be justified if there existed a state of siege, which was not the case in Canada, he said. Surely the one law that citizens deserved to be involved in determining was the one that exposed them to possible death. Trudeau was particularly scathing about Prime Minister Mackenzie King and his manipulation of the conscription issue. (Trudeau remained loyal to his anti-conscription position in later years. As late as 1962 he described the 1942 conscription referendum as one of the most devastating instances of English Canada's injustice and perfidy towards French Canada.)[30]

An intriguing motif in these essays is that of Trudeau's communitarian and traditionalist view of Quebec as the sentimental homeland of French Canadians and as their primary territorial state. Trudeau employed a "two-nations," dualistic vocabulary although he did not apply it in the cause of special jurisdictional powers for the province. Nonetheless equally apparent is the degree to which he was pulling away from conventional Quebec nationalism. The great proposition in these essays was about the need for change in Quebec. Quebec's culture, he believed, was too conservative and its religious institutions irrelevant and atrophied. The essays also confirm—as if it ever could be doubted—that he displayed a deep passion for politics itself. For now, though, his political ardour he expressed as an emerging public intellectual. Already he had begun to posit a calculus of political action; politics must take account of facts and realities; idealistic and utopian thinking was not relevant; and political action must somehow match idea to context. But it must also be about thinking clearly. If idealism by itself was not enough, equally a directionless, reactive, survivalist politics was inadequate too. The challenge he threw down to Quebec was to transcend both its cultural and religious conservatism and its political sectionalism in favour of a larger common good. He dared Quebec to secure the particularities of its identity at the same time as it pursued the broader good of a variegated and cosmopolitan world.

II

Canadians today identify Trudeau so overwhelmingly with his period as prime minister that, in regards to "history," they usually think of him as having lived and made history rather than having written about it. Yet, before he entered parliament, he was a historian of no mean ability. But Trudeau mainly used history for political purposes, which is not to say that he bent history to his own political ends. Rather he used it, he thought, as an ostensibly objective scaffolding to give foundation and structure to his political views. He held that historical claims in support of political positions must be scientifically and factually grounded. He was a positivist. He espoused a proto-Popperian view that held that historical investigation should at least be capable of disconfirming received political positions and perhaps it could establish more; above all historical "knowledge" could not be a rationalization of some preconceived, doctrinaire, or unempirical position. Nationalist historiography, he contended, was a particularly extreme instance of such rationalizations.[31] Trudeau the historian was a demythologizer, an iconoclast, and a provider of counter-narratives but not in order to create new myths of his own. Myth must be contradicted by fact and not be replaced by another myth.

The necessity that Trudeau had for a definite account of history is obvious. Politics in Quebec has always been centered on the meaning of its past and an investigation—sometimes a witchhunt—into who the villains of its piece have been. Ramsay Cook has put it well: "French Canadians, a most historically-minded people, have turned to the past for the explanation of their plight."[32]

Professional history-writing in Quebec had begun in the nineteenth century but it was only after the Second World War that there was established the infrastructure of a university-based discipline: the Institut d'histoire de l'Amérique française in 1946 and one year later, *Revue d'histoire de l'Amérique française*. Abbé Groulx, from his position in the University of Montreal where he had begun lecturing in 1915, was the moving force behind many of these initiatives. After 1945 the department there, and the one at Laval too, expanded substantially. These two centres became separate encampments from which platoons emerged to do battle over the meaning of French Canada's past. Ronald Rudin explains this well in his *Making History in Twentieth-Century Quebec* (1997).

What came to be called the Montreal school regarded the Conquest after 1760 as a horrible tragedy. The victorious British had been "merciless conquerors" bent on overcoming the French.[33] French Canadians were excluded from commerce, the professions, and government. But colonial domination brought resistance. The Catholic Church assumed the mantle of protector of the French Canadian "nation" and, in time, French Canada produced its own cadre of political leaders—Joseph-Louis Papineau, Louis-Hippolyte Lafontaine, Honoré Mercier, Henri Bourassa, and Maurice Duplessis—who stood up to their British and Canadian masters. Rudin sees the major exponents of the Montreal school as not just Groulx but Guy Frégault, Maurice Séguin, and Michel Brunet.[34] The Laval school was different.[35] It rejected British culpability and held that French Canada had been responsible for its own backwardness. After the Conquest it had turned inward and become deeply submissive to clerical authority. Its clerical, professional, and political elites set their face against enterprise and capitalism, and modernity in general. In the view of the Laval school there was no French-Canadian bourgeoisie in large part because there had been no such class before 1760. A mainly agricultural society had been held back not by the English but by French Canadians themselves and their lack of initiative. Far from Quebec's history being a story of the devilry of perfidious Albion, the British had introduced the rudiments of liberal justice and political democracy. Their influence had been "benevolent." They had pioneered industrial, urban, and capitalist modernity. Rudin considers the principal champions of the Laval view to have been Marcel Trudel, Fernand Ouellet, and Jean Hamelin. In time the two schools were joined by other schools, to which he gives the labels of revisionist and post-revisionist.[36] Revisionism put forward an interpretation of Quebec's development as one that was "normal," that is, similar to other contemporary Western societies. French Canada generated its own class of entrepreneurs and its farmers had indeed developed commercial markets. It was neither priest-ridden nor anti-capitalist and it was hardly a stranger to liberalism and democracy.

The Montreal and Laval schools did hold some views in common. Both fixed on the Conquest as the formative event in Quebec's history and they shared the conviction that the central question about French Canada had to do with explaining why its culture was different from that of English Canada and the United States. This emphasis on Quebec's distinctiveness led to a preoccupation with its early history as an agricultural society and resource frontier. Trudeau too spent a lot of time talking about the Conquest and its aftermath. But his most auspicious historiographical achievement—his contribution to the collection of essays about the Asbestos strike—was to carry forward Quebec's history into the late nineteenth and early twentieth centuries and to offer conclusions about its industrial and urban experience and especially about its working class. Like the Montreal school, including Groulx, Trudeau believed that French Canada had survived the Conquest through great pluck and perseverance. And with the revisionists he emphasized the role of economic class and the identity of the province as a multi-ethnic territory. Certainly he believed that French Canada was "different," but to the point of being backward and reactionary. In this regard he was at odds with the Montreal school. Rudin places Trudeau unambiguously in the Laval school.[37] He subscribed to a version of the "benevolent" English thesis and he wanted the province to embrace modernity. The fit is not perfect however. He shared *some* views with the Laval group, especially those to do with the idea of the benevolent English and of French Canada's responsibility for its own inadequacies. And it is true that, when, in his later years, he sought out a historian to represent his own sense of the past, he settled on Fernand Ouellet, from the Laval school.[38]

Trudeau's historical method was not that of a solitary scholar slaving away in some dusty archive. Instead he mined the work of those who had so slaved away, and to great argumentative effect. His historical writings are distinguished by the breadth and thoroughness of his reading. He mastered the secondary sources and combined them with his own enquiries in the one archive where he did undertake prodigious original research, namely contemporary newspapers as well as secular and Church-sponsored journals such as *L'Ordre Nouveau, Rélations, Laurentie, La Revue Dominicaine,* and *L'Oratoire.* And of course, as the 1950s proceeded, he was increasingly able to make use of the articles that appeared in *Cité Libre.* He foraged relentlessly for information and insight. Unpublished works made their way into his bibliographies as did statistical sources such as unemployment and census data from the Bureau of Statistics in Ottawa and various Royal Commissions and government agencies. His technique was to overwhelm the reader with evidence—sometimes excruciatingly detailed evidence—that he believed was factual and objective. Trudeau should be seen as being in the vanguard of a new, post-Groulx positivist historiography.

His historical method, then, was more than derivative though certainly it was indebted to particular individuals: in the early 1950s Jean-Charles Falardeau, Everett Hughes, and Frank Scott. By mid-decade he would mention his debts to Falardeau again but also to Maurice Tremblay and Mason Wade.[39] In the mid-1950s the works of some of the rising generation of postwar academic historians appeared among his sources, in particular Fernand Ouellet, Michel Brunet, and Marcel Trudel.[40] But to the proposition that Groulx was the father of "scientific," professional history in Quebec, Trudeau would have disrespectfully demurred. By the 1950s he saw Groulx as an ideologue rather than a historian, and as a purveyor of an account of the past at the service of nationalist politics. He was a peddler of sectarianism, an anti-capitalist, and an advocate of authoritarian and Church-dominated practices. Groulx, he said, believed that Quebec's deepest destiny was to be led by someone like Eamon de Valera, Benito Mussolini, Engelbert Dollfuss, or António de Oliveira Salazar. Groulx, for Trudeau, personified the narrow-mindedness of nationalist thought in its absolute rejection of "English," "socialist," or "materialist" influences. For Groulx, compulsory school attendance regulations and liberal divorce laws were to be rejected, not because of their inherent defects, but because they were the bastard offspring of "Protestant" parliaments.[41] Trudeau knew whereof he spoke for some of these opinions he himself had held in an earlier time, as he also had held a more admiring opinion of Groulx himself. But by the 1950s that was long ago.

With the founding of *Cité Libre* in June 1950 Trudeau was provided with a secure and dependable medium through which to publicize his ideas about Quebec's past and its possible future. Capricious and conformist editors, especially those with Catholic journals like *Relations*, would no longer be obstacles to the publishing of his ideas, if only because *he* was now the editor. His first essay in *Cité Libre* appeared in its first edition. Entitled "Politique functionelle," it was about French Canada. Equally suitably perhaps, since it was to be the first volley of his grand campaign, the article was extravagant in its intellectual ambitions and in the dramatic, sententious tone of its author's voice. What the article announced was the arrival on the Quebec scene of someone who saw himself in a heroic mode daringly addressing his people. Trudeau summoned French Canada to do nothing less than to reimagine itself and to set forth on a completely new politics. Here was a radicalism determined not just to get to the root of things but indeed to dismiss the idea of roots altogether. It had all the brashness of Paul-Émile Borduas's famous 1948 manifesto, *Le refus global*. Indeed both statements marked an important turning point in Quebec's intellectual life.

Trudeau began with a consideration of the Conquest. In essence his argument was that French Canadians' reaction to that

formative event had led them into a cul-de-sac. They had nobly
resisted ethnic and religious assimilation but this had drained
them of intellectual vitality and political imagination. Sometimes
a heroic resistance could "degenerate" into a "beastly stubborn-
ness," Trudeau observed. Having struggled unrelentingly, French
Canadians had ended up believing that virtue always lay in a state
of "negation." In Quebec, Church and State had been less interested in making friends and more in denouncing their enemies: the
communists, the English, the Jews, imperialists, centralizers, devils,
free-thinkers, and such like. In Trudeau's view, the Québécois must
embrace the "new" and the "positive":

> We must submit to methodical doubt all the political categories
> which have been bequeathed to us from previous generations.
> The strategy of resistance is no longer useful to the flourishing
> of the City. The time has come to borrow from the architect the
> discipline which is called "functional," to renounce the thousand
> preconceptions by which the past encumbers the present, and to
> build something new for mankind. Let us throw over the totems
> and break the taboos. Or even better, let us consider that they had
> never existed. Coldly, let us be intelligent.[42]

For this new project Trudeau prescribed an alternative social
way-of-knowing. French Canada should learn to think in the whole
and in a scientific spirit. He personally felt bound to demonstrate
to the Québécois that political science—he presumably saw himself
as practising such a modern discipline—was not the equivalent of
"magic" and that altogether it was necessary to "empty our language
of all emotional content. . . . [S]o many words . . . fill us with enthusiasm or indignation without reason."[43] Trudeau's own contribution
to the establishing of a dispassionate sensibility was to challenge
the sacred idol of the "autonomy" of Quebec as the *sine qua non* of
its political identity, "our first article of faith."[44] Quebec should take
account of wider global contexts and embrace co-operative intergovernmental arrangements. Some things were better handled

at the federal level. Quebec would do well, he thought, to pursue more "centralization" in, for example, fiscal and monetary policy and in labour standards. Abroad there could be many opportunities for international collaboration. The unity of humanity was emerging and this stood in stark contrast to the predicament of a province mired in a self-induced independence and isolation. Trudeau perceived a societal breakdown of almost apocalyptic proportions:

> In the name of autonomy, our rich province is satisfied with a reduced standard of life; our workers are content with inferior salaries; our cities are getting filled with brothels and outrageously expensive shacks; our population is ravaged by tuberculosis and high levels of infant mortality; our bureaucracy is a graveyard full of incompetent down-and-outs; our educational budgets serve our students little and give advantage more to road contractors: and our national resources are exploited for the profit of other countries.[45]

The dispiriting story of a French Canada immovable in its conceits and illicit habits was something to which Trudeau returned in an important essay after Maurice Duplessis and the Union Nationale had again triumphed in the provincial election of July 1952, "Réflexions sur la politique au Canada français," published in December. Trudeau began with disturbing candour, in words that have acquired an almost mythic resonance: "*Il faut expliquer notre immoralisme profond*" ("It is necessary to explain our deep-seated immoralism")[46] The Québécois were ostensibly a Christian people yet in one important respect—their relations with the state—they "are passably immoral":

> We corrupt public officials, we blackmail our representatives, we put pressure on the courts, defraud the public purse and turn a blind eye when it suits us. And in regards to electoral matters our immoralism is truly sordid. The farmer who would be ashamed to enter a brothel sells his soul each election for a bottle

of homebrew. And the lawyer who presses for the maximum sentence for the thief who steals from the alms-box in the church nonetheless takes pride in having added two thousand fictitious names to the electoral lists.[47]

Trudeau was equally reproving of the Church's role in buttressing this so-called Christian society. Catholics, he observed, were rarely "pillars of democracy." They had difficulty adapting to any arrangement based on the counting of votes. Where they were in the majority they tended to support authoritarian regimes and, where their numbers were few, they accepted the separation of Church and State as a "last resort" and devoted themselves to pursuing the particular good of the Catholic Church. They were distinguished neither by their morality nor by their political clear-sightedness. This was why in Quebec there was little respect for electoral rules:

> These are Protestant and Anglo-Saxon preoccupations whose profound importance is overlooked and whose immediate usefulness is translated into the bottle of whisky received, the parish hall built or the contract signed to build a road.[48]

For Trudeau, such deep immorality—he called it *"incivisme"* or lack of good civic values, especially a lack of regard for the common good, while elsewhere he referred to it as the absence of *"un État civil"*—had a historical etiology.[49] It had all begun at the Conquest. The administration of New France, he said, was authoritarian and so was local government. After 1760, English political forms were imported, particularly representative government. But there was a fatal flaw in the relations between the two cultural communities. To ensure the successful common governance of two language groups there needed to have been established an "entente" or "common good" based on "equality." (This became a crucial concept with Trudeau.) From 1763 until as late as the Union governments in the 1840s, he continued, an association founded on equality was rejected by the English. And so the fatal resolve of French Canada became cemented in place: representative government would be embraced but only for pragmatic or "opportunistic" reasons and democracy would be celebrated neither as an ideal nor as an "ideology" but as a means to simple "survival." French Canadians stood prepared to use any stratagem to protect their ethnic interest in the face of English intransigence and aggression. Later, using Gérard Pelletier's phrase, Trudeau postulated that throughout the English regime French Canadians had suffered under an endless "state of siege."[50] With this, politics in French Canada congealed in a mould of national self-defiance—in a word, nationalism. It was the amoral protectiveness of a beleaguered, permanent national minority. The Church did not publicly approve of such behaviour but it did not oppose it either. It simply turned a blind eye.

So, according to Trudeau, whatever political diversity existed within French Canada had been subordinated to the fundamental imperative of preserving its cultural existence by methods of unanimity and conformity. Quebec's politics, of whatever stripe, was uniformly and unconditionally nationalistic. The distinctions between Bleu and Rouge, Tory and Clear Grit, and later between Liberal and Conservative, were subsumed into an overarching ethnic imperative. "Ethnic rights" came to trump economic, philosophical, and ethical considerations. This was even true of French-Canadian support of Laurier after 1896 and of Bourassa after 1911. The Great Depression offered a new politics of principle when, with classical liberalism in eclipse, citizens looked to the state for aid. This was especially the case in English Canada with the emergence of the CCF. But in Quebec the "old brains" prevailed and conservative nationalism won out. In 1936 Duplessis successfully convinced Quebec voters that the provincial Liberals had sold out to "les Anglais." Defeated in 1940, four years later he played the nationalist card again, re-winning power and then retaining it in 1948 and again in 1952. The federal elections of 1940 and 1945 had fallen under the same rubric: French Canadians voted for nationalism, against the English and their war.

Trudeau's 1952 article was seminal and provided the general framework for his thinking about Quebec for the rest of the 1950s and early 1960s. He would periodically quote from it although there would also be some elaboration or alteration of terminology and viewpoint. His subsequent observations appeared mainly in seven essays he wrote between 1954 and 1964: "Obstacles à la démocratie" (1954), "La province de Québec au moment de la grève" (1956), "Un manifeste démocratique" (1958), "Some Obstacles to Democracy in Quebec" (1958), "La nouvelle trahison des clercs" (1962), "Democracy in French Canada" (1962), and "Federalism, Nationalism and Reason" (1964). A predominant theme running through all of them had to do with the anti-democratic ethos of French Canada and the remarkable fact that French Canadians had been the only people who had ever attained democracy without having to fight for it.[51] They had received it as a gift but, strangely, they had not wanted it. At first they had spurned it but then they discovered how to take advantage of it. As for the "Whigs of Westminster and the reformers of Upper Canada"[52] and English Canadians in general, they genuinely believed in democracy but they preferred to keep it for themselves and to deny it to French Canadians.[53] Indeed the unrelenting preference of the British regime, Trudeau said, was for the "assimilation" of the French. But the French substantially out-numbered the English, at least until the mid-nineteenth century, and so through a combination of a demographic *force majeure* and propitious political circumstances the French had blackmailed the British into conceding liberal legislation and representative gov-ernment. The good fortune of the French came not from British generosity but from the happenstance of circumstance, for British governors believed they needed French-Canadian goodwill in the face of hostile American colonies and later an expansionist United States government. The Quebec Act (1774), which gave civil rights to Catholics, was one such important concession. The power of num-bers continued and so the Constitutional Act of 1791 provided for the inclusion of both language groups in the Assembly. The impera-tive now for the Colonial Office in London and its administrations in the Canadas was to find ways to limit the effects of what they had conceded:

> Chief Justice Sewell, in 1810, produced all kinds of schemes to reduce the influence of the majority. He proposed high property restrictions upon the franchise which would permit the English-Canadians to vote but not the French. He proposed a union of Upper and Lower Canada so that the French majority would be reduced as much as possible. Governor Craig [Governor from 1807 to 1811] tried to implement the same schemes.[54]

Other cunning stratagems followed in the 1820s and 1830s, Trudeau observed.

The fourth side of the quadrilateral of colonial governors, English merchants, and French farmers was the Catholic Church. According to Trudeau, the hierarchy of the Church viewed democracy as an abomination and the French Revolution as even worse. Mercifully, in the Church's estimation, the Conquest had at least kept French Canada from being infected by revolutionary republicanism. Its task now was to protect its flock from home-grown Canadian democracy. And so a convenient convergence of interest had emerged between British administrators and Catholic bishops. After difficult beginnings, both powers found it advantageous to work out a *modus vivendi*. Loyalty was bartered for religious freedom, and the Church was as good as her word. During the wars of 1775, 1812, 1914, and 1939, the Catholic hierarchy preached submission to His Majesty's government: they even launched an appeal against the Fenian raiders in 1870. And at the time of the 1837 rebellion, they used their powers to check the Patriotes.[55]

But the grip of the Church was not total, Trudeau went on. French Canadians produced their own secular, political leadership that demanded representative government. French Canada's fondness for "democracy," however, was always opportunistic rather than principled, Trudeau contended. It emphasized the defense of the national interest to such an extent that in effect it pursued "self-determination" rather than "self-government."[56] Between the two Trudeau always held the latter to be a higher form of democracy. Self-government was a broadly democratic concept, the other a "narrow" ethnic one. But nationalist self-pro-tectiveness had been significant enough to produce Louis-Joseph Papineau and the Patriote rebellion of 1837, the political initia-tives of Louis-Hippolyte Lafontaine in the 1840s, and George-Étienne Cartier in the 1860s, and, later, those of Wilfrid Laurier and Henri Bourassa.

In Trudeau's account, assaults on the cultural integrity of French Canada had begun as early as 1763 and had continued unabated. Assimilation had been the policy of early governors as it was of the Durham Report in 1838 and of the Union governments from 1841 to 1867. Even after Confederation, by means of "representation-by-population," English Canadians had never ceased waging a war on Francophones and their rights.[57] In the early 1960s Trudeau believed that English Canada's bloody-minded chauvinism continued. If he is sometimes thought of as having been too critical of his French compatriots and too submissive towards the English and their apparently superior political and legal manners, then his many denunciations of the unchecked effects of the English Conquest establish a very different conclusion:

> The generations succeeded each other. The hope of assimilat-ing the French Canadians faded away (although right up to 1948, immigrations laws continued to favour immigrants from the United Kingdom as opposed to those from France). But the attitude of superiority by English-speaking Canadians towards French Canadians has never disappeared.
>
> At Ottawa and in the other provinces, this nationalism wears the pious mask of democracy. Because, as English-speaking Canadians became more numerous, they took to hiding their intolerance under the pretence of majority rule; thanks to this rule they were able to suppress bilingualism in the Manitoba Legislative Assembly, violate rights acquired by separate schools

in several provinces, savagely impose conscription in 1917, and break their word in 1942.

In Quebec, "where they had the money if not the numbers, our Anglo-Canadian fellow-citizens have often given into the temptation of using immoderately the means at their disposal." [Trudeau here was quoting from his own 1952 article.] That was how, in politics, Anglo-Canadian nationalism took the forms of what André Laurendeau has so admirably christened with the name of "the theory of the negro-king." Economically, this nationalism has consisted essentially in treating the French Canadian as a milch cow [*un cochon de payant*]. Sometimes it demonstrated its magnanimity by putting some straw men—with well respected names—on boards of directors. These men always had the following characteristics: first, they were never bright enough or strong enough to get to the top by themselves, and secondly, they were always sufficiently "representative" to beg the negro king's favor and flatter the vanity of the tribe. Finally, in social and cultural matters, Anglo-Canadian nationalism expressed itself, quite simply, with contempt. Whole generations of Anglophones have lived in Quebec without finding some way of learning three phrases of French. When these narrow-minded people seriously insist that their jaws and ears aren't made to be adapted to French, what they really want us to believe is that they refuse to corrupt these organs and their small minds by putting them at the service of a vulgar tongue.[58]

III

Perhaps Trudeau's most accomplished single historical project was his essay, "La province de Québec au moment de la grève," which appeared in 1956 in *La grève de l'amiante* (*The Asbestos Strike*). The book was a collection of nine essays by liberal and social democratic intellectuals, including academics, journalists, lawyers, and trade unionists. Trudeau also contributed an "Épilogue." Trudeau was the editor of the whole project. Even by his standards his own essay was a long one—ninety-one pages—and heavy with footnotes,

131 in all. It is fundamental to an understanding of his theorizing about French Canada.

Trudeau's subject matter was, of course, the historical significance of the miners' strike at Asbestos in 1949. Its immediate effect, he said, had been to divide the Church, to consolidate Quebec nationalism's attachment to tradition, and to reinforce the Quebec state's antipathy towards unions. But offsetting these effects and of greater importance, he thought, was the role of the strike as the harbinger of a new socio-economic order and proof of the emergence of a mature, unified working class. But such auspicious conclusions were secondary in Trudeau's mind to the central question raised by the strike: with the workers coming into their own and industrialization encompassing such a large part of the province's economy, how was it that Quebec's intellectual leaders remained so stuck in outmoded forms of thought and practice? To solve the puzzle Trudeau undertook a searching analysis of the intellectual culture of the province's elites between 1900 and 1950 and of the public discourse that underpinned the socio-cultural and political institutions of the province in the twentieth century. His conclusion was that in Quebec ideology and institutions constituted a system fundamentally oriented to avoiding "reality." Its dominant cultural codes and the political structures they sustained were in thrall to abstractions. They exhibited all the symptoms of a collective repression of the actual and a yearning for the world of dreams and sublimations, "an idealism that almost borders on schizophrenia."[59] Trudeau, the Freudian psychoanalyst, as it were, put French Canada's leaders on the couch and invited them to confront their fantasies, projections, and avoidances.[60]

So what Trudeau formulated was an account of Quebec's history in the service of political praxis. History intimated where society might possibly go and it warned against too dreamlike a wandering into the future, but in this case it cautioned against an obsessive nostalgia for what had gone before. Consider, for example, his observation at the end of his "Épilogue":

> Regarding the past, I must say that it only interests me as a means of influencing future things and in the sense of Gide when he wrote: "The present would be replete with every future if the past was not already projecting a history on it."[61]

Or, think about the broad, suggestive sweep of the conclusion to his main essay:

> The [Asbestos] strike . . . can only be considered an upheaval, and its causes and effects can only merit analysis, because it happened in a society incapable of averting it, powerless to control it, and heedless of its profound significance.
>
> Our ideologies, made up of a mistrust of industrialization, a withdrawal into the self and a nostalgia for the land, were no longer in step with our ethos. Pressured by anonymous capital, beset by foreign influences, we were displaced into a modern shambles where family, neighborhood, and parish—those pillars that traditionally keep our society from crumbling—no longer offered the same support. In industrial society, under capitalism, ignorance and insecurity, slum housing, unemployment, illness, accidents and old age needed other remedies than those offered by the local school, good neighbors, individual charity and private initiative. Yet our social thought had only conceived of solutions that were so inadequate to the problems that the best it could do was to take shape in the programmes of organizations that were artificial, trivial and debilitating. As for our living institutions, those whose very essence required them to stick pragmatically to reality, they were obliged to renounce any ideology, or see their vitality sacrificed.
>
> So how have we survived our torments? In fact, by thumbing our noses at all ideologies. Paradoxically, our ethnic group entrusted with a providential mission and the honor of doctrine, owes its survival largely to its "materialism." For peoples are not doctrinaire, fortunately. Their lives unfold in the here and now; and the urgent requirements to earn one's daily bread, and

to satisfy one's present needs, make them constantly seek out empirically what is possible. Certainly, a people can revolt, storm the barricades, endure a siege (in the psychological as well as the military sense), in short it can rise briefly to the heights of heroism. But by definition for most individuals heroism cannot be a permanent condition. That is why a sound instinct leads peoples to reduce the contradictions between their systems of thought and their plans of action; in the same way they pragmatically cut away those values that postulate heroic opposition and constant failure to adapt to normal daily events.

That is why in the social sphere our people have never—during the half-century preceding the Asbestos strike—followed the official line of the social postulates of nationalism. There was hardly any movement back to the land or a trend to establish cooperatives; small businesses withered away, corporatism remained in limbo; and the Catholic trade unions did not destroy the other unions. On the contrary . . . the province went through an era of intense industrialization, scarcely different from what was happening in countries that were less messianic than ours.[62]

Trudeau's account was a chronicle of the discrepancy between reality and idealization. The "facts" were that Quebec had gone through a social transformation between 1900 and 1945 so that it had become an industrial and urban society and this had occurred at the same pace and to the same extent as Ontario. But if other important factors were considered, Quebec's inferior performance was all too evident. Although by 1941 Quebec was in fact even *more* urbanized than its sister province, its wage rates and employment levels were lower. Admittedly Ontario had had several natural advantages: closeness to supplies of iron and coal, proximity to western Canadian markets, and better communications. Even so, in Trudeau's view, Quebec had also contributed to its own relative backwardness. Through its self-idealizations and cultural delusions it had inhibited its own social and economic development. Its collective mind had prevailed over its socio-economic matter.

Trudeau placed these "facts" in a theoretical framework. Modern industrial capitalism established given "realities" so that certain "rational" policies had generally arisen to mitigate its distresses and deficiencies: a democratic polity, an active state, a welfare system to deal with poverty and social inequality, technology and science to increase productivity, public education, large scale production, and the supervision of big business by the state in its function as the custodian of the general interest or, as Trudeau preferred to call it, the common good.[63] Trudeau put it succinctly a year later: "[A] strong and democratic state is the only worthy regulator of a powerfully industrialized society."[64] To elaborate his point Trudeau explored the relationship between the "dominant values" or ethos of a society and its institutions.[65] Given socio-economic structures—such as industrialization and capitalism—generated values of urbanism, private property, the profit motive, and markets, and these displaced the values and institutions that had gone before. Such realities had inevitably generated a widespread response from citizens who had increasingly come to recognize that to be widely beneficial, such an order required certain other values, loosely defined as socialist or dirigiste. Public opinion suggested them but did not determine them. And so there had come to pass the political dialectic of contemporary, liberal democracies. The competing values of market liberalism and social democracy and the socio-economic structures underpinning them, must in a perfect world produce a corresponding set of institutions in church, state, education, and culture. It need not be a perfectly isomorphic relationship but there had to be some correspondence between values and institutions, or else there would take place a systemic disjuncture between popular values, socio-economic practice, and lived experience on the one hand and public and private institutional leadership on the other. Otherwise institutions risked becoming obsolete and irrelevant. For Trudeau the predicament of Quebec was worse again. It inhabited the intellectual universe of neither industrial reality nor a social democratic one. What predominated in the mental universe of the Quebec clerisy and its political allies were images of traditional society, insularity, and conformitarianism, and, to boot, an aversion to technology, science, industrial capitalism, the state, socialism, and democracy. French Canadian social thought mainly extolled a simple ruralism, and a conservative, ultramontane type of Catholicism: puritanical, incurious, and authoritarian.

Trudeau observed that three dominant reactions to urban-industrial modernity had occurred in Quebec. The first had been that of institutions that had become "bogged down" in a purely "theoretic" system of thought, in this case a refined and ethereal French-Canadian nationalism. Here Trudeau produced a roll-call of the famous cultural and often church-sponsored institutions of the time: La Société Saint-Jean-Baptiste, La Ligue des droits du français, L'École social populaire, and L'Action nationale. Their embrace of tradition, parochialism, and anti-democracy were for him forms of social escapism and of little relevance to the socio-economic world around them. The second reaction was that of those who had sought to place one foot in the contemporary world while keeping the other firmly rooted in the past. This was the stance of the official Church, the universities, the professions, and the trade unions. Trudeau mentioned Edouard Montpetit and Esdras Minville, two well-known social scientists—and Abbé Groulx too—as instances of this, individuals who after the First World War had sought to come to terms with the new society but who in the end had capitulated to the old nationalism. It was true, Trudeau conceded, that some elements in the Church had recognized the altered social circumstances of workers living under industrial conditions, and recent papal encyclicals had to some extent attempted to rethink the social doctrine of the Church. But things were twisted in Quebec:

> The social doctrine of the Church which in other countries opened a broad way to the democratization of peoples, the emancipation of workers and social progress in general was invoked in French Canada in support of authoritarianism and xenophobia.[66]

It was not that the Church had grudgingly and belatedly fallen in with abstract, theoretical nationalism; in most cases it had directly initiated and sponsored it. Conservative nationalism, then, Trudeau believed, lay behind the Church's main prescriptions for renewal: a return to the land, an emphasis on small business, corporatism, co-operativism, and confessional Catholic trade unions. But business was now large in scale; the clash of interests among economic cartels could only be resolved by a democratic state; co-operativism only worked well in the countryside and among fishermen but not in the cities; and confessional trade unions flew in the face of international industrial unions and the multi-religious and secular nature of the working class.

In the schools and universities, Trudeau maintained, attempts had been made to articulate a more progressive response. Social science departments and social institutes had been established before and after the First World War and the discipline of industrial sociology had been introduced. Universities had founded schools of architecture and engineering and so on. But, all in all, educational reform had been compromised by the overbearing influences of the nationalists and the bishops. Witness their successful resistance to technical schools and to legislation requiring compulsory education:

> As for the teaching of history, one can say that our institutions have done everything they can to prevent often very serious and capable men from raising their discipline to the level of a social science. Our first historian, F.-X. Garneau, undertook the writing of his *Histoire du Canada* in a spirit of nationalist recrimination; and a hundred years later the holders of the chairs of history in our two French-speaking universities could still enthrall the cultivated public by discussing the question of whether our history should promote nationalism or a spirit of bon-ententisme. . . .
>
> It is really not worth it to deal with our French Canadian faculties of law. Harried lawyers go there to teach students how to find their way around the various codes of the province of Quebec.

All notions of a sociology of law have been carefully pushed aside, the great traditions of the philosophy of law are unknown there, the rare courses in public law are appreciated not a whit, and they ignore the names of Jean Bodin and Jeremy Bentham. With such training it is not surprising that we have gotten to the end of the first half of the twentieth century without the Quebec Bar having come to terms with the industrial revolution: for example in 1949 there still does not exist in Quebec a family court; nor a legal clinic, nor a legal-aid system to deal with the difficulties of a disadvantaged proletariat.[67]

In this environment new ideas and speculation went disregarded and unexplored:

There is something positively prodigious in the constancy whereby our official thinkers have circumscribed all of the social science of their time. Judging from their writings it is no exaggeration to say that until just recently they ignored all of general juridical theory from Duguit to Pound; all of sociology from Durkheim to Gurvitch; all of economics from Walras to Keynes; all of political science from Bosanquet to Laski; all of psychology from Piaget to Freud; and all of educational theory from Dewey to Ferrière.[68]

Trudeau's third type of institutional response were those of the Quebec state and, especially, the political parties. His argument here took a very subtle and intriguing turn. Political leaders in Quebec since Laurier, including Duplessis, had without exception practised a basic pragmatism and expediency, he said. Because politics in French Canada had been dominated by the imperative of defending the "nation" and holding the English at bay, its politics had become emotional, passionate, non-rational, and non-ideological. The Québécois rejected "thinking" about politics altogether. It was all about a sort of instinctual defensiveness. But, curiously, this anti-intellectualism also prevailed in politicians' attitudes towards nationalism itself, especially the "theoretic" kind that had predominated in the first half of the twentieth century and which was so much the object of Trudeau's scorn, the type expressed by Groulx, La Société Saint-Jean-Baptiste, and most of the Church. Quebec's politicians saw through the sham of this conventional "idealistic" mindset. But what they could never avoid was its demagogic appeal. And so the politicians' stance became one of "paying lip service" to and "manipulating" nationalist mythology. If such tactics did not work, then they could always resort to machine politics or to dispensing "home-brew."[69] Quebec's politicians, Trudeau seemed to say, were the least impressed by nationalism of any part of the elites. They avoided it if possible and, if not, they deflected it and tried above all to get on with the real business of society and the state. But they could not avoid it altogether and certainly they could not afford to be seen as unsympathetic to it or, worst of all, against it. For Trudeau Quebec's politicians did not "think" at all but that at least was better than thinking too much and in the wrong direction, which was the abiding defect of the intellectual nationalists.

For much of the modern period, said Trudeau, it was the Liberals who had succeeded most completely in riding the wave of French-Canadian nationalism. After 1891 they had been the major force in Quebec's federal politics and provincially too they had held uninterrupted power from 1886 to 1936. But the Depression had challenged Liberal dominance. The federal Conservatives had done well in Quebec in the 1930 election and rumblings of discontent had surfaced among provincial Liberals too. By early 1936 a section of the Liberals, led by Paul Gouin, concerned over the power of big business and the misery of the unemployed, founded the Action libérale nationale and campaigned for social reform and the nationalization of the electricity trusts. They joined forces with a provincial Conservative group led by Maurice Duplessis to form the Union Nationale, which went on to win the 1936 election:

[Duplessis] became leader . . . on the express condition that he nationalize the Montreal Light, Heat and Power. But once in office the tory leader thought better of it and the program of social reform for the most part lapsed into a rhetorical and conservative nationalism. . . . Mr Duplessis, in power since 1944, played the nationalist card so regularly that he prevented the social question even being posed. So much so that in the election of July 28, 1948 French Canadians, believing once again in their obligation to "save the race" from the "federal centralizers," elected 82 conservatives who took themselves for nationalists but who were actually the representatives of high finance and to a lesser degree the professional, bourgeois and agricultural classes.[70]

Even Duplessis, then, was more manipulator and exploiter of nationalism than its authentic voice. Nationalism was a subterfuge for what was basically the big business agenda of his government. But nationalism could not be dismissed.

Yet Trudeau's intriguing conclusion was that it was in fact the provincial state and its politicians who in a backhanded way had been the ones who had responded most satisfactorily to the realities of Quebec's socio-economic circumstances:

The Quebec state adapted better than our theoreticians to the reality of a province that was industrializing rapidly. Of course, the actual adaptation suffered frequently from delays for if the thinking of legislators was inadequate, their own interests as well or those of their financial backers led them to resolve definitively the social and economic problems of industrialization in the most conservative manner possible. . . . But in spite of everything our legal system was less cut off from reality than our idealist rantings might have led us to fear. It is why in spite of our "providential mission" and our pathological hostility towards outsiders' legislative schemes, Quebec lawmakers have ended up more or less plagiarizing what was produced elsewhere more adeptly and more expeditiously. M. Henri Mazeaud was right when he said that social and economic pressures make different rights evolve in the same direction.[71]

And so, surveying Quebec's legislative history, Trudeau found that the pragmatism of Quebec's political elite had been strong enough to give birth to a welfare state, of sorts. Social and labour legislation had been sufficiently progressive to constitute a departure from the received prescriptions and ideals of a clericalist, nationalist culture:

> The Quebec State has evolved to a rhythm and in a direction very different from those envisaged by our theory-loving institutions. It is the case that the State cannot govern without taking account of the real relations of forces that exist in a country. . . . Ideological forces have only had the effect of diverting and slowing down the process.[72]

In a long article written in October 1958, "Un manifeste démocratique," Trudeau presented a slightly different perspective on the Quebec state. He called it a "fallen state," one whose moral core had been hollowed out or which had collapsed. It had no claim to being a civil state, that is, the embodiment of "civisme" and the "common good." The various premiers of the province, he said, had been merely "epiphenomena," doing the bidding of "international capitalism and Quebec clericalism." Politicians had spent all their energy devising ways to stay in power but they did not control the real political agenda. This interpretation was a harder-edged, more radical critique than that of his Asbestos essay. It was more frankly Marxist in its view of politicians as puppets of big business rather than clever manipulators of nationalism in a pragmatic adaptation to socio-economic reality although his earlier view had had a "soft" Marxist materialism to it too. Perhaps it was that two more years of Duplessisme had made him more critical.[73] Theoretically, though, the two positions were not altogether at loggerheads. Both presumed the hegemony of church and capital in the province. Where his analyses diverged was over the extent to which the political class has been independent of bishop and businessman. Both accounts presumed that the political class did not have a free hand.

IV

A useful point of entry into Trudeau's political thinking about Quebec and its relation to the rest of Canada is to see him as being in a constant, restless search for an overarching moral framework, a common good that would be suitable to a people and a province living in a world of growing diversity. Ever the practical moralist, Trudeau's preoccupation was with devising methods to obtain co-operation in the midst of abiding social differences. The terminology of the common good he usually expressed as *"le bien commun"* to which he opposed *"l'intérêt particulier"* or *"le bien particulier."* He also employed phrases like *"la volonté générale"* and *"le contrat social."* When he wrote in English he used terms like "the general welfare" and "the common end," both of which were less Rousseauian sounding. This idea of a common good, however denoted, provided him with a definition of a moral order that somehow encompassed every person and group. The idea spoke to the aspiration of a moral unity amidst ethnic diversity and other politically relevant differences.[74] But what was it? Was it a principle of fairness or of communitarian living; or was it more like a *modus vivendi* in which, to use Bernard Williams's phrase, there was an "equilibrium based on perceptions of mutual advantage?"[75] Whatever it was, in its absence, there had persisted French Canada's endless predicament under the British and Canadian regimes.

This sense of a missing accord Trudeau had first significantly broached in that formative essay on Quebec of December 1952. There, unexpectedly perhaps, he linked it to the question of the operating norms of the British parliamentary system.[76] Parliamentary government worked best, he said, on the basis of two political parties, a government and a government-in-waiting both of which accepted "an identical common good." Later on he talked about the ideal arrangement of parliamentary governance as a duality of a "progressive" party and a "conservative" one.[77] Parliament, he said, was an adversarial system par excellence: the opposition believed that the government was wrong and that it could do better and so it criticized the government "systematically" and "piteously" in the hope that the people would be persuaded to place it in power. But such antagonism did not necessarily produce anarchy because the opposition party was typically involved in parliamentary committees and in the passing of legislation and so, willy-nilly, it became a participant in the way-of-life of the state.[78] If there happened to be more than two parties, Trudeau said, this usually worked to the advantage of the governing party and increased the likelihood of an executive-dominated parliamentary system. When third parties emerged Trudeau hoped that they would quickly replace one of the existing ones and thus re-establish the bipartite arrangement. He went on: when a political party governed under a parliamentary system, it brought forth a set of "means"—he referred to these on another occasion as a "technique of government"[79]—which were normally within the ambit of an overarching common good, this in spite of the fact that the two parties offered policies that were in disagreement with each other.

Clearly his view was that the differences between the two parties took place within a common consensus of values. But this "common good" that the British had exemplified is unclear. Was it the rule of law? Was it the ideals of liberty having to do with habeas corpus and other principles of liberal justice such as innocence before guilt, freedom of speech, and so on? Was it what Trudeau referred to in 1947 as the "agreement-to-disagree" principle so that the criticism of a government was not tantamount to treason? Or perhaps the common consensus could be seen in Britain's vaunted affinity for what he called "moderation and respectable realism"? Or maybe it was the principle of representative government itself? Might it have been what Laski once referred to as the implicit consensus between both political parties over the maintenance of the existing system of property even as the progressive party sought reforms within it?[80] The consensus in that case would have been an agreement to reject revolutionary economic measures. Probably, for Trudeau, it was all of these things.

But Trudeau might have explained things further. The emergence of a consensual, judicious British system he did not locate in a particular epoch. Is it the post-1689 constitutional order of habeas corpus and constitutional monarchy? Is it the late eighteenth-century parliamentary order of Fox, the younger Pitt, and Burke; or the more middle-class representative system of the 1832 Reform Act? Of course, it was not until almost one hundred years after the Reform Act that the British parliament was established on the basis of universal adult suffrage. If Trudeau was pressing a radical agenda—and he was—it seems odd that he would deduce notions of "normal" parliamentary performance from an aristocratic or a middle-class dominated era. However, Trudeau was likely pressing a left-wing but still Whiggish view of the supposed progressive tendencies of the British constitutional order, a "mother-of-parliaments" account of the cumulative accretions of democratic government and liberty from epoch to epoch, all leading upwards and onwards towards liberal rights, universal adult suffrage, and eventually the election of a socialist government. This was one of the ways he thought about the matter in 1958:

> In England . . . the Labour Party arrived in power, for five years, after almost a half-century of efforts; but this party itself was indebted before that to almost twenty years of Fabianism which itself was based on almost a hundred years of philosophical radicalism. This radicalism was in turn the fruit of six centuries of evolution towards democracy.[81]

For Trudeau the obvious difficulty in applying the British model was that in Canada deep linguistic and ethnic cleavages prevailed. French Canadians were a substantial minority. Even when they had been a numerical majority, they had been under-represented in legislatures and colonial executives and in effect had been treated as a minority, while, later, with the balance of immigration favouring the British, the French had become a clear numerical minority albeit an irreducible one as well. What Canada needed was a common good, an "entente" between the English and the French by means of which each would agree to treat the other as an equal. To elaborate the issue Trudeau took up the one instance in modern British parliamentary history of a struggle over ethnic diversity, the Irish question. Endlessly deprived of a chance to constitute in themselves a majority government, French Canadians had developed two strategies, said Trudeau. One was to imitate the example of the "Irish at Westminster"—the reference was, no doubt, to Charles Stewart Parnell's Irish Parliamentary Party in the late nineteenth century—and "sabotage" parliament and agitate for "Laurentian home rule." And the other one was to play the parliamentary game but without ever quite believing in the principles that lay behind it:

> It was with mental reservations that [French Canadians] adhered to the social contract: they did not believe that a "general will" could be born without an ethnic entente. And not being able to aspire to have a place as equals in a Canadian common good, they secretly focused everything on the pursuit of their particular good. That is to say they formed a community within a community. To preserve the first they connived to break the rules of the second. Trickery and compromise dictated their choice of parties or alliances: from the time of the Union government the people seemed uninterested in any ideology save nationalism. . . .
>
> Alas, in practising cheating one becomes a cheat. A subtle casuistry justified us in breaking the rules of the political game and so it is that eventually everything slid outside the bounds of morality. We have so successfully subverted the Canadian common good to our French Canadian particular good that we lost the moral sense of our obligation to the former. And, apart from moments of crisis (Riel, separate schools in the West, conscription) when we instinctively rallied to ensure our particular good in our survival at the heart of the wider community, each of us came to believe in the rightness of the pursuit of our own particular good even to the detriment of that larger community.

That is to say that our civic sense was perverted and we became opportunists.[82]

Another family of ideas informed Trudeau's account of the common good and this grew out of his reflections on democracy and the working class. In the late 1940s and early 1950s talk of democracy was impossible for him without mention of the rise of the working class, or "the proletariat," as he sometimes called it. His view of capitalism emphasized the hierarchical structure of its economic power and the degree to which it produced social inequality. Hence the importance of a positive or distributive state as a means to greater economic fairness. Much of Trudeau's language on this subject was Marxist-like. It seemed to him that there was, in spite of setbacks, an upward arc of workers coming to a consciousness of their own "interests." The working-class embodied the large and surging "sociological" forces of industrialization and urbanization. But in a number of crucial ways Trudeau parted company from Marx. He did not believe that the proletariat constituted a universal class, the attainment of whose interests would be the fulfillment of humanity's. Trudeau accorded an important place to class and to class conflict in his imaginary but he did not see class as necessarily the primary factor to the exclusion of other sources of group identification. And history, he believed, was more than an endless story of class warfare with an inevitable, perfect outcome.[83] He doubted that there was some imminent incursion of what he called a "proletarian messianism" or a "revolutionary mystique" that would sweep the workers to power.[84] Industrial workers had a particular interest and it was a significant one but there were other interests in society and governments must take these into account. However insofar as the workers did have an evident interest and given the size of their numbers, they deserved considerable attention from the state. His quarrel with the Duplessis government and with most other governments in Canada was that the workers had been largely overlooked, taken for granted and governed against their will. Part of this state of affairs, Trudeau conceded, derived from the inordinately rural bias of the electoral system in Quebec and in other provinces. But Trudeau was clear that the workers would win a better future if they persevered in intelligent electoral and industrial activity: founding their own parties, educating their fellow workers, establishing enlightened and disciplined trade unions, *and* changing the electoral rules of the game. He sometimes used revolutionary language but it is clear that he always considered himself a committed parliamentary socialist and a devotee of free, collective bargaining.

For Trudeau the rise of working-class politics contributed to the idea of a common good: workers were increasingly moving beyond nationalism. The Asbestos strike, for example, had taught them that the enemy was not the English, the Protestants, or the Jews but the capitalists and the financiers, and these latter were not distinguished by any nationality.[85] Workers had brought a new moral energy to the political order and promised a "cleansing" of the established legal and political stables. With history going their way and with the power of numbers behind them Trudeau sometimes implied that the workers constituted the "people" against the "ruling class" and the "elites" of financiers and capitalists so much so that democracy in itself become for him synonymous with *social* democracy. He was saying that the workers and their interests were *very* important and social democracy was indeed the best type of regime, but not just for workers.

The script of a radio broadcast on Radio-Canada in June 1956 caught much of the moral impetus behind his idea of the common good as an ideal democracy and of the workers as the invigorating spirit of a new social democracy.[86] Trudeau saw democracy as encompassing much more than elections.[87] He argued that traditionally in Quebec and elsewhere political parties and elections had failed to ensure democracy, understood as the effective and enlightened consent to government. Elections had not brought "self-government," as he frequently put it, nor had the Québécois pursued the common good, understood as respect for the rights and the equality of all citizens. Political parties had become mere

aggregators of interests and machines to win power. These electoral organizations, "by ideology, tradition and interest," had
retarded the emancipation of the new industrial proletariat and
the legitimate prospects of the farmers too, all to the advantage of
the "high bourgeoisie." He went on: Quebec had failed to provide
an election law that would give proportionate representation to
rural and urban voters; neither had it provided an equal voice to
poor as well as rich candidates nor an equal hearing to government
and opposition forces. As an antidote to all this Trudeau advocated
a new party/movement that would include concern for the interests of all classes, especially the "popular" classes and that would
not be financed by the privileged and "the great lenders of funds."
Even though he was already in discussions over the birth of a new
political movement, he nonetheless ended his talk with an exhorta-
tion to his listeners to support for now the Parti social démocratique (PSD), the provincial branch of the CCF, as it was called after
its change of name in August 1955.[88] Indeed within a few months
Trudeau shifted his support towards this new party/movement,
the Rassemblement, and later the Union des forces démocratiques.
However if he was changing his sense of what were the best means
of reform, his principles remained intact because social democratic
ideas prevailed in the manifesto of the Rassemblement. With the
Union his emphasis was a little different: without doubt democracy
prevailed as the indispensable minimum of a common good. But
at the same time he believed that there could be several legitimate
kinds of democracy, from liberal democracy to socialist democracy.
Whatever type it was, it must provide what he called "self-government." And certainly it must overcome the kind of corrupt, manipulated, and sectional electoral system that presently prevailed.
Democracy as self government, of whatever kind, was the *sine qua
non* of a Canadian common good and not the "self-determination,"
so-called, that Quebec had opportunistically practised. In Canada
English and French should pursue "self-government" together.

Trudeau returned to this subject in August 1958 in "Some
Obstacles to Democracy in Quebec." There he dwelt on the

identical historical dilemmas he had identified in his 1952 article by reiterating the same stark alternatives of the Irish option: to make Parliament unworkable as a prelude to a possible separation or to use and abuse Parliament while never quite believing in it:

> Parliamentary democracy I take to be a method of governing free men which operates roughly as follows: organized parties that wish to pursue—by different means—a common end, agree to be bound by certain rules according to which the party with the most support governs on condition that leadership will revert to some other party whenever the latter's means become acceptable to the greater part of the electorate. The common end—the general welfare—which is the aim of all societies may be more or less inclusive; and may be defined in different ways by different men. Yet it must in some way include equality of opportunity for everyone in all important fields of endeavour; otherwise "agreement on fundamentals" would never obtain. For instance, democracy cannot be made to work in a country where a large part of the citizens are by status condemned to a perpetual state of domination, economic or otherwise. Essentially, a true democracy must permit the periodic transformation of political minorities into majorities.
>
> In Canada the above conditions have never obtained. As to ends, the French Canadians would never settle for anything less than absolute equality of political rights with the English Canadians, a demand which . . . was never seriously considered by the Colonial Office before the advent of responsible government, nor by the English-speaking majority since then.[89]

This statement offers a modicum of clarification. In Trudeau's mind probably the common norms of parliamentary government are specific to a "democratic" time. As well, it gives a more precise definition of the common good or general welfare for which he yearned. It was about equality of political rights, presumably meaning the right to vote, freedom of speech and association, and language rights. It was about the importance of social inclusiveness and it invoked the social democratic side of his thought in his claim about the importance of equality of opportunity and an end to economic domination—although he was not explicit about how much economic equality there must be and what the overcoming of economic domination would entail. But he did quote approvingly from a 1949 work by Elton Mayo, *The Social Problems of an Industrial Civilization*, about the difficulties representative democracy faced under conditions of extreme inequality and group differences.[90] Rousseau for one had insisted that the common good required a levelling equality and a political community that was small in both territory and population and simple in its use of technology. Whitaker dwells on this in his critique of Trudeau. But there is no sense of these aspects of Rousseau being present in what Trudeau expressed. Perhaps this was because Trudeau was seeking a common good for a large, urban, highly technological industrial society—very different from what Rousseau prescribed.

Four years later Trudeau again returned to the dilemma of those stark options that lay before French Canada. This time he offered a somewhat different account and a slightly altered terminology. In his 1962 essay, "La nouvelle trahison des clercs," the choices were seen as between "the separatists or independentists" on the one hand and, on the other, "the constitutionalists." The first were little different from the earlier "Laurentian home rulers." Noticeable, however, was his description of the second group. In his earlier description of federalist "opportunists," Trudeau afforded them only limited virtue in their single-minded, amoral nationalism, for, in general, their resistance to Anglophone power had brought with it the nasty habits of political cynicism and narrow-mindedness. Within the earlier version even the more politically prepossessing defenders of French Canada's interests—Lafontaine, Cartier, Laurier, and Bourassa—Trudeau saw as monochrome nationalists, hardnosed and sectional to a fault, too particularist in their world view and largely bereft of a sense of a larger Canada. However, by the early 1960s, the very same

French-Canadian leaders had become transformed into heroes and pioneers of what Trudeau called "polyethnic pluralism," "ethnic pluralism," and the "multi-national state."[91] Indeed Trudeau's complaint at this later juncture was not that they had displayed too little regard for Canada and had connived at village-pump nationalist politics but rather that they and their successors had been too hesitant and unimaginative in perfecting the model of a pluralistic, federal Canada. Trudeau now contended that all along it had been the leaders of French Canada who had most believed in Canada. Their only fault had been that they had been too cautious. They had, as it were, wisely loved Canada but not well enough.[92]

With this shift there emerged in Trudeau a new respect for Confederation and the British North America (BNA) Act. What he had described in his immediate postwar writings as a serviceable but inadequate constitutional compromise that should be reformed through a more modern division of powers, he now saw as an achievement of immense foresight and brilliant, civic common-sense. Here the influence of Frank Scott, the McGill constitutional expert, and his views on the BNA Act are evident:

> I am inclined to believe that the authors of the Canadian federation arrived at as wise a compromise and drew up as sensible a constitution as any group of men anywhere could have done. Reading that document today, one is struck by its absence of principles, ideals or other frills; even the regional safeguards and minority guarantees are pragmatically presented, here and there, rather than proclaimed as a thrilling bill of rights. It has been said that the binding force of the United States of America was the idea of liberty, and certainly none of the relevant constitutional documents let us forget it. By comparison, the Canadian nation seems founded on the common sense of empirical politicians who had wanted to establish some law and order over a disjointed half-continent. If reason be the governing virtue of federalism, it would seem that Canada got off to a good start.[93]

Here one notices the pre-eminence Trudeau accorded to values like prudence, compromise, and empirical hard-headedness. The Fathers of Confederation were atheoretical, practical, and pragmatic. But also to be noted is that in his view the federation they had built was a work of "reason."

Yet, Trudeau continued, in spite of the overall success of Confederation events had not always gone well. Two centuries of French–English relations had produced an unhelpful stalemate in which neither group properly embraced the other. This was especially frustrating given that in the nature of their relationship neither could assimilate nor overcome the other. So Trudeau now recommended to both of them a calculative posture in which each would coldly and self-interestedly determine whether they would be better off remaining stubbornly attached to their sectionalisms. He believed that by the early 1960s French Canada had done much to sort out its side of the question. It had moved beyond its past identity as a "monolithic folk society" to become more open and receptive to democracy. The Second World War had had something to do with it; the Québécois now travelled more outside their province; and urban life too had played a part drawing them away from "their traditional family and parochial milieu." The Church was also becoming more interested in modern, democratic thinking.[94] A sign of the times was the defeat of the Union Nationale. Writing in the late summer of 1962 about the federal election of that year, Trudeau even found optimism in, of all things, the electoral successes of Social Credit in Quebec.[95] He joined together the Créditistes' breakthrough with the PC's success in 1958 and Lesage's victory over the Union Nationale in 1960 to hypothesize that there was emerging, at least in Quebec, a turn towards "democracy" and "ideology" and a move away from traditional party loyalties and the old ethnic politics of protecting the nation:

> [In 1958] Quebec had at last learned the first postulate of all democratic action: when the government considers itself irreplaceable, that is exactly the signal that it must be replaced. . . [In 1960]

Quebec . . . learned the second postulate of democratic action: what is at stake in elections is not simply the replacement of one elite by another: it is the substitution of one political ideology (or, more precisely a technique of government) by another. . . . On the 18th June 1962, Quebec completed its democratic apprenticeship. In giving a quarter of its votes and one third of its seats to Social Credit, Quebec—for the first time in its history—proved that the rise of a third party, in opposition to the traditional parties, was possible. An important portion of the electorate went beyond the lesson learned in 1958 (rejecting *all* traditional political elites) and beyond that of 1960 (opting for a completely different ideology) demonstrating that it had learned the third postulate of democratic action, namely that at a certain point of deterioration replacing the government and its ideology by those of the opposition is not enough; it is necessary to innovate completely.[96]

Trudeau warned, however, that this breakthrough might not be permanent. Nationalism had not disappeared and might lead to authoritarianism. Yet he also believed that traditional forces were in retreat.[97] French Canada still had some house-cleaning to attend to, but by the early 1960s it was a much more progressive society.

It was English Canada that had the more difficult choices to make. English-Canadians must cease their aggressive nationalism and overall intransigence, or risk sinking the federal ship altogether. However, if they acted prudently, they could successfully bring about an enlightened future of almost cosmic significance:

I insist on one thing certainly: that the nationalism of British Canadians has a lot to do—or rather to undo—before the pluralist state can become a reality in Canada. But I am tempted to add that that is *their* problem. The die is cast in Canada: there *are* two ethnic and linguistic groups; each is too strong, too well entrenched in the past and too well supported by a mother-culture, to be able to crush the other. If they both collaborate at the heart of a truly pluralistic state, Canada can become a special place where there will be perfected a form of federalist government suitable to tomorrow's world. Better than the American melting-pot, Canada can serve as an example to all those new African and Asian states . . . which must learn how to govern their poly-ethnic populations with justice and freedom. . . . Canadian federalism is a formidable experiment. It can become a brilliant tool to build the civilization of tomorrow. . . .

To repeat, the die is cast in Canada: neither of the two linguistic groups can assimilate the other. But one or the other, even one *and* the other can lose it all, destroy itself from within and die of asphyxiation. And so, through a fair reversal of fortune, and as it were a pledge to the vitality of humankind, victory is assured to the nation which renounces nationalism and enjoins all its members to direct their energies to pursuing the broadest and most human ideal.[98]

Trudeau, then, at this point in his thinking, in the early 1960s, referred to the common good more as a practical, judicious "compromise." But, even as this prudential, calculative idiom crept into his language, he could not resist proffering something more morally exalting.[99] His realism was never without idealism. English and French Canada should shrewdly assess their interests to be sure but if they miscalculated each would miss out on one of the most exhilarating adventures of contemporary times: living together in difference. "Canadian federalism is an impressive experiment and can become a thing of genius in fashioning the civilization of tomorrow," he concluded.[100]

In general Trudeau's version of the common good was far removed from communitarian precepts, be they derived from Rousseau or Charles Taylor. He was a pluralist at heart and so Rousseau's emphasis on the general will as the pursuit of a unitary or identical end—what Taylor has called his "unanimist" depiction of democracy—could not be his. Trudeau was more concerned with thinking about differences that could be brought into some kind of partial unity. Even so, for him the common good did presuppose common governance in some things and a shared national policy based on common values. Unlike Taylor, Trudeau did not quite use the language of social embeddedness being constitutive of the individual's identity. He did however employ an Aristotelian language, about society being the completion of the individual person and of society being crucial to human flourishing. This suggests an account that took him beyond the Hobbesian perspective of society as being little more than an arrangement of mutual self-interest. For Trudeau the individual had obligations as well as rights.

But what he clarified with one hand he muddied with the other. For there were also his formulations in the early 1960s about Confederation necessitating the prudential and empirical calculations of two trapped scorpions who had better learn to get along or they would destroy their common habitat. This suggests that the social contract that Trudeau envisaged for Canada might have been more like a *modus vivendi*, to use Bernard Williams's language, and a matter of mutual convenience. When Trudeau resorted to such language Hobbes comes swimming back into the picture. Yet in many ways Trudeau's political thought owed a great deal to Laski and Mounier, both socialists. It was also indebted to Maritain, a Thomist/Aristotelian social democrat, with his emphasis on justice as the common good and of society as ideally constituted by mutual friendship and the fulfilment of the individual person. It is important not to push Trudeau so far away from the Rousseauian and communitarian pole that, by implication, he falls into the clutches of atomistic individualists. Trudeau was somewhere in the middle. He was his own man and he provided a version of community that was some distance beyond atomism while falling short of a Taylor-like, "thick" communitarianism. For Trudeau "society" was important but it was of qualified importance. There were limits to the applicability of community in a society of great diversity and even more so in one composed of persons and citizens with consciences. But his view was that some measure of community must undergird Canada and, as Maritain and Laski emphasized, the common good was not vitiated by the existence of diversity.

Recall his critique of French Canadian nationalism, that it had been sectional, narrow, self-serving, and ultimately immoral. In positing the virtue of anti-nationalism, Trudeau was recommending a social contract that would be broad-minded, generous, and respectful of the Other, one open to co-operation and collaboration. Above all it presupposed that all relevant groups would regard the whole of Canada as their moral home, not in every matter but certainly in the important matters that they shared. Sectional thinking and selfish posturing were anathema as were cynical political manipulation and what Trudeau later called "blackmail." Reciprocity and sympathy of some kind towards the Other must prevail, as must consensus of some kind, and maybe what Maritain drawing on his Aristotelian roots called friendship or *philia*.[101] Part of this would be an understanding of equal rights between the French and English in matters of language and culture, "absolute equality" as he put it in 1965.[102] It was also about some kind of equal recognition and mutual respect between the two groups, as well as a "vital minimum" of economic well-being.[103] But his claim was that a legitimate political order presupposed a profound measure of democracy. Trudeau called it "self-government" although he did not mean by it direct citizen participation in the making of law. But Trudeau's proposal was on the face of it a radical, improved version of *representative* democracy, one that required that the relationship of the governors to the governed be one in which all legitimate interests would be taken into account so that the governed would have an ongoing power to determine the general direction of government policy. Parliamentary democracy could produce a sort of general will, was his overall claim.

V

Regarding some of Claude Couture's criticisms of Trudeau's views, it is evident that Trudeau did espouse a theory of modernization. His belief was that industrial capitalism had superseded aristocratic, feudal societies and that the logical response to this was to build a system of socialism of some kind. These stages of development he believed were more or less universal, at least within the West. About the criticism that he believed that Quebec was composed of some kind of unified, homogeneous cultural essence, Trudeau never held that Quebec was lacking in alternative economic and political practices and ideologies. Trudeau mentioned Étienne Parent's liberalism and that of the Rouges in the nineteenth century, and the co-operativism of Father Lévesque and trade unionism and socialism in his own time.[104] What he concluded, however, was not that these were alien or un-Québécois but that they had not hitherto been of any major political significance. They existed within a hierarchy of power and were marginal and subordinate to the Church, the nationalists, and the often supine political elite. He also included in this ruling class the English commercial interests whose privileges were tolerated and in some cases embraced by the French Canadian troika of bishop, nationalist, and politician. If Trudeau seemed to see Quebec as unitary, homogeneous, conformitarian, monolithic, and anti-democratic, it was not because this was its "essential" character; rather, it was because this was what its historic system of power had determined. Trudeau, unwittingly perhaps, expressed an analysis later made popular by Antonio Gramsci, the Italian Marxist theoretician, who in his theory of hegemony established the idea of how culture reinforced the effective power of particular groups.

It should also be noted that Trudeau was remarkably adept at his own version of the sort of post-colonial analysis favoured by Couture. He was hardly a simpering apologist for the English masters and their treatment of their French subalterns. French Canadians, Trudeau asserted, had been stigmatized and stereotyped as an alien Other, and the discriminations against them he abhorred. But he refused to overlook how French Canadians' experience of colonialism had produced a kind of moral fecklessness at the heart of their culture. Consequently French Canada and Quebec had denied to themselves the liberatory possibilities of liberal democracy and socialism. Trudeau knew about André Laurendeau's theory of the "negro king" and by the early 1960s he had read Frantz Fanon, one of the important contemporary theorists of Négritude and post-colonial liberation.[105] The subject matter of colonized peoples, corrupted by their own leaders in the name of "self-determination," became one of Trudeau's abiding themes. How to overcome empire's lingering depredations was something that reverberated throughout his thought in the 1950s and early 1960s.

There is a final puzzle about Trudeau's thinking on Quebec that might be solved. At times he argued that the problem of the province's politics, indeed of Canada's too, was that its politicians were not "ideological," and that they did not sufficiently reflect on the purposes of their vocation. The idea can be traced as far back as that original lecture in Paris in 1947 when he claimed that the basic deficiency of Canadian politics was that political parties were not distinguished by a clear grounding in philosophical principle and everything about their policy was "fuzzy." Ultimately what Trudeau wanted was a politics of coherent principle. But it must be one based on "realities" too. The possible contradiction arose because of the complimentary things he said about the politicians of pragmatism—Lafontaine, Cartier, Laurier, and Bourassa, Duplessis too in his controversial way—who had found a way of side-stepping utopian nationalism and had come to terms with the non-nationalist realities of their society. Trudeau made the same sort of claim about ordinary citizens in Quebec, who had learned to make the most of their circumstances by overcoming the dissonance between their received beliefs—often of a religious or nationalistic kind—and their actual social world:

> So how have we survived our torments? In fact, by thumbing our noses at all ideologies. Paradoxically, our ethnic group entrusted with a providential mission and the honor of doctrine, owes its survival largely to its "materialism."[106]

Trudeau had put it even more succinctly two years earlier in his brief to the Tremblay Commission: "Living comes first; philosophy comes later."[107] Trudeau, it seems, was applauding politicians and citizens who were literally "thoughtless," unideological, or even anti-ideological. On the face of it, this seems to be a contradiction, prescribing ideology yet praising politicians who rejected it. Maybe there is a resolution. Instead of an either/or view of the matter, perhaps what Trudeau was expressing was a descending scale or a double-track of preferences. What he was saying was that if he could not have the ideal—principle or ideology founded on realities—an unintellectual pragmatism based on socio-economic circumstances was the second-best type of governance and citizenship. Indeed he may be said to have advocated two realisms, one the "intelligent realism" of his ideal and the "unthinking realism" of his second-order concerns. One admits the usefulness of theory and the other pursues an atheoretical, pragmatic contextualism. What Trudeau wished to avoid at all costs was a third possibility: namely an idealism that was altogether dismissive of social realities. This he felt was the posture of much of traditional intellectual nationalism in the province and the object particularly of his scorn in *The Asbestos Strike*. (Later it became part of his critique of the socialism of the CCF and the NDP.) Always Trudeau was critical of an idealism that was utopian. Indeed he may be said to have been consciously and conspicuously anti-utopian. It is not that Trudeau himself was beyond all utopianism and idealism for we will argue later that, understood a certain way, there *were* such elements in his world view and political practice. For the "intelligent" guidance of his pragmatism had to come from some kind of moral source and sometimes he was inconsistent. But idealism and utopianism by themselves were not what distinguished his outlook. On balance he was a pragmatist *and* an idealist so that greater care should be taken by his critics when they refer to him as a Jesuitical thinker, a Cartesian, a believer in reason before passion, or some other type of rationalism. A precise reading of Trudeau's "rationalism"—if that is the chosen depiction of his intellectual method—will see him as being exceedingly careful and thoughtful about the limits of theory in politics. John Turner—later Trudeau's political colleague—talked of Trudeau as someone who was not an "empiric guy." Turner was not the only one to misread Trudeau. In fact there was a good deal of materialism, pragmatism, and realism in Trudeau's thinking. This made him a fairly "empiric guy," actually. Understanding Trudeau in this way, the disposition of his political thought reveals him as being less of a political philosopher and more of a political activist. His thought was guided by what existed and was fashioned primarily as a prelude to policy, the basis of action. To use Maritain's phrase, Trudeau espoused a "practical philosophy."

Church and State

———— • ◆ • ————

The civil power bears the impress of majesty: this is not because it represents God. It is because it represents the people, the whole multitude and its common will to live together. And by the same token, since it represents the people, the civil power holds its authority, through the people, from the First Cause of Nature and of human society.
Jacques Maritain

I

Trudeau insisted that his Christian and Catholic beliefs were integral parts of his life and so it is an instructive task to excavate the evidence for his religious convictions. However this is not an easy proposition because he was very guarded about speaking of them. What we do know is that Trudeau grew up in a household of conventional Catholic piety. His mother was an especially observant member of the Church and he was very close to her, especially after the early death of his father. Family influences were reinforced by his Jesuit teachers at Brébeuf. As in political matters, Trudeau's religious perspective changed after 1944 as he moved into the wider world. Mounier, Maritain, Berdyaev, Kierkegaard, John Henry Newman, and Teilhard de Chardin provided compelling examples of an alternative Catholicism and Christianity and there were other unorthodox Catholic theologians who impressed him, such as Yves Marie-Joseph Congar and Marie-Dominique Chenu. Michael Higgins, a historian of Canadian Catholicism, recounts a story by Father Michel Gourges, Rector of the Dominican College in Ottawa, who told of how, when he was prime minister, Trudeau invited Congar to 24 Sussex Drive and how the latter was struck by Trudeau's familiarity with his work, especially his book, *Jalons pour une théologie du laïcité* (*Lay People in the Church*). Higgins also states that Trudeau would visit with Chenu when he was in Paris.[1]

In the postwar period, under the pressures of an increasingly secular age, many Catholics severed their connection to the Church, some becoming unbelievers and radical humanists. Not so Trudeau. He sustained a faith in Christianity and Catholicism even as his overall intellectual disposition became more progressive. He regularly attended mass and religious retreats; at the LSE he was involved with the Union of Catholic Students collecting books for Catholic universities in Germany; on his global trek in 1948–9 he often stayed with priests and missionaries and in Burma he gave a lecture to Catholic girls in a convent; he constantly expressed concerns about the state of Catholic missions in places like India and China and the competence of missionaries in the field. Until as late as 1950 he sought the permission of his bishop to read works on the Index of Forbidden Books. His love affairs with Thérèse Gouin in the mid-1940s and with Helen Segerstråle in the early 1950s—both of whom he came close to marrying—were predicated on the idea of a Catholic union, which was the nature of his eventual marriage to Margaret Sinclair in 1971. Yet Trudeau's Catholicism was of a very dissident kind.

Inevitably his new religious views became entangled in the often rancorous debates in Quebec in the 1950s. But, strangely in one so drawn to public controversy, Trudeau insisted that his religious views were his private matters. Evidence from friends and lovers is telling. One of his closest friends, Jacques Hébert, said that Trudeau did not talk with him about religion, while Allan MacEachen, a Catholic from Cape Breton and Trudeau's cabinet colleague and desk-mate in the House of Commons for several years, recalls that Trudeau "never discussed questions of faith and resurrection and so on."[2] Trudeau was notably more open and forthcoming with his female friends yet his long-time girlfriend from the 1960s, Madeleine Gobeil, claims that he "rarely" broached the subject of religion with her.[3] However, Trudeau

was not beyond talking about theological subjects when they did
come up, as John Godfrey affirmed when he recalled discussing
personalism with him in the middle of the Canadian wilderness
on a canoe trip in 1979.[4] Margot Kidder, the actor, who was one
of Trudeau's girlfriends, did on one occasion extract some kind of
confession of faith from him:

> Once I asked him why a man of his intelligence would continue
> to believe in the Catholic Church. "I use it as a place of medita-
> tion," he said. "And I *do* believe in most of it. I don't believe that I
> have to go through some priest in order to talk to God. I'm more
> than capable of talking to [God] directly all by myself." And that
> was that. End of discussion.[5]

Here was one revealing moment—a non-conformist and
"Protestant" one at that—but it was brought to an abrupt conclusion, consistent again with Trudeau's conviction that his personal
faith was no-one's business but his own.

There was another moment. In an interview in 1971, Trudeau
talked of religious belief as "essentially a communication between
a man and his God. . . [and] the most personal thing of all." He
went on to talk of how he had been influenced in his formative
years by the Christian existentialists—Mounier, Kierkegaard, and
Berdyaev—and how they had induced in him an aversion to metaphysical questions. A person's religious sensibility, he said, was best
discovered through his rootedness in the world:

> I rarely discussed, probably because of language difficulties, meta-
> physics with the various religious people of other groups I'd meet
> with [on my travels]. But I'd very much try to see how they were
> incarnated, how their particular soul was incarnated or took roots
> into reality. I was inclined to judge the validity of a man's faith
> more by the depth of his roots in reality and brotherhood and
> love. So I felt more at home, shall we say, with some Zoroastrians
> in the Far East, than I did with some Catholic missionaries.[6]

Trudeau's phenomenological and personalist language is to be noted and also the idea of incarnation.

An anticipation of his postwar attitude towards the Catholic Church was his essay, "La promesse du Québec" in April 1947. There he expressed what would become that settled motif of his thinking, of how French Canadians had turned to the Church after the Conquest only for it to impose a reactionary and xenophobic conformity on them, so that "the forces of emancipation," as he put it, must to be pursued largely outside the Church.[7] However, the essay was never published, so it was that the first religiously centred, public controversy in which the newly progressive Trudeau was involved had to do not with politics but with art and culture. In March 1945 in Paris, *Les enfants du paradis*, a film by the French director, Marcel Carné, had received its first showing. Made under the dangerous circumstances of the Nazi occupation, it was set amidst the picaresque theatrical and criminal underworld of the Boulevard du Temple in Paris in the early nineteenth century. The film told the story of the several loves and betrayals of a free-spirited courtesan, Garance, played by the famous actor Arletty. It included an especially captivating performance by Jean-Louis Barrault, the famous mime artist, as Baptiste, one of her lovers. Innovative and controversial, plebeian in its subject matter, realistic in its representation of society, sexually frank for its time, and profoundly artistic, it has been recognized as a film for the ages. But in Quebec after the War, the censor's office prevented it being shown at the University of Montreal.

Trudeau and his friend, Roger Rolland, had seen the film in Paris and were enthusiastic about it. They were appalled by the turn of events back home. On May 1, 1947, the Montreal morning paper *Le Canada* published a letter from them in which they criticized the censor for denying young men and women an opportunity to witness brilliant art and an extraordinary spectacle of life in all its fullness, its ugliness, and its beauty.[8] The film, they conceded, was not suitable for young girls but then the same could be said of the poems of Baudelaire and Rimbaud; it did not glorify vice and it was an impressive instance of mime and dramatic dialogue but especially of the many sides of actual life. What fundamentally irritated the film's critics, they contended, was its depiction of sexuality. Chastity, Trudeau and Rolland admitted, was important and the sanctification of the flesh to the glory of God was central to the Christian message. But chastity was not all that Christianity stood for. Especially in Quebec "sexual self-control" had come to subvert everything else and love of God and one's neighbour had become of secondary concern. They reminded readers of St. Paul's admonition that without love a Christian is nothing. The two young men talked knowingly and confidently about such things.

Their letter drew criticism from a local Jesuit priest, Father Jacques Tremblay, and other readers too weighed in against what seemed its disturbing heterodoxy. And so Trudeau and Rolland offered a further clarification. But this time the editor, Guy Jasmin, judged the contents to be completely beyond the pale:

> I am sure that if you were to re-read it, you would realize that your comments on the state of opinion in Quebec are most inopportune. Permit me to add that I doubt very much that any French language newspaper in Canada would allow it to be published in extenso.[9]

The unpublished letter said much about what they termed their "religious mentality." Trudeau and Rolland reiterated that art was part of the broad stream of life in which young people should be immersed, but that in Quebec educators believed otherwise because the art in question was tainted by the "carnal":

> In effect religious education in Quebec is based on a unique dogma: that sexuality leads to eternal flames; and as a corollary, it is necessary to obey the clergy at all times. As a consequence it concentrates on recruiting for Christ only old maids, flabby parishioners, feeble church wardens and psychopathic priests. However, we believe that Christianity is a religion of virile men

and healthy women; and we refuse to be castrated. From a religion based on sublime acts of boldness and generosity, we have
gone to a lot of trouble shaping people who are preferably rigid,
constipated morons.[10]

Such dismissive criticism of the piety of the average Catholic recalls
Mounier's rebuke of the French petit-bourgeois church.

They continued: in Quebec Christianity had become a comfortable religion, indeed "an opium of the people." In its stead Trudeau
and Rolland offered a Christianity that was a bold, liberating risk
that bought temptations and dilemmas because it engaged life in all
its fullness, "art, science, thought and love." Did those responsible
for educating the young in Quebec not understand that the gospel
of Christ was an unsettling, immoderate one; that Christ had come
not to bring peace but the sword? Christianity was a disturbing
and provocative venture in an uncertain world. They ended with
a gnomic touch quoting from the Book of Ecclesiastes: "for no-one
knows if they are worthy of love or hate."[11]

Thus Christianity was a religion of risk and danger. Immersed in
the real world the Christian was confronted with difficult choices;
virtue as virility or manliness presupposed courage and determination and a kind of aggression, the opposite of the supposed feminine virtues of humility and passivity. Virility meant as well that
male sexuality was natural and God-given, and in a relationship,
no doubt with a "healthy" woman, a "unitive" view of "affective"
and loving sexuality would exist.[12] In Trudeau's and Rolland's hands
the idea seems to have been an indictment of chastity and celibacy.
Yet Trudeau himself at this time was unmarried, and likely had not
slept with a woman, so he had not altogether complete experience
of his subject. And from the evidence of his sessions with the psychoanalyst Georges Parcheminey in the winter of 1947—the very
time of his writing the letter—it was something about which he was
anxious and unsure.

Trudeau had been introduced to Sigmund Freud's ideas in 1944 by
Thérèse Gouin. She was as intellectually precocious as him—maybe

more so—and perhaps it was on her recommendation that he bought
Freud's *A General Introduction to Psychoanalysis* (1920) while he was
at Harvard. With her encouragement he sought out a psychoanalyst
when he arrived in Paris. Parcheminey invited him to write down his
dreams, so the record of these and his analyst's conclusions are of
course an exceedingly revealing document.[13] Friends and family figured frequently in his dreams, his mother rather than his father, and
his friend, Rolland, appeared constantly too; water and swimming
were central motifs—apparently significant to Freudians—and the
Church appeared only to a small extent. As well, and, quite predictably for a twenty-seven-year-old, unmarried man, Trudeau's dreams
contained many references to young women as attractive, beguiling
creatures, present and pressing but in the end unobtainable. As a
good Catholic and a dutiful son, the unmarried Trudeau had kept
his sexual instincts in check, though maybe not his inner fantasies.
Sometimes faith and passion came together in a sort of serendipitous
if still slightly frustrating moment as when he wrote in May 1947 to
Thérèse Gouin back in Montreal:

> If you would be my mistress, we would share the room [of my
> hotel] together beneath the garret, between the dusty walls.
> The bed is low and rough, but your arms would be soft and your
> mouth welcoming. . . . Every morning we would find a lost corner
> of Notre Dame [Cathedral] and ask for pardon.[14]

And in one of his dreams Trudeau recorded something even more
explicitly erotic: "In kissing T[hérèse] she feels the erection through
her dress. [She] says that marriage is possible."[15] Parcheminey's overall conclusion, as Trudeau recorded it, was that, while he did not
exhibit neuroses, he did have an inferiority complex, evidenced by
his tendency to "aggressiveness in real life, toughness etc [and] wak-
ing fantasies (which are often expressed in my case by a desire to
be elsewhere)."[16] That is, he had a constant need to prove his "virility," as Parcheminey put it. Trudeau, it seems, was sublimating his
sexual drive in unproductive ways. His analyst concluded that his

complexes would likely be overcome by the "normal achievement of virility; i.e. through marriage."[17]

Trudeau's and Rolland's commentary on *Les enfants du paradis* was almost like a gloss on Mounier's argument in *L'affrontement chrétien* although the valorizing of a vital Christianity over a formal, cosmetic one was present in Maritain too. Trudeau and Rolland castigated a flaccid and conformist Catholic piety in the name of a "virile" Christianity. They also used terminology similar to that of Mounier and Nietzsche in their description of conventional Christianity as a "castration." Trudeau and Rolland did not quite refer to Catholicism as the false religiosity of the "petit bourgeois," as Mounier had, but like him they were unmistakably dismissive of the current configurations of Catholic devotions. Later, in 1952, Trudeau did refer to Catholicism as a "bourgeois" Christianity.[18] Mounier-like too were their emphases on Christianity as a hazardous adventure in an uncertain and dangerous world and on Christian discipleship as presupposing some kind of "aggressive" posture. Their views also implied some notion of sexuality as an embodied gift of God, again like Mounier, and a rejection of the Manichaean bifurcation of flesh and spirit. A year later, in a piece published in *Notre Temps*, Trudeau returned to the theme of the complacency of traditional Catholicism:

> It is no longer a faith, but an insurance policy to get into paradise, paid for through a number of ostentatiously good works. Charity has fallen from our hearts and orthodoxy has filled our brains with pride. Our pharisaic religion is a doctrine of immobility: ah, it is a veritable opium of the people.[19]

Trudeau submitted this piece from London where he was listening to lectures at the LSE by Dorothy Pickles on post-revolutionary French thinkers including liberal Catholic ones such as Hughes Felicité Robert de Lammenais.[20]

Trudeau's religious sensibility in the late 1940s crystallized around an uncomplicated rendering of the Gospel, at the centre of which was a very human and existential Christ who preached straightforward truths about love, brotherhood, and freedom. Christ was the evangelist of a kind of social liberation. In his travels through Eastern Europe in 1948 Trudeau became aware of corruption in the Church and he witnessed how low in the esteem of the laity it was held. He wondered if the Church in Hungary had become too privileged and bourgeois and bereft of a social mission. He was troubled by the large number of priests he met who were prepared to risk a new world war in order to defeat communism. And a recurring refrain from his travels in the East was how stinting Catholic priests could be in their practice of charity. Trudeau stated that he had personally experienced instances of this, when dishevelled and dirty from his back-packing he was frequently thought to be "a vagrant in search of food" and not altogether welcomed by them.[21] Trudeau complained about the politically regressive views of the Church in the mission field. Writing about the Chinese Communists' accusation that foreign missionaries had been "spies in the pay of the capitalists" and "Chiang's [Kai-shek's] men," Trudeau agreed with such judgments:

> Would the Chinese Church have been transformed so quickly into a national church, separated from Rome, if the missionaries had counted less on the protection of foreign governments whose very presence in China, in itself the opposite of a Christian presence, constituted an offence against *all* Chinese; and if the missionaries had been more able to live in poverty, that is to say closer to the hungry people to whom they were teaching the Gospel of poverty? Finally, if the hierarchy had become Chinese sooner?[22]

A liberatory Christianity was a powerful motif in Trudeau's postwar world view so much so that it became one of the poles in his account of the universal dialectic of the time: the great contest between Christianity and communism. Trudeau conceived in imperial terms the universal truth and validity of the Christian message and its eventual political triumph. However, his Christianity was a very open and inclusive one, neither sectarian nor proselytizing. In his conception (as he once put it) two Jews who were Marxists, Léon Blum and Harold Laski, and likely either agnostics or atheists, could be seen as "righteous men who fought to uphold the Christian sense of human dignity."[23] Within this perspective—and at its heart was the theology of personalism—Christianity was the idea that all persons could live its message existentially and through a lived reality and not necessarily through belief in specifically Christian propositions. Nonetheless, if only because of its assumption about Christianity as the origin of the fundamental insights about the person and the mysteries of the Incarnation and of humans created in the image of God, personalism asserted that Christianity laid special claim to being a definitive expression of religion. Within this perspective the West too was somehow superior, since it was the civilization that had nurtured Christianity.

Trudeau's interest in a practical, political Christianity had been aroused at Harvard and had led to his choice of a doctoral subject about the inter-relations of Christianity and communism. Trudeau was not hostile towards Marxism and he believed that much could be learned from it. But he remained a strong religious believer and he had confidence not just in the rightness but in the actual ability of the Christian gospel to overcome Marxism's increasing appeal.[24] Reflecting on communism's particular indictment of religion as the opium of the people—Trudeau sometimes used the very same terminology as we have seen—he concluded that a classless society might paradoxically advance the cause of Christianity: "For myself, I want a classless society because I believe that untied from material concerns, mankind will even more pursue God."[25] Trudeau was persuaded of the likely triumph of Christian, Western values even in the inhospitable terrain of Asia. Marxism was weighed down by its doctrine of class warfare and its practice of harsh proletarian rule:

> The proletariat would be the worst of all dictators. . . . The contempt a poor person has for someone even poorer [than himself]

is more dreadful than his hatred (and often his meanness) towards the rich.[26]

In contrast Christianity promised the liberation of the slave and the downtrodden in the name of a universal brotherhood: "Christ alone offers us the means to bring all men together as perfect friends. The revolution of the future should be one of brother-hood, or it should not be at all."[27] In his notebooks about China in 1949 Trudeau expressed well this idea of Christianity as a liberating religion. His dependence on the presuppositions of personalism is again to be noted:

> The great revolution of Christ would have been worthless for refining civilizations without its social corollary of altruism. The complete difference between East and West is that in the West respect is given to the other as having his own dignity. Of course [human] nature is the same without doubt and there, as here, people want to burp when they want to, stare at foreigners, ask them the most personal questions but in the West we have come to respect more and more the intimacy of the person. Ever since Christ came to preach the gospel of love for one's neighbour, the doctrine has confronted several failures in its application but little by little, one by one, new areas have been opened up to the "inviolable person": abolition of slavery [and] of servitude, reli-gious tolerance, political liberty, [and] equality before the law.[28]

In an essay two years later he demonstrated again his disaffec-tion from established Catholic institutions and practices, though not from the core message, as he saw it, of Christianity. It was a satirical piece that was so far-reaching that it came close to collaps-ing into farce and anti-climax. "À Propos de Missions," was written in January 1952 while Trudeau was in Egypt and Sudan steaming slowly up the Nile.[29] Likely he considered it for publication by a Montreal newspaper—he had had other pieces published in *Le Devoir* by this time—but it was never printed. Trudeau structured the essay as a sort of dream—or maybe a nightmare—from which he was periodically awakened. Its main themes were the unconscionable inequalities of wealth within the global Church and the expensive, atrocious, rococo aesthetic sense of the Quebec clergy and parishioners.[30] The solution, for Trudeau, was for Canada to expel the Jesuits, sell all their earthly goods and invest the proceeds in missions abroad. This would have the certain effect of improving education in countries that were not as Christian as Quebec. With his tongue firmly in his cheek Trudeau observed that this would be a "simple case of marginal productivity according to economists." Other religious orders might follow suit including the Franciscans and even the Dominicans and as a consequence religious communities might be induced to take seriously their vow of poverty. He was not concerned that this would deprive Quebec of its many school-teachers in holy orders. There were many lay people waiting in the wings who had hitherto been systematically excluded from teaching. Many of them had been held back because the wages offered had been insufficient to support a family, as if, Trudeau slyly observed, celibacy were an invention of the Church to provide cheap labour. Religious houses had anyway been privileged by tax relief from a generous state. They should be made to submit to the same fiscal regime as commercial enterprises. Trudeau rubbed it in even further when he suggested that the loss of cheap labour in Quebec's schools could be made up by a special tax which "our very pious government" might impose: "A law for extirpating paganism abroad." This was presumably to pay the costs of a living wage to lay teachers at home to replace priests overseas. There is a Swiftian absurdity to all this.

Then, he said, his dream was interrupted and reality broke in although not in a manner that contradicted his central concern about inequality in the Church. Reality in this case was the dreadful circumstances of the mission-station to which Trudeau's journey had now brought him. Indeed, he said, it was true that the very poverty of foreign missions compromised the spread of the gospel. In this case the lack of money simply to buy a bicycle meant that many Catholics could not be reached by a priest to dispense the sacraments to them. Trudeau imagined how different things might be, back in Quebec, if instead of parishes vying with each other to worship God through statues and "pretty banners," they competed in matters of poverty so that they would build churches simpler in design and

> less defaced by marbled surfaces and carved wooden high-altars and enormous crystal udders [of chandeliers] which throw such a poor light on art that is so inferior.[31]

Under such circumstances, Trudeau reasoned, the basic message of the importance of charity would be reinforced and Christians would demonstrate their faith more credibly to the peoples of Asia and Africa. But something else brought Trudeau down to earth; this occurred after the Italian priest at the mission showed him the church he had helped build. It was an impressive edifice, especially in comparison to the mud huts nearby. Inside the church the priest proudly showed him a statue of St. Thérèse, complete with make-up, and adorned with red roses and a silver rosary. The priest explained how much his "simple" parishioners preferred it to the "cold and abstract religion of the Protestants." He explained that he had made the statue himself and had it cast in twenty-eight separate pieces. "'As for the Church it was built by our Brothers.' He adds laughing: 'The Italians are born masons.'"

It seems that Trudeau had travelled thousands of kilometres only to have confirmed for him that the frippery of church buildings in Quebec with their expensive, gaudy statuary and ornamentation was actually *de rigeur* in the mission-field too. It was as if Trudeau had rendered himself speechless. His homily on the need for poverty and charity descended into bathos. But he did allow himself the last word, though it was not altogether a convincing one: "At heart, I thought, the Canadian parishioner has still not evolved very much. And I would happily excuse a limited number of his pious frills . . . provided that the parish priest spends his nights casting statues, and vicars spend theirs gilding the Corinthian columns fastened onto the reinforced concrete of the pointed arches." It was an ending that was a whimper. Brutal church décor was alright, Trudeau seemed to say, if the priests produced it themselves. Perhaps he was allowing his idealism to be brought low by reality. Or maybe it was an instance of an imaginative experiment that had taken off successfully, but had not landed equally so. Yet there is no disputing the radicalism of his imagination. In his wholesale rejection—in theory anyway—of the institutional and iconographic evolution of the Church, its archaic décor and demotic rites as well as its serried ranks of priests and monks, he seems to have been living by his dictum of systematically challenging everything that was established. For Trudeau, the Catholic faith—probably more an ecumenical Christian faith—was summed up in the uncomplicated but testing requirements of charity and poverty. In the end, however, he did seem grudgingly to concede that the faith of the common parishioner might after all need to be reinforced by more traditional mythologies and images.

Did this make Trudeau an advocate of what Michael Gauvreau calls "an aggressive, male-centred spiritual elitism that was profoundly contemptuous of popular religious practice in Quebec"?[32] Given Trudeau's interest in "virility," the description of his Catholicism as male-centred has some applicability. As to whether his dislike for certain popular religious practices rendered him elitist is not clear unless disagreements about art and aesthetics are thereby a claim to personal superiority. Still, the obvious impression left by these early essays and letters is of the degree to which he was personally estranged from the Catholic Church in Quebec and its message and traditions.

II

In the summer of 1950, there began a more direct *public* confrontation with the Church. Trudeau had been incensed by the treatment handed out to Archbishop Joseph Charbonneau of Montreal after he had given his support to the Asbestos strikers the year before. For

his troubles, he had been banished by a conservative Church hierarchy to become a hospital chaplain in far-away Victoria in British
Columbia. Trudeau was privately apoplectic over the Church's reactionary behaviour and its duplicity in the affair since it had failed to
explain properly the reason for his banishment, he believed. He tempered his public comments about the incident but not sufficiently
to prevent himself claiming in the June issue of *Cité Libre* that the
Church was guilty of "shameful silence and awkward lies."[33] Other
controversial statements appeared. In the same month in the first
of his two articles on "Functional Politics," Trudeau listed all the
features of Quebec's public life that he thought deserved to be submitted to radical reassessment: the federal system, bilingualism, its
"so-called" elites, and "our religious and cultural infantilism." But he
stated baldly that a "definitive separation of Church and State" was
also something that should be considered.[34] More than that he did
not say but this was sufficient to raise the hackles of the bishops.

Then in a second article, the following February, Trudeau let
slip the phrase that would get him into very hot water. It came at
the end of his discussion of the arguments for and against the centralizing of Quebec's constitutional status. There he offered the
opinion that no matter what level of government was under consideration the modern state required the expansion of its bureaucratic capabilities so that a pressing priority was the accountability
of government to "free citizens" and their participation in the "the
general will." In Quebec, he believed, this meant that there needed
to be greater political education in "popular sovereignty" and
"self-government":

> It is especially urgent to understand this in Quebec, where we
> have been brought up to behave like slaves toward those in
> authority. We must redefine ourselves as that authority, so that
> the masters of discipline and the police resume their position as
> our servants. There is no divine right of first ministers and no
> divine right of bishops either. They only have authority over us if
> we are willing to let them.[35]

There it was: the seeming denial of the natural and divinely derived supremacy of the Church and the assertion that bishops only had authority if their flock somehow consented to give it to them. It was again only a sentence-long comment and, again, largely unelaborated but it subjected Trudeau to what became a steady drip of notoriety and condemnation. He was seen as a dangerous subversive, a near-heretic and close to public enemy number one. Critical comment about him—some public, some private—by important clerical opinion-leaders began as early as 1951; from Father Richard Arès, the editor of the Jesuit review *Relations*, and from Father Marie-Joseph D'Anjou, Trudeau's erstwhile Brébeuf teacher and wartime collaborator in would-be putsches. And in late summer 1951 Trudeau and Gérard Pelletier were summoned to a meeting with the new Archbishop, Paul-Émile Léger, to explain among other things Trudeau's "divine right of bishops" remark. Even so in December 1952 Trudeau chastised the Church and scandalized the hierarchy with his assertion that the Church was complicit in the province's "profound [political] immorality" and in late 1953, equally boldly, that the Catholic Church was no friend of democracy and had been a natural ally of authoritarian regimes.[36]

Usually Trudeau was cavalier and insouciant in the face of criticism and if anything dismissive of it. This changed when there surfaced the devastating attack by Father Léopold Braün over his participation in a conference in Moscow in April 1952. Trudeau had not been in any way secretive about his attendance there and indeed had published several pieces about his trip in *Le Devoir* and in talks on Radio-Canada. Months later, in the November issue of *Nos Cours*, Braün, an Assumptionist priest, attacked him for his views on the Soviet Union and especially what he perceived as his failure to confront the persecution of the Church under Stalin. Braün considered Trudeau to be a naïf, a communist fellow-traveller, and a dangerous subversive. The fact that his essay was published simultaneously in such other publications as *L'Action Catholique* and *Le Droit* suggested that there was a coordinated campaign against Trudeau by Catholic intellectuals. Trudeau himself believed so, as he also believed that the official hierarchy was actively working against him.[37] He was surprised by Braün's criticism and profoundly angry. What particularly got under his skin was his clever insinuation that he had been taken in by propaganda and had "swallowed snakes."[38] He was also furious at what he believed were the prevarications and manipulations thrown up by Catholic editors as they schemed to sabotage his attempts to get his rebuttals into their publications. Trudeau eventually resorted to direct action, visiting the editors in question, and on one occasion confronted Father Jean-Baptiste Desrosiers, editor of *Nos Cours*, in his office. Desrosiers started shouting and Trudeau pushed him into his chair.[39] Trudeau was capable of more than quiet rage.

Trudeau's more considered refutation of Braün and other critics came in May 1953, in "Matériaux pour servir à une enquête sur le cléricalisme."[40] The article was only secondarily an essay on church–state and clergy–laity relations. Primarily it was an attempt to set the record straight about what Trudeau regarded was the injustice meted out to him by Braün and his sympathizers. Trudeau was predictably at his vituperative best. They were "boors," he said, involved in an "odious attack" on him and Braün himself was venomous, dishonest, sophistic, inept, and stupid.[41] But Trudeau's anger did nonetheless have the effect of leading him to some interesting theoretical reflections on the limits of clerical authority.

Trudeau declared that he was anti-clericalist but not anti-clerical. In support of his position he immediately wrapped himself in the mantle of Jacques Maritain, quoting from his *True Humanism*: "The clergy do not have to hold on to the levers of command in matters that are temporal and political."[42] Trudeau recruited other, more traditional authorities—Pope Pius XI, a cardinal, and even his nemesis Father Arès, no less—in support of his general contention that there were limits to the knowledge, moral judgment, and competence of the clergy. Not only were priests without primacy in matters temporal and political but, if they did have a contribution to make in the secular domain, this was not because of their special spiritual and sacramental standing. For the Church was not necessarily competent in technical and non-religious matters. And, anyway, the Church must be respectful of citizens and resist the impulse to impose a theocracy in the manner of a parent or an elder over a minor. Trudeau was irreducibly opposed to those in the Church who claimed for the Church "a right of parental control of the Quebec people in areas beyond their competence."[43]

Trudeau conceded that the clergy were in a difficult position, especially in a society undergoing transition as Quebec was. If priests were content just to administer the sacraments, instruct the consciences of parishioners, and stay uninvolved in temporal affairs, they risked falling into a kind of "other-worldliness." But if they engaged "the real, in order to embody themselves as the fashionable word has it" then they risked transposing on the temporal world an authority that existed only in the spiritual. (It is instructive to see Trudeau using Mounier-like phenomenological language.) Priests should not presume that because they must be interested in all things human they should become involved in every temporal activity. Proponents of clerical primacy, Trudeau said, overlooked the fact that the Church was more than the clergy and that it included the laity. To confirm this view Trudeau quoted Yves Marie Joseph Congar approvingly, and Pope Pius XII too.[44] Trudeau was not opposed to priests participating in the world but they should do so in order better to pursue their sacerdotal calling. Priests' involvement in the temporal should be more like an "overture" to the temporal rather than a subsumption of it. If they did participate they did so not in possession of any special grace or wisdom but on the same basis as any lay person. Priests at work in this way did so as citizens and were in no way superior to other lay persons. If they uttered inanities, then they could be criticized just as forcefully as any other citizen. All of this brought Trudeau to his main point: Father Braün and his collaborators were interfering in political and civic affairs. Not only did they have no special authority in such matters but doing so in a manner that was devious and immoral was additionally offensive. Trudeau instanced other disasters that had flowed from the Church's ill-conceived compromise with secular powers: the crusade against the Albigensians, the Inquisition, the burning of Savonarola, the massacre of St. Bartholomew's Day, the revocation of the Edict of Nantes, and the persecution of Dreyfus. Evidently in his own mind Trudeau's contretemps with Braün was no less an instance of such persecutions. Trudeau also pointed out that when "the guardians of light" in Quebec had rained down denunciations and defamations on secular politics and politicians they usually had done so in support of the Union Nationale and international capitalism.[45]

If Trudeau's argument was more than a little self-serving and devoid of a sense of proportion, it did nonetheless reveal only too clearly his perspective on church–state relations and what were for him the especially dark moments in the history of the Church. (His references to the persecution of the Albigensians and the Huguenots and the dark chapter of the Inquisition were redolent of Lord Acton's criticisms of the Church.) Trudeau ended by calling on the Church, and by implication Father Braün and his friends, to treat their adversaries with charity and justice. Witch hunts, he said, had mercifully been largely absent in Canada but in this case the Catholic press in Quebec, with the imprimatur of Cardinal Léger, had done nothing less than to import an "epigone" of Senator Joseph McCarthy in order to denounce him for his views on the Soviet Union. Trudeau's plea was for tolerance and mutual respect. He believed that if anyone occupied the moral high ground in this controversy it was himself: "who has attacked who, in this affair?"[46] Especially when he felt blindsided, Trudeau reacted with a passionate intensity. If he practised Christian charity at such times it did not involve turning the other cheek. But what Trudeau never really addressed was the possibility that, if priests had no inherent superiority in discussing secular matters and engaged such matters on an equal plane with laypersons, this did not mean that priests were always wrong in what they asserted. Braün had to be dealt with on the merits of his argument. Trudeau could not simply dismiss him because he was a priest talking about politics. In fact he realized this and his responses to Braün did engage his specific claims, as we will see.

Three years later in *La grève de l'amiante* Trudeau was given a perfect opportunity to sum up what he felt was the principal failing of the Church in Quebec: its post-Conquest hegemonic infiltration of every nook and cranny of Quebec's life. What offended him was not just the lack of effective pluralism in French Canada but also the nature of the ideas that the Church had inculcated. In espousing nationalism and anti-industrialism it had been not just completely out of touch with the socio-economic circumstances of the province but, to boot, it was out of step with papal encyclicals and letters as well.[47] For Trudeau invoked a more progressive papal social doctrine going back to Leo XIII and his encyclical, *Rerum Novarum* (1891), which he saw as launching a tradition of greater respect for democracy and workers' rights. And so, in his view, the Quebec Church, and particularly the Jesuits, had been deaf to the Leonine tradition and had twisted it to suit their own purposes. Trudeau instanced how they had used statements of papal misgivings about capitalism to justify opposition to an English-controlled economic system, rather than opposition to capitalism itself; nationalism was the Church's dominant creed and so the hierarchy had concluded that a French-Canadian capitalism would be quite acceptable.[48] Trudeau took special delight in pointing out that it was the Church in Quebec and not himself that was out of step with papal teaching, although this particular view got him into trouble too. In a review of *La grève de l'amiante*, Father Jacques Cousineau more or less accused Trudeau of heresy for having made the unthinkable claim that the bishops in Quebec were in error in their understanding of the Holy Fathers. Trudeau, he said, had made an attack against "the infallibility of the Church and the inspiration of the Holy Spirit."[49]

Trudeau continued his goading of the Church in the essays published in *Vrai* between February and July 1958. In these his general concern was to challenge the legitimacy of the non-consensual state and to argue for a right of resistance to corrupt and tyrannical regimes. He made quite explicit his rationale for tyrannicide. The essays drew a number of adverse comments from readers, mostly clerics and editors of conservative reviews and newspapers.

His argument would certainly be offensive to some if only because he rejected the legitimacy of well nigh every ancient and modern regime, and gave such a high priority to conscience and consent. This was scandalous to those who adhered to the authority of St. Paul and his famous dictum in his Letter to the Romans that the powers that be were ordained of God and necessary for a Christian's well-being. In the sixteenth century such prominent Protestant theologians as Martin Luther and John Calvin had subscribed to the same doctrine and even in Catholic Quebec theologians and conservative nationalists were also partial to it. But, Trudeau wondered, why, if Christians held such a view,

> God conferred [authority] on Hitler and Stalin, and why in our democracies God expressed Himself through such intermediaries as those who stole elections and provided election slush funds.[50]

Nor did "natural law" offer a satisfactory explanation, he said. In most cases natural laws were the "artificial product of education" and were mainly convenient to those in authority.[51] Moreover,

> [natural law] does not explain the often contradictory diversity of forms of authority and laws. In some societies, it is the grandfather who rules; in others it is the mother; and in others still it is the eldest son of the queen; here slavery is illegal; there it is permitted; one country allows divorce, another does not; two years ago the Padlock law held sway in Quebec; today it has no effect. "The nature of things" does not offer much help in explaining why Maurice [Duplessis] is able to command Pierre [Trudeau], and why something permitted here is forbidden elsewhere.[52]

Here Trudeau was interpreting natural law either as an unchanging anthropological condition or as a human practice that prevailed everywhere, rather like some mathematical theorem or a scientific law such as gravity. Or maybe it was that he was conceiving of natural law as a rational ethical ideal, an "inclination" of conscience that prescribed a common aspiration after a universal good that was integral to a human being's nature or essence, the Thomist position. The fact that this universal truth had apparently been realized in such divergent and contradictory ways seems to have led him to doubt its existence altogether. Perhaps Trudeau was guilty of the mistake that Maritain calls "equivocity," of doubting the existence of a natural law because of the supposed varied and contradictory instances of its expression. Maritain—and Trudeau surely knew this—was a thinker who expressed the very idea of natural law that he was disputing.[53] Yet in other parts of these essays Trudeau himself employed a simplified Aristotelian/Thomist version of natural law in positing the benefit of living in society for the fulfilment and flourishing of its members. And good sense can only be made of other parts of his thinking if it was based on some idea of natural law; think of his defence of the inviolability and dignity of the human person, the suppositions he made about the existence of inalienable rights and his claim that "legal" laws and regimes must be judged against a standard of justice in order to discover if they might be legal or not. So Trudeau's thinking was not without some connection to supposedly indubitable ontological and metaphysical principles but he seems to have been increasingly uncomfortable explicitly invoking them, believing, apparently, that he could wall off legal and political matters from Christian metaphysics and suppositions. Trudeau formally conceded that the Church was supreme in matters of religious orthodoxy but this supremacy must be circumscribed and prevented from intruding on the important questions of politics and government.[54] Clerics could and should stay within the walls of their theological conclaves and not venture into the public square. Here is evidence of a decided secularism and French-like laïcité on Trudeau's part.[55]

Unsurprisingly clerical critics continued to pursue him. Father de Léry of Relations took him to task for advocating tyrannicide and implicating Jesuit thinkers in such a view; André Dagenais accused him of being a dangerous revolutionary; and Léopold Richer, founder and editor of the weekly *Notre Temps*, considered him an extremist.[56] Trudeau was if anything rather amused by such accusations. He even contributed to the welter of criticisms by making his own revelation: he knew of "a worthy, highly-educated lady—incidentally a very pretty lady—who is spreading a rumour among her circle that my theories make me a communist."[57] Others alleged he was a Protestant. Trudeau's view nonetheless was that yet another conspiracy was being hatched, masterminded once more by the Jesuits, and that the criticisms on which it was based were little more than a mishmash of logic-chopping, ignorance, and wilful misrepresentations. In defending himself Trudeau took special satisfaction in publicizing the idea that it had been Jesuit thinkers who had been among the pioneers of the view that there was right to assassinate tyrannical rulers. These Jesuits had been part of a broad trend of enlightenment, he said, advocating the separation of the spiritual and the temporal spheres and the development of a more advanced account of the venality of kings and the rights of the subject:

> I regret that such a rapid incursion into the theology [of tyrannicide] would have sufficed to give a bad conscience to the Jesuits at *Relations*. Of course I was thinking of [Juan de] Mariana when writing my article but also of [Francesco] Suarez and of the great Cardinal Bellarmine who did so much to establish a distinction between the spiritual and the temporal in regards the authority of the clergy. Equally I was thinking of their long-ago predecessors such as William of Occam who established the foundations of theories that limited the despotism of princes. Put simply, theologians (including certain Jesuit ones) have played a large role in the evolution of political thought, and it is in large part due to them that the liberty of the citizen has been able to prevail over the absolutism of kings.[58]

Trudeau's argument might be seen as a hymn of praise to the idea of an academic engagement with history in the cause of a progressive, modern understanding of individual liberty and responsible government. At bottom Western history had been about the unfolding and enlarging of the ideas of consent, social contract, and popular sovereignty:

> These theories go back to the very origins of political thought. One finds traces of them in Plato, in Epicurus, in the *lex regia* of the Romans and in Cicero. For these the authority of the State proceeds from the collective power of the people. The doctrine of the *Contract of government* was completely accepted in the Middle Ages, particularly during the Investiture Controversy. . . . But in its modern form the doctrine of contract is expressed for the first time—Oh the irony of names—by Duplessis-Mornay, the likely author of the *Vindiciae contra tyrannos.* After this Huguenot there were three Jesuits who were inspired by the theory of the contract: Bellarmine in Italy, Suarez in Spain and in England Parsons who used it better to prosecute the struggle against Elizabeth. In the seventeenth century contract theorists abounded: Althusius, Grotius, Pufendorf, Selden, Parker, Milton, Prynne, and Lilburne, then finally Spinoza, Hobbes and Locke. The doctrine was equally present in the United States with Paine and Jefferson, then finally in France with Rousseau; not to mention Germany with Kant and Fichte.
>
> The theory of popular sovereignty has spread abroad even further, if that is possible. Let us only recall such precursors as St. Isadore, and such tyrannicides as the monk John of Salisbury and the Jesuit Mariana. The idea that authority ascends from the will of the governed has deep foundations in the middle ages. Thus in the school of John of Paris: "*populo faciente et Deo inspirante*"; Marsilio of Padua and St Thomas Aquinas held that God is only the "*causa remota*" of authority; William of Occam saw the "*imperium a Deo et tamen per homines*"; and for Nicholas of Cusa, the head of State is "*quasi in se omnium voluntatem gestans.*" Then would come the Jesuits who in order to deny the transcendental doctrine of the State became almost unanimous in affirming the doctrine of the original sovereignty of

the people, above all Suarez, but Molina, Schmier, Victoria and Vasquez as well.

One more time, I do not pretend that all these thinkers developed an identical form of thought, far from it. But it is to the credit of all of them that they developed systems which—requiring various forms of participation or popular consent—imposed limits on political authority, protecting the freedom of the citizens and ensuring the full flourishing of persons. Why am I being reproached for pursuing in a more modest fashion the very same goals? Is it that freedom is not of concern among us? Or is it that no one considers it worth preserving?[59]

Vrai was not a tabloid newspaper but neither was it a high-brow journal so that it can easily be imagined what its good readers thought of an article composed of more than thirty often obscure names in the history of political theory and, to boot, a general disquisition on social contract theory. Trudeau was never backward in displaying his learning and critics will see in the above an instance of his habit of elegant name-dropping and showmanship. But, to repeat, another way of seeing it is as confirmation of his conviction that political practice should be based on intellectual insight. In this case it was almost certainly also a rhetorical device to rout his clerical critics, since the list seems to have been constructed to emphasize the medieval and Christian origins of consensual government and the social contract. Trudeau did mention scions of the radical Enlightenment such as Baruch Spinoza, Thomas Paine, and Immanuel Kant but his list leaves the clear impression that ideas about human rights and democracy have mainly derived from Christian—and certainly European—sources. In this regard Trudeau anticipated a contemporary debate about the Christian origins of liberalism, something to which his espousal of personalism also contributed.[60] Much of Trudeau's account he probably assembled from J.W. Allen's *A History of Political Thought in the Sixteenth Century* (1928) and G.H. Sabine's *A History of Political Theory* (1937), both of which he had read in McIlwain's class at Harvard fourteen years earlier.

III

Given Trudeau's reticence about his personal religious convictions, we should necessarily employ tentative language when talking about this aspect of his life. Nevertheless a solid truth is that he did practise his Catholic faith. But did he believe in all the traditional doctrines of the Church? Likely the answer is in the affirmative if we define them as being about his confidence in salvation through the Church and his hope in the Resurrection. But in other respects Trudeau was unorthodox. He was always opposed to ultramontanism. He likely did not believe that the Petrine commission gave a unique primacy and monopoly on truth to the Roman Catholic Church, atop of which sat an infallible pope. Trudeau could be very rude about infallible anythings. When he excoriated "Pope Pearson" over the famous Bomarc issue of 1963 Trudeau expressed something derogatory not only about the Liberal leader but about the primate of the Catholic Church too.[61] Trudeau's faith was more of an inclusionary and latitudinarian kind. Generally he held that religious experience was something that Catholics shared with Christians from other denominations and indeed with the followers of all the world's religions, even perhaps with all persons. Recall Trudeau's comments earlier when he stated that Christianity was a religion of love and brotherhood and that religious experience was expressed in the rootedness of individuals of whatever faiths in love and brotherhood. Trudeau thought of religion functionally rather than doctrinally or denominationally. He was intellectually skeptical and likely he had little belief in so-called Christian miracles and the "white magic" of relics and such. Nor can he easily be seen as a follower of Marian devotion. And we know from earlier discussion how he felt about the baroque adornment of Catholic churches. He was not in step in any substantial way with the customary expectations and devotions of ordinary parishioners. Trudeau's religious sensibilities were non-conformist and questioning, and, in his openness to ecumenical possibilities, cosmopolitan and universalist. Yet he never *publicly* rejected the authority of the Magisterium of pope and bishops, at least as long as their pronunciamentos were expressed within their proper sphere. However, he was quite capable of being subversive and disputatious towards clerical authority in every other respect and of course he had a very narrow sense of what was its legitimate sphere.

Trudeau's main point was that an individual Catholic's conscience must be respected, by priest and bishop. He was adamant that within the civil sphere the Catholic Church and by implication other churches and religions too had no special theocratic or theological standing. The insights of common citizens, even those without religious faith at all, were in political matters as valid as those of the clergy and its superiors. The "secular" world, especially the world of politics, had its own sources of legitimacy and truth, and the Church should know its place and respect both the authority of the state and the religious and other rights of non-Catholic believers. Indeed it must respect the beliefs and practices of those who had no faith at all. Perhaps his crucial conviction was that all humans were persons and therefore possessed of conscience and capable of intelligent, informed political choice. What the Catholic Church could, however, rightly claim was the protection of the state because confessional freedom was the mark of a good civil order. But the state's protective stance was not to be partial and was to be extended to all denominations and religions. And it was not to be interfering.[62] This at least worked to the advantage of the Church because the duty of the state was not to determine the lawful, peaceful practices of the Church such as the appointment of its bishops and officers. Lord Acton and other liberal Catholics had put it well in the 1850s: the ideal was "a free Church in a free State."[63] Although Trudeau now and then appealed to papal and Episcopal authority in moral and political debate, this was typically a rhetorical ruse to win his arguments. Most of the time he was dismissive of official Catholic social thought especially in Quebec although, curiously, he did support some traditional church-based moral views. Thus he never believed in the rightness of divorce for himself; and, likely, he did not support an abortion for a woman in his life.[64] However, about public policy on such contentious matters he held that the state could not rightly impose religious principles on non-believers because in a pluralistic society there frequently existed differences about the nature of the good.

On political issues his views were much more markedly out of step with those of the official Church. His espousal of the importance of a social contract as the basis of the legitimate state was almost universally rejected by popes from Leo XIII down to John XXIII.[65] And given Trudeau's own account of the injustices of capitalism and private property and the merits of socialism, not to say the overall—albeit undulating—conservatism of the papacy on such issues, at least until the coming of John XXIII, it is predictable that Trudeau was in radical disagreement with most papal thinking on such subjects. Trudeau's views on sexuality were particularly unconventional, and his ongoing practice of affective, companionate sexuality, after he had experienced the joys of sexual intercourse (likely after 1950 or thereabouts) would certainly have raised the eyebrows of the Holy Fathers if they had known. In general, thinking about the Catholic Church in Quebec, Trudeau was not beyond labelling it "obscurantist."[66]

In the late nineteenth century a major shift had occurred in the Church's thinking leading to the establishing of Thomism as its official theology. This too found Trudeau out of step. From his Brébeuf days and from his exposure to Maritain and Étienne Gilson, he knew his Thomism well but there is no evidence that he used it as a systematic metaphysical grid to buttress his moral claims. His thinking now and then betrayed a Thomist influence, as we have noticed, but only somewhat. Instead such consistent metaphysics as Trudeau espoused he more frequently found in Berdyaev, Mounier, and Maritain. The last named was, of course, a Thomist but Trudeau was selective in his absorption of Maritain's thought. He took from him the idea that society was a divinely decreed place of human fulfilment but that the state was a sphere that possessed its own human scheme of legitimacy. In other ways too there was a Thomist/Aristotelian touch. When Aquinas said that the good ruler should follow neither his own interest nor any sectional interest, Trudeau was in complete agreement and of course it was the basis of his own idea of a common good.[67] But that was all. In general Trudeau's Catholicism, while in personal practice expressed as one of devotion and conformity, in other respects was idiosyncratic or even heretical, although we can see in retrospect that it dovetailed with much of the Church's reform movement including Pope John XXIII's implicit personalism in his encyclical, *Mater et Magistra* (1961).[68] Trudeau's conception of the Church was less that of a hierarchical, sacerdotal communion and more that of a practical community of the laity who advanced social democracy as the hallmark of Catholic engagement-in-the-world. But Trudeau remained insistent that his personal faith need not be asserted in public. Politics could be justified without reference to theological first principles and Catholics and non-Catholics could collaborate together in common causes as citizens of equal standing in a secular, liberal state. Their common civil language did not presuppose a common theological vocabulary or common presuppositions. As a consequence any notion of a separate identity that a Catholic-centred politics might express through Christian Democratic parties or confessional trade unions had no purchase on him at all.

IV

Perhaps the most important religious dimension of Trudeau's thought was his personalism, although here too things were incomplete and indeterminate, and of course very private. Personalism in the hands of Mounier and Maritain presupposed a Christian metaphysic and for all of Trudeau's protestations that he did not approach religion metaphysically it is likely that his account of personalism presupposed Christian premises. Mounier for example asserted that the individual with a conscience was a specifically Christian insight and that this provided more than a materialist, non-religious account of the self. Persons were created in the image of God; God had become incarnate and taken on a human form in Christ; persons were centres of spirit and conscience; and humans' capacity to exercise free will and choice was a divinely prescribed capacity.

André Burelle is one recent critic who has taken Trudeau seriously as a personalist. In the late 1970s he was one of Trudeau's constitutional advisers and speech-writers and later, after Trudeau's death, he wrote a scathing critique of what he believed was his shift in thinking after the 1980 referendum, *Pierre Elliott Trudeau: l'intellectuel et la politique* (2005). However Burelle *is* impressed by the personalist perspective of the early Trudeau. He sees it as the great prescriptive presence in his world view before he allegedly gave in to American republican individualism in the early 1980s. For Burelle personalism regards humans as distinguished by intelligence and will; they lived in love and knowledge; the person was a universe within him- or herself, giving the self to others; the person thirsted for the absolute; and at the centre of the self were conscience and freedom; humans represented the priority of spirit over matter. Above all Burelle sees personalism as a protest against the abstract, disengaged individualism of liberalism with its notion of the universal person with equal abstract rights. Instead, for personalism, the individual was rooted in the materiality of existing culture. Persons belonged to real communities; and they established their identity dialogically through their dealings with others. Burelle's account of personalism with its Taylorite-sounding additions he deduced mainly from Mounier and Maritain and can usefully be compared to Trudeau's.[69]

Trudeau's account fits Burelle's type in some respects but not in all. Trudeau's was less religiously couched and less emphatic about the claims of community. Certainly his world view was not that of atomistic individualism and there was a sense with him of a common good that was more than an aggregate of sectional or individual goods. Particularly in the *Vrai* essays of 1958, as we shall see in the next chapter, Trudeau's belief was that society was essential to human fulfilment; the freedom of the individual was necessary but it coexisted in relationships with others; society presupposed co-operation, mutual aid and collaboration; and it provided the possibility of an invigorating collective pursuit of justice for all; society was a place in which human will and intelligence were guided and educated by common cultural endeavours that enlarged the citizen's understanding and provided greater personal fulfilment. Now and then Trudeau's language moved closer to the language of liberalism, that the common good was a sort of compound private value in which individuals recognized that, in order to pursue their own goals, they must accord a similar respect to others. In step with this way of thinking, the welfare state became a scheme of "co-insurance," as Trudeau put it as early as 1950: "All citizens in the equitable society are co-insurers of every citizen against collective disasters."[70] But in general Trudeau's ideas were only modestly communitarian: each was responsible for the other and for the common good; society was where we developed as moral beings; the well-being of each presumed justice for all. If Trudeau did not trumpet the joys of community in the manner of Mounier and to some extent Maritain, nonetheless his was a version that went beyond liberal individualism. That said, with Trudeau there is always the sense that he gave priority to the "individualist" side of personalism and to the role of conscience and individual choice in moral matters, although always he made it clear that to act freely was never simply to do what one wanted. He was especially sensitive to the many ways in which the state and the community imposed measures that contravened personal judgment and diminished the dignity and uniqueness of the person.

And of course there was Trudeau's noticeable reticence about proclaiming personalism's roots in Christian theology. As time went by Trudeau offered a more secular-sounding personalism, one that eschewed mention of the suprapersonal world of soul and spirit and of human beings incarnated in the image of God. Did he nevertheless hold to these precepts privately? Likely he did but he seemed not to have wanted to articulate them publicly. The Charter of Rights and Freedoms, arguably Trudeau's greatest triumph, talks a little about God when in the preamble it states that "Canada is founded upon principles that recognize the supremacy of God." It also guarantees freedom of conscience and religion and the right of free association, all of which have obvious religious implications. However, the inclusion of God in the Charter was not something that Trudeau personally approved since it offended the idea of the neutrality of the state. But in the end he agreed to it to accommodate conservative religious opinion. But there is perhaps another religious immanence in the Charter. The Charter talks variously of "citizens," "individuals," and "everyone," but significantly it also mentions "persons" and asserts that all persons are of fundamental moral worth. It does not explain, however, why this is so. In the Mounier/Maritain tradition of personalism persons are worthy because they bear the image of God and their freedom and dignity are divinely decreed. Persons therefore possess dignity and so deserve rights. Probably Trudeau believed similarly though he did not say so publicly. If he did so believe we might say that he did have an ontology of the person and that this ontology presupposed a theology. But if these existed they were implicit. His extreme privacy about such matters means that we cannot say for sure.

Socialism and Economics

<hr>

Obviously there is no need of fighting to overcome this single tyrant,
for he is automatically defeated if the country refuses consent to its
own enslavement: it is not necessary to deprive him of anything, but
simply to give him nothing; there is no need that the country make an
effort to do anything for itself provided it does nothing against itself.
Étienne de la Boétie

I

Already familiar with socialism during his time abroad and certainly embracing it after his return to Canada in 1949, Trudeau
became decidedly a man of the Left. In July of that year, in a letter to
Gérard Filion, editor of *Le Devoir*, he argued for a new federal party,
more radical than the Liberals, which would emphasize social and
economic justice and avoid becoming enmeshed in conservative
nationalism.[1] Accordingly Trudeau became not just a supporter
of the CCF in the 1950s but a member too.[2] His involvement went
deep. He gave money to the party, participated in its retreats, and
gave lectures at labour summer schools and CCF youth soirées at
the home of its Quebec leader, Thérèse Casgrain. He attended the
CCF National Convention in Toronto in August 1952 and became a
"research consultant" for the party in April 1956.[3] Especially through
his friendship with Jean Marchand he was well connected with the
trade union movement in Quebec. He represented unions in arbi-
tration hearings in places far away from Montreal and often rode to
them on his motorbike wearing a leather jacket, looking more than
a little like a cross between James Dean and Marlon Brando. He was
prepared to stand for the new union-sponsored party that Pelletier

and Marchand had bruited on the eve of the 1952 Quebec election and which was to run candidates in several working-class ridings.[4] Later there came his involvement in a project of the Fédération des unions industrielles du Québec (FUIQ) to establish a socialist party in Quebec in 1954–55.[5] These came to nothing but they are instructive of how much Trudeau was committed to working-class causes at the time. He was also involved as a researcher and counsel for the FUIQ and he prepared its response to the Tremblay Commission in 1954.

Such connections, and there were many more, flowed logically from his political beliefs. Trudeau became a socialist though, ultimately, of an avowedly democratic and undogmatic kind. His socialism was very much in the tradition of the British Fabians and the Labour Party, and in Canada of the CCF. It was parliament-centred, political-party based, gradualist, meliorist, and non-violent but radical in its critique of big business. There was much of Laski in this. And like him Trudeau was open to an unemotional and unprejudiced intellectual engagement with Marxism and the Communist governments of the Soviet Union and China and sometimes he said things about them that implied that he was more than a gas-and-water democratic socialist. But his settled opinion was that for Canada—he had other thoughts about the Second and Third Worlds—a democratic kind of socialism was preferable and that such a socialism drew on its own prepossessing traditions of Christianity, Fabianism, Swedish-style social democracy, and liberal democracy in general reaching back into European history. In the debate in the 1950s over revisionism and the question of whether public ownership and nationalization were indispensable means to socialism, Trudeau came down on the revisionist side. There were no indispensable means, he believed, only ones that were more or less effective in bringing about socialism's central goal, which was the control of private property in the name of the common good. Trudeau now and then entertained the idea of a sort of impending economic cataclysm that would result in capitalism's collapse but for the most part he eventually placed himself squarely in the Keynesian camp, believing that fiscal stabilization would mitigate the wild swings of production to which capitalism was prone. Trudeau discussed Marx's labour theory of value—and he employed now and then language that talked of ending economic exploitation—but his view of economic class was mainly what is called a distributivist one: the workers were exploited because the system of distribution was unfair and unequal, rather than because of the nature of production itself. Finally, he placed the development of socialism within an overarching historical inevitability of human improvement, although by 1953, as we shall notice, he had concluded that history's trajectory might not be quite as unambiguously progressive as he had thought.

Trudeau's backing of the CCF in the early 1950s was given with his eyes wide open. His support was never offered unconditionally or uncritically—witness the consideration he gave to running for union-based parties in 1952 and 1954, and his proposal of an alliance with nationalist voters after the federal election of 1953—but it was given in a generally clear-headed way because he knew that he was siding with a political movement whose vote at the national level was modest and in Quebec was either miniscule or non-existent. He knew only too well that because of the opposition of the Catholic Church and the subservience of Quebec's politics to nationalism, almost by default the CCF had been founded by "the English" and that it bore a stigma of otherness. Writing in 1952 Trudeau hoped that the new leader, Thérèse Casgrain, would erase the "English air" around the party.[6] What sustained Trudeau in these unpropitious times was a sense that these were still early days for socialism. Britain and France had demonstrated its popularity and if Canada's politics was somehow continuous with theirs—and there seemed little reason to doubt this—there was indeed a promising and perhaps glorious future awaiting it here.

In December 1953 Trudeau spoke on "Socialism in Quebec" at a union retreat.[7] The speech is a snapshot of his thinking at the time. He was brutally frank in pointing out the failures of the CCF

and laid out its dismal electoral record in the province in both federal and provincial elections: 2.8 percent of the vote in 1944—he
left out 1945 for some reason—0.5 percent in 1948, 1.1 percent in
1949, 1.1 percent in 1952, and 1.6 percent earlier in 1953. Trudeau
felt that the conventional explanations of these failures—the
combined impacts of the Church, nationalism, and the province's
conservatism—were now losing their effect. The Church had
withdrawn its prohibition against voting for the party and more
and more in the twentieth century Quebec had demonstrated a
growing acceptance of dissent. Instead he believed that the CCF
and socialists themselves bore some responsibility for the demise
of the party. In a nutshell, the CCF had failed to present itself in
a manner that respected French Canadians' yearning for identity:
"[The] CCF has never stood for Quebec as a province (centralizing force) and has never stood for French can[adians] as a people
(English force)," his notes abbreviatedly put it. Trudeau conceded
that Quebec was "behind the times historically and ideologically"
but it was also that "progressive thinking outside Quebec didn't
include respect for our ways (religion and language.)" Then he
offered a telling cryptic comment: "[Mackenzie] King understood
better than Woodsworth or Coldwell."[8] Somehow King with all his
faults had been more sensitive to French Canada's cultural aspirations than the two most important proponents of Canadian democratic socialist orthodoxy. But Trudeau concluded with a measure
of hope. The province was moving leftwards and efforts were being
made by French Canadians "to formulate progressive thinking in
our own language, by our people." The question now was whether
this new ferment of ideas would be captured by the Liberals or
independents rather than the CCF. Ultimately it depended on
the CCF: "Can it be less doctrinaire, and accept Fr. Can ways of
thinking and living: religion, language, politics?" Could the CCF
embrace the idea of "state control" from Quebec City rather than
Ottawa? And could it adapt its policies on questions like divorce,
the flag, the Vatican, and bilingualism? Such comments revealed
Trudeau's profound regard for a politics that incorporated regional

and provincial perspectives. He developed this perspective more completely in his essay, "The Practice and Theory of Federalism," in 1961.

In the middle of his CCF period, in February 1954, Trudeau took part in a debate at the University of Montreal on socialism and capitalism. The notes of his speech, five pages of foolscap, make clear that his defence of socialism, before "a few hundred students," was more than a brief disquisition.[9] Ever able to attract attention, *Le Devoir*'s report of the event gave pride of place to him.[10] His co-debater, Roger Dehem, a neo-classical economist at the University of Montreal, and Paul Lacoste, the moderator, could hardly have appreciated the subheading of the story: "Pierre Elliot [*sic*] Trudeau at the U of M." But then they likely would not have wanted to be associated with its larger headline: "Fear leads to fascism, and fascism to revolution."

Trudeau's speech ranged far afield and conveyed well his familiarity with socialism's many traditions and nuances. What is clear is that he spoke as a self-conscious socialist, albeit a moderate one. Capitalism, he said, was integral to "commercial societies" and had emerged out of the "ruins" of feudalism. A rising bourgeoisie, speaking ostensibly in the name of the masses, contested the privileges of monarchs, aristocrats, and ecclesiastics and demanded commercial freedoms. Later, especially in his 1962 article "La nouvelle trahison des clercs," Trudeau theorized that the bourgeoisie had allied itself to centralizing monarchies of the time, which was Laski's emphasis too. Capitalism, Trudeau now went on, had been in the ascendant since 1750 but had been in decline since the First World War. Over time it had developed an increasing concentration of economic power, the reaction to which had been a politics that sought to use productive resources for "the common good" and not for the profit of the capitalists. But socialism was not a monolithic strategy. The means to achieve it were several: "control or public ownership of the means of production; control by central authority, co-operatives, municipal [ownership] and anarcho-syndicalism." The "ideal" was justice understood as the redistribution of wealth and the "means" required presupposed "limits on private property." Trudeau did not call for the abolition of private property altogether.

Trudeau seems to have wanted to emphasize the antiquity of socialism for he began his speech by observing that the idea of socialism was as old as Plato and that it had an impressive genealogy drawn from many sources: the Stoics, Thomas More, the Anabaptists, Campanella, Harrington, Rousseau, Sombart, Proudhon, and Marx. The revolution of the eighteenth century—no doubt Trudeau meant the French revolution—was an alliance of "the bourgeoisie and the people" in pursuit of freedom and equality but a "crisis" arose. With liberalism not quite able to realize a universally egalitarian society, contemporary socialism was born. Trudeau mentioned the most important "applications" of socialism in his own time as Marxism, Fabianism, and social democracy. Marxism he condensed as an economic theory of surplus value that posited an inevitable clash between concentrated wealth and the increasing misery of the workers, a clash that would lead to the breaking apart of existing social structures, the coming of a classless society, and the withering away of the state. The exemplary Marxist state was Russia, he said. Then there were the Fabians. They represented a "pragmatic" socialism, Trudeau said, with little of Marx and more of the Christian gospel. Their emphasis was less on the class struggle and more on parliamentary action centred on political parties. It could best be observed in Britain, and indeed in Saskatchewan, he said. Social democracy, quintessentially found in Sweden, he saw as the third type and stood for the separation of ownership and control and proposed a mixed economy with a crucial participation by co-operatives and unions. Summing up, Trudeau said that socialism was not opposed to property as such but rather that it favoured expanding property ownership to everyone.

On the question of whether socialism was to be achieved peacefully or not, Trudeau was a little unclear. He noted that both capitalism and liberalism had been established by force and some socialist regimes had emerged in the same way. However, in his estimation, the three versions of socialism did not necessarily require violent methods. Even with Marxism Trudeau drew a distinction between Marx's and Lenin's views on the subject. Marx himself had not necessarily preached revolutionary violence, he said, but this had been the view of his Russian disciples. This distinction, we have noticed, was Laski's although he was not alone in holding it. Whether force was required, Trudeau said, depended on how Big Business reacted. If it resisted the workers' demands, authoritarianism and fascism were possible and this would likely induce workers to become violent in turn, another theme from Laski. Later, in his *Vrai* essays, as we shall see, Trudeau expatiated further on this dilemma by emphasizing that there was a right of resistance to the tyrant but that under democracy there could be no countenancing of violence as a method to win political power.

But the emphasis of his 1954 speech was a different one. Its special preoccupation was with what should be done when a powerful interest exercised a sinister control and was bent on a kind of despotic counter-revolution. In other places too Trudeau expressed concern that even under a system of universal suffrage, with competing political parties and parliamentary processes, there were all sorts of devious stratagems and structural advantages that those with power might use to get their way. But if the circumstance was one of impending fascism then Trudeau implied that popular resistance or the application of emergency powers by a people's government were legitimate responses. He concluded his 1954 speech by bringing the discussion back home. He made it clear that he was not advocating an immediate socialism for Quebec. A dominant motif in his thought was about how ideas needed to be fitted to context. An idea may be abstractly "true" but that was not enough to ensure its acceptance and applicability. Mainly Trudeau's purpose on this occasion was educational: to popularize the great idea of socialism. But Quebec was not yet ready for it, he said. It still had an unfulfilled rendezvous with democracy. For socialism in a society unprepared for it could easily turn into totalitarianism. Later in the debate Trudeau was asked about the question of nationalization and his reply was, again, that Quebec was not ready for it, if only because it did not have a sufficiently large corps of trained administrators. This became a theme of his in the late 1950s and early 1960s and shaped his response to René Lévesque's proposal to nationalize the private hydro companies in the province. For now Trudeau recommended that Quebec should "perfect its democracy" and press for "welfare" in the form of "housing, health and education."

In his speech Trudeau also intimated that the governments of the Soviet Union and China should be understood historically and were legitimate forms of socialism. He said nothing about their possible invalidity or deformation except to imply that Lenin had somehow misunderstood Marx's ideas on non-violent change. But in Canada Trudeau's view was that there were clear alternatives to Marxism and to violence so that against the background of his support for the CCF at this time, his accounts of Fabianism and social democracy have to be seen as his preferred versions of socialism. But also to be noted is that Trudeau was never without a sense of possible political and economic breakdowns and the need for extreme methods in response to them although as the decade unfolded his understanding of social change became more immediatist and less apocalyptic.

Trudeau's socialism was never an exercise in abstraction but always one bent towards practical application. His concern was with conceiving a form of socialism that fitted given contexts, be it Canada or China. For now Quebec was at the centre of his concerns. There his support of the CCF/PSD changed markedly after the 1956 provincial election. To the notes and drafts of his 1953 speech on "Socialism in Quebec" with its tabulation of the popular vote going back to 1944, Trudeau returned in 1956, pencilling in the derisory outcome of the recent provincial election in which the PSD had won 0.6 percent of the popular vote. Before that election Trudeau had encouraged Quebecers to vote for the PSD, clearly not to any great effect. Duplessis had prevailed for the fourth consecutive time and, including his term in office in the late 1930s, for a fifth time overall. Trudeau had seen this coming and even before the election was over he was making alternative plans. Some new strategy must be adopted to rid the province of Duplessis, one that moved beyond the PSD. He did not cast the party into outer darkness but he would now balance his loyalty to the democratic Left with a commitment to more broadly based, non-party initiatives.

The first of these was the Rassemblement, founded, formally, in September 1956. It was an attempt to draw together the Quebec centre-left, including the Liberals, into some kind of common alliance. Members of the PSD were of course involved. Thérèse Casgain claimed that she had taken the initiative in calling the first meeting of the organization in April 1956—Trudeau's memory was that it was on the 14th—and that Trudeau was the co-chair of the meeting.[11] Trudeau recalled that there were over a hundred people present and that an organization had been put in place by the end of the second meeting on June 23, three days after the provincial election.[12] The Rassemblement recruited neo-nationalists like André Laurendeau and some trade union leaders (although Jean Marchand was one trade unionist who was conspicuously absent). Trudeau saw it as a movement and as an oppositional coalition; it was to be more than a party although it might become one.[13] Mainly it was conceived as somehow non-partisan. However it was to have a manifesto to which all members would subscribe.[14] The eventual "Declaration of Principles" was adopted at the September meeting when the movement also assumed its name.[15] The manifesto was a decidedly social democratic document. Trudeau wrote the original draft more or less singlehandedly.[16]

It began with an affirmation of democratic ideals: society existed so that individuals might realize themselves; authority was rendered legitimate by individual consent; the individual person possessed inalienable rights; and parliamentary politics and a system of competing political parties were essential political arrangements. These were of course fundamental premises in Trudeau's political imaginary and were almost a perfect foreshadowing of what would become the main argument of his essays in *Vrai* in 1958. But in addition to political ideals, the Declaration talked of practicalities: the purpose of economic activity was to meet human needs; private enterprise by itself was incapable of guaranteeing general prosperity; there was a need for fairer distribution and greater social collaboration through a welfare state, trade unions, and co-operatives; workers should enjoy equal rights and farmers stable markets; and technology should encourage greater productivity. An allusive statement mentioned the priority of "democratizing enterprise" in order to overcome "the dehumanization of work." Regarding the overall "means" to these ends, the Declaration was open-ended, implying that it was impossible to stipulate in advance the ideal economic modalities. Public ownership was not rejected but it was not prescribed either. But certainly economic planning was necessary. The Declaration also talked of the importance of spiritual and cultural fulfilment and it made a strong statement against the politicization of educational and cultural affairs. Education, it presumed, must become a responsibility of the state and not of the Church.

On international matters the Declaration enunciated a strong belief in the individual's "ultimate allegiance to the human race" but this was counterbalanced with an equally strong statement on subsidiarity: as much as possible, political authority should be organized at the local level. This was especially important, it said, in cultural matters. In the case of multi-ethnic societies the diverse cultures that composed them should have equal rights to free expression and development. It also talked of the importance of federalism as a way of balancing local and regional imperatives against the overarching national unity necessary for economic prosperity. For good measure the Declaration attached as a codicil the complete statement of the United Nations' (UN) Universal Declaration of Human Rights (1948), to whose formulation both Maritain and Laski had been contributors.

Overall the balance struck in the Declaration was between realistic practicality and cautious idealism. Planning and measures of "dirigisme" were necessary, though these must be subject to democratic controls, and liberal democracy must necessarily advance towards social democracy. Trudeau put it well in October 1958 in his essay, "Un manifeste démocratique":

> [It] seems evident to me that the regime of free enterprise is confirmed as being incapable of satisfactorily resolving the problems which are posed in the areas of education, health, housing, [and] full employment etc. That's why I am personally convinced that in the face of the upheavals guaranteed by automation, cybernetics and thermo-nuclear energy, liberal democracy will not for much longer be able to meet the growing demands for justice and freedom, and will have to evolve towards the forms of social democracy.[17]

Intimations of Trudeau's gravitating towards a realistic account of socialism had begun even earlier, just after the federal election of August 1953, which the Liberals under St. Laurent had won handily. His commentary on that election may be taken as the symbolic moment at which he began to move towards accepting Keynesianism as the economic paradigm suitable to contemporary social democracy. Trudeau had been exposed to Keynes as early as his time at Harvard but embracing his insights took several years to materialize. In the immediate postwar years, if anything, he was a sort of Marxist who held that capitalism was a fundamentally chaotic and unstable system likely to produce periodic recessions and depressions and with them the political calamities of fascism and Nazism. As a more stable and enduring economic order took hold in the 1950s and workers' wages expanded Trudeau took practical note of Keynes. His article "Fluctuations économiques et méthodes de stabilisation" in *Cité Libre* in March 1954 and the FUIQ's brief to the Tremblay Commission in the same month revealed him explaining Keynesian possibilities.[18]

Classical economic theory, Trudeau observed, held that recessions and depressions were self-correcting and that the equilibrium of production and demand was automatically achieved. But the evidence was to the contrary, he said, and as well there must now be

taken into account the role of monopolies and trade unions holding up prices and wages and introducing rigidities in the economy.
Trudeau advocated the classical Keynesian solution of government
as the sustainer of "effective demand" through stimulating purchas-
ing power by lowering taxes, running deficits, making expenditures
on public works and social welfare, and developing state enterprises. As well government should reset monetary policy by having the Bank of Canada buy up government debt, making available
deposits to the banks which in turn would improve the availabil-
ity of investment capital to business. (Here perhaps was an early
version of what has become known nowadays as quantitative eas-
ing.) Trudeau articulated one of the guiding principles of Keynes
when he reminded his readers that the operation of a complex fiscal
and monetary policy under modern conditions was not like running a grocery store where simple issues of profit and loss were all-
consuming. But he also pointed out that Keynesianism had
two sides. Stimulation was one but when inflation rose and the
economy was growing rapidly it fell to government to reduce
demand and spending. Trudeau's FUIQ brief to the Tremblay
Commission in March 1954 may also be seen as part of his symbolic
conversion to a Keynesian synthesis about "stabilization."[19]

II

Regarding the *political* means to socialism, what we have called the
Vrai essays were especially important for understanding Trudeau.
Between February 15 and July 5, 1958, at the invitation of his friend
Jacques Hébert, the owner and editor of the weekly *Vrai*, Trudeau
published twenty linked articles on politics and democracy. The
essays were collected in 1970 in book form as *Les cheminements de
la politique* and published the same year in English as *Approaches
to Politics*. Though not unacademic, they were written in a popular style and permitted Trudeau ample opportunity to indulge
his penchant not just for grand theory but for satire and derision.
Predictably he used them to expose yet again, and with blistering
candour, the failings of the illegitimate, undemocratic regime of

Duplessis. More abstractly and a little sinisterly, Trudeau also discussed tyrannicide and the right—indeed perhaps the duty—of the citizen to kill the tyrant. Indeed one of his critics, André Dagenais, editor of the Quebec weekly *Salaberry*, believed he had caught him in the act of encouraging his readers to assassinate Duplessis. Of course Trudeau rejected the accusation. While the essays were highly contentious and spoke to political immediacies, they were nonetheless a fairly significant exercise in abstract thinking. After his brief to the Tremblay Commission, his contributions to *La grève de l'amiante*, and his 1965 essay "Le Québec et le problème constitutionnel," they were perhaps the most extended treatment he gave to any political subject matter in this period. What they revealed was the spacious sweep of his imagination, his deep historical understanding, and, strangely in one so embedded in the here-and-now, the idealism of his prognostications. But of course a realistic stance was significantly evident as well.

If there was a single text upon which Trudeau built his fiery, provocative sermons, it was Rousseau's famous dictum about how man was born free and everywhere was in chains. In step with this Trudeau repeated many times about how humanity had been subjected to devastating oppression but had overcome it in the end. Shifting Rousseau's emphasis a little, he posited another paradox that, although society was a place of human bondage, it was a natural condition. Society, then, was good but its politics were invariably bad. Rejecting the idea of an original state of nature and a historical social contract, Trudeau offered a gloomy account of things, at least at the outset: "man is born in society without being consulted and he continues to live there because he has hardly any other choice."[20] Life in society was "a given thing" ("*une chose donnée*"). However the misery of such a condition he quickly dispelled. A glorious future lay before human beings, one in which freedom and rights would be accorded to everyone. These rights were the traditional liberal ones: free speech, freedom of thought, freedom of association, free assembly, equality before the law, and a right to a fair trial under an impartial and independent judiciary.[21] All humans were free and equal and each had "an infinite value in himself and is bound by his own conscience."[22] Liberty was a "free gift," "a birthright"; our rights existed prior to the existence of the state—to that extent he believed in a state of nature—and were "inalienable"; we enjoyed these rights within an orderly society and the purpose of society was the fulfilment of everyone, "so that each can realize himself to the maximum"; society existed to ensure the recognition of each person's "dignity." Since we were each free and the keeper of our own conscience, our life would only be fulfilled if we exercised our judgment as morally informed, self-determining beings: "For an action is only good and can only have a moral value if it is freely willed, that is to say chosen by the enlightened conscience of he who exercises it."[23] This was a crucial axiom for Trudeau.

Such reasoning has obvious affinities with personalism and with the idea of the person as the inviolable node of conscience and self-determination. However, unlike Maritain and Mounier, as we saw previously, Trudeau did not explicitly locate the identity of the free person within any theological realm or metaphysical framework. He said nothing about the existence of a soul at the centre of the person where conscience, social obligation, and knowledge of the love of God intersected. Probably the only occasion in these essays he invoked a religious precept—and it is not an inconsiderable one—was in his account of the necessity of living in society:

> It is in this sense that one can say that authority, philosophically speaking, comes from God, or from the nature of things, since God has created man with a nature such that he must live in society, that is subject to a political order.[24]

The benefits of a civil society, according to Trudeau, were many and among them were the ones that Thomas Hobbes had described: security and peaceable social intercourse; the fostering of trade; the untroubled practice of religion; and the development of culture.[25] Trudeau invoked Hobbes quite explicitly.[26] Without the state, anarchy and egotism would prevail; without society and the sovereign we might as well live by ourselves in the woods as wolves. Trudeau seems to have overlooked the fact that wolves are very social animals but his point is clear. But for Trudeau living together under a state offered much more, namely the provision of a number of collective goods that could not be achieved individually. Here Trudeau went beyond Hobbes. Indeed we understand Trudeau better if we see him walking less in Hobbes's footsteps and more in those of Aristotle, Aquinas, and Maritain and of socialists and social democrats like Mounier and Laski. Social life and the state made possible relationships of "co-operation" and "mutual aid" and a "common good." To fulfill these imperatives, the ambit of government must be broader than that of the simple watchman state. Properly legitimized the state could expand its sovereign reach and provide social goods such as education, "economic emancipation," public welfare, social housing, and the protection of the weak, to name a few. As well, for Trudeau a proper function for the state was, in the name of the common good, to overcome the powerful particular interests that dominated and controlled government. On this issue Trudeau even recruited Karl Marx to his cause, quoting him about how the state under capitalism was an instrument of the capitalists to exploit the workers. Something similar, said Trudeau, had been held by St. Thomas More when he claimed that commonwealths were "a certain conspiracy of riche men procuring their owne commodities."[27] In the same cause he even summoned up the authority of Aquinas and the pastoral letter of Quebec's bishops in 1941. (Trudeau was a master polemicist.) Despite the state's appalling history as an engine of oppression, Trudeau's claim was that it could become a means to the flourishing of its citizens. There was no limit to what it might do if it was consensually based. Some version of social democracy or democratic socialism was clearly presumed by him.

Informing the essays, then, was the idea of the state as an institution that *planned* for the well-being of the whole society and so it was that government was not just a punitive engine of law-and-order but also a centre of creative intelligence accomplishing many other things. Such ideas resemble what Friedrich Hayek called the rationalist constructivist view of government and what Roscoe Pound referred to as social engineering. Here was how Trudeau put it:

> Now the State is precisely the instrument by which human society organizes itself and expresses itself collectively. A sovereign society which fears the State is a moribund society which has no assurance of the usefulness of its existence as a group.[28]

Here Trudeau was talking not of a society that feared the state as an instrument of security but one that feared it as a means to broader social justice. Trudeau held to a view of law and government that went beyond a liberal one. This persisted with him. In May 1967, when he was Minister of Justice, Trudeau talked about his department as a kind of "planning [of] the society in which we will live tomorrow."[29]

Democratically constituted—and that was the crucial point of his *Vrai* essays—the state can and must embrace whatever its citizens consented to or wished to attain, always, that is, as long as citizens respected each others' consciences and the rights of minorities:

> In all stable, self-governing societies the State is essentially a creation and expression of the people who compose that society. In other words, the State is exactly what the people wish it to be, and has the reality which they wish to accord to it. Its authority is limited by the extent of a collective consent to obey it; and it can only exert a force to the exact extent as the citizens lend to it.[30]

Or, as he put it later in these essays, though with a slightly more liberal inflection:

> It is important then to begin to banish from our political morality every conception to do with the idea that it is the first minister

who would give us bridges, roads and schools in the province. These things are works of which society has need, which it gives to itself and for which it pays the taxes. The first minister gives nothing at all . . . ; quite simply he works in the service of the State as an instrument by means of which the society gives to itself.[31]

And so for Trudeau the ideal state would register the wishes of the people, whatever they were, and not just function as an instrument of constraint. The law would rule and the people as the makers of the law would obey themselves. The law's role was educative and in obeying the law the citizen was aligning with the common good.[32] This again is some distance removed from the traditional liberal theory of the laissez-faire state and is redolent of what Rousseau prescribed, except that Trudeau did not posit an abstract, transcendent general will that was separate from the real, existential volitions of actual citizens. It was not so much a liberal conception as a social democratic one that he was expounding. Trudeau went on to say that the only ground on which the democratic state could behave coercively was when particular, sinister interests used force against the common good and usurped the role of the state as the provider of order and peace.[33] The last point was a foreshadowing of Trudeau's stance during the October Crisis of 1970. It was also a distinction central to Maritain, Mounier, and Laski.

However, arriving at the happy outcome of a social democratic civil order was perhaps a little unexpected because, as we know, another crucial part of Trudeau's theorizing in these essays was of the state as oppressor. For it was, he said, that the eternal tendency of the state was to exact an oppressive conformity from its subjects either because they cowered before its power or were gulled by its manipulations. Trudeau talked of a "psychological disposition to obey." Humans were morally inadequate. Typically seeking their own comfort, few were moved by injustices that did not affect them directly; or it was that the subjects of the state were usually duped into believing that its authority was divine or natural and must be obeyed. A sort of sullen moral lassitude and deference characterized most citizens: they were cowardly and stupid, Trudeau concluded. Trudeau then invoked a dramatic quotation from Blaise Pascal. This choice of inspiration presumably did not go unnoticed by the Church leaders in Quebec, given that the seventeenth-century French theologian and mathematician was a friend of the Jansenists and a critic of the Jesuits. Echoing Pascal, Trudeau declared that the laws of most states had been little more than rules for administering lunatic asylums. The madmen who ran the state had mistakenly considered themselves kings and emperors.

Here was a very anarchist-sounding version of the state and civil society. Trudeau refused to grant any legitimacy whatever to historic governments, even as simple vessels of public order. However, by his own admission the citizen, whether cowed or deceived, could hardly be the reed on which democratic mobilization could successfully lean. Yet Trudeau placed great confidence in the people. Democracy was after all growing in acceptance in the modern world, he reasoned, and the people possessed the priceless advantage if they chose to use it and this was their capacity to withdraw their obedience. Perhaps more significant in the history of human governance, Trudeau said, had been not so much the overweening power of government but the submissiveness of the citizen. In the end even oppressive governments could not survive if their citizens chose not to consent and obey: "For a man or a group of men is never sufficiently strong to impose its authority on a population that does not wish it."[34] On the ethical question of obedience to an unjust authority Trudeau was very clear: humans possessed a right to overturn a corrupt social order:

> [Rebellion] is not to be condemned. On the contrary it is often indispensible to restoring justice and liberty among men. For society is made for man. If it becomes corrupt men have a right to overthrow it. Humans live in society in order that each can realize himself to the greatest extent. Authority's only justification is to permit and nurture an order which favours such a realization.[35]

Later in these essays he said:

> And if the only sure means to re-establish a just order is to make
> a revolution *against tyrannical and illegal authority* [Trudeau's ital-
> ics], well then it's necessary to do it it.[36]

The French and Russian revolutions were proof of this proposition, he believed.[37] Violence was justified if it was employed to overcome a regime that was "rotten, tyrannical, illegal and vicious."[38] He
denied that he was making a facile, capricious case for civil disobedience and tyrannicide. If "prudence and circumspection" had been
tried and if circumstances were extreme, resistance and revolution
were justified. Tyrannicide and civil disobedience were "exceptional measures to which one can only generally have recourse as
a last resort against illegitimate and tyrannical governments."[39] In
fact Trudeau took pains to emphasize that peaceful action was to
be preferred and that peaceable change was the special virtue of
democracy.[40]

Now, there seems a contradiction in all this. According to
Trudeau the people are both vicious and virtuous. Worse than that,
the contradiction is not even equipoised between the two for his
claim seems to be that the people are normally disposed towards
conformity and altogether uncaring of others. Yet he was hopeful. Humans *were* capable of identifying with the pain of others.[41]
Humanity *was* capable of imagining justice as a collaborative venture, and as acts of social solidarity and collective engagement:

> It is clear that in a society of egoists, each would want a govern-
> ment which would favour himself personally, even at the expense
> of the well-being of others. Each would therefore promise his
> support to a government which as circumstances provide will
> give him a bottle of beer, a refrigerator, church paving [and] a uni-
> versity grant. But a society of egoists is quickly turned into a soci-
> ety of slaves. For a man by himself is hardly capable of unsettling
> established governments which are not in any way weakened by

a single discontented citizen who no longer consents to obey the authorities. He will simply be imprisoned. To live in freedom citizens must therefore seek their good in a social order which would be just for the greatest number. In effect only the greatest number has the power to make and unmake governments. Thus men can only live freely and in peace if their society is just.[42]

And so Trudeau went on to offer an encomium to the democratic state as an instrument of the creative participation of the people, "creative liberty" as he called it:

For if it wishes to establish an order to which the citizens will consent to adhere, the State must not only explore their needs, it must also encourage them to demand those things that they consider just. In this way democracy will become a regime in which all the citizens will *participate* [Trudeau's emphasis] in government. The laws will reflect in a certain way the desires of the citizens and take advantage of the particular wisdom of each and in this fashion the social order will incorporate in a sort of way the complete richness flowing from all the human experience of the citizens.[43]

Thus democracy became for Trudeau an exercise in the mutual, progressive education of the moral sense of the citizen and her government. The solution to the political predicament of humanity and especially of Quebec was more democracy, which was the burden of another of his important statements at this time, "Un manifeste démocratique" in October 1958. Democracy was consensually based; it offered an opportunity to change governments without resort to violence; it respected the rule of law; it founded government on the common good or the general will rather than the sectional goods of particular groups; it respected individual rights; and it adhered to a consensual, popular, and participatory idea of sovereignty. The idea is almost pure Laski, as articulated in *A Grammar of Politics* and in the lectures that Trudeau had listened to at the LSE in 1947–48. Trudeau's reaction then had been to declare facetiously that such a version of democracy would involve too many meetings. For Laski recognized that if sovereignty was to be genuinely representative of the popular will then more than just traditional voting in parliamentary elections was required.

Hitherto, then, in the *Vrai* essays Trudeau's account of democracy and the social contract seems to have motored along unswervingly towards participatory, populist, and plebiscitary destinations, sounding more like Laski's early version of participatory pluralism than the theories of Locke or John Stuart Mill with their emphases on "democracy" as a representative and indirect system centred on the state. Towards the end of the essays, however, Trudeau began to apply the brakes and offer a more traditional and hierarchical account of where the journey was taking him. Modern democracy, he reasoned, mobilized the consent of everyone but it did so in an increasingly technically complicated world. Because of this, whatever else theories of social contract and popular sovereignty might entail they did not require direct democracy and plebiscites.[44] Simply put, for Trudeau, the people could not understand technical questions and so they should defer to experts who could. Parliamentary democracy was a system in which leaders were chosen by the people but the latter's active role was limited to choosing between two or three "general collections of ideas and tendencies" offered by competing political parties and their leaders.[45] In the absence of unanimity—almost inevitable in a complicated society—the victorious experts would usually be those favoured by the majority of the people. The majority principle, Trudeau conceded, perhaps with some embarrassment, was at best a "practical" and "conventional" guideline because there was no certainty that ninety-nine citizens knew the truth better than one single person.[45] No doubt this was his homage to John Stuart Mill and his conception of the heroic, individual critic as it was perhaps as well a niggling recognition that virtue inhered not in numbers but in right thinking. Nevertheless, in Trudeau's mind, though not perfect, the majority principle did have practical value. Invoking democracy's

precept of individual equality and admitting a passing though limited affinity for utilitarianism, he claimed that the "happiness" of 51
percent is more important than that of the other 49 percent.[46]

For Trudeau, then, democratic politics was a two-stage process: first, the election and, second, the period of government,
with the latter being about the implementation of what the government estimated was the will of the majority rather than being
about consulting the people directly or being instructed by them.
Quite explicitly he denied that popular consent required a direct
system of democratic rule and a muscular measure of popular participation. The consequence was that his model of the isomorphic
relationship of the people's will to that of the government's policies was left looking more like a glance across a great divide rather
than a close identity between the two. For we have now increasingly come to see that representative democracy gives the initiative
to the elites who dominate and control the public in all sorts of
effective ways, although this is something that in another context
Trudeau indicated that he knew only too well. Writing in 1961 he
talked of the power of bureaucracy and cabinet over parliament and
the courts, and of cabinets' own limited ability to control the hand-
ful of significant decision-makers in its midst.[47]

Thus setting out with an uncompromising account of democracy and the utopian ideal of government founded on the explicit
consent of everyone, Trudeau allowed elements of realism and
practicality to creep back into the picture. This was his wont. Ideals
must coexist with practical reality and they must not supplant it. In
his mind, in an age of increasing technological complexity, democracy was all about a Westminster-type, two-party competition, with
universal adult suffrage and majority popular rule albeit within a
system that must accord respect to the rights of minorities. Such a
system found a place within it for hierarchy and elitism. His ideal
of a perfectly confected scheme of consensual and popular sovereignty he put on hold and in effect he admitted that it was a utopian
plan for a very long march, if at all. The risk that dogged him was
that along the way realism, if not handled well, would make him

cautious and conventional, and, practically speaking, conservative. In his ideals Trudeau was a political anarchist who could only sanction a consensual state; but his realism turned him into an advocate of the British parliamentary system, on its best behaviour to be sure, but still far removed from what democracy might become.

III

Yet Trudeau was not without radicalism. Demonstrating his continuing affinity for left-wing ideas was his essay, "Economic Rights," which he presented at a conference in Ottawa in December 1958. Here he argued for an understanding of rights that went beyond the traditional civil libertarian paradigm with its emphasis on the protection of individual immunity freedoms—freedoms from the incursions of the state and other citizens and so on—in favour of a version of rights as empowering and providing citizens with circumstances and opportunities to live a life of personal fulfilment. Trudeau classified economic rights into two kinds: consumer rights and producer ones. "Man has a right to a share of the total wealth of society, sufficient to enable him to develop his personality to the fullest extent."[48] Consumer rights—he was talking of rights to levels of material consumption rather than protecting the consumer from market fraud—"imply that no man . . . should be entitled to superfluous or luxury goods, until the essentials of life are made available to every man."[49] Turning to Canada, it was a popular misconception, he said, that a general affluence was pervasive. On the contrary, one study had established that the vast majority of wage-earners there lived below a decent standard of living; depressed areas and "sub-marginal groups" continued to exist in the slums of large cities and among the "Indian and Eskimo" populations; the country lacked a comprehensive social insurance system; and the private enterprise system was biased because it failed to satisfy such "collective needs" as medical care, hospitals, urban renewal, recreational facilities, and roads and public services. Trudeau added an international dimension as well by commenting on the existence of a significant degree of hunger in the world:

The existence of the above-mentioned shortcomings makes it impossible for many citizens to exercise their human rights in non-economic fields. For instance, the cost of education and medical services prevent all citizens from having an equal chance to develop their intellectual and physical capacities. The high cost of litigation, in the absence of a universal system of legal aid, makes a farce out of the right of equality before the law. And the cost of conducting elections nullifies our high-sounding platitudes about political equality.[50]

Trudeau understood "producer rights" to be provisions that secured safe jobs, protected from employer discrimination, with fair remuneration and reasonable working conditions. He was especially concerned about "technological unemployment" and "the gigantic upheaval of workers" wrought by what he referred to as the third industrial revolution of automation, cybernetics, and thermonuclear power. As a consequence the government must become more involved in retraining and redeploying workers. Of course for Trudeau it was axiomatic that the attainment of his egalitarian vision presumed strong trade unions. Workers must be able to defend themselves and this certainly included a right to strike. But Trudeau went further and advocated what has later come to be called anti-scab legislation:

> In the same way that Capital can say: "Unless we make a sufficient profit in a given area, we will withdraw our investment, and there will be no more employment," likewise Labour must be able to say: "Unless we enjoy reasonable working terms in such-and-such a firm, we will withdraw and *there will be no more operations* [Trudeau's emphasis]." In other words, the right to strike must include the assurance that workers will be able to protect their jobs against strike-breakers and court injunctions.[52]

Trudeau also advocated industrial democracy in the work place.

And then he concluded with a comment of impressive moral advocacy: a new age was necessary, with new values. The "liberal" "bourgeois" era with its antiquated definition of property must be transcended. There must be a "transvaluation of values" that would bring in a new society.[53] For Trudeau the phrase likely derived from Laski although its origin derived from Nietzsche's denunciation of Christianity as a religion of weakness and humility, the very foundation of Mounier's critique of Catholicism in *L'affrontement chrétien*:

> It is the minds of men which must be changed, and their philosophies. For economic reform is impossible so long as we cling to economic concepts which were conceived for another age. The liberal idea of property helped to emancipate the bourgeoisie but it is now hampering our march towards economic democracy. The ancient values of private property have been carried over into the age of corporate wealth.
>
> As a result, our laws and our thinking recognise as proprietors of an enterprise men who today hold a few shares which they will sell tomorrow on the stock market; whereas workers who may have invested the better part of their lives and their hopes in a job have no proprietary right to that job, and may be expropriated from it *without compensation* whenever a strike or lock-out occurs, whenever they grow old, or whenever Capital decides to dis-invest.
>
> That same erroneous concept of property had erected a wall of prejudice against reform, and a wall of money against democratic control. As a consequence, powerful financial interests, monopolies and cartels are in a position to plan large sectors of the national economy for the profit of the few, rather than for the welfare of all, whereas any planning by the State, democratically controlled, is dismissed as bolchevism [*sic*] or worse.[54]

Trudeau thought highly enough of this essay to submit it to the *McGill Law Review*, where it appeared in 1962. It was published more or less verbatim though with an additional introductory paragraph that elaborated the argument of the original essay. His new remarks reiterated—no doubt for the benefit of lawyers reading the *Review*—that a civil liberties approach by itself was inadequate. The early modern legal and political revolutions, he said, were about the removal of the "fetters" of medieval rules and prescriptions and, to be sure, economic development in the early modern period was stupendous, but it was in the cause of an "economic Darwinianism" shot through with a "maximum self-assertion," with benefits only for some. Now people had come to realize that "civil rights availed them little against such realities as economic exploitation or massive unemployment."[55] The lesson was not that civil liberties were inconsequential but rather that they must be supplemented with economic rights:

> If the law was to be, as Dean Pound put it, "a continually more efficacious social engineering," it would have to provide a framework from which many of the existing causes of social friction and economic waste would be eradicated, and within which many economic 'necessities' would acquire the dignity and authority of "rights"[56]

If any single essay established Trudeau's identity as a socialist, it was this one. In it he distinguished between a negative and positive liberty and favoured both; there was a Marxist-sounding language though his argument was always subject to the priorities of democracy. Likely he had not yet read John Kenneth Galbraith's *The Affluent Society*, which he did in 1959, but there was an anticipation of its insights about how under capitalism there was a discrepancy between private affluence and public squalor.[57] And in its account of the nature of property the essay seemed to mirror C.B. Macpherson's intuitions about liberal possessive individualism though another likely source here was Laski's consideration of the same theme in his work on European liberalism. (Macpherson had been Laski's pupil too.) The reference to Roscoe Pound is suggestive and confirms once again that Trudeau had moved beyond a traditional liberal view of the state and civil society. Trudeau's argument against the market was an argument against monopolies and the effects of allowing private profit to destroy egalitarian priorities especially in regards to public goods like health, education, and public parks. There was again his frank recognition that planning was indispensible and his sense that capitalism had corrupted the political process. There was a regard for something called the common good. Above all there was a radical commitment to the cause of workers and their unions and to new, democratic arrangements for the workplace. This was not a completely Marxist theoretical framework but it was a socialist one, although in its refusal to make public ownership an absolute requirement it was more social democratic in temper. But it was a deeply subversive and oppositional problematic nonetheless.

Earlier, in May 1958, Trudeau also provided a significant commentary on the issue of foreign ownership. It came in his essay on the *Final Report of the Royal Commission on Canada's Economic Prospects* which had been established by the St. Laurent government in April 1955. The report was released by the new Conservative government of John Diefenbaker in April 1958, only to be "pointedly ignored" by it, as Denis Smith, author of an important biography on Diefenbaker, put it.[58] (Walter Gordon, who chaired the Commission, would go on to fame and some misfortune in the 1960s as Minister of Finance under Lester Pearson and principal Liberal advocate of the new economic nationalism.) The report itself was cautious in its conclusions, recommending greater Canadian shareholder participation in foreign-dominated businesses, increased Canadian participation in technical and management positions, and greater disclosure of the operations of foreign subsidiaries in Canada.[59]

Trudeau's response a month later, "À propos de 'domination économique'" was an intriguing mixture of practical and radical thinking, underlining again the degree to which he reverberated between the poles of practical action and radical reflection.[60] Foreign ownership he considered a serious problem; however, not

unexpectedly as an internationalist, he regarded foreign investment as part of the normal development of modern economies.[61]
Sometimes individual nation-states were debtor nations, he said,
but then they became creditor ones. But as the title of the essay intimated there could be relationships with investor nations that left
the host country "dominated." He did not exactly use the language
of imperialism though his mention of the American-sanctioned *coup
d'état* in Guatemala in 1954 on behalf of the United Fruit Company
implied that domination could have highly coercive implications
indeed. But, to repeat, the perspective he offered was of foreign
investment having an almost natural ebb and flow. The British had
industrialized by employing their own capital resources and savings
but had gone on to become creditors through investment abroad.
The United States had begun as a debtor nation but since 1914 had
become very successful in investing abroad. The British had invested
in Canada but their holdings were in bonds that did not bring direct
control; Americans had invested in Canada, especially after 1945,
and they had gained a controlling sway over a number of economic
sectors through equity ownership. What had recently aroused concern about American practices, said Trudeau, was the US government's insistence in late 1957 that the Canadian branch-plant of the
Ford Motor Company be forbidden from trading with Communist
China, thus revealing the nexus of American ownership abroad and
the imperatives of the American state. The United States, Trudeau
alleged, was an especially problematical adversary given that it
was not necessarily committed to freer trade, had been shrewd in
exploiting the advantages secured by its control of patents, and had
also been adroit in recruiting intellectual and scientific talent from
abroad. For Trudeau the special dilemma of Canada was not that
it had been in receipt of foreign capital but rather that it had come
to depend on it so rapidly and that it had been concentrated in the
strategic sectors of the future: mining, chemicals, oil and gas, auto-
mobiles, and industrial production in general. The over-determin-
ing nature of these investments had produced a controlling sway
over crucial national economic decisions:

The foreigner will decide if our oil-wells will be developed or closed down, if our minerals will be processed here or elsewhere, if our factories will be automated or not, if our products will be exported to the world market or not, if our workers will be free to exercise their right of association or not. The foreigner will decide . . . and will pocket the profits: in the post-war years, for example, 55% of dividends paid by Canadian companies were distributed to non-residents.[62]

Foreign-owned companies had also been remarkable for their high levels of retained earnings, which of course they had re-invested in their enterprises. Canadians desired liberation from such domination, Trudeau concluded. The question was, though, how far were they prepared to go to do something about it? Both the Liberals and the Conservatives, and the CCF too, were apathetic and non-committal. Economic domination was necessarily intertwined with political domination and so the political community needed to galvanize itself before it was too late.

Yet Canada was not without bargaining power, Trudeau claimed. The United States was running out of natural resources and Canada had a monopoly in some of them; Canada was an important market for the surplus goods produced by American industry and as well it provided opportunities for American profit in an environment of political security. These advantages should be mobilized by the country's leaders in order to direct capital into other channels, for example into social spending on schools, housing, and hospitals rather than factories and manufactures. Trudeau was making a complicated argument here. Priority, he said, should be given to social spending but it should not be forgotten that levels of social spending were connected to commercial and industrial development; commerce and business paid taxes that helped pay for social expenditures. And depending on the economic stage the country was passing through foreign investment could help or hinder. In a time of full employment foreign capital competed with domestic capital and drove up salaries and prices and increased the cost of social investments. Trudeau recommended that priority be given to a slower, more considered development of the country's natural resources. Canadian decision-makers needed to challenge the preconception that they must be developed as quickly as possible. There should be a slower rate of exploitation, especially of non-renewable ones, and a cycle of exploitation established that was not so emphatically given over to booms and busts. Canada was nevertheless in a position to negotiate "toughly" with the Americans over the following: employing more Canadian technicians and specialists in domestic industry; processing more Canadian resources at home; and investing more intensively in sectors where there existed a Canadian comparative advantage. Also, greater encouragement should be given to the unionization of Canada's work force. Finally Trudeau could not resist a tug on the beard of the foreign lion: if foreign capital became more cautious about investing in Canada then it might well choose to invest instead in other less fortunate countries thus promoting the well-being of people abroad!

However his final comments were steeped in a sober realism that he thought was all too often lacking in Canada's public and its leaders, and in Gordon's Royal Commission too. If greater encouragement were given to Canadian investment in Canadian enterprises then certain "corollaries" followed: Canadians must save more and invest in the dynamic sectors of the economy. If not, then government must become active in buying shares so that companies would become in different ways "nationalized." Trudeau's conviction was that if Canadians were serious about economic liberation they must become believers in planning and economic ownership by government. But he doubted that the elites and their publics were prepared to embrace such positions.

Once again Trudeau was exploring the interplay of high principle and effective action. In general, he said, there was nothing wrong with foreign investment but investment in general represented foregone consumption; the Americans had restrained their demands and saved more in order to invest abroad and Canadians would have to do the same. Canada had grown rapidly in the postwar years in part through foreign investment but with alarming consequences. It would be difficult for the country to confront its foreign dependence. Here spoke a social democrat who believed he was worldly-wise. Ill-conceived policies might prove useless and some policies—albeit well-meaning ones—would require significant and immediate sacrifices by some. Trudeau's account of foreign domination was intelligent and informed. In many ways his account anticipated the analysis of the branch-plant economy and the multi-national enterprise that became canonical in the late 1960s and 1970s after the publication of the Watkins Report in 1968—originally set in motion by Walter Gordon—and in the critiques by the Waffle group and NDPers like Charles Taylor and Ed Broadbent and such other economic nationalists as Kari Levitt, Abe Rotstein, and Denis Smith. Indeed Trudeau's insight that the Canadian state would be crucial to buying back Canadian industry prefigured the viewpoint of the Waffle group about how the fecklessness of the Canadian business class made necessary a statist policy of planning and ownership, in other words socialism. But, again, Trudeau's emphasis was that high principle in itself was not enough. The world's complexity had to be also acknowledged, in this case the inertia of public opinion and of society's governors. The logic of his position was that if the right prescriptions were lacking—and that was how he thought of Walter Gordon's *Final Report*—and if public opinion was not prepared for sacrifices and daring interventions, then it might be better to do nothing at all. In the real world, an idea might be theoretically right but this did not in itself justify its implementation.

IV

Another extensive essay elaborating Trudeau's socialism and the concatenation within it of realism and principle was his "The Practice and Theory of Federalism" in 1961. This was not so much, as its title suggested, about the Canadian constitution and federalism—federalism was a benefit, the BNA Act had much to recommend it, and co-operation between levels of government was an inevitable feature of the Canadian constitutional order—as it was about what he called "democratic socialism" and how it should adapt to the highly regionalized cultures of Canada.[63] Overall it was a more considered and less acerbic piece than other comments he made about the Left at this time as it morphed from the CCF to the NDP. He even had some kind words for left-wing idealists in his claim that "dreamers," "doctrinaires," and "theoreticians" were necessary to educate the party in the goals of socialism.[64] What socialists lacked, however, was a certain strategic sense. Trudeau never claimed that politics should be without principle. But if principle was what must inform political "application," it required an appreciation of context too.[65] This was again the emphasis of his position.

The argument of the essay can be summarized in five propositions. First, there was his general claim that socialism could be attained through a variety of means. Its goals had to do with egalitarian provisions, ensuring "everyone ... the good life" and "making available to all what we desire for ourselves," as Trudeau put it.[66] However such general ideals were useless unless they were actually achieved, he said. Conceiving ideals was not the same as attaining them, and simply desiring them had the same defect. Political ideals were realized neither through some indeterminate process of history nor by political willpower alone. There needed to be an intelligent, apposite selection of effective means. The various contexts of democratic engagement meant that democratic socialists must constantly assess the adequacy of different means and their relation to their ends. "For example, the nationalization of the instruments of production is now being considered less as an end than as a means, and one that might in many cases be replaced by more flexible processes of economic control and redistribution."[67]

Secondly, federalism was a "fact" in Canada; it was a "*chose donnée*"—how Trudeau loved that phrase—but the democratic Left had yet to come to terms with this. Traditionally the CCF had believed in central planning and had reasoned that the larger the territory over which planning was exercised, the more efficient and the more redistributivist would be its effects. This had led to its preference

for Canada-wide schemes of policy-making and for a centralizing, unitary version of federalism. Consequently the CCF was ill-
disposed towards the provinces and towards the idea that regional
and ethnic imperatives were as important as class-based ones. But,
said Trudeau, in a society of manifold regional-cultural identities
where provincial power mediated strong localist perspectives and
vice versa, provinces could be as important as the federal government. A radical policy could be as successfully pursued at the provincial level as at the national. Trudeau favoured neither level in
principle. The matter was one of contingency and circumstance.

> My plea is merely for greater realism and greater flexibility in the
> socialist approach to problems of federalism: I should like to see
> socialists feeling free to espouse whatever political trends or to
> use whatever constitutional tools happen to fit each particular
> problem at each particular time.[68]

His third point was that socialism, pursued democratically,
would be hedged around with restraints, but it could also gener-
ate opportunities. Democratic socialism proceeded gradually, step
by step, and the basic question must always be: "just how much
reform can the majority of people be brought to desire at the present time?"[69] Democracy constrained the idealist and the utopian
although he conceded that such people were necessary in politics. But the emphasis in democratic socialism must be as much
on strategy and tactics as on goals—perhaps more so, since goals
tended to be more nebulous and citizens less easily convinced of
their value than practical achievements. If actually existing democracy was one reality that must be recognized, equally the variety
of social and cultural cleavages in Canada must also be taken into
account.[70] In effect, he was repeating something he had said as early
as 1947, that Canada was a sort of sociological federation as well as a
constitutional one. There was not just one majority in Canada but
several regional ones as well. For Trudeau, then, the federal division of powers was an opportunity for socialists to win power in

the regions and to build "bridgeheads" that would make easier the winning of power nationally.[71]

Fourth, he contended that socialism had different meanings in different parts of the country, a view he had articulated as early as 1953. It was absurd for Canadian socialism to insist upon a single, unvarying, countrywide definition. Socialists should come to terms with Canada's diversity and its federal constitution. One type of left-wing political party in Canada, he continued, had been the tightly disciplined national one that sought to preach the same message everywhere. The risk in this was that, given cultural diversity, either the message would become unacceptable to some of its members over time or the party would never be able to recruit many members in the first place. This was the Quebec problem in a nutshell. What a party like the CCF had not been able to achieve, since it was immured within its unerring pan-national purpose, was to vary its message across the country or even to appeal to a narrower regionalism. What had been the CCF's abiding mistake, the NDP now risked repeating. It would always have a small band of disciples but, unless it changed its ways, it would be difficult for it ever to become a major party.

However, if the Left embraced federalism it could build up autonomous provincial parties through offering local versions of socialism. Regional success might invigorate the party. This would involve adjustments, however, in what the national party articulated as its policy:

> The policy of the national party will thus be the result of a compromise between the most and the least advanced socialist thinking in various parts of Canada.

Trudeau implied that this better model could already be observed in the Liberal Party:

> It is perhaps no coincidence that during the twentieth century . . . the one national party that has been strongest and governed

longest is the party that has traditionally stood for provincial rights and embraced in its ranks such provincial free-stylers as Taschereau, Hepburn, Angus Macdonald, and Smallwood. For even while the Liberals at Ottawa were riding the wave of centralism, Liberal leaders in provincial capitals were stoutly defending the cause of autonomy.[72]

Trudeau's inference was that a national party of the Left should place a greater emphasis upon its provincial sections and their distinctive views and at a minimum the regional party should see itself as more than the local voice of the national party:

> Just as each province must evolve towards political and economic maturity in its own good time, likewise radicalism in different parts of Canada must be implanted in different fashions. For a time, parties with the same name may find themselves preaching policies differing in scope from one province to the other. Perhaps even parties with different names may preach the same ideology in different provinces.[73]

Here Trudeau was suggesting further ways to understand the political implications of pluralism. The first was that the national policy of a political party might be a compromise between the extremes of its different sections and local positions; and the second—the Liberals were an example of it—that the national party might ideally embrace centralism at the same time as its provincial sections emphasized provincial autonomy. In the second case the Liberals had embraced one extreme federally and another extreme at the provincial level, both at the same time. Its national position, far from being a compromise of a variety of regional variants, was actually an "extreme" one. The happy compromise in that case might have been something along the lines of balanced federalism at the national level but that was precluded by its decision to be centralizing at the federal level. Then there was a third possibility—parties of different names in different provinces might believe the same thing.

There are, then, ambiguities here. However conceived, Trudeau's immersion in pluralism is hard to reconcile completely with the time-honoured priority he typically accorded to philosophical coherence as a desirable feature of a Canadian political party. He seems to say that, in actuality, practical, well-adapted socialism—indeed any political idea in Canada—entailed diversity and contradictoriness, indeed the opposite of the idea of a national party that preached the same thing everywhere and at every level of government.

Trudeau's final, fifth proposition was that the type of theory that socialist politics in Canada must necessarily presume was "pragmatism." The latter accepted the realities of both federalism and democracy and should make strategic choices within them. The other word he used was, of course, "realism." But his pragmatism/realism had a clear, normative framework. It presumed the goals of socialism and was fuelled by the ideals of progressivism, what Trudeau called "justice, freedom and change." But it must be constrained by realities, especially the reality of democracy. Progressives tended to exaggerate the people's desire for socialist ideals. Here they must learn to be pragmatic as well: "The true tactical position of the *democratic* socialist is on the left, *but no further.*"[74] Trudeau used the same epigram elsewhere.

V

Some final comments on Trudeau's socialism and his economic views in the late 1950s and early 1960s. According to Christina McCall and Stephen Clarkson, Trudeau at this time was "less than wholehearted [in his] flirtation with socialism."[75] Referring to the article on "Economic Rights" they point out that in the 1950s "while he was managing his family's substantial trust," Trudeau "affected" a socialist analysis.[76] His offence was that he was, like Friedrich Engels, a rich socialist, and presumably an inauthentic one. However, taken at their face value, Trudeau's essays at the time, and especially the ones on economic rights and foreign domination, confirm him as an intellectual socialist. He emphasized the failures of capitalism and the need for state intervention on behalf of workers and the poor. What was also patently absent at this time—indeed throughout his later life—was any avowal in principle of the unalloyed merits of markets, laissez-faire, free enterprise, and capitalism. But his socialism was always coupled with realism and a sense of moderation and so his pragmatism inevitably affected how he viewed and behaved towards the existing reality of capitalism.

McCall and Clarkson have other complaints. Continuing the theme of Trudeau as a shallow or ersatz socialist—Reg Whitaker is of a similar mind—they allege that whatever left-wing proclivities Trudeau might have displayed were anyway irrelevant because under the influence of Albert Breton and a small, informal Montreal-based policy group, Le comité pour une politique fonctionelle, he jettisoned such views between 1962 and 1965 in favour of neo-classical, free market, and American economic ideas.[77] The Comité had come together in 1962 and was the brainchild of Albert Breton, a professor, and Marc Lalonde, a Montreal lawyer and activist, who, having met one day by chance in Outremont, conceived of an informal discussion group that would challenge the shibboleths and habits of Canadian politics, particularly what Breton called the "obscure and dangerous forces at play in Quebec." The several founding members had been intrigued by Trudeau's original articles on political functionalism and in some part their project became to imagine how his early abstractions might be shaped into policy prescriptions.[78] At the time Breton held a position in the Economics Department of the University of Montreal and regularly met with Trudeau. He has characterized his relationship with him at the beginning as being one of teacher and student:

> We talked about [separatism], but mostly about federalism. Pierre got me to read The Federalist Papers. Reading, I made notes, prepared questions which he answered. As in other areas of life, Pierre had a most powerful memory: he could and did quote from the Papers from memory. I was having no influence on him; I was being educated.[79]

However, there is no doubt that Breton influenced Trudeau in his thinking about nationalism, particularly with his 1964 article, "The Economics of Nationalism."[80]

Undoubtedly Breton was an exponent of classical economic theory. He espoused a materialist, utilitarian account of human motivation in which self-interest and economic motives were predominant. He believed in free trade and market allocations and what has come to be called rational choice theory. His life-work was mainly given over to understanding the circulation and competition within government systems of "public goods" like security, tax revenue, and organizational power. He suggested especially that the rational choice theory of *private* market analysis could be productively used to make sense of the phenomenon of *public* goods. As Breton put it: "[I] applied the methodology of neo-classical economics to the analysis of non-economic problems."[81] Nationalism was one such public good and Breton's conclusion was that it was a sort of epiphenomenon that masked the class-based motives of middle-class technocrats. This idea certainly appealed to Trudeau, but that was all.

Trudeau signed his name, as did Albert Breton and five others—Raymond Breton (Albert's brother), Marc Lalonde, Claude Bruneau, Yvon Gauthier, and Maurice Pinard—to two articles produced by the Comité: "Pour une politique fonctionelle" in May 1964 in *Cité Libre* and an extensive piece in the same review in July 1965, "L'agriculture au Québec." Both essays were generally dismissive of nationalism and were predisposed towards "universal" values; Trudeau had held such views for a long time. On economic matters the two articles did not necessarily extol free markets unless it is held that in their eschewing of a statist economy they were thereby prescribing a free enterprise one. If anything the dominant mindset of the essays was radically reformist and modernizing, with a technocratic bent towards rationalization. For example in the article on agriculture in Quebec what they advocated was a system-wide development of larger farms and greater mechanization and capitalization. The article opposed subsidies but presupposed an enabling role by the state sorting out the problems of low-income farmers. A crucial premise of its analysis was that the issue was not unique to Quebec but was part of a pan-Canadian problem.

The other essay, the manifesto of the group, mined similar themes. It also called for a fresh approach to policy-making and a greater adaptation to change. It called for a style of political communication that was less emotional and propagandistic and more oriented to clarity and precision; a more developed welfare state was presumed, with economic planning but also free trade. Overall its themes were about the importance of rigorous "objective" analysis, honesty, problem-solving, and "rationality" in decision-making. Most of these perspectives, again, Trudeau had espoused since his earliest articles in *Cité Libre*. But there was no extolling of free markets, *per se*. Private markets were presumed to be part of the economic landscape but the overall approach was a mixed one, partly directive and statist and partly market-oriented and voluntarist, but above all driven by the imperative of solving actual problems.

If McCall and Clarkson's argument about a liberal turn at this time by Trudeau is a weak one, it is perhaps because they do not understand his fundamental method. They seem to believe that Trudeau was moved by pure ideas. Their model is a rationalist one of Trudeau as a sort of all-powerful Zarathustra whose beliefs were revealed in his actions. If his behaviour changed, this must have been because his beliefs had altered. But this is to overlook the emphatically pragmatic streak that had existed all along in Trudeau's thinking. If it was that politics for Trudeau was a tense, dialectical interplay between theory and practice, then one understands his action not just by establishing what he believed but by appreciating the circumstances and situations he confronted and his calculus of engagement. It does not always follow that a given action expresses a given value or belief. That Trudeau as Prime Minister was slow to act on the issue of foreign ownership—a criticism particularly made by McCall and Clarkson—does not mean that he did not believe it was a problem. That he did not eradicate capitalism and markets in his time does not mean, as Whitaker,

McCall, and Clarkson allege, that he believed fundamentally in capitalism and markets. It is quite possible to believe that when Trudeau joined the Liberal Party in 1965 he did so not as a newly enlightened liberal (as McCall and Clarkson would have it), but as a socialist of a social democratic sort who saw no better course of action to achieve his beliefs.

Above, from left: mid 1940s; *Jeunesse Canadienne,* November 1947; June 1948. (All material in this insert is from the Trudeau Papers, LAC MG 26-02. Box and file, from left: 11.2; 8.22; 8.22.)

Above, from left: 1948; 1949; September 1951. (LAC MG 26-02. From left, 8.22; 11.2; 12.3.)

Above, from left: June 1952; March 1960; Charles Taylor, Election Campaign card, 1965. (LAC MG 26-02. From left: 12.3; 13.10; 14.13.)

Trudeau's life-studies. (Trudeau Papers, LAC: n.d. 14.13.)

7

Trudeau Abroad

———— ◦ ◆ ◦ ————

Of generalizations injustices come. They become "degeneralizations."
Pierre Elliott Trudeau

It is a clever man who can foretell the shape of Chinese politics.
Pierre Elliott Trudeau

(T)he second reason for my preference for federalism (is): "To govern is to foresee."' I mean that any political formula worth the name is by definition oriented toward the future. Now, the future is the rapprochement between peoples; it consists in pooling the wealth of the world; it is the march towards unity or it is atomic warfare.
Pierre Elliott Trudeau

I have a liking for people and I try to understand them. . . . I feel that governments in most lands, even those we don't agree with are generally trying to govern, no matter how misguided they may seem, for the good of the people. . . . I believe in the social contract. It isn't applicable in these quasi-totalitarian countries but, still, by going to these lands you see such different social and economic situations that you realize your political standards are not necessarily applicable there and you see especially how dependent you are . . . when you are bumming through China with just a little packsack and you can't speak the language; you feel how much you need the friendship and the co-operation of the people. Otherwise you will just starve to death out in the rain. But people like you if you come there rather humbly and if you make them feel you are not trying to run anything but you are asking them for their friendship . . . By travelling I've come to the conclusion that the world is such a diversified place that we

*need institutions that are democratic and forms of government
which permit the co-existence of various ethnic groups [and] various
linguistic communities.*

Pierre Elliott Trudeau

I

Although a paragon of consistency on some things—one thinks
of his opposition to nationalism and his advocacy of federalism—
Trudeau was not so on everything. He did have a genuine interest
in other countries and their peoples and a desire to explore and
understand them, but he was not beyond casting a cold eye on their
practices and folkways. Trudeau was the consummate romantic
traveller exulting in the unique and eccentric experiences that he
encountered yet he was a restless and candid critic too. There were
other contradictions. Steeped in what he regarded as the authoritarian culture of Duplessis's Quebec and persuaded that the state
was invariably a conspiracy of the rich and powerful to exploit and
control the people who in any event were usually submissive and
conformist, it is more than a little surprising to hear Trudeau talk
of the general tendency of governments everywhere to "[try] to
govern . . . for the good of the people."

Trudeau's appetite for world travel was insatiable. Beginning
with his earliest periodic trips to the United States, then to Mexico
in 1944, and to the United States, France, and Britain for further university education, Trudeau voyaged to far-flung places almost every
year. In 1948–49 there was his famous trek through Europe and the
Near and Far East, and to Egypt and Sudan, and the USSR in 1951–52;
Pakistan, India, Indonesia, Australia, and New Zealand in 1954; Ghana
and other parts of West Africa in 1957; Israel, Vietnam, Persia, and
Taiwan in 1959; China in 1960; and Cuba in 1961. And these were only
the high points of his journeys. He was a regular visitor to Europe for
vacations in Italy, Spain, Yugoslavia, and France and for political conferences such as that of the British Labour Party in Margate in 1955
and of the Socialist International in Hamburg in 1959.[1] Trudeau was

a self-described *"flâneur"* and bohemian. An attentive observer, he loved to float, detached, across and above life's surfaces. In a sense he was profoundly superficial. He was inordinately self-contained and adventurous too. He yearned to rise to meet the open road, voyaging he knew not where and confronting he knew not what. His love of white-water canoeing expressed this sensibility perfectly. There was something especially inspiring for him in pursuing the foreign, the exotic, the mysterious, the erotic, and the dangerous. His was an attempt to measure himself against the weight and the edge of the world; or as he once put it, "to test the elasticity of my bonds."[2] Speaking on Radio-Canada in September 1952 he reported his excitement at confronting a new land:

> I had ceased to wonder about the unbelievable good luck that found me in this impenetrable Russia; and with my forehead pressed against the frozen window I would gaze, now at the night plains, then the sombre outline of the forest, and the occasional pale light of a genuine *izba* [Russian log house] where real Russians lived. I was flooded with that joy that new sensations bring: the first time one tastes a mango, the first sight of the Taj Mahal, the first underwater dive, the first kiss. . . . It was my first visit to the USSR and I kept quiet to savour all the emotion.[3]

The ultimate of courage was to risk all, or almost all, in pursuit of adventure, secured by little more than one's intellect and ingenuity. In 1949 in China he hoped to be present when the Communists took over:

> Red armies are forming up and down the Yangtse [*sic*], everyone here seems to admit that it is only a question of time before they arrive in Shanghai. I sure would like to be here for the kill and see their operations at first hand.[4]

There was a sensual dimension too. He was intrigued by the erotic friezes on Hindu temples in Nepal; in China in 1960 he flirted incorrigibly with his Communist guide as he had done earlier in the USSR; and then there was the beauty of Vietnamese women: "Satin tunics down to their waist and beneath them long, billowing, satin trousers ... their hair tied back, waist-length."[5] Sensuality had its gastronomic aspects and Trudeau relished the delicacies and sometimes the indelicacies of foreign cuisine. On his trip to China in 1960 a serving of slugs went beyond even his stomach. But mostly his journeys were intellectual and moral adventures and in them he reached for deep explanations of things, for "spiritual and intellectual simplification," and for a "key" to the complexity of human relations and "the simplicity of being," as he put it in 1948–49.[6] Trudeau's ambition was somehow to achieve a kind of primary knowledge of the world and to enlarge his literary imagination and moral acuity in a boundless encounter with universal humanity. With his emerging socialist consciousness, he wished to identify with the common man and small nations and peoples of the world.[7] His was an intensely deep search for meaning and virtue. Life's surfaces were abundantly captivating but so were its depths.

He took great risks: during the Israel–Palestine–Arab conflict in 1948 escaping from agitated Arab irregulars who thought him a Jew; in Cairo dealing with an angry crowd seized by the belief that he was a British citizen; nosing close to Vietminh insurgents in Indo-China; skirting the chaos of revolutionary Shanghai; swimming the Bosphorus; and resisting the fast-moving current of a northern Canadian river; to name just a few. Certainly there was exaggeration in his reporting but there were moments of real danger too.[8] Participating in such experiences took great courage and sometimes produced exceptional investigative journalism but it could also represent foolish bravado. Think of his running with the bulls in Pamplona and his venture to row to Cuba from Florida in 1960. Here was a strange mixture of the genuinely heroic with the potentially farcical and preposterous. It was as if he believed that his life could only be justified if it was lived with theatricality at the edge of risk, tempting *fortuna* and never taking life too seriously, the tightrope artist traversing the gorge who on completing his walk announces that life is noble and beautiful but also faintly laughable. Risk was courted for the hell of it and to allow an exciting story to be told. Through self-imposed exigencies Trudeau believed also that he might discover the extraordinary and the exquisite, perhaps even the absolute, amidst the everyday. It was an important part of his sense of transcendence. He needed extremes. It was an especially solitary and individual compulsion too. He willed to be alone in and against the world. This was often difficult for the women who loved him.

But Trudeau did not always travel alone and not always without female companionship, and as time went by he travelled in greater physical comfort, staying in hotels, some of which were quite luxurious. On his first Asian trek he depended on the hospitality of Catholic priests—not always provided, he said—and roughing it and staying in hostels. In Saigon he talked of sleeping in "a makeshift dormitory [that was] hot, noisy and crowded."[9] There were communities of the moment he moved in and out of, some of them not altogether enjoyable to be part of. In Cambodia he described squeezing into a "Chinese bus":

> Till 8 p.m. we travelled in the sickening heat, and between some of the most filthy Orientals I have yet had the honor to meet. In all my travels, I have never had such a disgusting trip, at times I was hoping that the convoy would be attacked and a few of us killed off, to make room for the rest.[10]

(Trudeau's humour could be dark.) Evident also was his inclination to break away, go it alone, and test himself. In China in 1949 he climbed up a mountain on a rainy night to reach a Taoist monastery, and in 1952 he tricked his Communist minders and wandered alone through the streets of Moscow. He also recounted escaping his guides, hiding behind a pillar in Tiananmen Square in Beijing in 1960, and being "swallowed" up by the crowd during the celebrations of the Chinese Revolution:

He participated [Trudeau reported] in strange dances, in frenzied music, in spontaneous skits, in sweet flirtations; he described exotic orchestras, whimsical costumes, unusual friendships, and new scents; he told of jackets of imitation leather, black pigtails, curious children, laughing adolescents, [and] convivial and joyful men.[11]

Trudeau never asked himself whether everyone could live lives of such spontaneous and privileged abandon and, if he had, he would likely have doubted that they could and, anyway, he was uncomfortable with the idea of others following him. But it was an absolute necessity for him. Here were measures of self-absorption and solipsism but also of bold questing. Trudeau exemplified a kind of "heroic individualism."[12] Was it a sort of warrior complex that he exhibited: assertive, virile, and unambiguous? Yet though touched more than a little by an aggressive Prometheanism that challenged the gods and by an erotic inclination that thumbed its nose at sexual convention, Trudeau's inner and outer journeys, for all their adventurousness and sometimes recklessness, were undertaken within a Christian horizon. He was an avid disciple of Jesus, but also of Siddhartha and Casanova, with Cyrano de Bergerac thrown in for a dash of humour.

Perhaps because of his many personae and the evident success with which he explored them, there is a temptation to mythify Trudeau. Indeed he was a human being extraordinaire and a cosmopolitan par excellence. Yet he was, inevitably, a person of partial and incomplete judgment and insight. We should avoid the tendency to see his world travels and his account of global affairs—or indeed any part of his life and thought—as emerging immaculately from a perfect understanding. Even his cosmopolitanism was a work in progress and especially on his first world trek there is much to suggest that he had not totally left behind the narrow nativism of a conservative, Catholic Quebec. Equally there was evidence of an impressive opening to the future. But even in this he could never be a complete master so that he too was subject to the contingencies of time and its surprising ambiguities and gyrations.

II

And so one day in June 1948 Trudeau departed London with little more than what he could put in a backpack and headed eastwards.[13] He travelled by boat and train and, at first, in the company of two companions. He would not return to Canada until ten months later. Early in his journey he attended an international socialist youth camp in Ebensee in Austria and visited a displaced persons' camp in Salzburg. In Poland he visited the site of the Auschwitz concentration camp. Another early destination was Otwock, near Warsaw, to participate as an observer at "a conference of intellectuals," as he described it.[14] The conference was a meeting of the World Federation of Democratic Youth, which was almost certainly a Communist-inspired organization and part of the overall strategy conceived after September 1947 by the newly established Communist Information Bureau (Cominform) and its director Andrei Zhdanov, Stalin's cultural commissar and guardian of socialist realism.[15] Its goal was to recruit left-leaning and independent intellectuals to the cause of peace and economic co-operation and to bolster Soviet interests in the emerging Cold War.[16] If Trudeau was initially not aware of the Otwock conference's connection to Moscow, he certainly was by the time he had attended it. His attendance there was, however, revealing of his political inclinations at the time. He was a man of the Left.

It was the time when, as Winston Churchill famously put it, the Iron Curtain was clanging into place and separating a vauntedly liberal-democratic West, led by the United States, from a communist East with the Soviet Union at its summit. Wartime allies were becoming peacetime enemies. In March 1947 President Truman had enunciated his famous doctrine of "containment" and its support for "free peoples" against communism. Western Europe now became more deeply antagonistic towards communism and sought greater security through NATO and through economic integration and initiatives such as the eventual European Coal and Steel Community in 1950, the forerunner of the European Economic Community.[17] The Cold War intensified western Europe's resolve to place itself more emphatically under the American security umbrella. Consequently the postwar popularity of Communist parties in the West declined and this particularly had ramifications for their participation in the French and Italian governments. The Soviets and their allies were active as well. The USSR consolidated its hold over eastern Europe and established the Cominform. A Communist coup followed in Czechoslovakia in February 1948; and in the very month Trudeau set out on his journey, the Soviet Union began a blockade of West Berlin. All were auguries of the new, deeper fissures opening up across the continent. Europe's future was uncertain. Three years after the war, displaced persons' camps still existed, cities remained in ruins, political and economic reconstruction proceeded only slowly, and hanging over everything was the ominous foreboding of the nuclear age, with the United States having already demonstrated the destructiveness of the atomic bomb in August 1945 and the USSR poised to acquire one in 1949. What was true of Europe was true of the Middle East and Asia. A great political ferment was abroad along with deep antipathies.

Trudeau journeyed through Austria, Hungary, Yugoslavia, Bulgaria, and Greece, and on to Turkey, Lebanon, Syria, and Palestine. He arrived in the Middle East soon after the declaration of the new state of Israel in May 1948 and the outbreak of war between Israel and its Palestinian and Arab neighbours. Trudeau moved on to Iraq and then Persia and Afghanistan, Nepal, Pakistan, and India, the last two still recovering from the pogroms and dislocations brought on by independence and partition after 1947. He tried unsuccessfully to enter Kashmir. After that it was from Kolkata across the Bay of Bengal by ship to Rangoon, Burma, and then to Thailand, Cambodia, and Vietnam. In Indo-China there was civil war and revolution, with the Vietminh under Ho Chi Minh increasingly in the ascendant and throughout the region a palpable sense of things falling apart. Trudeau moved on to Hong Kong and then mainland China where the civil war was coming to an end with the Communists under Mao Zedong finally triumphant with the proclamation of the People's Republic of China (PRC) in October 1949. Trudeau regretted missing the final apotheosis of the revolution, having already boarded a ship in March to return to Canada.

He had moved through a troubled and shifting landscape where danger was ever present so that he might not have survived at all and, if he had, he might have become a hopeless cynic. Indeed such sentiments were not beyond him. Writing about the war in Vietnam he talked of the suffering and atrocities committed on both sides in the name of "elusive righteousness and honor":

> This is indeed a strange war: on one side you find patriotic fighters for freedom for self-determination, coupled together with cynical Stalinists and bloodthirsty thieves. On the other side, you find bewildered idealists joined together with greedy Imperialists and disguisting [*sic*] knaves. Politics thy name is mud.[18]

But his comments mainly affirmed a progressive understanding. History was moving upwards and the people were finally entering history. But progress was not inevitable. The Great Powers with their imperialist ambitions constituted powerful vested interests and he wondered whether local revolutionary elites possessed sufficient competence and public spirit to lead their peoples towards true equality and freedom. While Trudeau sought above all to be dispassionate, generally he tilted towards the new left-wing order in what would come to be called the Second World of the Communist bloc and the Third World of the underdeveloped nations of Asia, Latin America, and Africa.

Trudeau travelled with strong convictions, or it was that his travels brought out in him strong convictions. The times were an extraordinary moment in which long established struggles would be resolved. It was, he thought, the epoch of a world-historical struggle between Christianity and Marxism as both ostensibly vied for dominance of the global community. Trudeau thought

in universalist terms, yet he was only too aware of cultural particularities. He was seized by the divergencies between what he
called "East" and "West" and he hoped to promote a "synthesis"
between them.[19] Cultures were coming together, naturally, or it
was that Trudeau thought they ought to come together in some
intercultural compromise. The fate and well-being of one part of
the world involved the other. Trudeau seemed to overlook the fact
that Christianity and Marxism—the main contending forces—
both represented Western forms of thinking so that in effect the
great struggle was going on within the West for dominance of the
rest of the world. If challenged, he would likely have argued that
the East embodied auspicious cultural achievements that could
enlarge the experience of the West. But much of his actual commentary in the late 1940s was critical of Eastern practices and
norms. The East was for Trudeau a place of incompleteness and
inadequacy. He was seized, unconsciously, by a sort of "orientalist" perspective as Edward W. Said put it in his famous work,
Orientalism (1978). For Trudeau the East was a place imagined by
the West where Western preconceptions were destined to play out
and prevail. But, providing a counterbalancing and contradictory
tendency within him, the East was more than a geographic cat-
egory. It also encompassed peoples and societies who had suffered
under the imperialist yoke: the Middle East and Asia, of course,
but also Africa and South America. That is, for Trudeau the East
was a shorthand for the Third World. His Christian socialism,
then, represented an interesting and paradoxical mixture of religious and secular themes of universal justice but expressed within
mainly Western and Christian categories. Trudeau thought globally—how prescient he was in this—but he carried within himself
a kind of Western nativism. He wanted to learn from the East,
especially from their religions; but the East had much to learn
from the West.

Trudeau's version of Christianity at this time, we noticed earlier, was a gospel of love, forgiveness, and justice. Concerned for
the fate of the Catholic Church he worried over whether, in its

presently unreformed condition, it was capable of attaining such high ideals.[20] Trudeau was guided by the message of personalism—that eminently Christian and Western idea—about the dignity of the individual and the importance of altruism, political liberty, religious tolerance, and equality before the law. (Trudeau did not include a belief in economic laissez-faire as part of personalism's inheritance.) As he journeyed he saw himself as a kind of Christian pilgrim. His travels took him to the Holy Land, where he was very aware of treading in the very places that Jesus Christ had trod. He lamented the hatreds let loose in the world and mused on the parable of the Good Samaritan and the question of who was one's neighbour.[21] Above all this pilgrim sought a revelation of moral simplicity amidst the complexities of the world. At one point in his notebooks he announced that the central purpose of existence was "to put into men's hands the conditions of happiness." Christianity, he believed, was fundamentally a crusade against poverty and a yearning for material equality which, once achieved, would permit humanity better to drink from the deep wells of spirituality. The spiritual was important to Trudeau but no more than the material; the two were interrelated and equibalanced. Some got the balance wrong. The Church was perhaps too spiritually inclined; and, like Mounier, he held that a central deficiency of Marxism was its overly materialistic world view. Mankind did not live by bread alone but bread for everyone was a fundamental necessity

A Christian social ethic must, therefore, prevail but it should be sought democratically and peaceably. Change imposed from on high through aristocratic or authoritarian methods never succeeded because ruling classes were inevitably self-serving. However class conflict was to be avoided even though his main point was that what most ailed humanity was material deprivation and political oppression. The problem with those who single-mindedly fought the class struggle was that invariably they came to express a narrow, vindictive ethos in turn. Instead there needed to be a "fraternity of classes" in pursuit of a common good. Trudeau was not making a case for protecting the rich and powerful. His perspective was indeed a radical, egalitarian one but he wished to eschew the nastiness of actual class struggles, especially those prosecuted by communists. Ensconced in power the newly liberated poor could be as brutal and wicked as anyone, he maintained. In contrast a social democratic Christianity embodied his concerns: it was inclusive and open, pacific and loving, and it preached respect for all persons. History was moving in the direction of popular rule and Christianity had a chance to compete with Marxism and to prevail. Trudeau was open to exploring what other religions had to say about such fundamental things. The East, he felt, was particularly a place of spirituality and mysticism; this was its mystique. But for now he said little on such topics, and the little he did say was not always positive. Confucianism, he said, was a conservative political doctrine that entrenched established social status and control and led to authoritarianism; and Hinduism was greatly compromised by its sanctioning of castes. As for Islam it was "a religion of form and not of the heart." His contention was that Christianity was central to the winning of a democratic and socialist world. For Trudeau, even dressed in a more progressive garb, Christianity and the Church still had decidedly missionary roles to play.

Trudeau's early concern about communism was that it was essentially opportunistic. It had taken advantage of the collapse of the postwar order to become by default the voice of a rising humanity. People supported the communists because they offered the "illusion" of being their partisans. Liberty was on everyone's lips and the people were prepared to die for a "beautiful idea" and the happiness of future generations: "It is the curious power of an idea which has no regard for transcendence," Trudeau said. But communism brought injustices and shortcomings of its own. In Eastern Europe it had installed the cult of personality in Stalin's Russia, Tito's Yugoslavia, and Dimitrov's Bulgaria, and its version of democracy presupposed a majoritarian tyranny such was its disregard for the rights of minorities and its eagerness to eradicate fascism and vested interests. In Asia it was taking advantage of the unpopularity of the imperialists to lead wars of national liberation that cleverly combined nationalism with socialism. In these situations especially, said Trudeau, it exploited the mystical tendencies of Oriental people and their willingness to die for a cause.

To repeat, Trudeau sought to be even-handed in his judgments and he recognized communist successes wherever they did occur. The governments of Poland and Czechoslovakia had some legitimacy, he said, because they provided a higher standard of living, while in Vietnam the Vietminh had organized their "liberated" areas in support of social and economic development. But communism everywhere was sectarian and violent and anti-democratic, he said. At bottom it might well be that Ho Chi Minh was an opportunist. At the conference in Otwock Trudeau had noted the use of propaganda methods and the manipulation of proceedings by those behind the scenes in the cause of producing some kind of unanimity. He worried about the Communist coup in Prague —it was a "*coup de force*" he said—and he was concerned about communist and Soviet political manoeuvrings in Poland and Hungary. Yet Trudeau never concluded that communism was a flawed doctrine to be rejected altogether or to be resisted to the point of elimination so that on his world trek in 1948–49 it is evident that the seeds of his future conditional engagement with communism were being germinated. Nevertheless, even though encouraged by French and British retreats from empire, especially in Asia, Trudeau was sufficiently moved by doubts about communism's fitness to rule that he argued in favour of a controlled withdrawal by the imperial powers and for the UN to play a role as mediator and guarantor of what he hoped would become a new democratic order.

If he felt that the imperialist powers must not depart too quickly, he was nonetheless utterly convinced of their lack of political legitimacy, especially in the Near East and Asia. He would in early 1952 turn his attention—and with similar conclusions—to their role in Africa and especially British imperialism in Egypt and Sudan.[22] For now Trudeau did not go deeply into the roots of imperialism but clearly he saw it as driven by the desire for political power and economic advantage; and it represented a misplaced sense of cultural superiority towards the colonized. If there was a difference between the British and the French it was only in small details: "For the English the native is a child under their guardianship. . . . For the French the native does not exist at all." Imperial powers were essentially conservative and self-serving, and of course mercenary and exploitative. He offered no sense of their having contributed to the well-being of their domains. (His argument that in Canada the English had transmitted a kind of liberalism to French Canadians sticks out as a great exception but his main point there was that it had been French-Canadian pressure and other contingencies that had forced Britain's hand.) The United States, the most recent addition to the imperialist club, was no different, he thought. In throwing its support behind Chiang Kai-shek, the leader of the Nationalist Party (Guomindang) in China, it was protecting big business, sanctioning corruption, and aligning with vested agrarian interests. His special anxiety for the Catholic Church in China was that it was too close to Chiang and the Americans.

He continued: imperialist states were slippery in their diplomatic habits. The British had played both sides of the street in Palestine, garnering Jewish support through the Balfour Declaration in 1917 to establish a national home for Jews in Palestine; however, at the same time, they were promising freedom to the Arabs. Britain always took care not to jeopardize its commercial and strategic interests in the region—its military bases, the Suez Canal, and its access to Arab petroleum—by offending Arab countries. And of course empires in general had a vested interest in keeping their colonies in endless tutelage and underdevelopment. In little ways they exhibited arbitrary power: thus France had taken advantage of its position in Syria and Indo-China to use these places as a dumping ground for the "dimwits" of its colonial service. Yet, even as he condemned Western imperialist countries, Trudeau leaned over backwards to avoid criticizing any incipient Soviet and Chinese imperialism in Europe and Asia. Moscow, he said, tended not to send its citizens to occupy other countries but rather trained foreigners in the Soviet Union before returning them to their homeland. And it only dominated govern-ments whose territories were contiguous with itself or which were geographically part of its zone of influence. Even there it had not been established, he said, that Soviet domination had been trans-lated into economic slavery. Trudeau doubted that the economies of Soviet client states would be impoverished in order to enrich the USSR.[23]

In the emerging world order, as revealed in his travel notebooks of 1948–49, Trudeau was unmistakably on the side of the poor and dispossessed. He was fervently anti-imperialist and anti-colonialist, even invoking a Fanon-like Freudian insight about how the purpose of imperialists, or as he also sometimes called it "the metropole," was to inculcate a collective inferiority complex in the conscious-ness of the native. In some local conflicts such as that between the Jews and Arabs he tended to see virtue and vice on both sides. But he condemned wholesale the Great Powers—all of them imperial-ist—with the single exception of the Soviet Union.

Edward Said has exposed a type of Orientalism that depends on scientific, rationalist, and materialist methods to represent an Orient where collective phenomena are catalogued and given an objective status in reality.[24] Such "descriptions" inevitably contain judgements about the morality and cultural adequacy of the Other and intimate that the identities of Oriental groups are invariable and unchanging "generalizations" that produce "immutable laws."[25] "Orientalism assumed an unchanging Orient."[26] This way of think-ing draws the inevitable criticism that it engages in overgeneraliza-tions and stereotypes; complexity is overlooked and preconceptions are imposed. Much of this has been driven by political imperatives, according to Said: "knowledge" has invariably been the handmaiden of power so that Orientalism has been an accomplice of European penetration and domination of Asia and the Middle East.

Trudeau, we know, was decidedly anti-imperialist so that this last part of Said's critique cannot apply. But he was also an uncompromising positivist and from such roots derived his ten-dency to generalize and perhaps to overgeneralize. No doubt as well Trudeau carried within him cultural residues as a French-Canadian Catholic educated by Jesuits and exposed to popular lore about the East. The Jesuits had had missions in China for a long time and among them there circulated a conventional wisdom about the peoples of that part of the world. On his first grand trek Trudeau gained knowledge of a sort about the East from priests in the mission field, a large number of whom were Jesuits. Trudeau's own reading would also have made an impression on him, especially French authors who dealt with the East: André Malraux, André Gide, Paul Claudel, Paul Valéry, and others. We know as well that Trudeau as a young man was exposed to avowedly anti-Semitic writers like Alexis Carrel and Charles Maurras and that he had talked critically in his youthful play, *Dupés*, of the role of Jewish shopkeepers in Montreal crowding out French Canadians. (We now know more about anti-Semitism in Quebec at this time through the work of Esther Delisle and Mordecai Richler.[27]) But care must be taken in estimating how all of this might have applied to Trudeau. He deserves not to have his views speculatively presumed just because he read certain books and grew up in a French-Canadian Catholic culture. But, from his first world trip, what we do have is fairly extensive evidence of his views on the cultural dispositions of such groups as Arabs, Jews, and Chinese. He talked about other groups as well. Bulgaria was a poor country and the smells in the third class compartment on the railway, he said, were more disagreeable than anywhere else; Turks were bad drivers and could not speak without raising their voices and could never raise their voices without shouting; and Hindus disliked foreigners. But in exploring Trudeau's attitude towards the Other, we will concentrate on his views of Arabs, Jews, and the Chinese.

Interestingly Trudeau himself gave evidence of being well aware of the tendency of some to overgeneralize about human groups to the point of misrepresenting them. In one of his radio broadcasts about his Russian trip in 1952, he commented about the need to develop a way of talking about the Soviet Union that would avoid harsh imputations of failures and inadequacies and instead would advance the cause of "human fraternity." He was resolved, he said, to talk of the USSR as an "ordinary" country inhabited by people just like Canadians, in other words people with similar successes and failings.[28] By way of illustration he mentioned a number of stereotypes that prevailed in Quebec about foreigners:

> In China there are the missionaries that eat grasshoppers; in Africa there are the lions that devour the reverend fathers; in the Indies it is the people being crushed beneath the wheels of the juggernaut. And in Russia . . . it would certainly be the stories of the GPU [the Soviet secret police] brandishing the knout in the shadow of the Kremlin.[29]

Then, he said, there was the popular stereotype that Americans and Europeans sometimes held about French Canadians,

> as the uncivilized progeny of sex-starved settlers and wanton women, with a little bit of Iroquois thrown in, jabbering a hideous patois and led by pot-bellied and superstitious priests.[30]

Generalizations, Trudeau concluded, could veer into parody and insult.

On one occasion Trudeau did talk about nativist stereotypes to which he had been exposed in his youth. His comments appeared in the introduction to his and Jacques Hébert's book about China, *Deux innocents en Chine rouge* (1961). In words of biting satire, words which Trudeau himself likely wrote, he talked of the prevailing view of China as a place

> swarming with little yellow men, famished, cunning, and more often than not, sinister. Among all the fears by means of which paranoid educators sought to terrify us in our youth— Freemasonry, the Protocols of Zion, Bolshevism, American

materialism, the Red Heel, Chiniquy and what else?—the yellow peril has a place of choice.[31]

And so, said Trudeau, they had learned from "missionary propaganda" that China was a country of "paganism, plagues, floods, famines and terrifying animals . . . [and] a people that fed its children to pigs."[32] More recently terrifying preconceptions had come from China's staggering population growth and the fact that all these hordes of people were now communists. In this regard Hébert and Trudeau seem to have anticipated Said's insight about how a stereotype can be inculcated in a population and reproduced as a kind of transgenerational, collective unconsciousness. Clearly, by 1961, Trudeau believed he had escaped childhood influences. But what had been his own thinking up until then?

In his notebooks of 1948–49 Trudeau talked about the peoples of the East in two main clusters. In the first, in the course of discussing the interaction between Chinese culture and communism and whether Mao and Marxism would prevail, Trudeau revealed some interesting attitudes. It is hard to predict the outcome of the Chinese situation, he said, but events seemed to favour the Communists. The Guomindang represented reactionary interests and, in supporting Chiang Kai-shek, the United States was backing the wrong horse and helping prolong the civil war. And so his next question became: once triumphant will China assimilate Mao and Marxism or will it be the other way around? Trudeau, showing the wide extent of his reading, referred to Mao's famous essay of 1940, "The New Democracy," with its argument about how China, although an agricultural society, would overcome the necessity according to Marxist theory of proceeding first through a capitalist, industrial revolution before entering upon socialism. According to Mao, under the leadership of the Chinese Communist Party, China could proceed quickly from feudalism to the dictatorship of the proletariat—what Marxists later have called the principle of "combined development." But, in the view of Trudeau, in the great historical battle between indigenous forces and those of "alien insurgents," the homegrown ones had usually prevailed. China had assimilated the Huns, the Mongols, the Tartars, and the Manchus and it likely would do the same to "the Reds," he said.

Trudeau laid out a number of cultural impediments to possible Communist rule. Chinese culture was unruly; the Chinese had tried to develop a system of law inspired by the Swiss and the Germans but

> it does not stick to a people without order; whose spirit is absolutely incapable of accepting the rigour of a contract; who ignore syllogisms but who reason by way of juxtaposition; who have nothing of a deductive nature and who don't know how to move from principle to application.[33]

Case law might work better in China but political and linguistic disunity made it difficult to collect and effectively disseminate data on cases. The Chinese tendency to disorder rendered it a place where force and bullying held sway. It reminded him of a natural Hobbesian society where everyone was out to get the most for themselves. In the general anarchy such a society, he concluded, was better adapted to authoritarian rule and perhaps that suited the Communists. But other cultural tendencies militated against their successful rule such as the importance in China of family and kinship loyalties and the individualism of small farmers.

The second cluster of comments, entitled "Reflections on the Orient," was, as the title suggested, more general in its geographical perspective but it also referred to China. It was less focussed on the political context and more like a taxonomy of intriguing cultural characteristics of peoples of the Orient. "Egotism," Trudeau announced, was the word that most easily came to mind when thinking about the Orient. To talk of Oriental politeness was to express the most monumental of jokes, he said. Orientals were driven by "face" which seems to have meant for him an amalgam of avoidance of social disgrace and humiliation, making an impression, and enjoying the humiliation and discomfort of others. He also mentioned Oriental arrogance and self-importance and their tendency towards ridiculous ostentation. They lacked sympathy especially towards those who were their social inferiors. They were strangers to altruism. Even their famed politeness was a façade and only exhibited to select people. In front of strangers their egotism took over:

> They shove you on the stairs, move in front of you in the door-way, push you in the crowd, walk intentionally between you and the object you are looking at in a museum, staring at you with the most shameless curiosity, snorting and coughing as loudly as they possibly can, spitting and blowing their noses almost over you, burping and farting in your face, shitting and pissing in front of you, just as if you didn't exist and as if you were a brute with no understanding.[34]

Here was utter frankness on Trudeau's part, to the point of utter disgust. There was more. He repeated his claim about the tendencies of Orientals to be cruel towards their social inferiors and to be "boot-lickers" towards those in authority. Now he added a new dimension. It was not just that Orientals had a capacity for cruelty and an enjoyment of others' sufferings but also that Westerners and white people showed precisely the opposite tendencies. He told the story, originally disclosed to him by a Catholic priest, of how in Rangoon, in Burma, someone who had been attacked and splashed with acid and was in excruciating pain was met with unconcern by his own people; it took the arrival of a white person to wipe off the acid. There were other, similar stories. One was of a child swept away by the current and the Chinese hardly raising a hand to help him—again, it was a white man who saved the day. He also told of a sampan breaking up on rocks in the Yangtze River and spectators considering this a matter of mirth. Trudeau wondered if Marxism could succeed in a society bereft of the ideal of disinterested, collective service. He admitted that his judgments were a bit harsh and he balanced them with some descriptions of the positive qualities of Orientals: Chinese were a cheerful people much given to laughter and among friends and family, they were deeply loyal. In that case, Trudeau argued, they might be willing to take a chance on communism, reasoning that if they had friends and family in high places they would be protected. In other words Chinese culture was disposed towards nepotism.

Trudeau's comments about Arabs and Jews were also mainly offered in the context of a discussion of political circumstances, in this case the Palestinian–Arab–Israeli War of 1948. Trudeau was well aware of the Jewish question and the Holocaust, having travelled so extensively throughout Europe in the months just before his arrival in Jerusalem. In displaced persons camps he noticed that not all Jewish refugees wanted to go to Palestine, but many did. Palestine, however, could not accommodate an endless number of Jewish immigrants, he believed. Some Jewish survivors were sympathetic to communism though they were in a minority and most Jewish refugees did not want to return to the Soviet Union and eastern European countries like Poland. Trudeau completely understood how it was that a Jewish "chauvinism" about a homeland in the Middle East had developed; but he also took a broad view of the conflict and showed a concern for the interests of Palestinians and Arabs as well. He wrote,

> Before the misery of the Jews, I fall into line with the necessity of a Jewish state. But in "Arabie" I see what misery and injustice half a million refugees creates. And my convictions oscillate.[35]

But he was decidedly contemptuous of Britain's policy towards the region.

About Jewish people, Trudeau evinced a mixture of sympathy and stern candour. Once again he displayed a tendency to provocative generalizations that rubbed up uncomfortably against his usual tolerance and skepticism. He acknowledged the unimaginable suffering of the Jews but he felt obliged to mention their faults. He observed that around the displaced persons' camps there often thrived a Jewish black market. The inmates had been banned from commerce, he said, and had turned to illicit trade.

> In every city the black market is located near the synagogue or DP camp. And from one city to the next, people give you the (approximate) address (and a vague name: Sam, Abe, etc.), so that Jewry truly constitutes an international agency for information and commerce.[36]

Speaking of Poland, Trudeau explained that there were perfectly understandable reasons why the Jews there had turned to trade and money and had been stigmatized and marginalized by the wider society:

> Their fate was to perform unpopular tasks: they took care of loans at exorbitant rates of interest because Christians were prohibited from doing so; they formed the merchant class in Poland, since all land was still under the yoke of feudalism, and whenever things went wrong, it was easy to designate them as exploiters and scapegoats. This partly explains the harsh anti-Semitism that still characterizes the Polish people.[37]

Trudeau covered similar ground in a short essay entitled, "L'affaire palestinienne," almost certainly written in 1949 but never published.[38] It began with a declaration of sympathy for the Jews. In one displaced persons' camp for Jewish young people, as many as 90 percent were orphans; and he mentioned the horrors of the Warsaw ghetto. But then his argument pivoted and moved in another direction:

> Of course, they have committed a lot of wrongs on their side. And at first they gave rise to anti-semitism by their terrible spirit of the tribe; one knows that, where passes a Jew, a thousand will follow; and this thousand will never assimilate to their surroundings for

fear of weakening their attachments to the tribe and to international Jewry.³⁹

Of course, such ideas were mainstays of interwar European anti-
Semitism even if they did not express its most extreme insinuations,
but Trudeau pressed the issue further. To assertions of tribalism
he added a comment about Jewish cultural insularity. He knew,
he said, of a "well-educated Jew" who lived in Warsaw who, even
though she was seventy years old, did not know a Polish person and
could not speak the Polish language.⁴⁰ He went on: "The Jews seem
to inhabit a 'secret' language which in central Europe unites them
and distinguishes them." He was happily surprised that he could
talk directly to the Jews he met in Bulgaria and Turkey but it was in
Spanish: "These people, even after five centuries of being expelled
from Spain, have never ceased to speak Spanish." Trudeau did not
make clear whether such Jews were to be commended because they
had once learned to speak the patois of their land or were to be
faulted for not having learned Bulgarian and Turkish in the intervening five hundred years of exile. In any event the tone of censure
continued. Turning to Palestine Trudeau went on to observe that
the Jews had not behaved irreproachably there either. He instanced
the "abominable violence" of the Stern gang and the Irgun, two of
the Jewish guerilla resistance groups in Palestine. But Israel's regular troops in the war had conducted themselves badly too and had
used dum-dum bullets and six-inch mortar shells in civilian areas.

As for the Arabs, Trudeau offered some understanding of the
rightness of their cause, for there were limits to the capacity of
Palestine to accommodate all the Jews of the world. Perhaps he had
an inkling of competing nationalisms in the region and how these
would affect the possibility of peace. Ultimately he believed that
Arab incompetence, disunity, and fecklessness would vitiate their
endeavours. They were, he said, terrible in their hatred of the Jews
but they seemed to have been more respectful than the Jews of the
interests of civilians in the war. But Arabs had a dark side. Trudeau
instanced their practice of honour killings and their bloody brawls:

"But give them the least opportunity to think well of you and their generosity knows no bounds." But the neighbouring Arab nations were disunited and they pursued divergent goals so that they were incapable of preventing a Jewish state in Palestine. Arabs seemed to talk a good line but were, practically speaking, ineffectual: "A people, wily, ambitious, tenacious, rich and materialistic confronts a people divided, passive, careless, and backward."

What to make of these categorizations? They covered a range of human activities from the public hygiene of Orientals to the etiology of Jewish suffering. Trudeau expressed them as insights acquired through direct personal observation or through the supposedly evidence-based observations of others. Perhaps he was too trusting of the veracity of the latter, and too willing to build on hearsay. In almost every case they were generalizations about large and complex collective phenomena. Of course they could be thought to have been simply intellectual shorthand for describing more complex phenomena, what has been referred to as "communicative expediency."[41] And so his claim would be not that all Chinese expectorated in public but that it happened there noticeably more than he was used to witnessing in, say, Outremont. Also it should be noted that Trudeau was aware of divergencies from putatively general categories of behaviour. And so some Jews were Communists and not small traders, and not all Arabs were bloodthirsty. And yet his point, presumably, was that he was assembling claims based on palpable evidence of cultural difference through the predominance, although not necessarily the generality, of cultural features in particular groups.

Turning Said loose again on Trudeau—to some extent this is what happened in the critique provided by Couture—Said would contend that someone like Trudeau represented a type of essentialist, Orientalist thinking in which the characteristics of a given group are deemed to be inherent and unchanging. Trudeau's defence would presumably be that he was asserting no such thing since his disposition was that of the positivist sociologist abroad, noticing unusual and astonishing facts that were objective and true but which could change. But this would not exempt him from criticism because Orientalism also posits a "scientific" sub-type of thinking, a "scientific" essentialism. Even if Trudeau's claims were contingent ones that by no means assumed an unchanging identity, Said might still contend that what Trudeau was expressing was a diachronic essentialism whereby, while the identity of the group may indeed change over time, nonetheless it continued to presume an overarching derogatory identity.

Trudeau, then, sometimes expressed a visceral dislike for the behaviour of certain collectivities and sometimes he articulated simplified accounts of what were in effect large and complicated phenomena. In this he implied a kind of objectification, an "aura of apartness," as Said puts it.[42] He *was* capable of a certainty of judgment and sometimes of a moral insensitivity too. Trudeau desired to embrace the Other in all his splendour and uniqueness, except that the Other sometimes disappointed or appalled him. At the same time he was anxious to make sense of other peoples and to understand them in a sociological way in the belief that positive knowledge would provide a basis of useable public policy. To undertake political change through applying large, explanatory categories was one of his fundamental imperatives. Yet, even as there existed a tendency towards a generalizing and insensitive positivism, there also existed in him an anti-colonialism and a universalism that was open to the concerns of everyone. The peoples of the East—even with their sometimes regrettable features—were worthy of respect and should be accorded justice and equality by the Western powers. Yet the new order was to be a Christian one. Trudeau mixed several discordant elements. There were remnants of a clericalist nativism at the same time as he was exploring and expressing a new, controversial ethos of leftist cosmopolitanism.

III

The part of Asia that eventually occupied a good part of Trudeau's early political attention was a country that he did not visit in 1949. Korea had been occupied by the Japanese as early as 1910 so that with Japan's defeat in 1945 there was a strong expectation that its former independence would be re-instated. In conferences at Cairo (1943), Tehran (1943), and Yalta (1945) the Great Powers had provided guarantees of Korean sovereignty and territorial unity. However such prospects were not immediately forthcoming at war's end because the country was re-occupied, this time with the Soviets taking over the northern half of the peninsula and the United States the southern part, with the 38th parallel agreed upon as a demarcation line. How to implement guarantees of independence became the complex question of the moment given that the two occupying powers were of very different political complexions and would soon be fighting a cold war. Though both had made a commitment to Korean unification, each sought such an outcome only on its own terms. Each negated the interests of the other and so each came to accept, pragmatically, that it could only attain half of what it wanted, at least for now. In its sector in February 1946 the USSR began to set up Peoples' Committees under the Communist leader Kim Il-sung and in the south the United States sanctioned a very rough-and-ready liberal-democratic regime under the autocratic Syngman Rhee who came to power in August 1948. So was set up in the south the Republic of Korea (ROK) and the following month the USSR established in the north the Democratic People's Republic of Korea (DPRK). Korea in effect became partitioned.

Official thinking in Washington did not consider the peninsula part of an indispensible American strategic perimeter in Asia and the Pacific, and indeed the Americans went on to withdraw their troops from the peninsula as the Soviets had already done.[43] In China by 1949 the Communists had completed their political revolution and Chiang Kai-shek had withdrawn with his Nationalists and his government—the so-called Republic of China (ROC)—to offshore Formosa or, to give it its Chinese name, Taiwan. The United States expected Chinese and Soviet pressure to be focused there rather than on Korea. And so, unexpectedly, the Korean War broke out on June 25, 1950, when, with the indirect support of the USSR and the PRC, the North Korean army invaded the ROK and swept all before it. The United States won support from the UN for an international force to resist the invasion, an outcome made possible by the abstention of the USSR in the Security Council in protest over the continued seating of the ROC as China's official representative in the UN. The Americans led the UN operation in Korea. General Douglas MacArthur and his troops landed in July and by September they had pushed into the North. This triggered the entry of troops of the PRC coming to the aid of the North Koreans. MacArthur talked extravagantly of taking the war to China, literally, and possibly using nuclear weapons. This was too much even for American official opinion and in April 1951 President Truman relieved him of his command. On the battlefield by July 1951 a stalemate was established and an uneasy truce took hold, again around the 38th parallel. Only two years later would a formal armistice be signed. Altogether it was a vicious, bloody war with many civilians killed and many refugees. The Koreans lost 10 percent of their population, civilians and soldiers, while 37,000 Americans were killed and over 500 Canadian soldiers too. It was a war that has still not been properly concluded.

By late summer 1949 Trudeau was employed in the PCO in Ottawa advising the federal government mainly on constitutional matters. However what piqued his interest more was the onset of a nasty war in Asia that had the potential to blow up the world. Lester Pearson was the Minister of External Affairs in St. Laurent's Liberal administration at the time and he oversaw a policy that dovetailed with the American view of the conflict: the bipolar logic of the Cold War, the hegemonic position of the United States, and the need to punish Communist aggression. Trudeau acceded to none of these positions. His thinking instead was shaped by the neutralist and third-way perspectives expressed in the late 1940s by Emmanuel Mounier, Harold Laski, Maurice Duverger, Étienne Gilson, Hubert Beuve-Méry, and by journals and newspapers such as *Esprit* and *Le Monde* in Paris.[44] Trudeau disagreed fundamentally with the Atlanticist and anti-Soviet views of such commentators as Raymond Aron and Jacques Maritain.

Trudeau first voiced concern about the war in August 1950 in a letter to Jules Léger in the Prime Minister's Office (PMO). His terse, unflattering comment on a speech by Lester Pearson was that it was "without an original thought, little current history and [full] of propaganda."[45] Dramatically Trudeau announced that "Asia is being lost." He believed Europe might still be saved though it would only be through a policy of independence and neutralism. In the tight-knit world of the PMO, PCO, and the Department of External Affairs (DEA), such views would not have gone unnoticed. His second set of comments no doubt drew even greater attention. Pearson had given another speech, on April 10, 1951, in Toronto, on "Canadian Foreign Policy in a Two-Power World." On April 28 Trudeau wrote to Douglas LePan and Pierre Trottier, advisers in External Affairs, rejecting Pearson's contention that the war had been the result of deliberate policy by the "hard-faced despots in the Kremlin, [who were] men hungry for power and world domination."[46] Presumably Trudeau had access to correspondence within the Canadian diplomatic service for he went on to use information from communications from John Watkins in the embassy in Moscow and from Chester Ronning, the chargé d'affaires in Nanking to challenge Pearson's views. Watkins and Ronning, he observed, had mentioned the more or less sensible policies of the Soviet Union and the PRC in improving living conditions in their countries. The Soviets, according to Watkins, were war-weary and "naively proud of their primitively-democratic institutions" while Ronning spoke of the "progress [being] made . . . for the benefit of the Chinese people as a whole."[47] Trudeau pushed his argument to a final and perhaps absurd conclusion. If Pearson was unaware of these reports, he said, he was failing in his job; or if he was acquainted with them and was not following their advice then he was discounting it, in which case he was guilty of retaining two diplomats who were "gullible soviet stooges"; or if he believed them and still held that the Communists were guilty of starting a war, then he was misleading the public. Trudeau concluded by accusing Pearson of a lack of courage, not the last time he would say such a thing:

If Mr Pearson had that courage, would he not acquaint the public with facts which might tend to open an avenue of comprehension and sympathy towards the potential enemy. Or because our world is fractured, must we regard it as our duty to rent [sic] it completely asunder.[48]

It was an impossibly indiscreet and impertinent letter.

For the Nemnis, Trudeau's position did not betoken support for the communist side because they see its emphasis as lying in that suggestive phrase about opening an avenue of comprehension with the enemy. This interpretation dovetails with their overall tendency in *Trudeau Transformed; The Shaping of a Statesman, 1944–1965* to defend Trudeau from being thought of as a dangerous radical and leftist; hence their consistent tendency to diminish the influence upon him of Mounier who was prominent in the European criticism of an American-led, Cold War polarization of Europe and the world. We will deal with Trudeau's attitude towards communism later. For now it should be noticed that, in addition to mentioning the importance of "avenue[s] of comprehension and sympathy towards the potential enemy," Trudeau also made use of Watkins's and Ronning's reports to support his view that these supposed "enemies," the USSR and the PRC, were in fact making substantial advances for their people, which does not quite fit with the Nemnis' view of Trudeau as a non-radical. Trudeau's views may not have made him a communist but they did take him some way towards aligning himself with what actually existing communism was doing.

More followed. The following month, while still in the employ of the PCO, Trudeau anonymously published an essay on the Korean crisis in *Cité Libre*, "Positions sur la présente guerre." It was a long piece, ten pages in length, and it showed Trudeau at his intellectual and rhetorical best with bold theorizing and extensive historical knowledge and iconoclastic conclusions. Likely his comments helped solidify his resolve to resign from the government, which was what he did four months later. The article has had mixed reviews from two of Trudeau's recent biographers. John English hardly mentions it at all, while the Nemnis give it greater attention but fail to explore its complexity and subtlety. Actually the essay tells us much about the fundamentals of Trudeau's account of global affairs in the early 1950s. Written in May 1951, it was published just as the war was coming to its ambiguous dénouement so that most of the war's horrors and devastations had already taken place. Trudeau began with one of those ascending, crystalline syllogisms that he was wont to make: war was not necessarily the greatest of evils and peace was not the absolute good. The goal ultimately was justice. History he saw in terms of a tragedy, with humanity staggering from war to war, each new victory leading to a new holocaust. Without knowing the final outcome of this "cold war," millions were suffering throughout Korea, said Trudeau. It was important to take a stand. Evil was too powerful to take a pacifist attitude:

> We do not wish to affirm a priori that the just can always be defended without recourse to force. We are pacific rather than pacifist. That is to say, we accord to peace the benefit of the doubt: we see in it an aspect at least partial to justice (which war can never be); and if one resolves to break it, then that can only be possible in the name of a larger justice.[49]

In interstate relations, then, Trudeau was not a pacifist, even if he was pacifically inclined.

Regarding the North's invasion of the South, which had caused the war, Trudeau agreed that defending the territorial integrity of a state was a noble cause and insofar as this was what lay behind the resolve of the UN to come to the aid of the South, it would be an honourable motive. But he doubted that this was what had ultimately lain behind the decision. Instead the UN had acted out of "impure motives." Trudeau proceeded to list no less than seven instances of what he called "injustices." The Great Powers had acted arbitrarily and contrary to the Declaration of Cairo in 1943 in which they had promised the re-establishment of a sovereign Korea. Once ensconced in Korea the Western powers—presumably the Americans—had encouraged a "corrupt and reactionary" government in the South with aggressive designs on the North. As proof Trudeau quoted from General MacArthur who as early as August 1948 had talked about the arbitrariness of the division of the country and how this must be reversed. Moreover, he continued, the frontiers of a neutral China had been violated by the United States and by the UN when they had agreed to the separation of Taiwan from the rest of China, again in defiance of what the Cairo Conference provided. Trudeau then made a very general reference to the "repressions" and "atrocities" committed by MacArthur's forces in the North after the UN had broken back across the 38th parallel. He also criticized the extent of their advance right up to the Yalu River and the border with the PRC. Another injustice he believed was the action of the Americans in closing the door on a peace initiative by several Asian nations in January 1951 and later the insistence of the US Congress on recruiting as many as forty-three nations to support a declaration designating the PRC as an aggressor in Korea. Finally, there had been the belligerence of American leaders in threatening to take the war into the PRC and the surrounding regions.[50]

Trudeau's list was impressively detailed and, evidently, the result of much study and reflection. His position leaned emphatically towards the DPRK, the PRC, and the USSR. This is in spite of the fact that the North Koreans had launched an unprovoked attack with the blessing of both the Soviet Union and the PRC, and that the PRC had been involved in broadening the war. But, of course, when writing in May 1951, Trudeau had available in support of his argument the ominous musings of MacArthur about the necessity of not just winning the war for freedom in Asia but finally dealing with Communist China. At the time, it was not only the faint of heart who believed that Korea might be the cause of a Third World War.[51] In late November 1950, in the aftermath of President Truman's ill-judged comment about possibly using "every weapon we have," an opinion poll had found that 50 percent of Americans thought that another world war was imminent. For Trudeau it was the Western Great Powers that were principally to blame for the Korean debacle and his indictment of them was particularly driven by his outrage at their treatment of China over its loss of Taiwan and their insistence that the UN not recognize the PRC as the legitimate government of an undivided country. Indeed the UN did not come off well at Trudeau's hands. But principally it was the Americans who had failed to provide the moral measure of the needs of Korea and Asia. The US, he said, preferred the regime of Syngman Rhee and his protection of feudal agricultural relations over that of Kim Il-sung and his agrarian reforms. The Americans, he claimed, could not forgive the Chinese Communists for having forced the retreat of Chiang Kai-shek and his corrupt Guomindang to Taiwan. Overall, Trudeau argued, American policy was driven by international high finance. It sought to establish a capitalist "orbit" in Asia and was prepared to brutally punish any country that "wish[ed] to change its zone of influence."

Trudeau went on to imagine a more realist-minded interlocutor who in response to his possibly overly abstract argument might reason that history could never be returned to a "zero" of pure justice and that perhaps the binary divisions of the world of the Cold War had to be accepted and justice pursued within it. In that case, Trudeau agreed with accepting a more realistic perspective. All right. But had a sense of justice emerged from the breakdown of peace in June 1950, and had the extension of the conflict brought on by the intervention of the UN had as its purpose a greater good to justify the slaughter and devastations brought on by the war? His answer was powerfully in the negative:

> As for the good of Korea itself . . .[i]t is impossible to think that the lightning war set off by the North Koreans and the subsequent unification of Korea under a government at the same time communist, totalitarian [and] atheistic would have led for combatants, non-combatants and refugees to anything like the

collective and individual injustices, indiscriminate butcher-
ies, abominable destruction and unimaginable terror which has
effectively resulted from the UN intervention.[52]

Here was provocative reasoning on Trudeau's part. His claim was
that in spite of the North Koreans' precipitating the war and establishing an illegitimate regime, such things constituted a higher
good than what had transpired because of the UN's intervention.
What Trudeau expressed was reasoning based on the principle of
a lesser evil, although in this case it was reasoning undertaken in
retrospect rather than in prospect. Prescribing justice in retrospect
is always an easy matter and this Trudeau did not seem to notice.

Or was it, Trudeau continued, that the question of justice
should only be considered within the larger global framework of
the fate of freedom throughout the world? In that case, was the
annihilation of Korea the price to be paid to make Moscow understand that the West will go to any lengths, including war, to prevent the "sovietization of the World"? Here too Trudeau found his
opponents' reasoning weak. Asia deserved freedom and development but the West and especially the United States had failed to
understand the "mood" of Asia. This was more than an academic
mistake: it had practical global consequences. The United States
and their imperialist surrogates—the British, the French, and the
Dutch—opposed nationalism and liberation throughout Asia in
order to protect corrupt, plutocratic regimes. Trudeau continued:
a policy of aggression towards its "legitimate aspirations" will drive
decolonizing forces into the Soviets' embrace. A more advantageous
strategy would be to make peace with local communism in order to
defeat Stalinism. The United States was supposedly committed to
emancipation and self-government, except that it

wants the liberated nations to become American-style democracies, that is, respectful of private enterprise and great wealth. Thus
they contribute everywhere to protecting the most reactionary
feudalism and don't see that capitalism is a hollow formula in

countries where eighty percent are illiterate and where annual income is below $40 per capita.[53]

Asia wanted to build a different political order and Trudeau implied that it could not be a Western liberal-democratic one.

The root of America's failure, he continued, had been its "hallucinatory fear of socialism." Here Trudeau once again made use of ideas he had expressed in his earlier Asian notebooks about how communism would triumph if the West did not provide a fair and egalitarian way of meeting the aspirations of Asian peoples. If the only alternatives were alliance with Moscow or Washington, Asia would side with Moscow. Americans did not understand how "hungry people prick up their ears when socialists promise rice but remain deaf before offers of refrigerators and civil liberties." But there was a third choice, in Trudeau's view: encouraging local liberation movements that might be communist (but were not necessarily so) and which might become examples of alternative socialisms and escape the embrace of Stalin. The United States, he said, had failed to appreciate the lesson of Tito in Yugoslavia: socialist nations can be anti-Stalinist.[54] Also it had done its cause no good by refusing to recognize the Communist government in Beijing as the legitimate government of China. In so doing it had forced the PRC to align with the Soviet camp. Instead American policy should seek a sensible engagement with Beijing and the encouragement of Soviet–PRC rivalries. A further source of American failure, he went on, was its intensifying of racial antipathies by whites towards what were represented as the yellow races. Trudeau's conclusion was that the policy of the West towards Asia did not meet the standard of justice. The UN's intervention had been unjust and had made matters worse.

Just war theory seems to have informed Trudeau's account. The war should have been fought for the right intentions; the peace established should have been an improvement over the previous one that had been broken; and the military methods used should have distinguished between civilians and armed combatants. None of these conditions had been met in Trudeau's estimation. Perhaps the only criterion of just war theory that the Korean War might have satisfied was that it was waged by a "legitimate" authority, in this case the UN—except that on this occasion the USSR had chosen not to use its veto on the Security Council so that the UN had become little more than an alliance of Western imperialist powers and their satellites, bent on doing damage to nations that had the temerity to stand up to the West.

What of Canada's role in all this? It had been one of craven deference and non-existent fealty to principle:

> Faithful to a tradition which arises with the North West rebellion and the Boer War, Canada is always ready to courageously defend the strong against the weak. In matters of foreign policy, it has followed, it follows and it will follow.[55]

Canada essentially had become a "satellite" of the United States and the other Western powers. Of yet another speech by Lester Pearson, this one on February 2, 1951, Trudeau said that it represented "apathetic clairvoyance in the service of cowardice." He acknowledged the more advanced theoretical positions of the government: its support for mainland China's admission to the UN and its status as the legitimate government of the country; and its wisdom in advocating that the UN forces not occupy all of Korea and not declare the PRC as an aggressor. But what was to be made of its actions? By its deeds it had fallen into line with its allies. What Trudeau wanted was not conformity with other Western countries but independence, imagination, and courageous action, and, as well, a more open immigration policy and greater measures of foreign aid to Asia. What Trudeau especially desired was "a refusal to obey," in other words a Canadian foreign policy that would become more like that of the non-aligned movement led by India's Jawaharlal Nehru and Indonesia's Sukarno, which was beginning to develop at the time. Trudeau's view rejected categorically the logic of the Cold War because of its failure to meet the needs of the developing world and its tendency to reinforce American and Soviet hegemony within their respective spheres. He did not want American liberal democracy but rather socialism for the peoples of the planet; however, he preferred for it not to be along the lines of Stalin's kind. On the Korean War, Trudeau showed the extent of his socialism and took a position that was inordinately partial to the interests of the small nations of the world but also to those of the USSR—in spite of his skepticism about Stalin—and the PRC. If his position was not quite one of absolute defence of the geopolitical interests of global communism, it was not far from it.

IV

Notwithstanding his misgivings about Stalin and Stalinism, between April 3 and 12, 1952, Trudeau attended the International Economic Conference in Moscow. The origins of this Conference are a little unclear. According to the Nemnis it was the product of an organizing committee of "distinguished personalities" concerned about world peace, which had met in Copenhagen some months before.[56] But which sponsoring organization lay behind the committee or whether there was one at all, they do not specify. Almost certainly it was a project of one of the several groups that the Cominform helped establish in the late 1940s as part of its popular-front strategy among left-wing sympathizers in the West to help fight the Cold War. The conference Trudeau had attended at Otwock had been part of that larger design. Two of these groups were the World Congress of Supporters of Peace and the World Congress of Intellectuals for Peace, which held conferences in Wrocław, Poland, in 1948 and in Paris in 1949—the latter being the one at which Pablo Picasso's celebrated image of the dove was unveiled—and later in Sheffield and Warsaw. These two Congresses transformed themselves in 1950 into the World Peace Council, which proclaimed the Stockholm Appeal for Peace in the same year.[57] Trudeau himself believed that the Copenhagen Conference was somehow linked to the Stockholm Appeal and thus to the Moscow International Economic Conference.[58]

Some 450 delegates attended the Conference, drawn from forty-seven countries. Its ostensible purpose was to discuss economic co-operation and peace, and one of its concrete achievements was to establish a Committee for the Promotion of International Trade (which as it turned out failed to produce much co-operation because the United States refused to participate). In the charged atmosphere of the Cold War the Conference was inevitably a subject of intense controversy. But it does seem to have been a genuine attempt on the part of a number of public intellectuals outside the Soviet bloc to arrest what they saw as the rush to conflict and nuclear war. That said, 135 delegates were from the Soviet Union and many of those from abroad were members of local Communist parties. Independent, left-wing intellectuals only constituted a minority and many of these were what critics of the Soviet Union have called fellow-travellers—ostensibly independent leftists and progressives who nonetheless saw the Soviet Union as "a new civilization" (as Beatrice and Sidney Webb once put it) to be defended more or less unconditionally. Lord Boyd-Orr, political independent and winner of the Nobel Peace Prize in 1949 for his work on nutrition, was a noted delegate, as were others, including Piero Sraffa (an Italian economist and fellow of Trinity College, Cambridge) and three British economists: Joan Robinson, Maurice Dobb, and Alex Cairncross. (Dobb, a Communist, later became famous for having recruited the spy, Kim Philby, to the Soviet cause.) Maurice Hancock and William Garth Teeple, both members of the Communist Party of Canada, were part of the six-person Canadian delegation. Two others, Michael Freeman and Jack Cowan, had connections to the Party. Filling out the Canadian delegation was Morris Miller, Trudeau's friend from the LSE who had accompanied him to the Otwock conference in 1948, and Trudeau himself.[59] Not always sensitive to diplomatic niceties, Trudeau opined that the Canadian delegation was not of great consequence.[60]

Trudeau's own account of how he came to find himself in Moscow has that air of purposeful nonchalance and inadvertence in which he chose to wrap many of his actions. Alfred Sauvy, a well-connected left-wing French economist, had alerted Maurice Lamontagne at Laval to preparations for the conference, especially the meeting of the committee in Copenhagen in October 1951, and he in turn had told Trudeau. After further thought Lamontagne decided not to go, deeming it likely to be an exercise in Soviet propaganda. Trudeau, by contrast, though knowing about the dangers of being identified with a Soviet-inspired project, felt strongly enough about international understanding and collaboration to take a chance and he went.[61] He advertised himself as an economist and a correspondent for Le Devoir. His conclusion about the conference was that, although initiated by independent-minded, peace-loving people—as Joan Robinson put it, "we were not delegates from anyone, but a job lot of individuals"—it was clearly supervised by the Communists.[62] Trudeau admitted that he was not "naive" enough to believe that the Communists would risk losing control over its proceedings. But the built-in "Stalinist" majority, he said, used its bloc vote sensitively and allowed the development of a consensus and unanimity.[63] Although not much was done on behalf of greater world trade, Trudeau considered it a success in that it had challenged the dominance of both the United States and the USSR in their respective currency zones and had advanced an understanding of economic multilateralism through diversification and interpenetration. Thinking back on the conference Trudeau called for greater Canadian trade with the Soviet Union and, finally seeing a useful role for the UN, he called upon it to facilitate economic co-operation. Here were signs and wonders of an emerging initiative to counteract Cold War economic polarization, he believed.[64]

Trudeau remained in the USSR for a month and travelled as far as he was allowed. He was mainly confined to Moscow, but he did manage to get out into the provinces and visited Kalinin on the Volga River (about 200 kilometres northwest of Moscow) and the Caucasus through the Ukraine to Georgia and the city of Tbilisi. He would have liked to have gone to Tashkent and the fabled city of Samarkand, in what is now called Uzbekistan but then part of the USSR—fantasies of the mysterious East no doubt dancing in his head—but he was told by Intourist, the Soviet tourist agency, that it was not possible because there was no hotel there. Trudeau replied, a little airily that it did not matter: "I would sleep in the streets of Samarkand and dream of the great Tamerlane."[65] Trudeau claimed that he talked to many public officials and opinion leaders—judicial officials, academics, trade unionists, industrial employees, and agricultural co-operative workers—and, sometimes managing to escape his minders, he met average Muscovites and even visited the "louche" district of the city, he said.[66] Trudeau had several conversations with the Canadian chargé d'affaires in Moscow, Robert Ford, and attended mass on the four Sundays he was there. He spoke to the wife of the top American diplomat and indiscreetly told her, no doubt with a twinkle in his eye, that he was a communist.[67]

From the moment he had applied for a visa and got on the train in Prague to travel to Moscow, Trudeau was accorded the very best of treatment. In Moscow he was royally lodged at the famed Sovietskaya Hotel and given a car and an interpreter. But after the conference he insisted on making his own arrangements and he left the main hotel, ate in local restaurants, and often travelled on foot. However his eccentricities and drolleries were not always appreciated and eventually he exhausted his welcome. The abrupt manner of his final expulsion revealed the extent of the breakdown of his relations with the Soviet authorities. Trudeau had expressed an interest in travelling to Leningrad only to be told that there were no vacancies in the hotels there. So he informed the official that in that case he would sleep in the Hermitage, the famous art gallery, if need be. (Sleeping rough seems to have been a favourite response of Trudeau's.) In the event, his official overseer did find him a bed in Leningrad and, of course, not in the Hermitage. Trudeau then asked for a travel permit and was told to phone later but at the appointed hour the phone did not work. So he went to the official's office in person and the next day was informed that he had both a travel permit and a bed in a hotel but now there was no longer a seat on the train. Eventually a seat was found but now there was a problem over his permission to enter Finland. Trudeau now took great satisfaction in announcing that in fact he already had a visa to enter Finland. The official then made his next move and observed that if he went, he would still be present in Leningrad for several hours after the expiration of his travel permit. To this Trudeau declared that in that case he would travel there by plane, only to be told that his seat on the plane was taken. Clearly Soviet bureaucracy had lost patience with Comrade Trudeau. Summoned to appear at the bureaucrat's office, under an "enormous portrait of Molotov [the foreign minister]," he was interrogated about his plans to leave the USSR. Trudeau supposedly replied:

> What are your plans for helping me leave the USSR? For the last five days I have tried to leave by way of Leningrad and Kiev and you have systematically blocked my exit.[68]

He was told that he must now leave directly by plane through Warsaw and Berlin to which again Trudeau triumphantly replied that it would take at least two days to obtain the necessary visas to do so. According to Trudeau, his minder now personally took him to the embassies of Poland and East Germany at 8.00 p.m. to obtain the necessary stamps on his passport. The next day, he said, he was awakened in his hotel at 6.00 a.m. by two Soviet operatives, taken directly to the airport and put on a plane for Poland. Trudeau clearly found great amusement in all this seeing it as a complicated chess game. His satire on the impenetrable relations of bureaucrat and client was not as dark and menacing as, say, Franz Kafka's or Arthur Koestler's, but in its own mischievous way it was a highly subversive exposé of bureaucratic malevolence. But sometimes Trudeau's non-conformity could appear rather adolescent, and precious and self-important too.

His time in the Soviet Union provoked strong reactions back home. He was put on a blacklist that banned him from travel to the United States—no doubt the American ambassador's wife had spilled the beans about him being a communist—and the Canadian government could hardly have been amused by the news that one of its recent advisers had consorted with communists and fellow-travellers. In Quebec Trudeau was met with a veritable tidal wave of criticism from intellectuals; the Church did not hold back either, as we have seen. The Nemnis are no doubt right to say that Trudeau was not a communist and it may well be possible, as John English asserts, that Trudeau was by no means "a duped fellow traveller" and that he knew well that "liberty was the most precious individual good."[69] But, in all their complexity, what were his views? He may not have been a communist and he may have wanted to promote international dialogue and trade—it was an early version of peaceful coexistence and détente that he espoused—and he may have had strong views on the value of freedom but, remembering his comments on the Korean War when he had taken a very dyspeptic view of the Western powers, what were his opinions on the Soviet Union and the Cold War and how conventionally liberal were they?

In all Trudeau published seven newspaper articles about the Soviet Union in *Le Devoir* between June 14 and 21, 1952, and he gave four talks between September 4 and 25 on Radio-Canada. Politics aside, he showed that he was a pretty good travel-writer; he wrote with clarity and vividness though sometimes with too much sentimentality and perhaps he presumed too high a level of cultural understanding on the part of his readers and listeners, even those of *Le Devoir*. Predictably, he sought out unusual, dangerous, and forbidden experiences. His experiences of Moscow and the Caucasus described in his "Au sommet des Caucases," found him transported with wonder and amazement, a truly romantic voyager abroad in exotic and foreign lands. In general he showed little of his earlier fussy and irritated comments about the failings of different peoples and he seems to have taken to heart his own advice about seeking everyday realities and appreciating the common humanity of people. But this is not to say that he was uncritical.

The Soviet people were strongly resilient and nationalistic, he concluded, having endured so many wars and revolutions. From his hotel in Moscow, he said, he had seen some of the wooden

houses that had survived the great fire during Napoleon's invasion in 1812. More recently Germany's attack on the Soviet Union
in 1941 had inevitably reinforced Russian nationalism. Russians
had good reason to be suspicious of foreign governments and
they resented being pushed around, he affirmed. Culturally they
were very accomplished and he mentioned the achievements
of Tchaikovsky, Dostoevsky, Chekhov, Stravinsky, Eisenstein,
Nijinsky, Chagall, Shostakovich, and Mayakovsky. But Russians
were mystically inclined and a little dreamy, and sometimes lazy
too. Here he registered a commonplace preconception of the
Slavs as moody sentimentalists. Russia, he continued, was distinctive because it formed the marches and borderlands of the
West with the mysterious East, "the doorway through which the
vagabond peoples of the Plains enter into the western world." It
was through reading Paul Claudel, the French diplomat and poet,
Trudeau said, that he had been persuaded to go to Russia. He
quoted from Claudel's play, *Tête d'Or*, about passing through the
Caucasus and arriving at the edge of Asia:

> This is the threshold which opens onto the eternal North and
>   from whence comes the sun;
> this is the rampart, the hinge attaching Europe slantwise to the
>   Earth of Earth...
> For here...
> journeying upwards we have reached the level of the world and
>   here is where the slope ends.[70]

In this case, it seems, Trudeau was engaging in some kind of
reverse Orientalism, viewing the East as the fructifying source
of the life of the West, if only the West would allow it. In one of
his Radio-Canada broadcasts Trudeau invited his listeners—he
talked to them as if they were lovers—to wander with him through
the streets of Tiflis (also known as Tbilisi) and the mountains of
Georgia, where myths had been conceived, and where East and
West, and past and present converged:

I would love to wander around with you, especially in the old quarter, among ancient thermal springs out of which emerge well-scrubbed and laughing children; along the picturesque alleys which sing and throb to the beat of drums; on to the small medieval cathedral where old folk are at prayer; up to the high fortress of kings of ancient times; on to Mdhéta where one of the purest examples of a Christian church (5th century) is now scarcely used except by octogenarian nuns.. . .

But I promised to take you to the summit of the Caucasus. So let's climb up, by twisting streets, beyond the last houses and gardens, high above the minarets and the bell-towers, high above the green cypresses, high above the puffs of vapour from the thermal springs, high above the noise.

Here on the aerial strand where break the elemental light and the mythological tempest, here is the black rock to which Vulcan chained Prometheus, the divine protector of men. Here is the place Tête d'Or drew his last breath, victim yet conqueror of the fecund peoples of Asia. And here the resting place of the mother of Joseph Vissarionovich Djugashvili, also known as Stalin.[71]

Recalling his visit to the Bolshoi Theatre, Trudeau remembered "wandering"—the eternal *flâneur*—among the building's portals and mixing with a crowd drawn from many distant parts: the Ukraine, the Caucasus, the Urals, Uzbekistan, and Mongolia, Asia present at the very heart of Russian culture.[72]

This people with its strategic territory and its rich diversity were now subject to a communist order. Trudeau sought to make sense of the new reality and to challenge the stereotypes of the Cold War: that the Soviet Union was a totalitarian regime like Nazi Germany and that its citizens were beaten in the streets and terrorized. In fact, he claimed, the government had done much to improve material conditions and large investments had been made in schools, parks, and hospitals; new buildings had been constructed and there were new cars on the street. But there were deep inadequacies in the regime too. Religious freedoms had not been extinguished but with religious education officially forbidden organized Christianity would be denied to the young and would fade away. When he went to churches in the Soviet Union Trudeau noticed that he was surrounded by old people. In contrast the cult of Joseph Stalin was almost religious in its adulation of the great leader. Trudeau took note of new architecture in Moscow but regarded it as the expression of the soulless giantism and the propaganda of an overbearing regime. Citizens were compliant and docile but mainly because material circumstances were modestly better than they were used to. Certainly Soviet citizens were without influence over their political world and over the material goods that the state planners decided that they should purchase. Everything was prescribed and justified by the five-year plan and the planners along with the other personnel of the state lived a privileged existence with levels of income and status, not to say power, well beyond those of the average citizen. The privileges of the elite, Trudeau presciently predicted, would become self-perpetuating. A suffocating bureaucracy enclosed everything and the Soviet state was not beyond behaving nastily. The new revolutionary regime in its requirement of conformity and obedience was not much different from that of the czars:

> They have replaced the police by the military, the Czar's army by the Red Army, the Tcheka by the NVD; Stalin is regarded as an icon. The names and the symbols have been changed but where is the revolution?[73]

Trudeau's general perspective was that the Soviet Union represented some measure of social and economic progress; the people enjoyed "relative prosperity."[74] But there was still much to criticize and to reform.

These essays offer immense insight into the subtleties of Trudeau's perspective on the Soviet Union. Four in particular are worth examining closely: "Un peuple sympathique, mais conventionnel jusqu'à la nausée," "Est-ce pour ça qu'on a fait trois révolutions?," "Staline est-il poète?," and "Aux prises avec le politbureau."[75] The very titles are enlightening with their provocative declamations and cheeky insinuations. In the first Trudeau talked of the prevailing mood of the Soviet people. Overall they were compliant, he contended. Why would they criticize when everything was oriented to the common good even if the common good was defined by the state? But they were materially better off than they used to be:

> Moreover when the alternative is to believe or to die, it is not surprising to find a majority of them faithful [to the Stalinist cause], especially among a people well-known at the same time both for its capacity to bury its misfortunes and for its extraordinary superiority complex.[76]

Russians maintained a proud attitude towards everything that was Russian. This was the meaning of Pan-Slavism and it was now the meaning of Pan-Sovietism. Trudeau laughed, he said, when he heard Western politicians represent the Russians as living in the hope of being liberated from their "Stalinist yoke." As long as they felt threatened from abroad they would instinctively rally around their leaders. What the West should do is leave the Soviet Union to its own devices so that the regime would be deprived of the opportunity to claim that it was only rooting out counter-revolutionaries. In that case, in time there would likely take place a diminishing of the "rigours" of the Soviet state's behaviour, Trudeau believed.

The Soviet government maintained an intense hatred of foreign governments, according to Trudeau, but its inclinations were isolationist and non-threatening. In "Est-ce pour ça qu'on a fait trois révolutions?" his claim was that a distinctive feature of Soviet policy was that it eschewed foreign territorial expansion even as a method of mobilizing the Russian public and keeping them loyal. In this, he said, it was different from the regimes of Hitler and Mussolini. The Russian people had been through too much and they now wanted to reconstruct their country. Why would they build so many buildings if they were preparing for war, as Western politicians alleged?

The older generations remembered Czarism and were content with the present order while the young were enthusiastic about the future. Here Trudeau contradicted some of his other comments about citizens' grudging compliance with the regime. The young, he believed, were enthusiastic supporters of the government. Even so, he admitted, the revolution still lagged far behind the West: in the Soviet Union the ruling class was too privileged, the cult of Stalin was almost messianic, and to secure its revolutions it had "liquidated millions of kulaks, purged the revolutionary old guard and imprisoned an unknown number of political opponents." He went on:

> Comrades, look at liberal Canada, socialist Sweden and labour-ist Australia where capitalism has been breached little by little in the name of justice by organized workers. They believe sincerely in winning power while still respecting Christian values, democratic means and constitutional methods; they pursue a different interpretation of the gospel according to St. Marx; but is that a reason to detest them?[77]

Trudeau wanted the Soviet Union to become more open and pluralistic in its understanding of Marxism and socialism, and to embrace countries in which Titoism and Trotskyism prevailed. There should be greater solidarity between all progressive nations, he believed: in other words, a world of tolerant, mutually respecting socialisms.

The condition of the arts and of artistic freedom provided the theme of "Staline est-il poète?" The cultural traditions of Russia were too rich, Trudeau contended, to be totally subverted by Stalin and the Bolsheviks. The country had paid a huge price in achieving an industrial revolution in only thirty years when it had taken other countries 150 years or more. Yet he had witnessed, he said, intriguing attempts to integrate art into the common life. There were factories where on one side was a production line and, on the other, rooms where workers pursued dance, art, and choral singing. But overall he was unimpressed by public art in the Soviet Union. It was aimed at flattering the leadership. The orthodoxy of socialist realism with pictures of miners and young men with a heroic, elevated gaze, Trudeau concluded, did not move him and he was appalled by the story of an art gallery that had put in storage its collection of paintings by Cézanne, Gaugin, and Van Gogh in order to exhibit the art objects given to Stalin for his seventieth birthday. Official art, said Trudeau, was "irredeemably false." It was art that was external and which failed to look and explore within. Trudeau expounded an ethic and aesthetic of inwardness:

> I fear that the only purpose of these extraordinary performances [of opera, theatre, puppetry, and cinema] is to draw attention to everything that is exterior, and thereby to prevent attention from turning towards the interior and suddenly discovering the spirit and transcendence. Think of Shostakovich and Khachaturian condemned only to composing melodies that can be hummed; the filmmaker Eisenstein thrown to the side; Stravinsky and Chagall disowned by their own; [and] the suicide of the genius Mayakovsky.[78]

Then there was the amusing story that Trudeau used as a preface to his essay, "Aux prises avec le politbureau." During a meeting of the Politburo, he recounted, it was said that Stalin expressed concern about the disappearance of important state papers. The secret police was alerted but later Stalin found them in his briefcase. He explained this to Lavrentiy Beria, the head of the NKVD: "'Impossible' exclaimed Beria, 'Citizen Molotov has already confessed to being responsible.'" The story nicely captures the malevolence and mistrust among those who walked the "golden tightrope" of Stalin's government yet unexpectedly Trudeau used it not so much to throw light on such uncertainties but rather to corroborate his idea that the regime was not one that terrorized its people.[79] The story had been told to him by a Muscovite and a member of the governing party. Trudeau's point was that the regime was not based on fear and terror, for why otherwise would a Soviet citizen and Bolshevik have felt comfortable sharing such a joke with a foreigner? The police in the Soviet Union, he said, were in fact either too incompetent or too embarrassed by what they would ever have to do to be the guardians of a truly totalitarian country. Yet Trudeau went on to say that "he is under no illusion about the ability [of the police] to suddenly sow terror, witness in this regard the liquidation of the kulaks."[80]

Trudeau's understanding of Russian culture gave prominence to its traits of intellectual subtlety and "finesse." The Russians were inveterate chess-players, given to calculation and gambits; they responded and adapted to their opponents' strengths and were not beyond feeling strong enough to lose a game now and then. The West should appreciate that in dealing with them it should eschew a politics of force and accept that finesse would be a better response. A competition of ideas was better than a nexus of coercion. Trudeau again recommended some version of peaceful coexistence. He also believed that, because the Soviet Union was a paragon of finesse, it was capable of tolerating activities in its citizens even when it disapproved of them.

Overall, we might say that Trudeau had a soft spot for Russia and the Soviet Union. Russian culture was rich in beauty and creativity, he believed. It was different from the West, blessed by its relations with Asia but recurringly hurt by its proximity to Europe. He leaned over backwards to see the best in Soviet society although he was not uncritical of it, as fellow-travellers typically were. His claim that the standard of living was improving was less controversial than his contention that it was not a totalitarian society. He conceded that the USSR had an atrocious history as a persecutor of political dissenters and "class enemies" like the kulaks. Jacques Maritain had mentioned the camps for dissidents in his *True Humanism* which Trudeau had read; he was also aware in his own right of such camps and Stalin's systematic liquidation of his opponents. Trudeau's contention about the non-totalitarian nature of the regime was only plausible because he structured his argument in such a narrow, specious way. Thus it was that the Soviet Union was to be regarded as a non-totalitarian state because the police did not brandish the knout on Red Square and because a party member could freely tell a joke about Stalin and Beria to a foreigner. But these were minor matters. Even within his own account of things, Trudeau conceded that the regime was capable of imposing a dreadful terror if it chose to do so. That was surely the most significant thing and it was something to which he might have given greater place in his argument but did not. It was as if Trudeau refused on principle to deduce the kind of conclusions that other commentators in the West had arrived at.

Yet, contradictions and solecisms aside, the cumulative message of the essays was devastating in its criticism of the Soviet Union: its cult of personality, the arbitrary power of the *nomenklatura*, the lack of artistic freedom, and the state's capacity to terrorize its citizens. At the same time Trudeau's concern to open up avenues of comprehension and sympathy with the Soviet Union cannot be doubted. He was truly fearful that the aggression of the Western allies might tip the world into nuclear war, always an overriding concern with him. Dialogue with one's enemies was essential, he believed, and this could not be achieved if one was accusing them at every turn of every imaginable evil. Trudeau sought quite explicitly to avoid demonizing the Soviet Union. Yet in his commentary he hardly held back in his own criticisms. Maybe this was what he understood as the competition of ideas between the West and the Soviet Union. So we cannot say that Trudeau was a fellow-traveller. But he did in some areas give the Soviet Union the benefit of the doubt. He did not believe that it was so fundamentally illegitimate that it must be quarantined and isolated. Nor was it so suspect in its ultimate intentions that it should be boldly resisted. In the rarified atmosphere of McCarthyite opinion in the early 1950s, such a position was seen to be far too tolerant of Soviet excesses. In a way Trudeau *was* naive. He was worldly-wise enough to recognize the existence of the vested interests and entrenched attitudes that were in play on both sides of the conflict, especially in the US and Canada. Yet he could not resist offering a sympathetic understanding of the USSR, often contradicting himself. It might be said that he was not realistic enough, and perhaps he also overlooked the fact that, regardless of how delicately he put the issue, his words would be twisted and used against him. Moreover he often employed language that was playful and humorous and that made it even more likely that his opinions would be distorted. He was not a communist and his comments make it very clear that his socialism was of a democratic and constitutionalist variety. But he wanted the best for the Soviet Union even under its existing leadership. He did not want to topple the Soviet system. He wanted it to become more like what prevailed in Sweden under the Social Democrats or in Saskatchewan under the CCF. He seemed to have believed that such an evolution was possible.

The sharpest arrow aimed at Trudeau over the Soviet Union and the Economic Conference came on the religious question and was delivered by Father Léopold Braün. This appeared in the review, *Nos Cours* in November 1952, in his "Commentaire circonstancié sur les articles de M. Pierre Elliott-Trudeau: 'Je reviens de Moscou.'"[81] Braün had lived and worked in the Soviet Union between 1934 and 1945 and was an undying critic of the regime. By the early 1950s he was a militant Cold Warrior. His fundamental criticism of Trudeau's newspaper articles—he apparently did not hear the radio broadcasts—was about his "lack of elementary prudence" in his analysis of the Soviet Union.[82] Actually his position was even more categorical than that and he refused to grant any truth whatever to any of Trudeau's claims. So it was that he believed Trudeau was wrong in his assertions that there had even been economic progress and that in different ways the public supported the regime. Braün maintained that Trudeau had failed to draw out sufficiently the extent to which the regime was authoritarian and totalitarian. But mainly what offended him was that Trudeau had underreported the degree to which the Catholic Church had been persecuted. Braün contended that there had once been as many as fifteen hundred Catholic Churches in Russia in 1917 and now there were only one or two. He and Trudeau may have quarreled over how many had actually survived but whatever the number was, implicitly, they agreed that it was very few indeed. The Catholic hierarchy in the Soviet Union had been destroyed, Braün said, and by 1939 all of the Catholic clergy had been imprisoned except for a French Dominican in Leningrad and Braün himself.

In fact Trudeau had not overlooked the fate of the Church. He had pointed out the presence mainly of old people at mass and this he believed was due to the state's denial of religious instruction to the young. This was not good enough for Braün, who wanted something much more denunciatory to be said about the atheism that the government inculcated in those who belonged to the Pioneers and the Komsomol, the youth movements of the Communist Party:

> Is it a mere bagatelle . . . that the total extermination of the Catholic hierarchy of Russian can be passed over in silence in a series of seven articles?[83]

A similar rage characterized his account of Trudeau's other comments about such things as the regime's non-totalitarianism and the degree of support it had mobilized. Braün was driven by his sense of the enormity of the crimes committed by the Soviet state. There were, he said, between 16 and 20 million people in "concentration camps," and so how could anyone accept an offer to attend a conference on peace and co-operation made by such a government? Braün knew a great deal about the hidden workings of the Soviet system and he perceptively latched on to the likelihood that the Cominform had had a hand in the preparatory conference at Copenhagen.[84] How could Trudeau be so naive, he said, to believe that visas to the Moscow Conference were issued without discrimination? Braün was a very able antagonist and Trudeau was rattled by his criticism.

Trudeau responded in two articles entitled, "M. Pierre Elliott Trudeau répond aux articles de Père Braün," which he sought to place in the newspaper and journals that had carried Braün's original indictment.[85] Braün, he said, had misunderstood his humour and verbal style—he was a *flâneur* after all—and had distorted and overlooked many of the criticisms of the Soviet Union he had in fact made. Later on, as we have seen, Trudeau would make his own considered response to Braün and others in his "Matériaux pour servir à une enquête sur le cléricalisme," in May 1953. In a sense Trudeau could not win with Braün because it was not really what he had said that was so offensive but rather his action in going to the conference at all. Indeed an objective-minded comparison of Braün's text with those of Trudeau would establish that they did not in fact greatly disagree about the nature of the regime. One difference between them was in the tone they used; another was the fact that Trudeau did say some positive things about the USSR. In addition, Trudeau was dismissive of bellicose Western attitudes to the Soviet Union while Braün wanted to enflame them. Clearly they disagreed over the amount of contact there should be with the Soviet Union.

Nevertheless Braün did expose weaknesses in Trudeau's position. How could there be congress with a government that had killed so many of its citizens and kept millions of them incarcerated in camps, and how could a good Catholic have been so sparing in his criticism of Soviet treatment of the Church? Trudeau's response was that diplomacy was better than war especially if the war might be a nuclear one. But détente and peaceful coexistence were not his only considerations and his oversights to do with the "totalitarianism" of the regime and its relations with the Catholic Church cannot simply be explained by his interest in keeping open lines of communication. For reasons not altogether clear Trudeau did overlook or downplay some of the most shameful realities of the Soviet state. If technically he was not a fellow-traveller, was he not as close to being one as not to make much difference? Perhaps it was, as John English alleges, that Trudeau believed that the Soviet Union had gotten its social priorities right.[86] It was not an altogether illegitimate regime, in Trudeau's view. Later when he visited Moscow in September 1960 on his way to China, he again commented favourably on the social and economic progress of the country.[87] Certainly the Nemnis' categorical claim that "Trudeau had no affinity whatsoever for Soviet-style socialist or communist regimes" seems rather wide of the mark, a judgment that will become even more clear after we have considered his relations with Mao Zedong's China.[88]

V

Continuing the independent, neutralist, and anti-nuclear perspective of his Moscow essays, in August 1952 Trudeau gave a presentation at the Couchiching Conference of the Canadian Institute of International Affairs on "How Canadians can contribute to the defence of *human* values."[89] He stated boldly that the country's foreign policy had been inordinately "subservient" to other, more "senior" governments. Under Lester Pearson, Canada only interpreted London to Washington and vice versa. Canada was a wealthy country, he noted, and marked by British institutions and a bicultural and bilingual population. But Canada needed to throw off its political submissiveness and launch forth on a foreign policy based on principle; especially it should emphasize its cultural distinctiveness. Trudeau also commented on the American elections in October 1952, "Répercussions internationales des élections americaines."[90] It was not a shrill piece but it did express concern over the Republicans' foreign policy and particularly the views of their candidate for president, Dwight Eisenhower. Towards the Soviet Union Trudeau envisaged the Republicans, if they came to power, repudiating the policy of containment and the Great Power agreements entered into at Yalta in order to pursue what they saw as the liberation of eastern Europe. If Eisenhower was elected the world should be prepared for an anti-communist crusade. The Republicans were intent on substituting a politics of force for one based on compromise. Clearly from Trudeau's perspective the right wing in US politics had not learned any lessons about the perils of aggressively pursuing the Cold War and tipping the world into a nuclear Armageddon.

In late 1956 war did indeed break out, in this case in the Middle East between Britain, France, and Israel on the one side and Egypt on the other. This had been triggered by President Gamal Abdel Nasser's nationalization of the Suez Canal. Roughly at the same time a popular uprising erupted in Hungary against the Communist government and its Soviet protector. That these crises did not precipitate a nuclear confrontation involving the Great Powers was mainly because President Eisenhower did not behave as Trudeau had predicted he would. Eisenhower put pressure on the British, French, and Israelis to cease and desist. In Hungary he chose not to come to the aid of the rebels and so the uprising was put down with Soviet tanks. Trudeau's short piece in *Cité Libre* in February 1957, published anonymously, exhaled almost a literal sigh of relief that the worst had been avoided:

> For two days in November humanity tottered above the abyss. Today it seems to have resumed its uncertain progress but the stupor does not quite leave us of having stared into the face of nothingness. And thousands of corpses strewn across the soil of Hungary and Egypt remind us that several leaders and several governments have within themselves a power of life and death.[91]

Trudeau never ceased to be exercised by the nuclear question. In the early 1960s he would become an avid supporter of the Campaign for Nuclear Disarmament (CND), and concern over the issue would especially inform an essay he wrote in 1961, "La guerre! La guerre!," about the horrors of radioactive fallout and its effects particularly on children, and thus the necessity of an effective treaty banning nuclear tests.[92] The nuclear question would also be central to his denunciation of Lester Pearson, the leader of the Liberal Party, over the Bomarc issue in 1962, as we shall see. Writing about the Suez crisis in 1957, Trudeau for the first time had kind words for Lester Pearson, whom he praised for his work on peacekeeping, and also for Paul Martin, another Liberal minister, for his work at the United Nations. He also had praise for St. Laurent and his government for its defence of the interests of small nations against the Great Powers. In the matter of the Suez crisis Canada had for the first time asserted a position in foreign policy that was fundamentally different from that of Britain. Trudeau decidedly approved.

Throughout the 1950s and early 1960s, Trudeau remained a strong advocate of third-way neutralism, nuclear disarmament, and economic development in the Third World. After 1952, as he became more concerned with Quebec and the eventual gathering crisis of Canadian federalism, he became less vocal on international matters. But one country did preoccupy him and that was China, which was the subject of a book he co-authored with Jacques Hébert in 1961, *Deux innocents en Chine rouge*.[93] The work was a record of their travels there with three other Canadians in a five-week period in September and October 1960. They were guests of the Chinese government. It was a similar situation to his trip to Moscow in 1952 with Trudeau once again inhabiting the liminal world of fellow-travellers, political radicals, and iconoclastic eccentrics. He knew from the outset that his trip would be manipulated and intensively supervised by the authorities but this did not deter him. This time he was not so much interested in making a statement on behalf of international co-operation and peaceful coexistence—though these were hardly absent from his mind—but rather to promote the full diplomatic recognition of the Chinese government in Beijing and an appreciation of China's actual circumstances and predicament.

Countering stereotypes of China was also his and Hébert's concern and they began the book with a couple of homilies—we noticed them earlier—about ugly preconceptions of China that had become, they said, part of the unconscious Western mind, including in Quebec. China by these accounts was the land of the yellow peril, a place of inhumanity and cruelty, presently rendered more menacing by being clad in the garb of devilish communism. By now Trudeau seems to have moved beyond most of those earlier generalizations about Chinese and Oriental peoples and their poor public hygiene and wanton joy in the suffering of others. But, as we shall see, he still adhered to some preconceptions about China. The overall tenor of their book was that Mao Zedong was all-wise and that his Great Leap Forward was catapulting China towards social justice, industrialization, and Great-Power status so that it was bound to become an exemplar to the Third World. Trudeau never quite paid such compliments to the Soviet Union and, anyway, he believed that Stalin himself was up to no good with his cult of personality, a judgment he never quite made about Mao. That said, neither Hébert nor Trudeau parked their critical faculties at the airport when they got on the plane to Beijing. Both clearly were irritated by the cosseted nature of their treatment by tour guides and officials, which left them little opportunity to explore the country for themselves. Indeed their itinerary was confined to a narrow corridor of China. From Beijing they travelled by train south to Shanghai and then to Canton (Guangzhou) in the far south, returning roughly over the same route and including a visit to Hangzhou, the city of pagodas and Buddhist temples and the place where Trudeau had climbed through the rain and darkness to a Taoist monastery eleven years earlier. They also made a short trip northwards to Manchuria and to the Great Wall, near the capital. They were shown a variety of places—factories, communes, museums, and institutes—and several interviews took place with experts and representatives of the state. The whole thing was intensively managed. However, with a mixture of whimsy and condescension, Trudeau and Hébert brushed this off and strove to discern some truth behind the official obfuscations and manipulations. They might easily have concluded that the Chinese regime was an impossible one. Yet in the end they gave a very positive account of Mao and what he was doing.

But clearly Trudeau and Hébert were not uncritical. Demonstrating again his interest in architecture Trudeau observed of the Party Congress building on Tiananmen Square that its gigantic coffee-cake shape reminded him of Soviet buildings; it was colossal and pretentious. In a word it was "bourgeois." They noticed class differences between the railway compartments that the common folk travelled in compared with the plushly upholstered ones in which they themselves did; they doubted that Chinese workers could go on strike and intimated that Chinese rule in Tibet might not be completely benevolent though in general they gave high marks to the government's treatment of minorities; the vaunted intellectual and cultural freedoms of the Hundred Flowers Campaign in 1956 had allowed some popular discussion of different views, but only within the limits of socialism and subject to the control of the Communist Party; workers in rural communes, they observed, could not freely move to the cities; signs of poverty in Canton were duly noticed though they thought the streets of China were generally cleaner and healthier than elsewhere in Asia and the people materially better off than they had been. They were concerned about the government's treatment of the Church and concluded that there were severe constraints upon it as the authorities pursued official atheism. But the Church had had a hand in its present demise, they claimed, because it had inordinately supported the Nationalists of Chiang Kai-shek. But, as with Trudeau's commentary on the Soviet Union, they did not make religious persecution the central theme of their book. They did not overlook the role of propaganda and indoctrination in reinforcing the government's policies but this did not deter them from concluding that on balance the regime was a benevolent one and in general to be commended.

Trudeau was particularly concerned about the planning process in China and he grilled his guests about how it was that, in the absence of forces of supply and demand, prices were allocated, wages and production determined, and equilibrium established. He became fixated on incidents he had witnessed of tractor engines sitting in the open exposed to the elements and generators piled up haphazardly in corridors; he wondered how planning could succeed given such signs of over-supply and bottle-necks.[94] Trudeau pointed out to his interlocutors the rising standard of living of workers in North America. He was surprised that the director of the Shanghai Institute of Social Sciences had not heard of the "neo-Marxist" Harold Laski. Even without such knowledge, the director was supremely confident in his prediction of the impending demise of capitalism. Trudeau reiterated his point about a rising standard of living in the West, but the director replied that this was based on the exploitation of other countries, to which Trudeau observed that the Danes lived well and they did not exploit anyone. But this brought the response that although there might exist a progressive bourgeoisie it could not resolve the contradictions of capitalism. Trudeau was clearly being confronted with an official, unvarying Marxist line and he remained unconvinced that he was being given a credible explanation of how planning would solve all these problems. Yet, curiously, in the end it did not seem to matter because he was self-confessedly swept away by a sense of 600 million people rising up as one to successfully make a new world, even with an erratic, inexplicable system of planning.

Trudeau took as his frame of reference China's unique environmental and geographic circumstances and special historic problems and concluded that Mao's approach made great sense. It was as if he took seriously the advice he offered in his 1946 essay on political violence that to avoid violence the ruler must use the method proportionate to the desired end; it should be applied implacably and it should be subject to perfect control. Ends and means should be in harmony and political leaders must be prepared to sacrifice themselves to methods that would be effective even if they were personally unpalatable. China's context precluded liberal-democratic methods and if the goal envisaged was physical and economic security for the Chinese masses then Mao's policies constituted the perfect strategy. Yet Trudeau and Hébert must have suspected that an extremism of both ends and means was involved, the ends extravagant and the means destructive and ultimately ineffective. Their own emotions, they said, oscillated between "incredulity" and "enthusiasm."[95] But ultimately it was the latter that prevailed. They represented the skepticism of Western social democrats who nevertheless were impressionable to the point that they fell in with the utopianism of a country apparently on the march and certainly not to a liberal-democratic drummer. On China Trudeau represented the strange antinomy of the skeptical true-believer. In the Soviet Union in 1952 Trudeau offered Australian labourism and Swedish social democracy as alternatives to Soviet excesses. In China having publicized the example of Denmark—no doubt it was that country's social democratic tradition to which he was alluding— Trudeau retracted the suggestion and never once offered other Western liberal-democratic examples for China's edification. What he did underwrite was a party-guided but participatory system of charismatic leadership that risked becoming horribly oppressive, as indeed it did become. What Trudeau advocated was yet another version of Oriental despotism.[96]

Consider the more detailed justifications that Trudeau and Hébert advanced in support of Mao and his Great Leap Forward. Visiting a steel works they were disturbed to see evidence of wear-and-tear: the brickwork crumbling, scrap iron scattered haphaz-ardly, and tiles broken. But on reflection they were encouraged. China was doing what it could to industrialize as quickly as it possible:

> As a consequence construction workers have to form mobile teams that cover vast regions: they arrive quickly, build quickly and then move on elsewhere, and they don't have the time to return for fine-tuning or maintenance. Such a rhythm is imposed by necessity; if time were taken to produce perfect work, nothing would get started.[97]

The necessity of break-neck development also explained why much of the work was done by women and teenagers. But everything was justified if life was improving:

> It is always important to ask if the actual state of things is more acceptable than before and thus if the future plan provides for an improvement.[98]

When they talked to some of the workers, they believed they encountered a proud and beaming proletariat, the very oppo-site of the Western stereotype of slave labour driving China's industrialization:

The genius of Mao has been, by methods of persuasion of terrible effectiveness, to convince hundreds of millions of people of the grandeur and nobility of their task. Indeed we would say that the most remarkable achievement of the Chinese Communist Party is to have transmitted—or imposed—on the Chinese people confidence in the future and an active faith in its own future. The government has given the Chinese a job to do, *and it makes them do it*, [authors' emphasis] all of which is somewhat new compared with the Chinese fatalism and otherworldiness of the past.[99]

Trudeau and Hébert seemed uncertain as to whether the methods of the Party were coercive but whatever they were they conceded that they would not be acceptable in Canada. However in a context driven by dire necessities, "such attitudes will be swept aside as the pleasing scruples of comfortable people."[100] Indeed the Chinese model had wider application and would be increasingly imitated by the two-thirds of the world that went to bed hungry, they said. China was on the rise and, of course, there were casualties—witness the refugees fleeing to Macao and Hong Kong. But this was not going to deter the regime, which was only now getting into its stride. Trudeau and Hébert did not say it but their message was that revolution was not a dinner party, supposedly something that Mao *had* once said; casualties were to be expected.

Their sense of China's history and geography informed much of their view of the new order. China had been victimized by recurring devastations and famine. Life was inherently insecure and impoverished. In contrast Mao's China provided full employment and the workers were proud and possessed of a sense of human dignity:

Before this fundamental reality all the considerations of westerners about the arduous nature of work in China, about female labour, about the miserable standard of living, about the totalitarian regime are nothing more than ineffective quibbles.[101]

However they did notice that all was not completely well for in all their time there they said they had never heard one worker singing! But a society that provided work and survival for the masses subordinated all possible objections. There were no legitimate, practical alternatives to Mao's methods. And these, they claimed, were, anyway, not quite based on coercion and terror but propaganda and persuasion which after all were less oppressive but equally effective:

> Perhaps the most effective method of persuasion (and the least costly) is the local meeting. This is where the family is indoctrinated. The fanatics leading the hesitant. . . . Are they obliged to go to such a meeting? No more or less so than we Catholics are obliged to go to mass. Some of them go to the meeting with the enthusiasm and fervour of believers. Others attend, as with mass, in order not to commit a social offence. The result is that almost all the Chinese attend the weekly indoctrination meetings. Has there been a religion that preached its message with such effectiveness, using so many means?
>
> In our newspapers there is much talk of the terror that prevails in China. This is an inadequate explanation of the matter. Why massacre discontented peasants, thus alienating a whole region, when it is so easy to dispatch an army of propagandists who will transform the doubters into convinced Marxists and into zealous even happy workers? Doubtless the revolution has not been established without violence but why would they resort to that when they have found a better way: persuasion?[102]

It is curious to see the analogy they made between Maoist, agit-prop methods and the normal routines of the Catholic Church in Quebec. They were aware of the role of "fanatics" in mobilizing Chinese citizens but this did not lead them to doubt the validity of the official model. They conceded that indoctrination and group pressure were employed yet they never raised the question of the possible fate in such circumstances of doubters and dissenters.

By their estimation the Chinese people were altogether willing and happy conformists. They reiterated that it was the ever present threat of hunger in China that explained popular support for the government. Mao had vanquished the "menacing dragon" of hunger:

> That fact alone would be sufficient to explain the behaviour of this ancient civilization, about which it has been said that it would vomit up Marxism or that it would assimilate it as it has assimilated everything else that has come from outside. Mao has conquered hunger and it convinces the Chinese that this is due to Marxism. And so the Chinese have confidence in the regime. It is not a matter of believing promises: the management of water resources by means of dikes and dams, afforestation, land improvement projects, the mechanization of agriculture, industrial expansion, and above all the bowl of rice and the loaf of bread on the tables of China, these are the facts that every Chinese person can attest to at the tip of their chopsticks.[103]

The evident dislocations of the Chinese planning system they explained away sympathetically: somehow the dogged determination and discipline of workers and managers would be rewarded by eventual adjustments by regional and national planners; the sheer mass and impetus of the system would carry the day and, anyway, there were always alternative markets for goods that might have been over-produced:

> Obviously such a rudimentary economic process will engender enormous mistakes: gluts and bottlenecks. But these will be corrected in the next version of the plan; and as for inconvenient surpluses, these can be disposed of in markets in Asia and Africa. . . . We conclude that this is not the tidy model of planning taught in the great economics schools. But is it not the awkward and complicated awakening of a powerful industrial giant?[104]

Inevitably preconceptions about China were present in their analysis. One that Trudeau had spoken of in 1949 and that was repeated this time was about the prevalence of saving face.[105] But in 1960 the preconceptions were mainly of a different kind. China was mysterious and ancient, "as old as the world," as they put it; it had been beset by foreign powers historically and was more "aggressed than aggressor";[106] it was a poor land disadvantaged by geography and climate. Another powerful motif was the idea of China as incubator of an "organizing genius." Several times they referred to the building of those famous Pharaonic structures in China: the Grand Canal and the Great Wall. They spoke too of the immense physical scale required to overcome China's problems and of the need to employ the Chinese brilliance for planning and centralized administration. Thinking within such categories Trudeau and Hébert came to the conclusion that similar structures and policies were necessary in the present day: grand irrigation projects and dams and dikes, the communalization of agriculture generally, and the building of an industrial system almost from scratch. And to supervise these grand initiatives there needed to be a great brain and master planner, a role provided by Mao Zedong. Mao had succeeded to the centralizing and totalizing powers of ancient emperors:

> The Grand Canal which still unifies China from north to south and the Great Wall which crosses the country from east to west constantly bear witness to an organizational genius that has never been equalled even by the builders of the pyramids. As well they go back to a time when our wild ancestors dressed in the skins of animals were still running around the forests of Europe. It is true that for several centuries the feudal system of China, with the connivance of western capitalism, found profit in keeping the people in a state of disorganization and stupidity. . . . But here is a regime that shows the Westerners the door and sends the feudal powers to the scaffold. Ten years later China gives proof that it will be able to become the premier industrial power in the world.[107]

Their account of Mao emphasized his revolutionary proclivities and his willingness to use violence—at least in the early stages of the revolution—but he was also seen as a pragmatist who was capable of making tactical concessions like allowing a role for domestic capitalists, substituting persuasion for force, and ensuring that the "fanatics" were not completely in control. He was "that superb strategist."[108] In their estimation Mao became a kind of gentle giant and a mastermind too, the fulfillment of all of China's ancient wisdom, solving its predicaments in ways that had eluded previous rulers. To Hébert and Trudeau China's ecological necessities precluded any resort to liberal-democratic measures, though frankly they never really canvassed alternative possibilities. There was no mention of the rights of the person or the necessity of the rule of law, both themes from Trudeau's early reflections on China. They denied the relevance of such considerations not only by their contention that China's problems required grand solutions but by their conclusion that the liberal-democratic option had been utterly discredited by Chiang and the Nationalists and their corruption, conservatism, and alliance with the Americans. In contrast and in line with a common Western progressive view at the time, Mao was a kind of benevolent socialist Buddha, the saviour of the Chinese nation and the architect of an alternative modernity. Once in Tiananmen Square they had caught sight of him:

> Mao is one of the great men of the century, with his powerful head, his unwrinkled face, his gaze that of a sage touched with melancholy; in his tranquil face his eyes [are] heavy with having seen too much of the misery of men.[109]

It is hard to resist Yang Jisheng's characterization of Mao as the last Chinese emperor, just as it is hard to resist the conclusion that Trudeau would have agreed.[110] Trudeau was a Maoist, *avant la parole*.

Trudeau was an ambitious public intellectual who travelled both literally and imaginatively to the new political epicentres of the world: the USSR, Korea, and now China. Not only was he intellectually and physically bold but he was morally adventurous too in that he offered highly unconventional accounts of what was taking place. If Trudeau's political perspective was imaginative and daring, it was also that he wanted his world view to be worldly. There was no point in academic analysis if it avoided commitment, engagement, and effectiveness. The point was to change the world and sitting on the sidelines was not an option. However the risk in this was that he might come to conclusions too precipitously and with incomplete evidence so that commitment trumped caution and prudence. In the matter of China it turned out that there were large parts of what he claimed was happening that were misconceived or missed the mark. Perhaps Trudeau was too impetuous.

The Great Leap Forward was the zenith of Mao's utopianism. It was a cluster of interrelated policies that began to emerge in late 1957. The original idea had to do with water conservation: building large dams and irrigation canals. Armies of agricultural labourers were directed into such projects. But there were other parts. In the forefront of Mao's mind was a plan to make China, through rapid industrialization, an equal to Western economic powers like Britain and the United States. The famous development of backyard furnaces was integral to this. Part of the supply of materials to these furnaces was tools and implements used by farmers. Mao saw China as not just overtaking capitalist countries but also challenging the Soviet Union for leadership of the international communist movement. Indeed he aspired to make China a nuclear power—how ironic that Trudeau, the partisan of nuclear disarmament, would so intently support such a leader—and to achieve such a status he was prepared to countenance the most revolutionary of policies. If need be Mao was willing to export foodstuffs in order to barter or to earn foreign currency to pay for military and technological hardware.

Agriculture was also to be reorganized. In August 1958 there began the introduction of communes and communal messes and the eradication of what remained of private property relations. Mao took seriously the idea that the family was a bourgeois institution and that it was to be reconstituted. On average the new communes encompassed five thousand households and these were organized completely collectively, subject to the control of the central and local party. The Great Leap Forward depended on increasing agricultural production to feed the growing urban proletariat and to provide food for export for foreign credits. Foodstuffs were increasingly requisitioned by the state. New techniques, ostensibly at the leading edge of scientific farming but ultimately detrimental to greater productivity, such as deep-ploughing and close-planting were forced on communes. Actually the increased requisition of agricultural products was often to the advantage of foreign peoples. It was under the Great Leap Forward that rice became a staple foodstuff of the German Democratic Republic, whose margarine industry at the same time took advantage of supplies of Chinese edible oils.[111] Such agricultural products were exchanged for East German electronics and other technical products so that China might industrialize.

The Great Leap Forward was total in its ambition and involved the transformation of well nigh all sectors of Chinese society. It is now seen to have been a disaster that produced untold human suffering. The aims of the central planners were so extravagant that they were impossible to fulfill. The large and often unsuccessful water projects and the urban factories diverted workers from farming. The proposed new cultivation techniques often reduced agricultural yields. Farmers resisted communalization and the pig iron produced by the backyard smelters was frequently of little use, for example as ball bearings for barrows. Unfortunately this was something that was discovered only after useful farming implements had been melted down.[112] And suffusing the government's campaign were the methods of intimidation and coercion meted out by the regional and local party cadres as they pressed farmers and workers to meet the impossible demands of the central party. The whole system unleashed a multitude of unintended consequences. From two recent works, Frank Dikötter's *Mao's Great Famine: The History of China's Most Devastating Catastrophe, 1958–1962* and Yang

Jisheng's *Tombstone: The Great Chinese Famine, 1958–1962*, it is now known that perhaps as many as 45 million Chinese died from malnutrition or from suicide, murder, and torture.[113] As Dikötter puts it, "coercion, terror and systematic violence were the foundations of the Great Leap Forward."[114] In the end it produced "the near collapse of a social and economic system on which Mao had staked his prestige."[115] The worst period of the famine was between January and April 1960, in other words just before Hébert and Trudeau arrived in China. If a very dark cloud now hangs over the Great Leap Forward an equally dark one hangs over the reputation of its most complete perpetrator, Mao Zedong. James C. Scott, in a review of the above two works talks about Mao's "callous utopianism," his megalomania, and the "structural brutality" of the system he created.[116]

The response of the authorities to the gathering catastrophe was propaganda, manipulation, and violence. In some cases local party cadres even confiscated or censored letters to the central government in order to alert it to the famine conditions.[117] Instead the party spread the explanation that dislocations were due to the anti-revolutionary activities of rich peasants hoarding grain and rightist party members and citizens. The government initiated an especially nasty campaign of persecutions in 1959. Dikötter estimates that between 6 to 8 percent of the total number of lives lost through human causes were the result of torture and execution, 2.5 million in all.[118] Yang talks of a concerted propaganda campaign by the government to manipulate world opinion, part of which was to invite selected foreigners to visit China on guided tours, the very means by which Hébert and Trudeau had found themselves in the country.[119] By 1961 the truth about the extent of the human suffering was finally acknowledged by the central government and it relented in its opposition to capitalism sufficient to allow the return of private plots of farm land and local markets as well as the importation of grain from Western countries. In 1961 Canada provided about 40 percent of the grain imported to China from the West, some of which Canada helpfully shipped directly to Albania to meet China's commitments there under its foreign aid program.[120]

Of course Trudeau and Hébert were not able to draw informed conclusions about the Great Leap Forward because they were in many respects in the dark. When they did engage the subject they denied the seriousness of the famine and blamed reports of it on Western rumour-mongering. It is now known that the worst of the famine was in a band of provinces from Quinghai and Sichuan in the west to Anhui and Shandong in the east.[121] Thus in travelling from north to south, as they did, Trudeau and his group would only briefly have passed through this corridor and so they were largely segregated from any offending evidence. As it was the state and its cadres usually ensured themselves a more than ample supply of luxurious foodstuffs and Trudeau's and Hébert's book contained several accounts of sumptuous official dinners where delicacies such as lacquered duck were served. There was one inadvertent, mute witness to hunger when they noticed on one occasion some guests enthusiastically cleaning their plates; they concluded that they must have once known profound hunger. Maybe they believed that this had something to do with experiences of the Long March of the Chinese Communists, long ago. But, in recalling the moment, perhaps they inadvertently spoke more knowingly than they knew:

> When one sees with what ravenousness our hosts devoured everything in their dish, seizing with their nimble chopsticks the last grain of rice which might want to escape the carnage, rummaging through the carcasses of the fish to discover a mouthful of flesh, one has grounds for believing that these men have known hunger.[122]

Later in the book they did attempt a more direct response to the rumours of hunger but again they drew conclusions that showed how completely they were committed to seeing only virtue in the Communist government and its leader:

Isn't China enduring a famine at the present time?

Do you mean the famine delighted in by the western conservative press? The one spoken of with such cheerful compassion by the government of Formosa? It is true that dispatches from Hong Kong report a "shortage of supplies which in certain places borders upon famine." It is true that during our travels we have been informed about drought in the south and floods in the north, that there is no rationing . . . but that there has been a "controlled distribution" of foodstuffs. But it must be said that it would take much more than that to unsettle the government of Mao Zedong.

It has been reported in the West that the famine of 1932 in Russia had caused the deaths of millions of people. But that resulted in an increase of Stalin's dictatorial power. However famine has been not as common in Russia as in China, where it has been known for millennia. That takes nothing away from the tragedy of present food shortages . . . but if they are less frequent and less deadly than hitherto then that will be enough for the Chinese to recognize progress and to wish for [the government] to continue.

Even if present day famines are of equal seriousness they will cause less damage than in the past because there will be no financial sharks speculating on the misery. The means of distribution and apportioning (roads, trucks, personnel) are better organized today than in the past.

Conclusion: the Chinese will continue to listen to the professors of Marxism in their weekly meetings.[123]

The famine of 1958–61 might not have been the worst of all time in China but it was among the worst and much of it was the result of state policy.

VI

Trudeau's global travels and his prognostications about the international order between 1948 and 1965 brought him to some intriguing positions. In 1948 he started out with high hopes for a Christian socialism and for the spread of political democracy throughout the planet. He doubted that communism was the solution to the socio-economic dilemmas of Asia and the underdeveloped world. Over time his ideas became more secular and he came more and more to abandon the idea that democracy and liberal rights were applicable in what was increasingly called the underdeveloped or the Third World. China initially he had looked at critically through the lens of a Western nativism—or Orientalism—but by the early 1960s he was an admirer of the Chinese tradition and a celebrant of its straitened political ways. He came to see Mao as a hero of sorts. Throughout these years Trudeau was a decided critic of Great Power imperialism and exploitation. He aspired to speak for a community of mainly small, relatively powerless, and often misunderstood nations. His was a refreshingly dissident and unconventional outlook during the Cold War. Trudeau believed that there was a better way of running the world than the old imperialism and the balance of power that in an era of nuclear rivalries always had the potential to tip the planet into a general conflagration. His perspective was bold and confident and not in any way beholden to vested interests either at home or abroad. In his skepticism and dismissal of the pretensions and moral disorders of the Western Great Powers his equivalent today would be thinkers like Noam Chomsky or Slavoj Žižek.

For Canada he sought independence from the embrace of the United States and support for small and struggling nations who if they worked together, he believed, might act as a counterbalance to the lunacies of a bipolar world. Regarding the two emerging giants of the international communist movement, the USSR and China, he counselled the Western powers to show understanding and forbearance, and détente and peaceful co-existence. Trudeau was capable of profound criticisms of both of them, the USSR more so than China, but he never rejected the fundamental premises of their socialist state. He disdained Stalinism but never rejected the Soviet Union as a pioneer of socialism, and altogether he recommended a postwar order of respectful competing socialisms.

But that is the point; at the end of his intellectual and geographic journeys, by the early 1960s Trudeau clearly remained a convinced socialist. Theoretically he wanted a democratic socialism that respected individual and minority rights but he doubted that in the very different environments of non-Western countries there could be an actual application of liberal and democratic practices and ideals. This perspective stood at the heart of his argument about China and places like Cuba, Algeria, and Tanzania.

Even so his position is puzzling. Understood in its most simple terms it was that China's problems and by implication those of the Third World constituted circumstances of such poverty and insecurity that a liberal-democratic order could not succeed. For these countries had no democratic traditions and capitalism offered little possibility of success. In Trudeau's mind his was a counsel of acute moral realism, ends and means being appropriately coordinated. It was not that he abandoned all regard for the premises of personalism and the value of individuals and persons. His position remained that all souls were valuable but that in the actual circumstances of China this presupposed basic rights to life and survival, indeed the very economic rights delineated in his 1958 and 1961 essays on the subject. What were required in China were the methods of the Great Leap Forward. And in any case it was not that the *sine qua non* of personalism was always some version of liberal-democracy. Mounier, the great personalist, expressed more than a little regard for the Soviet Union, especially after 1945, and personalism in the 1930s had a checkered relationship with Nazism and other authoritarian governments. The fulfilment of persons, it seems, could be advanced through all sorts of regimes.

In an essay published in May 1964 Trudeau provided a remarkable insight into what informed his thinking on freedom in the Third World. In the middle of chastising young nationalists in Quebec he offered the following:

The progress of humanity is a slow advancement towards the liberty of the person. Those who are responsible for an abrupt

reversal of this direction reveal themselves as counter-revolutionaries. In some historical situations where the liberty of the person
has hardly been protected at all by established institutions, it can
then be that a genuine revolutionary can put the emphasis on
collective freedoms, as a prelude to personal freedoms: Castro,
Ben Bella and Lenin. . . . But when personal freedoms exist it
would be *inconceivable that a revolutionary would destroy them*
[Trudeau's emphasis] in the name of some collective ideology.
For the very goal of the collectivity is to better assure personal
freedoms. (Otherwise one is a fascist).[124]

Here Trudeau gave voice to a theoretical account of the very practical predicament that he had identified in China, namely a culture where institutions did not accord great respect for personal
freedoms but where the pursuit of survival and security through
collective means might lead to economic security and eventually,
presumably, the enjoyment of personal freedoms. This account
saw Trudeau asserting the ultimate value of personal freedom but
what was problematical were the means to attain it if a tradition
of personal freedom was nonexistent. His was an argument about
practicalities and modalities as well as about what was ultimately
valuable. On this occasion, Trudeau did not mention Mao as one
of the tribunes of collective freedom in the cause of personal freedom but he would have been a logical fit with the three leaders he
did mention. In his general thesis here, Trudeau was being optimistic and speculative. Even if it was, at the time of his writing, too
early—and it probably was not—to estimate the political trajectory
of Castro in Cuba and Ben Bella in Algeria it was not too early to
estimate the effects of Lenin. Lenin was well known for his disdain
for what he derisively called bourgeois freedoms and of course his
successor built on illiberal tendencies established already under
Lenin. (Trudeau seemed to concede this in his comments about
Stalin and the Soviet Union.) This was an interesting argument
on Trudeau's part as he struggled with the perplexity of what to
recommend in cases where there were non-existent traditions of

personal freedom, the rule of law, multipartyism and democratic elections. In his notebooks in 1948–49 Trudeau had contended that China would benefit from the application of these very rights and arrangements but by 1961 he had abandoned this perspective. There were places on earth where the social contract did not apply.

8

Federalism and Nationalism

———— • ◆ • ————

*(B)ecause it seems obvious to me that nationalism—and of course
I mean the Canadian as well as the Quebec variety—has put her on
a collision course, I am suggesting that cold, unemotional rationality
can still save the ship. Acton's prophecy . . . is now in danger of being
fulfilled in Canada. "Its course," he stated of nationality, "will be
marked with material as well as moral ruin, in order that a new
invention may prevail over the works of God and the interests
of mankind." This new invention may well be functionalism
in politics; and perhaps it will prove to be inseparable from any
workable concept of federalism.*
Pierre Elliott Trudeau.

*Who is so narrow-minded that he cannot envisage
several horizons?*
Pierre Elliott Trudeau

*The apparent universal ideological domination of nationalism today
is a sort of optical illusion. A world of nations cannot exist,
only a world where some potentially nationalist groups, in claiming
this status, exclude others from making similar claims, which,
as it happens, not many of them do.*
E.J. Hobsbawm

I

Inevitably Trudeau's perspective on postwar constitutional matters was shaped by the dual traumas of his youth and early adult-
hood, the Depresssion and the Second World War. Much of the

legal responsibility for responding to these had resided with the provinces except that they had been chronically handicapped in doing very much because of straitened economic and fiscal capacities. Circumstances were so bad that in the 1930s several of them had come close to bankruptcy. The Rowell-Sirois Commission, appointed in 1937 to investigate the crisis, concluded in 1940, *inter alia*, that a realignment of federal–provincial finances was necessary and recommended the "renting" by the federal government of particular tax fields in return for a system of subsidies to the provinces.[1] The war created a climate of support for the central government, except in Quebec, and in 1942 the majority of provinces agreed to exactly such a tax-rental arrangement. At federal–provincial conferences in 1945 and 1946 the federal government proposed an extension of the agreement. By 1947 all but Ontario and Quebec had signed on to the proposal. The pact was renewed in 1952 when the original seven signatories agreed, together with newly acceded Newfoundland, with Ontario finally signing on as well. Other constitutional questions pressed in on postwar policy makers. Until 1949 Canada's final court of appeal remained the Judicial Committee of the Privy Council (JCPC) in London; and in a similar vein Canada remained beholden to the parliament at Westminster for the amendment of its constitution. As well, many provisions in the BNA Act contradicted the country's status as a truly federal state: the federal power over the provinces of reservation and disallowance; a completely federally appointed Supreme Court and Senate; and a division of tax powers that seemed inordinately to favour the central government. Also present and pressing on political leaders were rising expectations about the social rights of Canadians. In these years the judicial resolution of federal–provincial conflicts was not a widely canvassed option, nor was the formal amendment of the constitution and the redistribution of powers easily useable either. So there arose, often through federal initiative, a prevailing though not necessarily unanimous inclination towards what was called co-operative federalism. The "new" constitution should be adjusted intergovernmentally.

Throughout all this Quebec was the principal objector so that the most significant cleavage in Canada remained the ethnic and linguistic one between the French and the English. Left outside the tax-rental system through its own choice Quebec continued to be taxed by the federal government in the fields of income and corporation taxes and succession duties but without financial compensation. With his conservative nationalism Duplessis was a constant thorn in the side of Ottawa. Among his complaints was that the federal government disregarded the constitution: Ottawa intruded too much on provincial jurisdiction. Canadian unity, then, not well served in the conscription crisis, continued to be in difficulty. And after 1960 a more secular, left-wing nationalism came to prominence and offered an even more portentous political challenge. With the new nationalism, as with the old, Trudeau was unceasingly exercised. Under the influence of Mounier, Maritain, and Laski traces of an anti-nationalism began to appear in him; as time passed they became ever more noticeable.

From Carl Friedrich and Charles McIlwain at Harvard he had also learned about the virtues of constitutionalism and bills of rights. He was conversant with K.C. Wheare's ground-breaking work, *Federal Government*, published in 1946, and he was also increasingly familiar with the homegrown, left-wing constitutionalism of Frank Scott and Eugene Forsey.[2] Scott was an early advocate of an entrenched charter of rights and, like Forsey, he developed a highly informed understanding of the principles at the heart of Confederation and the BNA Act.[3] In Quebec there was beginning to appear the works of non-nationalist, academic constitutionalists such as Paul Gérin-Lajoie's *Constitutional Amendment in Canada* in 1950 and Maurice Lamontagne's *Le fédéralisme Canadien: évolution et problèmes* in 1954. Trudeau knew of these. He read the primers and introductory political science texts of the time, the works of R.M. Dawson, J.A. Corry, and H.M. Clokie.[4] He consulted the *Independence Papers* of that intrepid Ottawa lawyer, J.S. Ewart;[5] he read extensively about the political history and jurisprudence of Canada, from constitutional authorities like A.B. Keith and his encyclopedic work, *Responsible Government in the Dominions,* and W.P.M. Kennedy's *The Constitution of Canada* to Canadian procedural and legal experts like J.T. Loranger, P.B. Mignault, Emery Beaulieu, and Aimé Geoffrion.[6]

But if anything especially set in motion Trudeau's own constitutional prescriptions it was Laski's account of the consensual and pluralistic foundations of authority in the modern state. Almost as the raison d'être of his intellectual endeavours Laski had taken concentrated aim at what he considered to be one of the great fallacies of European thought, namely the Hobbesian/Hegelian account of the state as sovereign dictator of society. Instead he argued for the inherently federal nature of society and the inevitably pluralist character of the state. It was the lived experience of people that lay at the base of political authority, Laski claimed. Out of their perceived needs arose a co-operation that was federal in its nature since it encompassed the people's many diversities; political unity was a derivative of these realities and was an endlessly manufactured thing; the direction taken by the state depended on popular consent mobilized by political parties in periodic elections and by organized groups in civil society. Trudeau echoed these arguments very closely in his *Vrai* essays, as we saw. It followed that if society was invariably diverse in composition, then, in regard to the question of nationality and its relation to government, the state could never be "the juridical personification of one nation."[7] Here was the fundamental error of nationalism. Trudeau, we know, had embraced such ideas by the time of his Paris lectures in 1947–48. Canada, he believed, was a "federated country" with a federal constitution. He recognized the degree to which the BNA Act prescribed a strong element of centralization but, like Wheare perhaps, he believed that if the written constitution was a quasi-federal one the actual constitution might well render it "politically federal."[8] Trudeau took an expansive view of Canada; it was a place that offered the multiple loyalties of region and nation, a truly intercultural territory with many subcultures, embodying what he referred to in 1950 as the ideal of "intercitizenship."[9] Yet it had an overarching integrity and unity too. And so in these early essays Trudeau was patriotic both for Canada and Quebec and he saw no contradiction between the two.

Between 1949 and 1965 Trudeau's ideas on federalism and the constitution appeared in two important sets of essays, one at the beginning and the other at the end of the period. The first included the position papers he wrote while in the PCO about the compact theory of Confederation and the idea of co-operative federalism. Other essays spoke to the pressing issues of tax rental agreements, federal subsidies, federal grants to universities, and Quebec's resistance to all of them. Also important were his submission to the Tremblay Commission in March 1954 and his essays, "De libro, tribute . . . et quibusdam aliis" in October 1954 and "Les octrois fédéraux aux universités" in February 1957. The second set encompassed Trudeau's response to the new nationalism in Quebec in the early 1960s: "L'aliénation nationaliste" (1961), "La nouvelle trahison des clercs" (1962), "Les séparatistes: des contre-révolutionaires" (1964), and "Federalism, Nationalism and Reason" (1964). There was also his intriguing essay, "The Practice and Theory of Federalism" in 1961. Always Trudeau was preoccupied by the predicament of Quebec but these two clusters embody also his more abstract considerations on federalism and nationalism. On the eve of his return to Ottawa and bringing his thinking to some kind of timely and, for our purposes, tidy conclusion, there was his significant essay in early 1965, "Le Québec et le problème constitutionnel."

II

In "Notes on the Compact Theory" in 1949 Trudeau took the measure of two prevailing interpretive accounts of the Canadian constitution: the compact theory and the view that the BNA Act was the product of an actual political process, what Trudeau called the "law" view. The compact interpretation, which had been aggressively advanced in the 1880s by two provincial premiers, Honoré Mercier in Quebec and Oliver Mowat in Ontario, was reasserted strongly in the 1940s and 1950s by Duplessis. It held that Confederation was a compact or an agreement between the original colonies who had determined its terms and who had then been succeeded in their political-legal identity by the provinces. A subargument had it that it was these provinces who had created the central government. The theory emphasized the autonomy and independence of the provinces within their spheres of jurisdiction and thus the overwhelmingly federal nature of the BNA Act. However these claims seemed to other commentators to be negated by provisions in the 1867 Constitution that delineated a clear federal primacy.[10] Compact theory's other significant assertion was that any alteration of the terms of Confederation necessarily required the consent of all the provinces. Against this view was the one made popular in the postwar period by Donald Creighton and Eugene Forsey who pointed out *inter alia* that Confederation was a process in which the colonies certainly participated but not in any determinative way and that the terms of such agreements as the Quebec Resolutions in 1864 were no more than advisory to the British government and parliament. The telling insight of such commentators was that the provisions of the BNA Act were never ratified by any of the original provinces and, in the case of Nova Scotia, they were actually rejected. If the compact theory was the authorized version of Canada's constitution, how was it that such amendments to the constitution as had taken place had been attained, in many cases, without unanimous provincial consent?

In an advisory brief written in 1949 Trudeau assiduously summarized the evidence for both views. If anything he seems to have seen more validity in the compact view. An impressive list of politicians in 1867 and afterwards, in Canada and Britain, he said, had favoured this account as had many constitutional and legal experts. Trudeau inclined to this interpretation perhaps because he favoured the view that a realized federation of strong but separate levels of government was what Canada had come to represent and that a federal state needed an original social contract or "fundamental law" that bound diverse peoples together. Yet he also listed the arguments against the compact theory:

> 1. It is difficult to identify the parties to the contract.
> 2. The parties didn't have treaty making powers.
> 3. The true function of the delegation to London was advisory in character.
> 4. In fact substantial changes were made and not referred back to the provincial legislatures.
> 5. John A. Macdonald says that the [BNA] Act must be hurried through without the provinces knowing too much about it (e.g. Ewart, *Independence Papers*).
> 6. The use of the word "treaty" in discussion was purely rhetorical.
> 7. The actual practice of amendment is definitely against the implications of the compact theory.[11]

His conclusion was that neither side's argument was sufficiently overwhelming to carry the day. Therefore elements from both should be included in ongoing constitutional discussions. But this was an advantage, in his opinion, because the idea of a compromise or a contract was the very thing that must underwrite a federal constitution and the terms of any amending formula:

> The Act of 1867 is a *law* of the Imperial Parliament; but a law based on a *contract*; and therefore the very meaning of the law is derived from the original contract. But that is tantamount to saying that the BNA Act is a *federal* constitution. Therefore jurisdiction is divided: the sovereignty of Ottawa is limited by certain constitutional provisions, just as sovereignty of the provinces is limited. And therefore an amending process should call for one party, or for several jointly, or for all unanimously according to whether sovereignty is exercised by one, many or all, in that particular case. Thus would end the extreme rigidity of the compact theory, and the extreme arbitrariness of the legal theory: by the simple admission that a federal constitution is no ordinary statute.[12]

Trudeau offered exactly the same view ten years later when he said that

> the Act of 1867 was a law of the Imperial Parliament, but a law based on an agreement between federating parties, and consequently a law which can be understood and interpreted (and eventually amended) by referring to the spirit of that agreement.[13]

Trudeau resumed the issue of the amending formula in a memo of December of the same year, "Federalism Revisited." He took as his starting premise that Canada was a bona fide federal state that claimed sovereign independence. But there was unfinished business. The JCPC had been retired as the final court of appeal but the Supreme Court left much to be desired regarding its impartiality, given that it was appointed by the federal government; and it was absurd that the British Parliament still was integrally involved in changing Canada's constitution. As part of an amendment package, he said, the provinces might be given some involvement in determining the number of justices on the Supreme Court and the manner of their nomination. With regard to a home-grown amending procedure, he laid out three types of legislative powers that might be subject to different formulae: areas of exclusive jurisdiction, subjects involving both levels of government, and finally areas to do with fundamental principles relating to the identity of the whole country, "that is to say, sections concerning matters of such vital significance to the community that upon their inviolability is founded the general will to live together as people of one country."[14] An instance of the last was the entrenchment of a bill of rights. In a similar vein he talked of the "sovereign people of Canada, federally united, wish[ing] to take the constituent powers to themselves."[15] Here Trudeau was using a republican language of democratic legitimation that was not always central to Canadian constitutional discourse. Amending areas of exclusive jurisdiction, he continued, would require only the agreement of the specific legislature or parliament; while areas of shared jurisdiction might entail the agreement of six out of ten provinces having 60 percent of the population with the federal parliament also required to agree; matters of the "general will" would presuppose unanimity or near unanimity. Trudeau proposed that the upcoming federal–provincial meeting should constitute itself a "constituent conference" for the purpose of agreeing to an amending formula. Its specific determinations would become "a general will" and might involve a ratifying formula of unanimity, or nine of the ten provinces having 90 percent of the population and if less than that, no lower than eight out of ten or 80 percent. He was not altogether impressed by the idea of involving the people directly in constitution-making: "the people are hardly good judges in matters of law." They should however be involved in ratifying a new amending formula: "the people would be directly appealed to through a series of plebiscites by province." Here it is not clear whether Trudeau was recommending plebiscites instead of the vote of a provincial legislature or as an addition to such a vote. For now he displayed a decided optimism about constitutional renewal though he was not without a sense of the inevitable wranglings that federal–provincial relations engendered.[16]

Two other memos followed for the attention of his superior in the PCO, Gordon Robertson: "Theory and Practice of Federal–Provincial Co-operation," written in June 1950, and "Federal–Provincial Co-operation" in September, the latter an amended version of the former.[17] In Canada, he argued, there were growing expectations of an enlarged and dynamic role for government in providing a welfare state; however, there was a disproportion between the financial powers of the two levels of government and their administrative responsibilities. Grants-in-aid by the federal government to the provinces to encourage the expansion of social services had had the unfortunate effect of inducing some provinces to provide a level of services that they could not afford and many had gone into debt. To deal with such problems Trudeau qualified the classically federal tenor of his previous views and argued that the formal realignment of jurisdictions was impractical because so much of the constitution was a series of overlapping jurisdictions

and because governments tended through the dynamics of offsetting power "to invade contiguous spheres of action." As well in
modern society complexity was everywhere. Neither was judicial
review necessarily the best way to deal with conflict. This led him
to what became a central contention of his account of federalism,
at least at this time: that intergovernmental co-operation was now
absolutely essential. If such a perspective was embraced, federal–
provincial relations, he believed, could be transformed:

> Often their [the different levels of government] dealings with one
> another have been nothing but a disguised attempt to gain more
> power. Naturally the result has not been greater understanding,
> but rather the development of a persecution complex, which in
> turn results in increased aggressiveness.
>
>   This psychological trend can only be reversed by creating a
> greater sense of security in all governments.
>
>   Confidence might rapidly be engendered if the good inten-
> tions and pious resolutions of Federal [sic] and provincial gov-
> ernments were rationalized and then imprinted upon political
> realities by institutionalization. Men have long discovered the
> value of the institution as a framework and a catalyst for their vir-
> tuous actions, and as a shield against their irrational impulses.[18]

He went on to advocate such structures as a permanent intergovernmental secretariat and regular intergovernmental conferences.
In exchange for establishing a bill of rights the federal government
might give up its traditional power of reservation and disallowance.
Above all he believed there should be a change of heart, especially
by those at the federal level so that the two orders of government
would treat each other with a sense of equality and mutual respect.
For example, they should both be involved in drawing up the agendas of intergovernmental conferences:

> The Federal Government would also be less tempted to act as the
> self-righteous victim who is being forced to centralize against its

will by the very inaction of the provinces. Nor would there be any repetition of the paradoxes of the 1945 Conference when the Federal Government, because it had greater financial resources, argued that it should bear greater social responsibility, and therefore that its financial powers should be increased. . . .

    If the Supreme Court in constitutional cases, and the Royal Commissions in joint questions, were given a really "federal" mandate, instead of a unitary one; if relations between Ottawa and the provinces, as characterised by one-way delegation of power, and by pressurized grants-in-aid, were to become really a two-way avenue of exchange; then there might be some hope of fruitful co-operation.[19]

It was an impressive but perhaps overly optimistic account of imagined relations between governments in Canada. Nevertheless these early papers do attest to the depth and reach of Trudeau's thoughts on these complex questions and his understanding of the many layers of the federal system in Canada. He expressed a firm belief in classical federalism: an effectively demarcated division of powers was an important aspect of a well-ordered government in a pluralistic society. But that was not all because a clear demarcation of powers could not always be attained and new demands were always being made of government so that Trudeau's conclusion was that the Canadian state—federal and provincial—was a many-sided architecture of immense complexity. But in that case, how easy would it be for the average citizen to follow federalism's arcane and intricate logic and unerringly hold particular levels of government accountable, as Trudeau also required? The question is germane because in another major statement on federalism Trudeau offered prescriptions that multiplied even more the intricacies of federal–provincial relations. This was the implication of his presentation in March 1954 to the Tremblay Commission.

    The commission had been set up by Duplessis in early 1953 as part of his ongoing opposition to Ottawa's conduct of postwar federal–provincial affairs, particularly its insistence on maintaining

tax rental agreements in return for federal grants. The FUIQ brief—
it was Trudeau who wrote it—was a long one of thirty-nine pages,
packed with statistical detail. It was here that he rehearsed many
of the arguments and methodologies that appeared in *La grève de
l'amiante* in 1956. Trudeau was in his element. He was representing a
non-confessional, international, and industrial trade union federation that through its affiliation to the Canadian Congress of Labour
articulated a national perspective and not just a Quebec one. He
was perfectly placed to make the case against Quebec nationalism
and provincialism and other ill-advised stances of Duplessis, yet
he spoke of a balanced federalism and was critical of the centralizing tendencies of the federal government. The brief demonstrated
again Trudeau's detailed grasp of policy-making. Federal–provincial relations could not be considered from a static position, he reasoned, because these were set in a changing environment. Not only
must the authority of different jurisdictions be respected but there
must be an acceptance of co-operation between different levels of
government and between governments at the same level too. But,
most importantly, there must be regard for the claims of social justice through equalization payments and economic stabilization, as
he called the new priorities of Keynesian planning and full employment. Trudeau was articulating a social democratic constitutional
vision. At the time only Scott and Forsey—Trudeau thanked them
for their advice—were comparable in their intellectual competency
and political convictions.[20] Trudeau's analysis was equally pioneer-
ing and scintillating.

In his brief Trudeau spoke with a special concern for the industrial workers of Quebec who, he said, were more poorly paid than
those in Ontario, who endured higher unemployment and inferior
healthcare and housing, and who lacked access to post-secondary
education. But questions of social injustice involved a constitutional dimension as well, he contended. Workers deserved a living
wage, a welfare state, and national standards of labour, but these
matters fell largely under provincial jurisdiction and were vulnerable to the divide-and-conquer mentality of big business as it played

provinces off against each other. Yet a provincial responsibility for labour was, Trudeau believed, wholly fitting: matters of contract were best dealt with locally. That being so, perhaps through inter-provincial agreement a common labour code might be established. And, if not that, then resort might be had to a formal constitutional amendment transferring labour responsibilities to the federal level.

Workers, then, had a fundamental interest in constitutional questions and were connected to a broader political world than simply collective bargaining and strikes. They were seized by broad concerns and values. It was a social democratic constitutionalism informed by personalism that Trudeau espoused:

> The Federation of Industrial Unions of Quebec is happy to come before this Commission of Inquiry into constitutional problems. For the constitution is the fundamental law which shapes the form of the State and determines the framework at the heart of which the nation [*nation*] is governed for the common good. And Canada being a sovereign and democratic country [*pays*], its constitution must express the collective will of its citizens and how they can reach out to govern themselves so that each can realize himself to the best that is within him. . . . However if [the Federation] appears, as much by this brief as by its daily activities to be pursuing more specifically guarantees of the material conditions of life, this should not lead to the conclusion that workers place spiritual concerns [*esprit*] second. On the contrary, they are just as concerned as anyone to ensure respect for all human values; and they consider that the very basis of civil and political society is the postulate of the inviolability of the person. That is why they wish, through the Canadian constitution, to remove from the realm of the arbitrary those fundamental requirements that flow from this postulate. In particular, they believe profoundly in a democratic system and in freedoms which are connected to it, principally freedoms of belief, thought, speech; freedoms of the press, assembly and association. They affirm the equality of all before

the law: and they hold that the reality of one nation, built on the union of two great ethnic groups, should be reinforced by a federalism that is intelligent and open.[21]

And so Trudeau set out a version of federalism that was, he believed, a balanced one, which avoided both centralization and decentralization and which addressed the pressing issue of justice for workers, a welfare minimum for all citizens, the promise of liberal democracy, and the pursuit of economic prosperity. Regarding the constitution, Trudeau summarized his concerns in three important principles. The first was fiscal proportionality. By this he meant that the division of financial powers should be proportionate to the actual division of jurisdictional responsibilities. Provinces, especially because they were in the front line providing the services of the welfare state, should have enough revenues to meet their obligations. This, said Trudeau, had not hitherto been the case. The second principle was that of financial equalization: there must be revenue distribution that would ensure "a minimum level of subsistence to all [of society's] members." He went on: "in effect, the cohesion of the political society depends on its will to assure the vital minimum for all its members regardless of geographic location."[22] This would entail a redistributive role for the federal government so that all provinces, including those with sluggish economies and below-average fiscal capacities could meet a minimum standard, without going into debt or imposing impossibly high tax levels. The taxpayers in richer provinces through federal equalization policies would be contributing to common levels of services throughout the country. Thirdly, there was the imperative that Trudeau called economic stabilization, ensuring that government pursued anticyclical policies favoured by Canadians in general, as Trudeau put it. His assumption was that there was an emerging popular consensus in favour of a Keynesian management of the economy. There must be restraining financial and economic policies in times of strong growth and inflation, and expansionary ones in a time of slow growth and impending recession. Ottawa should oversee the whole process, but it should do so in co-operation with the provinces. As with equalization, stabilization gave primary responsibility to the federal government. That was the major shift in constitutional practice that Trudeau was proposing. Only the federal level had a country-wide ambit of policy-making and possessed the jurisdictional levers that controlled banking, currency, and trade and commerce. The tantalizing question, he thought, was how to involve the provinces, for in many ways the two levels of government were driven by contradictory inclinations. In a recession the provinces tended to reduce spending and avoid indebtedness and in a time of inflation they were tempted to lower taxes and increase spending. And of course in Quebec and some other provinces, there was resistance in principle to any enlarged federal role.

What Trudeau proposed as a solution was a highly complex concatenation of intergovernmental agreements, all superbly and unerringly calibrated and realized, he believed. Under the existing tax rental agreements, he said, the level of subsidy must be fixed so as to take account of these many priorities. (He seemed to have overlooked the inevitable presence of scarcity, real or imagined, as well as political rivalries, although he claimed otherwise.) His system presumed co-operation all round. But how was it to be achieved? He repeated some of the recommendations he had discussed in his PCO days. There should be intergovernmental conferences at regular intervals and a permanent intergovernmental secretariat; governments should participate in these institutions as equals; and the agendas of their conferences should be the result of the participation of all governments. Later that year Trudeau floated ideas to do with the introduction of an interprovincial commission to prepare fiscal agreements and anticyclical policies in the area of public works and an intergovernmental credit organization to allow provinces to adopt deficit budgeting in a time of recession.[23] In 1961 he advocated a permanent committee of federal and provincial officials to make recommendations on fiscal policy.[24] His system was ambitious—perhaps even a little utopian—and yet something resembling it has become the norm in Canada in the last fifty years, although of course not necessarily working with any-where near clockwork precision.

In 1954, the pressing issue had to do with Quebec's continuing resistance to Ottawa's tax rental system. It was to fight this battle that Duplessis had set up the Tremblay Commission in the first place. Trudeau usually held no brief for Duplessis so that predict-ably on this occasion he especially opposed his call for the federal government to withdraw altogether from the field of direct taxa-tion. Said Trudeau, the BNA Act gave general powers of taxation including direct taxes to the federal government and as long as Ottawa raised them for genuinely federal purposes all was well. Direct taxes, Trudeau said, bore heavily on the rich—he approved of that—and were necessary for Ottawa to sustain its obligations in the areas of health, unemployment insurance, and old age pensions. But where Duplessis was right and the federal government delin-quent, he believed, was over the latter's ongoing direct taxation of citizens in Quebec even though the province had not entered into a tax rental agreement and was not in receipt of federal grants-in-aid. After Quebec had decided to introduce a provincial income tax, this had become an egregious instance of double taxation. The issue at its heart was about the "deductibility" of Quebec's federal taxes in light of their non-participation in the tax rental system. Such was Trudeau's desire to expose the injustice of Ottawa's treatment of the province that he went as far as to produce a second edition of his brief to the Tremblay Commission. Writing in February 1955, just after the federal government had announced that non-partic-ipating provinces could receive a 10 percent reduction in their fed-eral income tax payable, Trudeau concluded that the decision was unacceptable. It was unilateral and contradicted the government's own anticyclical principle because the offer was not conditional on the province maintaining existing levels of taxation—Trudeau believed the mid-1950s was a time of inflation—and of course it was an "injustice" because the amount in question was significantly less than what Quebec would have received if it had signed on to the agreements.

Trudeau's position in this debate was not always clear. What seems to have been the case was that he did not favour tax rental agreements as such, though he seemed to believe that they were justified as temporary expedients. In that case he held that it would be better that Quebec be brought into the present arrangements rather than that it stand outside them. As such, his priority was one of encouraging the federal government to realign the formulae to ensure general provincial participation. In other words Trudeau did see intrinsic merit in the principle of a common relation of the federal government to the provinces although earlier in 1950 he seemed willing to countenance consensually agreed delegations of power back and forth between Ottawa and individual provinces.[25] Above all he put his faith in the practice of a broad co-operation that would solve ongoing conflicts. It was almost a tautological truth: all would be well if there was sufficient agreement to make things well. On this occasion in 1954–55 he remonstrated with Quebec to embrace as well a package of changes that should, he thought, ensure its willing participation in the Canadian constitutional family:

> Thus the Province would well be able to declare itself ready to accept the inclusion of a declaration of human rights in the constitution on condition that there be extinguished the powers of reservation and disallowance. The Province might suggest a precise plan to repatriate the Canadian Constitution, and with it an amending formula, on condition that the Senate was made into an institution more federalist and less unitary, and on condition that the organization of the Supreme Court be made a part of the Canadian constitution rather than the product of federal statutes alone.[26]

Trudeau would continue to argue for this basket of policies for some time.[27] It has partial resemblance to the one that he offered Quebec and the other provinces after the defeat of the referendum in Quebec in 1980. What were absent later were those elements of intra-state federalism that pertained to the possible roles of the provinces in the Senate and Supreme Court. Trudeau exhibited continuity in his constitutional prescriptions but also willingness to horse-trade, at least a little. Also present, no doubt, was a disposition to take political contexts into account. Throughout the period we are looking at he held that there needed to be some provincial say in the appointment of Supreme Court justices. He would likely never have acceded to such an arrangement if the provincial government of Quebec were composed of separatists!

Trudeau was offered another opportunity to refine his views on the division of powers when in the mid-1950s Duplessis prevented the distribution of federal monies to universities in the province. Although he abhorred him as a dictator of sorts, Trudeau came to his defence in a strongly worded essay, "Les octrois fédéraux aux universités" in *Cité Libre* in February 1957. This was one instance when a Wheare-like emphasis upon the separateness of the division of powers under a federal system was relevant and appropriate, he thought. In other words the need for co-operation for Trudeau did not pre-empt an appreciation of separate jurisdictions where these could be clearly demarcated. A clear separation of jurisdiction was important, he maintained, because it was indispensible in ensuring that the citizens of a federation, who were after all the electorates of both federal and provincial governments, were able to hold each level accountable. No matter how proponents of federal grants to universities and of an unrestricted federal power of the purse argued their case—in other words that the federal government had authority to spend monies in whatever ways it chose or that universities were part of a federal jurisdiction—Trudeau concluded that their arguments ended in absurdity. The basic principle that must hold under federalism was that because the provision for a "common good" was divided between two levels of government, each should provide for it "as it decides itself," and each should avoid interfering in the business of the other.[28] If it did breach its jurisdictional boundaries this for Trudeau was telltale proof that the government in question had too much money and was taxing its people excessively. In the case of universities Trudeau believed that the provisions of the constitution were clear enough: it was a provincial responsibility. He continued by examining the arguments of others, for example about universities being part of the world of culture and thus of legitimate federal concern and about federal monies being properly spent on universities from funds that the federal government possessed though not from taxes but rather from the profits of crown corporations and such. Such arguments were specious according to Trudeau. Nor could spending the monies be justified according to Keynesian stabilization principles because, if anything, in an inflationary time the flow of monies should be reduced. The claims of equalization did not offer a blanket justification either: "I believe in equalization so long as it relates to that part of the common good assigned to the federal government."[29]

Trudeau's last point is ambiguous. While such a claim allowed him to seem consistent on the question of the division of powers, it contradicted what was surely the main drift of his own earlier case for equalization by means of which the federal government would make monies available to the poorer provinces for the financing of services in their own areas of jurisdiction. If the services were provided by the federal government in areas of federal jurisdiction these would anyway be provided universally and there would be a redistributive effect because federal taxes drawn from the more prosperous parts of the country would be paying for identical services in other parts. But this would have still left unaddressed the question of national minima in services provided by the provinces. Perhaps Trudeau believed that a provincial government spending monies from unconditional grants made available by Ottawa for equalization purposes was not an interference with the provinces' jurisdiction, given that the latter would have made the final determination of how exactly to spend them. But clearly such monies would, in all likelihood, be spent on matters within provincial jurisdiction. The matter is unclear. Anyway, Trudeau went on, spending on universities in the way the federal government had undertaken it could not constitute an equalization strategy because it was spending on universities *throughout* the whole country and not just in poorer provinces. However he did concede that there could be federal spending on university education to do with agriculture and fisheries since these were areas where the federal government did have a jurisdictional standing—but that was all. It was not very much. That the universities were underfunded did not justify Ottawa sticking its nose in provincial affairs.

What is most surprising was Trudeau's absolute dismissal of the idea of a federal power to spend directly in whatever areas of juris- diction it chose.[30] Foregoing such a power meant operating without the principal instrument whereby the federal government came to shape the modern welfare state in Canada whose subject-matters, especially health care and social assistance, fall so inordinately within provincial jurisdiction.[31] Four years later, in his essay, "The Practice and Theory of Federalism," Trudeau offered an even more categorical objection to an unfettered federal spending power:

> Professor Corry finds it 'extraordinary that no one has challenged the constitutionality of the assumed spending power before the Supreme Court'. . . . I share this wonderment; but I find it even more extraordinary that political scientists fail to see the cor- roding effect that the 'power of the purse' will have on Canadian democracy if the present construction continues to prevail, and in particular what chaos will result if provincial governments bor- row federal logic and begin using their own 'power of the purse' to meddle in federal affairs.

On this occasion Trudeau went on to refer his readers to his discus- sion in "Federal Grants to Universities."[32] Trudeau changed his mind on this issue. In *Federal–Provincial Grants and the Spending Power of Parliament* (1969), he proposed entrenching a federal spending power in the constitution, with certain conditions however.[33]

III

Setting in motion Trudeau's complicated account of federalism was his belief in pluralism. Perhaps, after personalism, it was the central ordering concept in his thinking, and, with economic class, the most important one in his account of the political sociology of modern Western societies. From pluralism flowed his antipathy towards nationalism. Pluralism was more than just an acceptance of the political reality that had it that societies were invariably diverse and differentiated. Pluralism generated its own intrinsic benefits: differences produced alternative projects and alternative individual identities and mutual curiosities, and they furnished important opportunities for cultural comparison and experimentation, which contributed mightily to the march of civilization. Federalism was the political derivative of pluralism. But nationalism stood in fundamental opposition to both. Pluralism was open and outward-looking, nationalism closed and introverted. Trudeau never strayed from such ideas.

Given the influence of Laski, Maritain, and Mounier, when he returned to Quebec in 1951 it was natural that he would enter upon an undying battle with nationalism. At first the enemy was conservative and clericalist but after the death of Duplessis a new kind of nationalism drew his attention, one that was more secular and "progressive." Trudeau had little time for either and in a series of sharply worded essays between 1961 and 1965 he engaged his new foe unrelentingly. In this case, apart from a passing mention of Maritain, he did not explicitly invoke the authority of his original mentors but instead another set of intellectual authorities. However his message remained constant, for these new authorities had mainly built their arguments on similar premises. Trudeau used the English historian E.H. Carr to help define the nature of the nation, as well as Elie Kedourie and his book *Nationalism* (1960) to the same effect. He was also familiar with the work of Hans Kohn who in 1944 had published an exhaustive study of nationalism, *The Idea of Nationalism: A Study in its Origins and Background.* He made mention too of the work of the English historian, Alfred Cobban, specifically his work *Dictatorship* published in 1939, a copy of which Trudeau had acquired at Harvard in 1944 and which he energetically marked up. And there were three other substantial influences on his thinking about nationalism in the early 1960s: Lord Acton, Father Joseph Thomas Delos, and Julien Benda.

Several intriguing commonalities existed among them. All of them placed the question of nationalism in a broad historical context, so that measured against the long view of things it struck all of them how recent and restricted had been nationalism's existence. As Trudeau put it, given its brief existence nationalism could hardly be considered a biological necessity.[34] It had emerged only in the late eighteenth century and had replaced a predominantly dynastic, aristocratic politics and international order, which were nevertheless somehow more dispassionate and civilized than what had taken their place. Nationalism was a contingent phenomenon whose emergence had greatly depended on social and political artifice and manipulation. Mostly Trudeau's sources saw the French Revolution as decisive. The revolutionaries had pioneered the idea of government and sovereignty as emanations of the will of the people, a unified people or nation. But not yet did the idea have an ethnic connotation. This began to creep in with the coming to power of Napoleon in 1799, "the first modern dictator" as Cobban succinctly put it, who ventured on a course of French imperialist expansion prompting inevitable resistance and counter-nationalism, particularly from the Spanish, the Russians, and the Germans.[35]

Napoleon's defeat and the re-establishment of the old dynastic order after 1815 slowed nationalism's development but by the mid-nineteenth century the idea of a state with specific spatial boundaries and tied to a particular ethnic group was growing in acceptance. After the spread of social Darwinism in the late nineteenth century what constituted the nation was increasingly given a racial, biological definition leading eventually to the horrors of Nazi Germany and the Holocaust. Almost all of Trudeau's sources were highly critical of the contributions of Germans to the idea of nationalism, especially those of Johann Gottlieb Fichte, Friedrich Wilhelm Joseph Schelling, and Johann Gottfried Herder and their conception of the nation as an organic unity that found its true expression through the state. The corollary of German romantic nationalism, Trudeau's teachers believed, was Hegel's idea of the absolutist state and Otto von Bismarck's successful implementation of the same. In their view nationalism valorized force and will so that, inevitably, it dealt oppressively with dissident and "inferior" minorities. German thinkers were not the only villains and Rousseau and Abbé Sieyès were also typically mentioned as individuals who had made a sinister contribution to modern nationalism.

Trudeau's sources also concluded that, in addition to the nation, another feature of modern political evolution had been the centralized state with its effective control over large populations. This however they generally regarded as a potential blessing since it had helped banish the old hierarchies of monarchy and feudalism. They thought that such a state, suitably democratized, was the necessary means to ensure individual rights and the good of all. But somehow it had all gone horribly wrong. Liberal democracy had been hijacked by nationalism. Liberal democrats had failed to anticipate the tyrannical, assimilative implications of democracy's doctrine of majority rule. As an antidote what was necessary was recognition by the state of a higher law than the will of the people, a natural law, "a divine, objective right" regarding the liberty of human conscience, as Acton expressed it, or as Delos put it the valuing of the person as the incarnation of the human spirit and human dignity.[36] All of them concluded that, if care were not taken, nationalism would produce a more effective absolutism and totalitarianism.

Through such authors Trudeau absorbed the ideas of people who were, for the most part, skeptical but unrepentant liberal-democrats who held that liberal nationalism had profound weaknesses but who also believed that these were remediable through federalism and a bill of rights.[37] Yet Trudeau's authorities, though profoundly critical of nationalism, did not dispute the importance of patriotism in the development of human personality and identity. While the organic and sentimental connections of citizens with region, religion, and nation might in the broad course of history be fated to disappear—Acton hoped they never would—or might become reconfigured in different ways, for now they were important instances of actual human affiliations. What must be avoided was not the existence of such identities but the assumption that one of them must provide the basis of the state.

Julien Benda was also important for Trudeau. An eminent French journalist and belletrist in the tradition of Joseph Ernest Renan and Charles Péguy, both of whom Trudeau also admired and quoted, Trudeau identified closely with his assault on the intellectuals of his day who (according to Benda) had sold out to the passions of class, race, and nation. Trudeau felt similarly about Quebec nationalist intellectuals in the early 1960s and he quoted him approvingly at the beginning of his essay "La nouvelle trahison des clercs." For Benda the true intellectual was personified in Leonardo da Vinci, Desiderius Erasmus, and Johann Wolfgang von Goethe, guardians of the universal, the spiritual, and the abstract in the face of the local, the material, and the irrational. Modern culture, Benda believed, egged on by its passionate thinkers, accorded value to pride, arrogance, and self-importance. Enthusiastic partisans of socialism and the working class had much to answer for too but especially so did those who set themselves up as doctrinaires of the nation. For Benda much of French philosophical thought had become little more than a crass celebration of the supposedly special or unique characteristics of a given people. Nationalist ideology was a kind of mentality of aggression so that nations and races could feel superior to others. "Our age is indeed the age of the intellectual organization of political hatreds."[38] What had come to pass was the "mystical adoration of the nation."[39] Nationalism, he said, even celebrated the vices of a given people simply because they were uniquely their own and not those of others.[40] Writing *La trahison des clercs* in 1927, Benda concluded despairingly—we now know how prescient he was—that "humanity is heading for the greatest and most perfect war ever seen in the world, whether it is a war of nations or a war of classes."[41]

Two things about Benda's analysis are especially pertinent to Trudeau's thinking. One was the uncompromising way in which he located nationalism within the human passions and in opposition to more rational and universalist beliefs and forms of belonging. And, secondly, there was his insistence that nationalism pursued comparisons with the Other precisely in order to establish a schema of hierarchy. All national comparisons were invidious. For Benda, nationalism was a force for conflict and domination. There were similar claims in Trudeau.

Someone else to whom Trudeau was indebted was another Frenchman, the Dominican father Joseph Thomas Delos, who in the interwar years was a professor of public law at the Catholic University of Lille where he wrote extensively about international law and colonialism. He later held a position in Father Lévesque's faculty of social science at Laval University. He was a vocal critic of Nazi totalitarianism and this was no doubt why, like Maritain, he remained on the Canadian side of the Atlantic during the war. In 1944 he published in Montreal a two-volume treatise, *Le problème de civilisation: la nation*. Trudeau made reference to this work in his own writing. In this he was unusual for Delos has gone almost completely unnoticed, certainly among the Anglo-Canadian intellectual establishment.[42] Some French-Canadian intellectuals did notice him however. Maurice Tremblay was one and he made use of Delos's book in his critique of French-Canadian nationalism. Trudeau spoke glowingly of Tremblay's article "Réflexions sur le nationalisme" (1959) too.[43]

Delos was an important contributor to what has been called the school of French Institutionalism, along with Maurice Hauriou and Georges Renard. With Renard, Delos brought a natural law and Thomist emphasis to its formulations. In general Institutionalism challenged the Hobbesian and Austinian primacy in legal philosophy and its ideas of an amoral legal positivism with its view of law as the command of a sovereign. Institutionalism sought to insert the group and the institution between the individual and the state and to reintroduce the idea of ethics to legal philosophy. In modern society groups established themselves as a "body," a "communion," and a "foundation."[44] Renard especially talked of the group having an "intimacy."[45] The existence of many groups raised questions of how their powers and interests would be reconciled and "balances" (*équilibres*) established.[46] This was the function of the state but groups themselves in their peaceful dealings provided social order. In their permanence and intensity groups became "institutions."

Delos particularly emphasized the extent to which institutions were one of the important "facts," "realities," or "*données*" of sociological inquiry; they were fundamental data that must be empirically analyzed in order to understand better the operation of the modern state. But just as the institution and the group must constitute an object of empirical investigation, so must be the institution of law itself. Here Institutionalism's distinct voice was that positive law presupposed a moral order. As Delos put it:

> Every legal norm, every juridical system is necessarily bound to principles of a higher ideal; . . . the order set up by positive law is always established with reference to a rational and moral conception—philosophical or metaphysical—of society and human relationships; . . . an aspect of law escapes us if we do not consider it in light of the moral principles inspiring it.[47]

Delos was a committed personalist and Thomist, and in *Le problème de civilisation: la nation*, he made reference to two works by Jacques Maritain that we know Trudeau also read, *Humanisme intégral* and *Les droits de l'homme et la loi naturelle*. Personalism provided Delos with an understanding of the moral basis of what was in so many respects a liberal conception of the state. The latter was not an end in itself but rather a means of "assuring the complete good of human life," as Delos quoting Aristotle once put it; or, as he put it in *Le problème de civilisation: la nation*, "The State is . . . at the service of . . . the common good . . . and the entire human community."[48] Informing the workings of the state, he continued, must be respect for the conscience of the person; "personality" was the highest stage of individual development so that the state's function was to protect "conscious, free, responsible persons."[49] With a foundation in natural law the legitimacy of the state did not derive from the expression of the "will" of its citizens but from its conformity to fundamental principles. Clearly Delos was a personalist, especially in the tradition of Maritain.

The nation was one instance of a community sentiment—family and region were others—by means of which individuals and groups had pursued their goals and made concrete their identity. This was well and good. However nationalism had sown seeds of disorder in its assertion that the nation and society were identical and that the state should represent the nation qua society:

> The nation is a community and not a society. . . . It is an error
> to presume that the nation in organizing itself becomes a state.[50]

For Delos the state represented the ethical ideal of the solidarity of society in support of the rights of all. It could not, without denying its basic function, become the representative of a nation, or of some other community group. Its work was to provide universal protection to all national groups, including those Delos called "*allogènes*," that is, non-native persons, or, as it can also be defined, strangers, minorities, or members of another race. He also made it clear that, if the state was under an obligation to protect national groups, it was not because the nation in question enjoyed rights as a group but rather because the individuals who composed it had *individual* rights.[51] (Trudeau made a similar stipulation.) Federalism too, Delos thought, had something important to contribute to the balancing of the rights of citizens in general and those of nationals in particular. Looking to the future he believed that a global order of states pursuing liberal imperatives would come to pass and, in collaboration with international institutions, would provide an international "society." For now, writing at the height of Nazi domination of Europe, Delos saw more immediate and terrifying possibilities, a deformed state transfixed by the Führer principle:

men absorbed by their quality of nationality; the nation identified with the State; the State identified with the Government; the
Government absorbed with the person of the Leader.[52]

Situating Trudeau in the context of such ideas underlines how
much he might indeed have come to associate nationalism with
collectivism and totalitarianism and with opposition to individual
rights.

In his essays on nationalism in the early 1960s Trudeau quoted
from Lord Acton on at least four occasions. He considered him a
"great" thinker.[53] In an interview with Barry Callaghan in 1968 he
confessed to an ongoing admiration of him but his familiarity with
him, he admitted, was limited:

> My knowledge of Acton is out of one or two books: his essay
> on freedom and power, and another, the title of which I don't
> remember . . . I don't claim to know Acton in great depth. Though
> he's a rather conservative Catholic historian, I especially like his
> humanist approach. I find he is always trying to explain things.
> He's trying to look for the mainsprings in society. I just can't read
> history which is a description of events.[54]

One of the works to which Trudeau was referring was Gertrude
Himmelfarb's collection of Acton's essays, *Essays on Freedom
and Power* published in 1948 and which included the 1862 essay,
"Nationality," from which he quoted so extensively. If he was famil-
iar with another work by Acton it was likely his *Lectures on Modern
History* published in 1906. However calling Acton "a conservative
Catholic historian" tells us much less than is helpful, and much less
than the extent of the uses to which Trudeau put Acton.

John Emerich Edward Dalberg-Acton, first Baron Acton, was
an aristocrat whose family held estates in Shropshire in England. A
Catholic at a time when Catholicism was still slightly illegitimate
in England, he was privately educated in Edinburgh and under
the personal tutelage of Johann Joseph Ignaz Döllinger, a Catholic

historian and theologian, in Munich. Acton's own intellectual life was mainly as an author of essays, published in British journals such as the *Rambler* and the *North British Review*. He was an active, Catholic intellectual and layman, and many of his essays were about the history of the Church. The zenith of his professional life was his appointment in 1895 as the Regius Professor of Modern History at Cambridge University and editor of the *Cambridge Modern History*. He is often famously quoted about his belief that "power corrupts," which he expressed in a letter to an English Anglican churchman who, he thought, had written too approvingly of the pre-Reformation English Catholic Church.

There are obvious continuities though some differences between Acton and Trudeau. Acton became a liberal Catholic and opposed the ultramontane movement of the mid-century papacy of Pius IX and the declaration of papal infallibility by the Vatican Council in 1870. What offended him was ultramontanism's centralizing tendencies, its rejection of scientific inquiry, and its opposition to an evolving tradition of theology. He was appalled by the Church's ongoing defence of the Inquisition and the other atrocities in which it had been involved, a theme that Trudeau picked up and used against his own clerical critics in the early 1950s. Trudeau was also critical of ultramontanism and no doubt he liked the fact that Acton had come close to being excommunicated for such opinions. But Trudeau was right when he said that there were elements of conservatism in Acton, who was a Burkean and believed that politics was an empirical activity requiring an appreciation of tradition and experience and a disdain for utopian abstractions. During the American Civil War he took the side of the southern states arguing that the abolitionists espoused an abstract agenda inconsistent with the tradition of states' rights. Only later did he reject the principle of slavery. A supporter of liberty in other respects, Acton was a cautious man who believed that change should be achieved gradually. He eventually came to believe in expanding the suffrage but he resisted votes for women. He sometimes made criticisms of laissez-faire economics and he did eventually say moderately positive things about the emerging socialist movement in Britain but above all he affirmed the importance of private property. His own politics took him into the House of Commons in 1859 sitting for an Irish constituency as a Liberal. Most of his political life he was a supporter of William Ewart Gladstone, the famous Liberal prime minister, and his project of Home Rule for Ireland. The obvious conclusion about Acton's politics is that he was a conservative liberal, in other words a Whig.

The conservative side of him was perhaps best on display in his view of the very thing that made him a liberal, the concept of liberty. In a sense he was a proto-personalist. Liberty and freedom of conscience were what humans were destined to enjoy:

> By liberty I mean the assurance that every man shall be protected in doing what he believes [is] his duty against the influence of authority and majorities, custom, and opinion.[55]

For Acton the idea of liberty was an ancient one and to its development even pagan thinkers like the Stoics had made a contribution. In later life he surprisingly expressed regard for the novelist George Eliot's project to establish an ethics based on atheism. The predicament of modern liberty in Acton's view was that it was under constant assault by its near relative, democracy. The French Revolution had let loose on the world a sovereign people exercising an absolute will. Its depredations included the destruction of such intermediate institutions as the Church, aristocracy, and corporation. The people now held complete power. Once allied to nationalism and the view that the state was the embodiment of a homogeneous nation, there were no limits to the people's ability to enforce their will, especially towards alien nationalities. Democracy's tendency was to remove any restraint upon itself. Hence its bias, as Acton put it, towards "Plebiscite, Referendum or Caucus, free play for the will of the majority."[56] Acton, like Burke, despised the idea of government founded on consent and social contract, concepts that in his democratic moments were enthusiastically favoured by Trudeau.

Democracy, then, had given birth to nationalism so that in a society composed of several nationalities democracy would necessarily produce the rule of the dominant one and the tyranny of the majority. For Acton what protected and guaranteed liberty was a complicated and dense system of offsetting centres of power in civil society. A realized democracy was about ensuring that there was no single centre of power; it was about sharing and balancing power between groups and corporations. Otherwise there was despotism, even if it was popularly sanctioned. "Free government" was the result of "long, manifold and painful experience," Acton said.[57] Federalism was crucial to the protection of liberty through the division of governmental power between different levels. For these reasons he was an admirer of the American constitutional system and of the Habsburg Empire where there had evolved a pluralistic order of counter-balancing centres of power.[58]

Reading Acton, Trudeau was exposed to the same theoretical binary posited by Benda and Delos, between the abstract obligations of citizens to the higher order of society and the liberal state, and their sentimental, affective attachments to subsidiary formations like the family and nationality:

> The difference between nationality and the State is exhibited in the nature of patriotic attachment. Our connection with the race is merely natural or physical, whilst our duties to the political nation are ethical. One is a community of affections and instincts infinitely important and powerful in savage life, but pertaining more to the animal than to the civilised man; the other is an authority governing by laws, imposing obligations, and giving moral sanction and character to the natural relations of society.[59]

Acton had no difficulty imagining a multi-national society governed by an overarching state where citizens' diverse, affective solidarities could be respected and protected. But one particular nationality and its way of life should never become the dominant one:

> A State which is incompetent to satisfy different races condemns itself; a State which labours to neutralise, to absorb, or to expel them, destroys its own vitality; a State which does not include them is destitute of the chief basis of self-government. The theory of nationality, therefore, is a retrograde step in history.[60]

These last ideas were at the core of Trudeau's political mentality and offer an anticipation of what he came to call "polyethnic pluralism."

IV

In providing his own account of nationalism Trudeau was well aware of the conceptual pitfalls lying in wait for him. Political enquiry was inherently contentious because of the imprecision and ambiguity of its terms. Quoting Humpty Dumpty in Lewis Carroll's *Alice in Wonderland*, he observed that in political debate a word often meant what the speaker chose it to mean. Politicians were masters of the slippery use of language, and this was especially true in the case of nationalism.[61] However, as diligently as he could, Trudeau argued as follows. The word "nation" had two important senses. One was a "sociological" one and the other a "juristic" or "territorial" one. Regarding the first, a nation was any ethnic group that was constituted by common language, customs, religion or history. Sometimes a common geography was important or a shared experience of exploitation or perhaps invasion by a foreign power. In this sense one could talk indeed of the French-Canadian or English-Canadian nations and of the Japanese nation.[62]

There was another sense, however, and this had to do with how the word was used in everyday speech when, for example, one spoke of the "Swiss nation" or the "United Nations."[63] India with its several languages and religions would be another example of this second conception.[64] Here the word denoted the existence

of a political entity that had a legal existence as a sovereign country or state. Switzerland had a sense of being united but it was
composed of several nations in the sociological sense, that is, at
least four language groups. India had many languages and several religions but it was a nation too. As for the "United Nations,"
it referred to an international organization of nations as territorial states, simpliciter. Integral to the idea was the emergence of
the modern territorial/juristic state as a centralized scheme of
government more or less effective in controlling and regulating
a given population and territory and claiming an untrammelled
authority or right to make the law; in other words the modern
state possessed sovereignty.

And what did Trudeau mean by nationalism? Nationalism
was the claim advanced, usually with emotional intensity, by
sociological nations to have and to control their own particular
government or state. This produced what Trudeau called the
"nation-state" (*état-nation*), or, as he also called it, the "national"
or "nationality state" (*état-national*). Thus a state or a nation in
the juristic or territorial sense might be based on a single nation
in the sociological sense like Ireland or Germany or it might be
composed of several sociological nations like India or Canada.
Some states were national states or nation-states while others were multi-national states. And so while some states were
founded on the principle of nationalism, others were not. The
confusion in Trudeau's usage came from his implying now and
then that the "nation-state" could refer to the territorial/juristic
state and to the "national-nationality state." However, usually he
used the term nation-state to be the equivalent of the national/
nationality state. And where and how had nationalism emerged?
It was especially in two essays that Trudeau attempted to answer
this question. Both were instances of Trudeau's powerful, nimble
and protean imagination. One, "La nouvelle trahison des clercs,"
was informed, but combative and controversial in style, while the
other, "Federalism, Nationalism and Reason," was sober and academic, presented initially to a conference of professors, although

even here Trudeau structured his argument aggressively in terms of contemporary political debate.

His account of the emergence of nationalism he mainly based on European and North American examples, including Canadian although he did make some reference to nationalism in Africa and he was aware of its history in Latin American and Asia. However it was mainly Europe that he had in mind when he thought about the subject. It was the story of the gradual evolution of new political concepts and structures out of feudalism. Social life had emerged originally in the family, the tribe and the clan but later these had been transformed into the local societies of medieval times. (Trudeau overlooked the internationalizing role of the medieval Catholic Church.) On such a foundation, modern ideas and economic forces had gone to work. Cultural intermingling had increased along with trade and commerce; localisms had been overcome by conquests and "militant religions" had increased their reach. Coeval with these was the consolidation of monarchical power by the end of the sixteenth century from which had emerged the modern state claiming absolute control or sovereignty. The growths of a bourgeoisie and of an aggrandizing, dynastic state were crucial to the development of nationalism.

In an earlier version of the course of modern history—the one that Trudeau had expressed in 1954—he presented a much more economistic account. The bourgeoisie had sought greater economic freedom and had made an alliance of convenience with the emerging monarchical state to overcome the feudal nobles and the Church and then, having helped establish the sovereign state, took control of it to ensure that capitalism prevailed. But in his "nationalist" account in the early 1960s Trudeau took a slightly different tack. The bourgeois–monarchy alliance was still intact but it was the bourgeoisie that eventually wins out, only to have to share its power with the sovereign people and nation in the name of democracy as the nineteenth century unfolded. If in the later version there was an economic aspect to nationalism it seems to have resided mainly in Trudeau's presumption about the economic basis of war and imperialism in the new nationalist era. In his estimation it was *political* events and ideas in the late eighteenth century that had been pivotal. The revolt of the American colonies and the revolution in France had set in motion the destruction of the old order. Kings and queens were supplanted by states somehow beholden to "the people." In the American case it was the idea of consent that had been crucial, not just consent as "the foundation of civil society" or as the process whereby rulers were held accountable, but consent as a means of defining the people's adherence to one territorial state rather than another.[65] American colonial independence had originated in the idea of "self-determination":

> Consequently, it might be said that in the past the (territorial) state had defined its territorial limits which had defined the people or nation living within. But henceforth it was to be the people who first defined themselves as a nation, who then declared which territory belonged to them as of right, and who finally proceeded to give their allegiance to a state of their own choosing or invention which would exercise authority over that nation and that territory. Hence the expression "nation-state." As I see it, the important transition was from the *territorial state* to the *nation-state*. But once the latter was born, the idea of the *national state* was bound to follow, it being little more than a nation-state with an ethnic flavour added. With it the idea of self-determination became the principle of nationalities.
>
> Self-determination did not necessarily proceed from or lead to self-government. Whereas self-government was based on reason and proposed to introduce liberal forms of government into existing states, self-determination was based on will and proposed to challenge the legitimacy and the very existence of the territorial states.[66]

Something similar had happened in France where the revolutionaries had asserted that the basis of government should be the "nation" or the people. But what were such entities? At first the revolution delineated a non-ethnic account but then it slipped into a definition of the French people as a linguistic entity. Revolutions that had started out as democratic ones became transformed into movements of nationalism. In Trudeau's terminology a movement of "self-governance" was replaced by one of "self-determination." Competing class interests were transcended in a common endeavour to advance the nation understood as a particular nationality:

> At first democracy did in fact open the ways first to the bourgeois classes, then much later to the working classes whereby all of them could participate in political power. The State appeared at that time as a means whereby eventually all classes, that is the entire nation, could assure peace and prosperity for themselves. And by a natural consequence everyone wanted this instrument to be as strong as possible in its relations with other nation-states [*états-nations*]. It was at that point that nationalism was born, out of the union between liberal democracy and the egalitarian mystique.
>
> But, alas, this nationalism, by a singular paradox, quickly distanced itself from the ideas which had presided at its birth. For as soon as the sovereign State was put at the service of the nation, it was the nation that became sovereign, that is, above the law. It meant little then that the prosperity of some would signify the ruin of others. Historically strong nations, those that had industrialized first, who had inherited strategic and institutional progress, quickly recognized the advantages of their situation. Rulers joined in alliance with the ruled, the haves with the have-nots and this unholy alliance proceeded in the name of nationalism to enrich and flatter itself at the expense of weak nations.
>
> Nationalist egoisms now gave themselves ever more exquisite labels: political darwinianism [*sic*], nietzschean mysticism, the white man's burden, the civilizing mission, pan-slavism, magyarization and all the other garbage that would justify the strong in oppressing the weak.
>
> But in every case the result was the same: nations that were dominated, amputated, exploited and humiliated conceived a

boundless hatred for their oppressors; and coming together in their hatred they invented against the nationalist aggressor a defensive nationalism. So was set alight a chain of wars which has not yet finished setting fire to the planet.[67]

The scale of the destruction wrought by nationalism derived from two principal factors: the increased involvement of civilian populations in the wars of the modern state and, secondly, the growing role of technology as a supplier of ever more efficient engines of destruction.[68] And making the carnage ever more intense Trudeau added that nationalism expressed an almost biologically based aptitude for intolerance and inhumanity. It is reminiscent of what Benda had claimed. Out of the seemingly gentle courtliness of dynastic warfare—as Trudeau saw it—there had arisen the terrifying Moloch of modern, total warfare:

Up until the end of the eighteenth century it was generally sovereigns rather than nations that made war on each other; and while the sovereigns waged war civilians continued to visit each other, merchants crossed the borders, men of letters and philosophers went freely from court to court, the heads of armies took under their protection the wise men of conquered towns. At that time war killed soldiers but respected civilization. Whereas in our day we have seen nations fighting Germany refuse to listen to Beethoven, others at odds with China boycott the Peking opera; yet others refuse visas or passports to scholars wanting to attend a scientific or humanitarian conference in an ideologically different country. Pasternak cannot even go and receive his Nobel Prize in Stockholm. The concept of nation which gives so little importance to science and culture in its scale of values cannot hope to place truth, freedom and even life higher than itself. It is an idea that corrodes everything: in peacetime the intellectuals become propagandists for the nation and their propaganda tells lies; in time of war the democracies slide towards dictatorship and the dictators herd us towards concentration camps;

and, finally, after the massacres of Ethiopia, there were those of London and Hamburg, then Hiroshima and Nagasaki, and so on to the final massacre perhaps.[69]

There is another important part of Trudeau's thinking that needs to be emphasized and that is his distinction between "self-determination" and "self-government." In one of the quotations above Trudeau refers to the American Revolution as an instance of "self-determination," rather than "self-government." The distinction links up with a definition developed in an earlier chapter in which he characterized French Canadians' resistance to the Conquest and their opportunistic, cynical embrace of democracy and rights as an instance of "self-determination." This was a typical Trudeauian use of the term. Self-determination constituted a form of resistance to an overweening nationalism, in this case that of Anglophone settlers, businessmen, the British colonial administrators, and, later, English Canadians; a subaltern nation had shown self-determination. But, in Trudeau's view, this had little to do with moral principle, at least not in the same way that "self-government" did, based as the latter was on reason, debate, and commitment to universal principles. A defensive nationalism was vitiated by its own group logic and the manner of the individual's association with it. Trudeau put it succinctly:

> [The values of the nation] are more private than public, more introverted than extroverted, more instinctive and savage than intelligent and civilized, more narcissistic and passionate than generous and reasoned.[70]

In short, attachments to the nation were primitive and irrational.

Here is, then, another instance in Trudeau of the binary of reason and passion, in this case that of an irrational nationalism confronting a rational humanism or cosmopolitanism. But it is instructive to realize how far he went with this distinction. Actions based on a group's will or determination were sectional and self-serving, and, in its attitude towards its own members, uncritical; towards others it was discriminatory and accusatory and, in the worst cases, genocidal. To found political action on irrational will was to submit to the logic of "power" rather than to that of deliberation and consent and it made nationalism inherently amoral at best, and, at worst, immoral. Nationalism's principle of self-determination had redrawn the map of the world but not in any rational way:

> The political history of Europe and of the Americas in the nineteenth century and that of Asia and Africa in the twentieth are histories of nations labouring, conspiring, blackmailing, warring, revolutionizing, and generally willing their way towards statehood. It is, of course, impossible to know whether for humanity there has ensued therefrom more peace and justice than would have been the case if some other principle than self-determination had held sway. In theory, the arrangement of boundaries was to be that no important national group would be included by force in the territorial limits of a state which was mainly the expression of the will of another group, and that this would be conducive to peaceful international order. In practice, state boundaries continued to be established and maintained largely by the threat of or use of force. The concept of right in international relations became, if anything, even more a function of might. And the question whether a national minority was "important" enough to be entitled to independence remained unanswerable except in terms of the political and physical power that could be wielded in its favour. . . .
>
> [I]t becomes apparent that more than language and culture, more than history and geography, even more than force and power, the foundation of the nation is will. For there is no power without will. . . .
>
> [W]e are bound to conclude that the frontiers of nation-states are in reality nearly as arbitrary as those of the former territorial states. . . . [T]he nations of today cannot justify their

frontiers with noticeably more rationality than the kings of two centuries ago; a greater reliance on general staffs than on princesses' dowries does not necessarily spell a triumph of reason.[71]

If Trudeau's argument is persuasive, it is hard to see any virtue at all in nationalism. Trudeau subscribed to a school of thought as Benedict Anderson puts it that insisted "on the near-pathological character of nationalism, its roots in fear and hatred of the Other, and its affinities with racism."[72] Predictably, about the new nationalists in Quebec Trudeau was never less than utterly critical. He knew many of them, he said, and some were earnest and nice but others were totalitarian-minded and anti-Semitic. Even with their leftist proclivities the separatists were "reactionary"; right-wing nationalist organizations outnumbered those of the Left and in any nationalist coalition the conservative ones would predominate; nationalism was fundamentally reactionary because it defined the common good in terms of the will of a particular ethnic group which made it "essentially" intolerant, discriminatory, and totalitarian.[73] Above all, he said, nationalists were economically incompetent. Nationalism stood for national self-sufficiency and it defied the logic of modernity, that interdependence was fundamental and inevitable: "treaties, commercial agreements, common markets, free-exchange zones, cultural and scientific accords—all are indispensable."[74] French Canada was not large enough by itself to deal with all the problems of the modern age. Separatists lived lives of self-delusion and narcissism, within a "hallucinatory frenzy," as Trudeau put it;[75] they fantasized about how brilliant French Canadians were as a people and how creative they would become after independence. Did they not understand that they already possessed—and had done so since 1867—all of the tools of their own liberation and creativity, if only they would use them?

At the heart of Trudeau's critique was the assumption that cultural progress and development were the results of intercultural interaction and exchange. This had informed his claim that it had been scientists, intellectuals, and traders that had played the crucial roles in the emergence of the modern state and of liberalism and democracy. It was indeed the basis of his own self-understanding as a public intellectual who challenged established conformities. The idea also informed his claim that French Canada had been advantaged politically through contact with British liberal-democratic ideas and it was integral to his argument in *La grève de l'amiante* that Quebec's government had built the rudiments of a welfare state through its interaction with other Canadian policy-makers. The same idea was present in "The Practice and Theory of Federalism," in his contention that social-ism in Canada was immeasurably advantaged, if it chose to be so, by having several regionally based versions of itself from which to choose. Nationalists, in contrast, saw creativity and development as a magical offspring of cultural homogeneity and political seg-regation. This was a false idea; innovation and creativity, in art as much as in practical matters, originated in rubbing against differ-ent ideas. Cultural openness and cosmopolitan relations were cru-cial. The sectarian tendency in nationalism offered only reaction and a kind of atavism and, of course, a dependence on emotion. Nationalism brought together the collective and the destruc-tive. It was inherently anti-liberal, and bred chauvinism, racism, jingoism, and totalitarianism. Indeed it was a kind of fascism. It was as if Trudeau posited in nationalism a Freudian death wish. And adding a new, decidedly economic dimension to his under-standing—and a class-oriented one at that—Trudeau argued that in Quebec nationalism was a kind of petit-bourgeois plot by a rising middle-class of alienated, self-serving professionals and intellectuals who sought to seize the booty of independence for themselves. Tweaking the noses of the new separatists in Quebec, Trudeau turned Frantz Fanon loose upon them claiming that they were just like the national bourgeoisies taking over in the newly independent countries of Africa who, once in charge, resorted to one-party rule, dictatorship, and petty self-importance. In Quebec, the would-be leaders of the tribe were bent on returning to the "wigwams. . . Separatism, a revolution? My eye. A counter-revolution; the counter-revolution of national socialism."[76]

But is the world imagined by nationalism so unremittingly disastrous? Trudeau had begun "La nouvelle trahison des clercs" with the dramatic declaration that "it is not the idea of the nation which is retrograde but it is the idea that the nation must necessarily become sovereign."[77] Was this an opening to another possible view of nationalism? Later in the same essay, in a similar vein, Trudeau talked of the nation as the "bearer" of

> definite values: a cultural heritage, common traditions, communitarian consciousness, a historical continuity, a collection of morals, which together at this moment in the evolution of human kind contribute to the development of the personality.[78]

So strongly did Trudeau seem to make the case for the informal nation in these statements that it is quite plausible to see in them the germ of a theory of identity that places him—at least in his engagement with the idea of identity itself—in the company of such as Charles Taylor. The latter's *The Pattern of Politics*, we have seen, is full of insights about the shifts in identity brought about by modernity. It seems that Trudeau too was asserting that it was through their rootedness in organic, sentimental communities that humans were provided with an understanding of who they were. However, if Trudeau did make a case for such an informal nationalism, he sanctioned the idea only to a limited extent. While such informal identities were real and actual and must be respected, he explained that they were provisional and only part of human experience at this moment; in time they would be superseded by more personal and universal identifications. The imperative of the "tribe" would necessarily be transcended.[79] Here was another instance of the interplay of the ideal and the realistic in Trudeau's thinking. The nation was destined to fade away but for now it had an immediate existence, so that the actual problem in Quebec was as follows: "without recourse to the absurd and retrograde idea of national sovereignty, how can we preserve the national values of French Canada?"[80]

Predictably his answer spoke to the advantages of federalism and the BNA Act. Regional power expressed through provincial sovereignty in Quebec permitted the expression of the "national" values of the French, as indeed other regional powers in Canada expressed the national values of the English. The division of powers established at Confederation was far-sighted and successfully divided responsibilities between a federal level concerned with matters that affected the whole Canadian society—foreign affairs, economic stabilization, international trade, navigation, postal matters, and money and banking—and a provincial level that dealt with matters of a local and private nature and matters of "ethnic" significance: education, municipal and local institutions, the administration of justice, marriage, and property and civil rights.[81] But, even as he implied, perhaps facetiously, that under federalism the provinces might legitimately become megaphones of a regional nationalism, English and French, he cautioned that a province representing a "national" view, so to speak, should not act as if it was the sole ethnic group in its provincial territory and it must avoid cultivating a "mentality of the nation-state at the provincial level."[82] Nationalism, wherever it raised its ugly head, was to be avoided. Indeed so fearful was Trudeau of the idea of federalism becoming an arena for competing nationalisms that he not only roundly rejected the two-nations view of Canada but on some occasions he preferred to talk not of nationalisms in Canada but of "regionalisms":

> The purpose of a federal state is not to encourage the development of conflicting nationalisms: it is to reap the human, democratic and administrative benefits which derive from friendly competition between divergent regionalisms.[83]

Altogether, for Trudeau, the better way was federalism, suitably supplemented by an entrenched bill of rights and to this he made special reference in his essay "Federalism, Nationalism and

Reason."[84] Here he couched his argument in terms of the central dilemma of the modern state and its need to achieve social unity and legitimation within the large territories and populations that it typically governed. Nationalists provided one answer, and this was to cultivate the nation and to make it the basis of the state. Or it might be that, having established a state, the government might use its power to cultivate a nationality that would bind together otherwise disparate peoples. Trudeau's conclusion was that both of these were lost causes because human populations would (or could) never be uniform enough to overcome tendencies to disintegration and separation and that nationalism through its dependence on emotion constantly risked picking fights with other nations. Given the world as it was with its many pluralisms and its need for interdependence and co-operation Trudeau saw no alternative to federalism. Federal societies had a further special advantage: they were unified around a more limited range of values. But there would need to be *some* common values or else why would different groups associate at all. Federalism required a pact or a consensus between the constituent parts; Trudeau sometimes called it a social contract or a general will. This made the integrative tasks of the modern state easier. But, even in its more limited tasks, federalism depended on the subtle skills of its leaders because it required the constant balancing of the contradictory forces of centralization and localism.

If "reason" prevailed, elites and citizens in a federal system would be realistic about their circumstances and prospects. If a given group did not wish to be separate and wished to associate with another, it must develop habits of compromise and mutual understanding. There must be something at the federal level that all parts of the country must agree to share; but too much "nationalism" in this respect might offend regional nationalists and undermine their willingness to remain in the federation. Equally too much nationalism at the regional level could offend the majority or cause the minority to separate and cast itself into an unfulfilling isolation. Federalism required the nurturing of a constantly calibrated balance: "The advantages *to the minority group* of staying integrated in the whole must on balance be greater than the gain to be reaped from separating."[85] And the majority group too must look soberly at its own interests and wonder if it would be truly better off if it remained intransigent and apart. The "reason" of federalism was calculative, prudential, and pragmatic; a never-ending, unsentimental linking of means to ends; it was a "cold, unemotional rationality."[86] Trudeau posited an instrumental account of reason, on this occasion.

Trudeau concluded his essay by saying that there were signs that reason was winning out in Canada, although nationalism with its emotive incantations was a dogged enemy. Passion often overwhelmed reason and led societies into disasters. Simply put, the world of technology, science, and international society could not be governed by the emotions and the old sodalities of the nation. But even as he confidently predicted the passing of the old norms and habits, Trudeau could not avoid mentioning again how antiquated and unattractive they were. In the end he seemed to see little if any merit in identities based on the nation:

It is possible that nationalism may still have a role to play in backward societies where the *status quo* is upheld by irrational and brutal forces; in such circumstances, *because there is no other way*, perhaps the nationalist passions will still be found useful to unleash revolutions, upset colonialism, and lay the foundations of welfare states; in such cases, the undesirable consequences will have to be accepted along with the good.

But in the advanced societies, where the interplay of social forces can be regulated by law, where the centres of political power can be made responsible to the people, where the economic victories are a function of education and automation, where cultural differentiation is submitted to ruthless competition, and where the road to progress lies in the direction of international integration, nationalism will have to be discarded as a rustic and clumsy tool.

No doubt, at the level of individual action, emotions and dreams will still play a part; even in modern man, superstition remains a powerful motivation. But magic, no less than totems and taboos, has long since ceased to play an important role in the normal governing of states. And likewise, nationalism will eventually have to be rejected as a principle of sound government. In the world of tomorrow, the expression "banana republic" will not refer to independent fruit-growing nations but to countries where formal independence has been given priority over the cybernetic revolution. In such a world, the state—if it is not to be outdistanced by its rivals—will need political instruments which are sharper, stronger, and more finely controlled than anything based on mere emotionalism. . . . [I]n short, if not a pure product of reason, the political tools of the future will be designed and appraised by more rational standards than anything we are currently using in Canada today.[87]

The sense of rationality that informed Trudeau's apologia for an "enlightened" federalism, particularly in this essay, was as close to being Hobbesian as Trudeau ever came. The good was subjectively and emotively defined and reason was no more than a calculating device to determine how best to achieve a group's sectional interests. But the direct source of this idea may not have been Hobbes but Albert Breton and his rational choice theory of nationalism with which Trudeau was familiar at the time.

But there was another sense of rationality at work in Trudeau. The clue here is to be found in returning to what he saw as the difference between "self-determination" and "self-government." The first, we recall, was based on will and force, and was irrational; the second was rational in that it pursued a form of governance that was based on the common good, the rule of law and the rights of all. This second sense, with shades of Aristotle and Aquinas, and of Immanuel Kant too, presupposed a society peopled with rational, purposive agents reflecting on their duty and choosing measures to realize the common good and the flourishing of every citizen.

Here the supposition was that everyone lived under an objective or universal moral law that affirmed the value of all persons and the obligation to seek justice for them. This was a kind of rationality very different from that of Hobbes and similar-minded thinkers such as David Hume and the tradition of utilitarianism.[88] Late in life Trudeau was asked by B.W. Powe to explain what he meant by "reason over passion." His reply was that reason was not rationality but "mind. . . . It's guidance and light. We would call it lucidity . . . intelligence." How mind might prevail over passions Trudeau said was a "mystery . . . [a]n enigma. I think of reason as being the call to justice."[89] Such an account of reason is hardly an instrumentalist one. Evidently Trudeau employed at least two senses of reason.

Does Trudeau's opposition to nationalism lead to any conclusions about how he conceived of human identity and how best it might be realized? If his claim was that identities rooted in the nation were irrational, was there an alternative account? There *was* one and it goes roughly as follows. The post-nationalist age, which is both imminent and urgent, will ideally be one in which citizens will increasingly see themselves as conscience-driven persons moving in a world of great diversity and opportunity and living the life of democratic participation and universal freedom. Each person will be constrained less and less by group affiliation and will be shaped more and more by individual judgments and commitments that will constitute the person's network of relationships and the informal, dialogical communities of the moment she moves in and out of. The freedom of the person to live according to conscience means that the identity of the individual will be one that is chosen and periodically revised and altered. There will exist no presumption of the superiority of communitarian identities but rather a series of encounters with the Other from which the person will derive opportunity for moral exploration, personal affirmation and cultural development. The social world presupposed by Trudeau is one that is individualized but not atomized. It will be international as well as local. The emerging global order will be ever more interconnected and open to all to participate in. Cosmopolitan citizens in their freedom will encounter other like-minded—though culturally different—citizens and out of these encounters civil society, domestically and globally, will emerge. Using Trudeau's favoured phrase, "polyethnic pluralism" will increasingly come to pass. Individual identity will be open and porous and changeable. If the individual wishes to belong to a community of, say, religion or nation, she will belong to these privately and voluntaristically. Above all no particular group will be given a privileged legal or constitutional standing. Living increasingly among cosmopolitan believers in the human ideal the appeal of nationalism will fade away and likely the appeal of other sodalities as well. The old forms of belonging will change radically but a pluralism of culture will remain and, if anything, will become more intense. Cultural identity will take much more protean and plastic forms.

We can perhaps best understand the implications of Trudeau's outlook on identity and groups by an examination of his views on First Nations people. In his writings between 1944 and 1965, Trudeau commented little on the indigenous question. His dismissive comments about French-Canadian nationalists' attachment to the "tribe" he no doubt would have made about Aboriginals people's attachments as well. A fuller disclosure of his position came early in his prime ministership. In the *Statement of the Government of Canada on Indian Policy, 1969* Trudeau's government challenged the Indian Affairs system in favour of an alternative arrangement that would have integrated Aboriginal people into Canadian society with all the rights of other Canadian citizens. The *Statement* did not attack the Treaties head on. However a society without the Treaties was almost certainly part of Trudeau's thinking. In a speech later in 1969 he talked of the invalidity of Indians, as he called them, having a "special status" and of "one section of the society hav[ing] a treaty with the other section of the society."[90] The *Statement* did not explicitly advocate the assimilation of Aboriginal people, though Trudeau believed that were they to become, as he saw it, full members of Canadian society and accorded all the rights of citizens, there would likely be some attenuation of their traditions. He said as much in his 1969 speech.[91] But the *Statement* also affirmed in a very dramatic fashion the importance of preserving Aboriginal culture. At the same time it implied that in a modern social order the preservation of cultural values should be sought privately and voluntaristically, under the protection, of course, of a government that ensured rights to free speech and free association. The adverse reaction from the First Nations' communities to the *Statement* caused Trudeau to back away from it. And in the 1982 Constitution, under Sections 25 and 35, the historic Treaties with First Nations were entrenched—this in spite of what he had said about the invalidity of group rights.

Similarly, regarding French Canada, Trudeau's course was to recommend further linguistic and cultural protections through statute and constitutional law, building on the limited entrenchments of bilingualism and Francophone educational rights in the BNA Act. The Official Languages Act was passed in 1969 and, in the 1982 Constitution Act, bilingualism was extended and further entrenched. In justifying his support of these initiatives it is not clear that Trudeau would have exactly shared Charles Taylor's belief that the continuation of the historic "expressive power" of the French-Canadian community was a good in itself. Trudeau took a different tack. With the more instrumentalist cast of his thinking in the early 1960s, recognition of Francophone linguistic rights was for Trudeau expressed more as a course of realism. As he put it in 1965, both linguistic communities were big enough to break up the country; and so necessity required recognition of Francophone linguistic and cultural rights.[92] But Trudeau's argument for federalism was not just that it made the governance of pluralistic societies easier or that it allowed pluralistic societies to survive but that cultural diversity was the stuff of progress. That is why it is reasonable to conclude that Trudeau must have believed that the continuation of a vibrant Francophone community was a necessary means to ensure the intrinsic good of cultural interaction and competition. But he was less communitarian-oriented in this than Taylor. Trudeau did not think that government had a basic duty to preserve a traditional culture, linguistically constituted or otherwise. For Trudeau the emphasis was more on the individual and his sovereign choices. As he once put it:

> I believe that the human person in his conscience is, in the last analysis, authorized to choose his scale of values, and to decide which forces will predominate with him. A good constitution is one which does not prejudge these questions but leaves its citizens free to orient themselves as they wish to their own destinies.[93]

Such individualism and voluntarism caused him to characterize official bilingualism as essentially providing *individual* rights rather than *collective* ones. The French-Canadian individual must be able to communicate with his government in his own language. But if he chose to associate with some other language community, then that was quite acceptable to Trudeau as well. In other words there were in principle limits to his willingness to support the preservation of a given linguistic community.

Did Trudeau, then, imagine and sanction the possible assimilation of the French-speaking community in Canada? In a sense he did not have to answer this question because his view was that French Canada was sufficiently rich and deep in cultural and demographic resources that it was assured of linguistic survival even without affecting adversely the linguistic rights of the Anglophone minority in its midst, and even if it afforded greater linguistic freedom to its own French speakers by for example allowing them to send their children to Anglophone schools and colleges. As he said,

> French is spoken by a greater and greater number of persons. . . . Short of a catastrophe or a genocide, it seems certain that in this corner of North America and regardless of constitutional upheavals, French will always be spoken.[94]

Taylor in contrast was much more concerned about the ability of the individual French-Canadian "self" to maintain his traditional identity since this "constituted" who he was and to achieve this he must be assured of both the existence and the continuance of a French community around him. Trudeau's sense of the self was much more dynamic and free-wheeling and less rooted in a traditional group identity. Thus Taylor and Trudeau did not quite agree on the "ontological" justification for French-Canadian survival, although both did in fact seek French Canada's "survivance."

Where they clearly disagreed was over the means to ensure it. Taylor believed that Trudeau's version of bilingualism was insufficient and that further initiatives were necessary, such as a special constitutional status for Quebec and greater protections for Francophone linguistic and educational rights in the province. Trudeau believed that going beyond established bilingualism as in Bill 101 (the PQ's language charter of 1977) exposed Anglophones in Quebec to unwarranted intrusions on their rights. As for special status Trudeau always believed that it would vest an unjustifiable group right in the legislature of Quebec and undermine the principle of the equality of the provinces. Yet events would make clear that Taylor too believed that nationalism could go too far and become discriminatory; witness his condemnation of the so-called Charter of Secular Values proposed by the PQ government of Premier Pauline Marois in 2013. Especially the Charter's requirement that public servants be forbidden from wearing prominent religious symbols while at work was, he said, clearly discriminatory towards Sikhs, Jews, and Muslims, the "unquebecois" minorities of the province. In the heat of this particular battle Taylor uncharacteristically employed Trudeau-like language and called the Premier an "ignoramus."[95] If Trudeau had lived long enough to consider this proposed Charter he would certainly have said something similar and concluded that all his historic concerns about the collectivist and reactionary tendencies of French-Canadian culture and nationalism had been confirmed. The PQ's subsequent electoral defeat by the Liberal Party led by Phillipe Couillard would have led him to rejoice that a more cosmopolitan ethos had finally been planted in the province.

V

Trudeau's essay of early 1965, "Le Québec et le problème constitutionnel," provides a convenient summation of his position on questions of nationalism and federalism on the eve of his entry into parliamentary politics. He composed it for a coalition of Quebec trade unions making a submission to the government of Quebec. At the time the political atmosphere in the province was one of escalating nationalist agitation. Now and then bombs were going off and the visit of Queen Elizabeth to Quebec City in 1964 was a hugely controversial issue. Lesage's provincial Liberals were increasingly assertive of provincial rights and were especially resistant to the Pearson Liberals' initiatives to do with shared-cost programs for healthcare, social assistance, and a Canada-wide pension plan. Regarding the future of the province the options championed by Quebec's political parties ranged from outright, even violent separation to more pacific but still radical revisions of the constitution. After the appointment of the Bilingualism and Biculturalism Commission in 1964, bilingualism was clearly on the country's agenda. So too was biculturalism, with its related idea of two nations within Canada and special status for Quebec. In these distempered times Trudeau's voice, in its affirmation of the status quo, sounded almost prosaic and archaic.

His essay was strongly pro-federalist and, in its social and economic recommendations, social democratic. It was militantly anti-separatist and disdainful of the idea of a Canada composed of two nations. All in all Trudeau saw little need to change much in the constitution. Putting as much distance as possible between himself and nationalism Trudeau evinced a decidedly internationalist outlook emphasizing the growing openness of the global order. Above all he was consciously and aggressively realist in his analysis. French Canada, he reasoned, was a linguistic minority within a mainly Anglophone federal state, set down within a continental sea of English-speakers. Another important "*chose donnée*," he pointed out, had to do with technological innovation in the new industrial age. Economies now increasingly thrived through their investment in research and development and whichever national economy dominated in this respect would have superiority in the size of its GDP and its capacity for growth. This was why the United States ruled the economic order. Realism dictated that national economies could afford to be neither protectionist nor resistant to capital and technological transfers. In such an environment Quebec could have no significant control over whether French became a major language of business in North America. It must somehow come to terms with being part of a continental economy. If anything, it should become more oriented towards developing multilingualism.

Trudeau, then, was impressed with American technological and economic success and partial to what was called at the time "the American challenge."[96] Yet it was an idea that had also informed his early functionalist commitment to universalism. But his position was not unreservedly in favour of openness. Thinking of social and economic justice he presumed that Canada must become a social democratic state in which economic security, a welfare state, and, indeed, some kind of protection of culture would be pursued by government. So his recommendation for Canada was not to blissfully embrace global forces, in this case mainly American ones. Justice required an interventionist state and, in regards to industrial development, direct investment in strategic domestic sectors. But this must be pursued intelligently. For the real world imposed trade-offs and tough choices. To finance social priorities there must be economic growth; and if foreign capital was excluded there must be some means of compensating workers for their lost jobs and income. Interference with cultural flows was also necessary "to ensure the survival of cultural values in danger of being swamped by a flood of dollars." But realism also established that cultures must embrace interdependence and the free flow of ideas.[97]

Trudeau's position sought to recognize the complex reality of actual circumstances and the principle of relative costs:

The great art here is not to expel foreign capital which would simply oblige us, so as not to go backward, to reduce our standard of living in order to replace foreign capital by domestic capital; but rather, on one hand, to use foreign capital in the framework of rational economic development and, on the other hand, to create home-grown capital and to direct it towards key sectors of the future: industry in an era of nuclear energy, cybernetics and the service industry. Movements of capital are just like movements of population: they are very sensitive to political decisions. . . . [I]t is crucial that in a commendable effort to change economic realities [*données*] the state not use legal or moral violence against its citizens. A healthy economic policy must not presume for example that workers are ready to accept a radical reduction in their standard of living for the pleasure of seeing a national bourgeoisie replace a foreign one in the management of firms.⁹⁸

The lesson was that national economies could not be sealed off; and there must be general openness to dynamic international flows. This was one of the few places where Trudeau seemed to accede to the benefits of free markets but, understood properly, his point-of-view was one of balance: his priorities were those of a social democrat. But, even as a social democrat, he was stating that a managed, closed economy was inconceivable.

Given its smaller size the same diagnosis applied even more to the notion of a separate, autarchic Quebec, dreamed of by nationalists. An alternative strategy, Trudeau thought, was for Quebec to take greater advantage of its membership of the larger Canadian economic community and become more open to the wider world. But this did not entail an end to the protecting of home-grown values. Even as French Canadians might become more open to multilingualism given the international context of the province, they should equally be prepared to make a greater commitment to the use of French not just in government but in business and finance. Perhaps he expressed his argument best when he asserted that there needed to be a cultural adjustment in Quebec so that French became the language of "[a] people . . . in the avant-garde of progress."[99]

Turning to contemporary constitutional proposals, Trudeau exhibited a cautious conservatism. With a few changes the BNA Act was wholly adequate to Quebec's needs. Almost presciently, he said, those who had devised the Act had divided jurisdictional powers so that the provinces were already in possession of those areas that dealt with "rising expectations" to do with education, health, welfare, natural resources, and agricultural and industrial matters. And through its original provisions of official bilingualism the constitution had established a sense of the "fundamental equality" of the two language communities. Building on this it was possible to imagine a successful expansion of bilingual rights in the civil service, the military, industry, and education. There were as well the natural ebbs and flows of centralization and decentralization in the history of Confederation. Canada was now going through a phase where the provinces were more and more in the ascendancy as evidenced by their increased proportion of spending by governments. Under Section 92, where provincial powers were delineated, Trudeau continued, Quebec had all the jurisdictional authority it needed to protect French-Canadian cultural values. And, if only because they were a majority in Quebec and possessors of the benefits of a federal division of powers, institutional life in the province necessarily had a French flavour. (Here Trudeau came close to articulating a view popularized later by Ernest Gellner and Will Kymlicka about the historic role of nationalism in creating a "societal culture" in which there predominated a "national" way of life into which citizens would be integrated.[100])

Trudeau's ultimate point was not that Quebec needed a new constitution but rather that successive Quebec governments had failed to use the powers it had under the existing one. Instead they had pursued chimeras of endless constitutional reconstruction:

The constitution is an insignificant factor in the state of the economic, technical and demographic inferiority which prevails among French Canadians in Quebec. If I am not especially moved to change the constitution, it is because I am especially moved to change the reality of things. And I don't want to afford the ruling classes [*classes dirigeantes*] any excuse to avoid solving the true problems until the day after the constitution is reformed.[101]

Besides, said Trudeau, constitutions were not the sort of things that should be regularly tampered with. Even so, the BNA Act was not perfect and its one major weakness, he believed, was that it had allowed English Canadians to escape their obligation to treat French Canadians equally. But that must now change. Turning to the nationalists in Quebec he sought to settle several scores. Quebec was not all of French Canada and there needed to be concern for French-speaking communities outside the province. French Canadians in general, he thought, would have better cultural protection under a Canada-wide bilingualism than under a special constitutional status for Quebec. But to demonstrate that his constitutional conservatism was not a stance of constitutional stasis, Trudeau offered a panoply of reforms (in addition to an enhanced bilingualism), most of which he had championed since the late 1940s. These included an entrenched bill of rights; the abolition of the federal power of reservation and disallowance; changes to the judicial system that adjudicated federal–provincial conflicts; and Senate changes to allow a more direct representation of the provinces. He also articulated support for modest measures of intergovernmental co-operation, although the burden of his position was that what Canada and Quebec needed most were politicians who explored the opportunities afforded by the existing division of powers of a genuinely federal system.

Trudeau's 1965 essay also allowed him to comment on what had been the most recent attempt—it would prove unsuccessful—to establish an amending formula: the Fulton-Favreau formula which had emerged from an agreement of federal and provincial justice ministers in 1961 and was revised in 1964 in Charlottetown by first ministers. The eventual proposal was complicated. It established different areas of the constitution that would require different rules of amendment. Changes in areas of exclusive provincial jurisdiction would require the agreement of all ten provinces, effectively giving each of them a veto; there was a class of intermediate matters such as education that could be changed by agreement of the federal parliament and two thirds of the provinces having 50 percent of the population; and there were provisions for four provinces and the federal government to delegate powers between themselves.

Generally Trudeau thought ill of the formula.[102] In part he saw it as a mechanism whereby, under the two-thirds provision, the federal government might "invade" areas of provincial jurisdiction. At the same time, he thought the provision for delegation would encourage a constitutional Balkanizing of the country leading to a situation where federal parliamentarians would be voting on legislation that did not apply to constituents in their own ridings and provinces. This would blur the sense voters must have of who to hold responsible in a federal system. Trudeau also believed that the overall formula might lead to isolating Quebec. If provincial leaders were concerned about retaining their powers, Trudeau thought that the prevailing informal trend towards decentralization should satisfy them enough. It would be better for the provinces to leave things alone:

> Our existing constitution, cleverly exploited, modified if it must be (but in a way which retains between the two levels of government a division of powers which will be generally the same between one province and another) creates a country where Quebec can be part of the ten against one in defence of provincial autonomy, and where French Canadians can struggle one-on-one to affirm the French fact in North America. At the same time, this constitution prevents Quebec from thrusting itself towards an excessive particularism which would only mean the extinction of

French Canadians living outside of Quebec and the development among those that live within its borders of a ghetto mentality.[103]

VI

There was a remarkable continuity in Trudeau's prescriptions about the Canadian constitution. He believed that federalism with bilingualism and an entrenched bill of rights was essential to solve the dilemmas of the rights of minorities. He had been brought to a skeptical account of democracy, because while it was a fundamental political good it could not be so considered if it produced majority tyranny. In this regard Trudeau's thinking had affinities with aristocratic thinkers like Montesquieu, Tocqueville, and most importantly, Acton, who saw liberty as protected less by democratic rights and more by the offsetting and juxtaposing of concentrations of power—in Trudeau's case, province against federal government and courts versus parliament—so that the good society would be a place where no one group would hold a monopoly of power. But if federalism was about the dividing of powers among great regional factions, it was nevertheless under its classical form an arrangement for ensuring that different electoral constituencies could be discerning enough to know which faction was responsible for what and so hold the relevant level of government responsible. However, this might in practice be difficult to obtain. Trudeau was well aware of the complexity, not just of the Canadian constitution but of industrial society in general. Recognizing the intricacy of things Trudeau advocated co-operative federalism but of course the difficulty with that is that it muddies the waters of democratic accountability even more.

In the period 1950 to 1965 it was the classical Whearean idea rather than the co-operative one that predominated in his thinking though never to the exclusion of the latter. But there was another dilemma. Trudeau was not just an advocate of classical and co-operative federalisms; he was also a social democrat. The constitution was a legal framework within which justice was to be sought, and not simply the justice of economic and social equality but respect for cultural diversity too. Justice, then, would be satisfied if there were established national standards of social and cultural well-being: a welfare state, Keynesian economic management, an entrenched bill of rights, and bilingualism. Provincial standards of cultural protection were necessary too. Trudeau exaggerated the extent to which these several policies could be achieved under the existing constitution while still adhering to the classical model. In all of his accounts of the existing division of powers Trudeau presumed that the provinces controlled all the major jurisdictions that would make possible the building of the welfare state: healthcare, social assistance, education, and urban affairs, to name the main ones. But how could there be national standards unless the provinces agreed to amendments that would allocate provincial powers to Ottawa—an unlikely proposition—or unless there were some intrusions on provincial spheres? And how could Ottawa achieve the latter if there was no federal spending power and no enticing of the provinces through the "fifty-cent-dollars" of shared-cost programs? As we shall see, Trudeau justified his decision to join the Liberals in 1965 in large part in order to stabilize and invigorate federal power against rising nationalism in Quebec and provincial assertiveness in general. But, as he said, joining the Liberals and relocating to Ottawa did not mean that he had set aside his social democratic priorities. The nub of his problem was this: how to respect provincial jurisdiction while all the while building a national welfare state? And how would it be possible to avoid compromises such as Lester Pearson's decision in 1965 to allow Quebec, with financial compensation, to opt out of the proposed Canada Pension Plan?[104] One way of squaring the circle would have been to presume that all provinces would agree to interprovincial programs on pensions, healthcare, social assistance, and so on. But that was as unlikely as achieving a formal amendment to transfer powers to Ottawa and Trudeau must have known that. Indeed he recognized later when he was prime minister that the realignment of jurisdictions was not only unlikely but undesirable given that so many of the issues that seized federal–provincial diplomacy related not to "either/or" situations but "in-between" ones, as he put it.[105] So there was no alternative but to continue pursuing co-operation and to deploy a federal spending power and the shared-cost program, as indeed happened with the two major achievements of the Pearson government's national social agenda—the Canada Assistance Plan in 1965 and the Hospital Insurance Services Act of 1967. But Trudeau was correct when he had said in 1957 that such arrangements would be an infringement of a strict interpretation of the Whearean model. But sometimes utopia must give place to realism and on these matters Trudeau became realistic too.

If Trudeau espoused federalism so determinedly, it was because he was so contemptuous of nationalism. Ethnicity of some kind was inherent in nationalism; and while not all nationalisms were actually genocidal, they were potentially so. The dangers in nationalism had in the modern age, he thought, been greatly increased by the geometric growth of the state's technical mastery. Certainly his account of the historical origins of nationalism bears the imprint of his times, especially the chaos visited on the world by the interwar totalitarianisms of Italy and Germany. If the young Trudeau took his time to register a sense of the historic significance of the Nazis, once he had done so it left an overwhelming impression on him. But was he right in believing that such an epoch tells us a great deal about nationalism? His was very much a conception of nationalism as an intellectual invention having mainly *political* origins and consequences. More recently Ernest Gellner offered a more anthropological paradigm of nationalism as a modernizing idea crucial to the building of industrial societies while Benedict Anderson in *Imagined Communities: Reflections on the Origin and Spread of Nationalism* provides suggestive insights about the role of print capitalism in structuring the consciousness of nationality. Nevertheless there is remarkable plausibility in what Trudeau specifically theorized. Eric Hobsbawm, no less a historian than either Gellner or Anderson, offers interesting confirmation of some of Trudeau's claims: that the paternity of the idea of nationalism lay in the French Revolution and that it was integrally connected with the idea of democracy. He also argues that nationalism did eventually develop a racist tendency and that it led to the genocides not just of Jews and other groups in the Holocaust but the killing of Armenians by the Turkish government after 1915 and massacres and ethnic cleansing by Greeks and Turks after 1918. Hobsbawm also mentions the class appeal of nationalism to a rising middle-class in Italy, Germany, and Ireland between the wars.[106] Trudeau's analysis shares with all three historians the sense that nationalism was a product of modernity and that political constructivism of some kind lay at the heart of its existence. With his fascination for the role of economic and technological factors in explaining history Trudeau's views might be thought to have natural affinities with Anderson's theory of the origins of nationalism. But ultimately Trudeau's argument was less about nationalism's history—though it cannot be left out altogether—than about morality and practical political prudence: nationalism is an unstable idea because it valorizes the sectional over the universal and it is especially problematic in the modern democratic state that purportedly exists to serve everyone. If the evidence of the interwar years and the Second World War is no longer decisive—yet how can it not be—there has since been heaped up a mountain of evidence from the Balkans and Rwanda in the 1990s to Ukraine and Syria and Iraq in the present about the continuing dangers of nationalism. What Conor Cruise O'Brien said about anti-Semitism, Trudeau in effect said about nationalism: be very wary of it because it is a light sleeper.[107]

To the Liberal Station:
Trudeau's Surprising Terminus

———◆———

As long as I have been following politics, I do not remember having seen a more degrading sight than those Liberals who changed their opinion with their leader, when they saw a chance to take power.
Pierre Elliott Trudeau

For political projects are essentially conditioned, not just in their background intellectual conditions but as a matter of empirical realism, by their historical circumstances. Utopian thought is not frivolous, but the nearer political thought gets to action . . . the more likely it is to be frivolous if it is utopian.
Bernard Williams

Good intentions, however, are no substitute for realism in pursuing a course of political action.
Pierre Elliott Trudeau

I

On September 10 1965 Trudeau, in the company of Jean Marchand and Gérard Pelletier, announced his intention to run for the Liberal Party in the upcoming federal election. For some this was news that was completely unexpected, not to say unwelcome. During the 1963 election Trudeau had said that he would be voting for the NDP. As for Pelletier he had been a vociferous critic of the federal Liberals— even more so than Trudeau—and had established an impeccable reputation for political independence. Pelletier himself recorded that there were three general reactions to their announcement:

rejoicing by some, disappointment from others, and, finally, a group that felt they had been betrayed.¹ Trudeau himself found the decision a "difficult" one.² The Liberals had wanted to recruit Marchand but the three of them had concluded a pact in the spring of 1965 that they would join the Liberals as one, or not at all. Predictably, given Pelletier's and Trudeau's past condemnations of the party, there were hesitations on their part while among the Liberal "big-wigs," as Trudeau was fond of calling them, there was outright opposition. It was not every day that a political party knowingly clasped to its bosom two of its most viperous critics.

What took place that fateful summer is not absolutely clear but based on Pelletier's memoirs, Michel Vastel's biography, and Peter Stursberg's oral history the following seems to have happened.³ Although Maurice Sauvé, a federal cabinet minister, was one federal Liberal notable who did not initially support recruiting even Marchand (calling it a "harmful intrusion"), by high summer he had changed his mind and wanted all three of them as part of his crusade to cleanse the Augean stables of the federal party in the province and to challenge its established leadership.⁴ Two other Liberal apparatchiks, Maurice Lamontagne and Guy Favreau, and some others in the Quebec federal caucus, wanted to recruit Marchand but had reservations about Trudeau and Pelletier. Matters came to a head at a meeting in the Windsor Hotel in Montreal on September 9. Favreau, Lamontagne, and Bob Giguère, the party's campaign director in Quebec, were present and possibly also Maurice Sauvé—memories were unclear as to whether he was there—and, of course, Trudeau and Marchand, with Pelletier arriving late from a speaking engagement in Winnipeg. By now Favreau and Lamontagne were under instructions from Prime Minister Pearson to accept all three. At the meeting Marchand, Trudeau, and Pelletier held the whip hand, given their unshakeable loyalty to each other. Marchand had already leaked to the media that they would announce their candidacies the next day. Sauvé was already on side and in the end Lamontagne and Favreau swallowed their pride and, although not altogether happy, fell into line, Lamontagne a little more easily than Favreau. And so the three "wise men," as they came to be called, were accepted for nomination by the Liberals, although such was the last-minute nature of the affair, finding a suitable Francophone constituency for Trudeau, which was his preferred alternative, proved difficult and in the end impossible. Almost exactly a month after the September meeting, as documentary film-maker Donald Brittain nicely put it, Trudeau was "gently parachuted" into the affluent, English-speaking riding of Mount Royal, with the sitting member, Alan Macnaughton, the Speaker of the House of Commons, equally gently pushed aside.[5] Trudeau was opposed for the nomination by Victor Goldbloom and two other candidates but he easily prevailed.

From Trudeau's perspective appearances could have been better. He had shown a prodigious—some said an indecent—aptitude for compromise in running for the Liberals, as others had in letting him run for them. How could he justify joining the very political party and its leader, whom just two years earlier he had condemned as representing the most "degrading sight" he had experienced in politics? And, as we will see, what he said then was hardly a departure from what he had said about them throughout the 1950s. And was there not great insensitivity in running against Charles Taylor, his friend and brother-in-arms?

Trudeau and Pelletier offered their own complex apologia in the October issue of *Cité Libre*.[6] Doubtless under Trudeau's influence the article began with a quotation from Plato. Originally Trudeau had wanted the following: "The punishment of intelligent citizens who are not interested in politics is to be governed by idiots."[7] But Pelletier insisted on something a little softer: "The greatest cost for those who are uninterested in public affairs is to be governed by people who are worse than themselves." This was closer to the original words of *The Republic* and, while it moderated his friend's more inflammatory version, it was still a provocative statement.[8] In any event, Plato, the benevolent absolutist and anti-democrat, oft-quoted by Trudeau, was now recruited to the cause of political participation. On the face of it, their message was straightforward: if you do not get involved in politics, then you should not be surprised if people much less qualified than yourself come to rule over you. Or, was it that they were simply saying with a perfectly modulated frankness that they were likely more honest and competent candidates than the "non-entities," "riff-raff," and "cheats," as they put it, who dominated Canadian politics?[9] This too would have been a suitably Platonic interpretation. Here, Trudeau was certainly speaking but perhaps Pelletier too, for an obvious inference is that they were referring, among others, to the Quebec Liberal Party leadership and Liberals in general and Pelletier had never been cautious in criticizing them either.[10] Yet such criticisms they gave forth at the very same time as they were joining that very same party. Perhaps Trudeau was telegraphing a subtle message to his friends and colleagues, who over the years had encouraged him to run, that they had been right all along about his suitability for public office. In the end it is hard not to see in the comment a very large measure of *amour propre*. Trudeau was shrill, impudent, and self-serving yet somehow, at the same time, charming and persuasive. His frankness was always disarming even when it was extravagant and disagreeable.

Trudeau and Pelletier went on to offer an analysis of two role-types: the person of thought and the person of action, not quite the same as Max Weber's famous distinction between the man of conscience and the man of responsibility but certainly close. The person of thought, they asserted, was bound to be critical of everything, to go to the limits of his critical quest and not to worry about making enemies or giving offence:

> It is why the authors of this present article have never put a safety-catch on their thought; so that in trying to prod politicians further down the road of progress we have said and written much that is critical of all of the Canadian political parties, without exception.[11]

They cannot, then, be legitimately criticized, they said, if they have ended up supporting one particular political party. For it is a necessary truth that, if they have done their job well, they would have criticized every political party, including the one they eventually joined.

The radical disjunction between the world of action and the world of intellect had not always been Trudeau's emphasis. In his writings in the 1950s, especially in *La grève de l'amiante*, he had held that thought itself constituted an important form of engagement in politics. Thought was to be the tutor of political practice; good politics required not just recognition of the limits of theory but equally an appreciation of how far politics was an exercise in informed, educated practice. John Stuart Mill, for one, had talked of the importance of deliberation as an ideal foundation for political action as he had of the importance of the heroic individual, not necessarily a politician, fighting the tyranny of conventional opinion. Trudeau never tired of preaching the virtue of Mill's insights, and, in a similar vein, it was the view too of Julien Benda with his notion of *"les clercs"* as ideally a spiritual check on the group passions roused by race, class, and nation and "the realism of the multitudes."[12] In 1962, when he had directly confronted the question of the role of the political intellectual, Trudeau summarized his views with an approving quotation from the American playwright, Arthur Miller: "The task of the true intellectual consists of analyzing illusions in order to discover their causes."[13] Or if another definition is instructive, drawing on Mounier's definition, Trudeau's stance in those early years can be described as that of the "prophet," that is, someone who challenged prevailing values and who, in ways that could not be predicted, did in fact have a powerful effect on actual politics. And if that was not enough justification of the lonely intellectual ploughing his radical furrow there was the example of Cyrano de Bergerac for whom Trudeau always had great admiration:

A man who does his own thing, who has his own ideals, and who fights anybody who tries to get in his way. Let's not follow conventions, fashions, or accepted opinions. Let's be ourselves and seek new truths for ourselves.[14]

Critic and prophet and perhaps the self-affirming, and sometimes self-aggrandizing, eccentric too, all spoke to the relevance of the public intellectual to political life. But now that he was poised to enter parliamentary politics Trudeau tended to diminish the role of the independent critic, implying that it encompassed a sort of full-bore tendency to criticize and little more, the intellectual as contrarian and gadfly. Trudeau was saying that the legendary, heroic individual, maker of history in his own right, prodding and pushing the stubborn multitude in the direction of progress, was not quite enough and that only the politician could truly change things.

In fact the two ideas may not be incompatible. Perhaps the heroic intellectual may shape history simply by formulating a compelling idea. But more effective again will be the seizing or winning of power in order to implement it. Michelangelo and Beethoven, through their artistic ideas, would be instances of the former and Joan of Arc and Queen Elizabeth 1 instances of the latter. John Stuart Mill mentioned these individuals and the differences between them in his work *The Subjection of Women* in 1869.[15] Or it might be said that in 1965 what Trudeau intended was not to cast off his earlier persona but to incorporate it into his identity as a politician. But having intellectual convictions in the first place would, according to this interpretation, have been indispensible. Trudeau with Mill and Mounier—and Laski too—prescribed an idea-based politics. The intellectual on her own may have had influence but the maiden-warrior and the virgin-queen seized with an important idea demonstrated the benefits of power.

Trudeau and Pelletier continued their self-defence with some reflections on the instrumental nature of politics. The political party, they said, was a morally neutral set of means and no more than a tool, and the test of its usefulness was whether it did or did not work successfully:

> Among the democracies that we know of, the political party is not
> an end but a means, not a goal but an instrument. Joining a party
> is like selecting a tool. One can criticize the choice and attempt

to show that the tool is not the most suitable for the chosen goal. But unless one raises party spirit to the status of absolute dogma one has no right to criticize this choice as some kind of treason or apostasy.[16]

In their further defence they offered the observation that they had not, in fact, altered their goals nor given up on their ideals:

> In the present case [we] are pursuing always the same goals and continue to adhere to the political ideologies that [we] have expressed for a long time in *Cité Libre*: a constitutional view respectful of the rights of persons and groups, a democracy centred on social progress, a federalism that knows how to reconcile a strong central power with autonomous and progressive provinces and a politics open to the left.[17]

They explained that they had chosen the federal Liberal party as the best means to these ends. Even so they themselves seemed a little stunned as to where their political logic had brought them. They conceded that their prior contributions to public debate were indeed "engagements" of a kind but now that there was a crisis in the country, direct political action was called for, something the intellectual *qua* intellectual could not undertake.

As they saw it, the crisis was a compound of three elements: a weak central government, rampant nationalism in Quebec, and an inadequate left-wing alternative. Present circumstances put in jeopardy the very ideals for which they had struggled since 1950:

> For fifteen years we have preached a personalist conception of society, the priority of the social over the national and a functionalist technique in politics. We hold these objectives as fundamental against those who refuse to engage in dialogue and who wall themselves off inside the absolute, who wrap themselves in nationalism and fight for its symbols. It is the struggle for our long-held objectives that now draws us into political action.[18]

They recounted what had always been their abiding concerns. One had been to invigorate provincial politics in Quebec. But now, with the defeat of Duplessis and the triumph of Lesage, the province was indeed stronger but the federal government, sadly, weaker. For believers in a balanced federal system all roads now led to Ottawa. There was an imminent threat to the Canadian political union. Who would fill the void at the centre? The Diefenbaker Conservatives were non-existent in Quebec and, anyway, in recent years they had demonstrated their incapacity to govern; the Créditistes now lacked any political thought whatever and were falling apart; and as for the NDP it had made the fateful error of defining itself in terms of the nationalist issue in Quebec and was unable to voice a clearly federalist position. While the new Canadian Labour Congress-sponsored party had seen some growth in support, it suffered under the same limitations as the old CCF. Basically the NDP could not be expected to make a breakthrough nationally. It was doubtful that it could obtain even a plurality of seats in the upcoming election. Thus the NDP was a net contributor to the very disunity and paralysis at the heart of the crisis. To sign on to the NDP was to do little more than to reinforce the age-old yearning of the Left for "dying with honour." And so, by a process of elimination, Trudeau and Pelletier came to the conclusion that the Liberal Party was the only option left for those who were moved by the twin preoccupations of

> a dynamic federalism and a socially progressive politics. . . . [W]e are bound to recall for those who condemn us the stern words of [Charles] Péguy addressed to the intellectuals of his time: "They have clean hands because they have no hands at all."[19]

Writing in 1993, Trudeau's recollections of that changeful summer were quite consistent with what he expressed in 1965 and what others remembered too.[20] He emphasized the crucial role played by Jean Marchand who, he said, had been courted in 1962 by both the provincial and the federal Liberals although the provincial offer was in the end "withdrawn." Discussions *had* taken place between Pearson's advisers and Marchand and he had insisted that, if he were to go to Ottawa, Trudeau and Pelletier must accompany him. But the Bomarc crisis had put an end to that.[21] Two years later defence and foreign policy were apparently less pressing issues. Now the emphasis was on domestic matters. In his *Memoirs* Trudeau also touched on the larger intellectual rationale for his jump to the Liberals. He had been, he said, an early supporter of the CCF and the similarity of its program to that of the British Labour Party was what had originally attracted him to it:

> But the excessive centralism of the CCF and its ignorance of French Canada bothered me a great deal. And later, when it swung to the other extreme, the NDP's support of the "two-nations" doctrine made me give up on it for good.[22]

Equally critical, he said, in shaping his decision had been the growing nationalism of Lesage's Liberal government and of Quebec intellectuals in general, and the sense that there was a vacuum of support in Ottawa for federalism. Here too Trudeau's position led by a process of elimination to the federal Liberals. But Trudeau conceded that they might not have been automatically welcomed by that party:

> Pelletier and I had on numerous occasions written scathing criticisms of the Liberals; I seem to recall one of my articles using the word "donkeys," not in a complimentary way.[23]

But Marchand's "unyielding" stance had won the day and so Trudeau joined what he had once called an assemblage of asses.

II

If Trudeau himself was convinced of the reasonableness of his decision, can it be said that his political itinerary before then led plausibly to such a destination? Was his new affiliation an improvised one, taking account only of his interests of the moment? Or was it the logical consequence of a long-term, consistent perspective?

In late 1947 the fundamental premise of his critique of party politics had had to do with its intellectual incoherence. Coherence was important, he thought, because it provided clarity of political purpose and policy; it afforded the citizen the chance to see alternatives to established ways of thinking and doing.[24] It was, of course, mainly Canada's deep regional and cultural differences that had led to a national politics mired in compromise and, literally, unthinkingness. The parties stole each others' ideological clothes and embraced positions they had erstwhile opposed. Everything was oriented to accommodation, tactics, and compromise, and, of course, winning and keeping power. In those postwar years Trudeau already noticed that the Liberals possessed the advantageous flexibility of being able to bend to the left to capture the popularity of ideas pioneered by the CCF. But at bottom the Liberals were the party of big business—the "bourgeoisie" as Trudeau sometimes called them—and its partisans in the professional and middle classes. As a corrective Trudeau came to propose new political initiatives and ideas: clear thinking and thought in the whole, an appeal to reason rather than to emotion and self-interest, and new parties and new non-party movements.[25] In his reflections on early postwar politics in Quebec Trudeau offered a similar perspective: the need for an intentionally theoretical approach to policy-making; new thought and new alternatives to the unspeakable Duplessis and his "cult of [the] infallible leader."[26] What was needed was a politics of the common good, he believed. The industrial and financial power of big business must be confronted, as must the power of the Church and nationalists. Thinking increasingly as a socialist, Trudeau held that in Quebec and other parts of Canada there were prospects of a new working-class politics. What informed his views was not just some kind of underlying political *ouvrièrisme* but a sense as well of the creative and surprising potentiality of the times.

Evidence of this appeared in unexpected places. Writing in 1952 about the prospects of the Parti ouvrier-progressiste—the

Communist Party in Quebec—Trudeau observed that in its opposition to "Church and Nation" the party was deeply unpopular.[27] But if the working class, he said, ran aground in its mission to cleanse Quebec politics or if there were a move towards fascism there might be a turning to the party. For Trudeau, Canada's communists too, it seems, were within history and capable of being favoured by its twists and turns. Raised against the background of the horrors of the Depression, the rise of Nazism and an atrocious war, and registering the influence of a sort of inchoate Marxism, Trudeau was capable of expressing pessimism about the postwar world as a place where catastrophes and chaos might recur. The viability of capitalism was not to be taken for granted and in a crisis the emergence of another Hitler or Mussolini was quite conceivable. Democracy was now triumphant but it might not always be so.[28] Laski in particular held that fascism was "the institutional technique of capitalism in its phase of contraction" and a similar idea lay at the back of Trudeau's comments about the possible return of right-wing authoritarianism.[29]

But mostly in the immediate postwar period Trudeau was optimistic. For Trudeau, history was on the move, in democratic directions. Colonized peoples were being liberated, and in Europe and North America, electorates were challenging established conventions. There was an element of North American exceptionalism too: the United States and Canada in particular were free of the entrenched rigidities of the old world. Here was a new place that was more spiritual and open to experiment. The potentialities of technology and science led to a similar optimism. He would never regard these as unreservedly beneficent: cybernetics were useful but they might also reinforce the bureaucratic and centralizing reach of the state and undermine government's accountability to legislatures. And, after Hiroshima and Nagasaki, the evidence was only too clear about the horrific consequences of the atomic age. Trudeau was profoundly affected by the idea that humanity now lived in an era of total war and possible annihilation. But about technology and science in general Trudeau was a sort of commonsensical

modernist. Science, technology, and industrialization increased
productivity to such a point that, if their fruits were fairly distributed, the poverty of untold millions could be overcome; and as well
machines allowed humans to avoid degrading work.[30] Technology
was so omnipresent that everyone must somehow live within it and
adapt to and accept its imperatives. He confirmed this view in an
interesting comment in 1970 about policy towards Aboriginal peoples. Trudeau talked of how important it was for Aboriginal people
to embrace the modern world. Integration with it was in a sense
inevitable and, while it did not come without problems, it was also
advantageous:

> The way we see the history of Canada and of the western nations
> developing, no small group of people can long remain outside of
> the mainstream of education, technology, urban living, and all
> these things (some of which have produced pretty awful results,
> I agree.) You cannot do this [that is, remain outside the main-
> stream] without paying a very heavy penalty in terms of the
> health of children, the education of minds, the freedom to move,
> the right to accumulate property and the right to be treated as an
> equal under the law.[31]

Trudeau was saying that modern life was unimaginable outside of
technological society, another instance of his view that the dominant material circumstances of the time had to be accommodated.
Mostly, however, Trudeau played the progressive card: technology
might be increasingly omnipresent and while it came with its share
of problems, generally its ministrations were agreeable.[32]

Trudeau also held to a strong belief in the progressive possibilities of democracy. It was the age of the rights of the person
and increasingly of "the sovereign people": civic-minded, rational,
informed, and active, the people at their best, so to speak. Laski had
said something like this and Maritain too. However Trudeau was
not a populist because, as we have seen, he saw limits to the public's capacity to vote knowledgeably on complicated issues. Nor was

he the sort of democrat who believed that the people were always right. A major theme of the *Vrai* essays was about how the people typically had been craven and lazy in the face of political power and only too submissive. But his settled conviction was that "the people," with all their limitations and handicaps, were at bottom the indispensible midwives of a decent and fair society. As he put it once, quoting Thomas Jefferson, if the people demonstrated a lack of enlightenment and discretion, the solution was not to take away their power but "to inform their discretion by education."[33] Once Trudeau had shed the conservatism of his youth he embraced the postwar democratic state as the provider of general well-being and justice: full employment and material sufficiency for all. Reaction and privilege would be held at bay by a progressive electorate. As important too for Trudeau was the notion of democracy as the crucial precondition of a politics of non-violent change, which for all his flirtation with the rhetoric of force and revolution, was his primary moral position in domestic affairs.

Even so, there were limits to how much Trudeau could have known about where history was going and how unerringly it could be pointed in positive directions. A progressive sense of history—Marxism is an obvious example—can offer what looks like iron-clad guarantees about how events will unfold but of course these are often unfulfilled so that continued belief in them becomes a kind of religious faith. For Trudeau, wise politicians and public commentators knew a different truth. Long before he entered active parliamentary politics—indeed it may be said to have been his fundamental political disposition all along—Trudeau's orientation was towards policy and action. Gérard Pelletier saw it all so exactly when he observed of his friend that he was, from the outset, practically oriented in his approach to politics.[34] Trudeau was not a salon intellectual and armchair dabbler in abstract worlds. In a sense he was not a philosopher at all. He used philosophy to point out philosophy's limitations. Certainly he did employ "methodical doubt"; he was fond of Plato's style of grand declamations; and undoubtedly he aspired to a politics of reasoned, literate, and coherent argument. But primarily his purpose was to use theory to illuminate and shape pressing policy questions. Such a pragmatic perspective was also continuous with his sense of action-in-the-world that was his debt to personalism, phenomenology, and existentialism.

But this meant that for Trudeau the direction that policy and action should take could never be crystal clear. This is not to say that integrating theory and practice was for him impossible and pointless. "Reality" itself provided a searchlight of a kind upon the way ahead. But reality, once it was observed in such pervasive phenomena as industry and cities—the lesson he drew from his writings about the Asbestos strike—could only take him so far. Reality was after all many-sided and complicated and hardly a perfect guide as to what to do. The "real" provided a sense of present context and present limits and an outline of the future—but it was a dim one. If only because he conceived politics from a fundamentally democratic perspective there would necessarily be vagaries and unexpected turns. It could never be known for sure what the people would sanction, whether they would be civic-minded and "sovereign" or self-serving and passive. Trudeau was, then, well aware of society's complexities and history's undulations. Life was uncertain and contingent even as it demanded intelligent choices from the political actor. Yet, for Trudeau, uncertainty always existed within a framework of possible coherence and progress. Political, social, and economic improvements might be irregular and erratic and they might be reversed; but they existed as real possibilities if humans chose to think clearly and were resolved to act.

III

After the essays of 1947–48, Trudeau's next significant scrutiny of national politics appeared only in November 1953, "L'élection fédérale du 10 août 1953: prodromes et conjectures."[35] His piece was extensive and thorough and established him already as a first-class journalist and political scientist. (How expert he was in so many different fields.) From Trudeau's perspective much had changed in the intervening years and the changes had not been for the better. What had begun as an epoch of fluid, creative possibilities had congealed into revanchism and reaction. The war and its aftermath, he said, had set in motion an invigorating democratic politics. In Africa and Asia movements of national emancipation and in the "free states" of the West there was talk of a welfare state:

> Three countries in the Commonwealth gave themselves labour governments. Socialism consolidated itself in Scandinavia and made progress in the main countries of western Europe. . . . The Republicans were easily defeated in the United States in 1944 and in 1948.[36]

But these advances had now been thrown back. The fulcrum year had been 1949.[37] Faced by the rise of the people, "the owner classes," had begun a successful counter-campaign. Aided by their friends in the press they had drummed into the public's mind the message that extravagant workers' demands had brought on inflation and the new welfare measures had increased the costs of production, adversely affecting the balance of payments and generally devaluing money. Part of this anti-socialist crusade was the contention that behind the scenes the Soviet Union was fomenting troubles in the West.

Depending on circumstances, he continued, the lurch rightwards had taken different forms. Where there had existed a deeply entrenched culture of socialism the shift had been limited but, even there, the centre of political gravity had moved at least to the centre. In countries where communists had been in government the shift had been more rightwards: socialists had split apart, as in Italy, or had been removed from office, as in France. In both countries, power had passed to anti-communist coalitions. In countries where the Left had not been well established and where, as Trudeau put it, the people had not yet thrown off a sort of political "inferiority complex," the voters had returned parties of the status quo, often led by strong authority figures such as Konrad Adenauer, Winston

Churchill, and Dwight Eisenhower. And there were new conservative governments in New Zealand and Australia too.

The same trends had affected Canada, he said. In 1944–45 it was as if "a wind blew from the left across the country." Unemployment insurance had been introduced in 1940 and votes for women in Quebec too. The results of the plebiscite in 1942 had shown that the federal government had been right to initially resist repudiating its election promises of 1940.[38] The Marsh Report in 1943 presaged the coming of a welfare state. And family allowances had been introduced: "The government reduced illiteracy, trained workers, created jobs, built houses, allowed trade unions to develop, stabilised prices and acted honourably towards soldiers."[39] But the political landscape had shifted, he said. In the last year of the war, the CCF had done very well all across the country but especially in British Columbia, Saskatchewan, Manitoba, Ontario, and Nova Scotia. Even the communists had enjoyed increased popularity while other movements and third parties had prospered. In Quebec there had been a rise in support for the nationalists and, in the west, Social Credit had flourished:

> But the same reaction after the war was manufactured in Canada as elsewhere. The elite invited the people to reflect on the prosperity created by "free enterprise," on the recession of 1948 brought on by the supposedly unreasonable demands of workers and on Marxism and its international consequences, the spy scandal [Trudeau is no doubt referring to the Gouzenko affair] and the war in Korea.[40]

As Trudeau saw it, "Grandfather" Louis St. Laurent and the Liberals' triumph in the federal election of August 1953 was proof of this ideological turn. They now dominated the federal scene. Supported by a newly affluent electorate and epitomizing political reliability and economic stability, they were the party of the status quo. If anyone stood in the way of reform it was the Liberals. And they were devious too: they were chameleons, adept at shifting to

the left or right if need be. They were the perfect centrist party play-
ing off the CCF and the PCs on either flank. Their propensity for
success was infinite. During the election the voters had seen them
as offering the advantages of incumbency and dispensing the "fruits
of victory." Quebec voters in particular had evolved special reasons
to stick with them. There the Union Nationale was regarded as protecting their interests in provincial matters while St. Laurent

> better than [George] Drew [the PC leader] looks after their con-
> federal interests . . . French Canadians are faithful to their history.
> They would never have belonged to the Conservative party had it
> not been for Cartier, or have belonged to the Liberal party had it
> not been for Laurier, Lapointe and Saint-Laurent [sic]. They have
> never adhered to a Canadian party; they prefer to be allied to par-
> ties to which they can form a semi-detachable wing.[41]

This last metaphor was one that Trudeau often used. He continued:
the outcome of the election had been miserable for the Left and for
minor parties in general. The CCF's share of the popular vote had
declined and it had lost seven seats. Only in Saskatchewan had the
party held on to its support, so that with Social Credit's success in
Alberta these two Prairie Provinces had become the radical excep-
tions to an otherwise Liberal sweep of the country. Trudeau saw
Liberal prospects as greater still, mainly because of the parlous condition of the PCs. The PCs in Trudeau's eyes were passing through
a sort of identity crisis that might marginalize them for a long time,
or at least for as long as the Liberals remained, Janus-like, as both
reformers and conservatives.

   Trudeau was especially concerned over the electoral misfor-
tunes of the CCF. Apart from Saskatchewan and parts of Manitoba
and Nova Scotia—he overlooked British Columbia for some reason—the roots of socialism had not gone deep, he said. Ontario
and Quebec, as the two most populous, industrialized provinces,
were crucial and there the story was not encouraging. Nevertheless
he felt that in these two provinces socialism was sufficiently well

established to take advantage of future economic crises, although a crisis may not be altogether desirable:

It is clear that if the Canadian economy were hit with a grave crisis, there would emerge social upheavals that would be ruinous for the old parties. But hoping for the best, let's wish that the new techniques of macro-economic stabilisation and the competence of our federal civil service will prevent such a cause for upheaval. Even so Canadian socialists have hardly much to base their hopes on from the results of the last federal election. . . .

It is certain that the further away one is from Saskatchewan the more difficult it is make sense of its socialist experiment: the owners of the means of information are careful not to inform us about that. But in Ontario the CCF was well known; it had almost tasted victory and yet it gained fewer votes in 1953 than in 1949. No doubt the date of the election worked against the CCF more than against the other parties since it fell during the period of workers' holidays. . . . It seems though that the progress of socialism in the province depends on a greater realization by the working class of its democratic power. That is more likely to occur when the tasks of increasing productivity and the contraction of markets and prices will no longer allow businessmen to increase simultaneously both salaries and profits. Then the parties involved would want to appoint the government as an umpire and for that they would consider choosing one more to their liking. In this respect, the strikes in northern Ontario are a sign of the times.

The same causes will have the same effects in the industrial sectors of the Maritime provinces. Moreover that's what explains the hold of the CCF over the miners of Nova Scotia. But these provinces are almost as ferociously independent-minded as Quebec. And for socialism to take root there it will have to be provincialist in tone. It is a paradoxical fact that it will perhaps not succeed there before it has made a breakthrough in Quebec: that would be its most sure proof.[42]

The situation was especially distressing in Quebec where the CCF had received only 1.6 percent of the vote. There, said Trudeau, socialism was non-existent. But there were signs of a hopeful future. He also noted that the decline of the Bloc populaire had left nationalist opinion rudderless and unrepresented. The Liberals presently dominated federal politics in the province but Trudeau wondered if they would survive the shock of a rising "proletarian mass." Neither workers nor nationalists alone could be effective, but if both of them united around a concrete program perhaps they could overcome their weaknesses:

> I am obviously not talking of this being done by adventurers for whom politics is a game but by sincere men who feel within them the burden of social and national injustices. I would love to see them discussing together the problem of the exploitation of national resources for the benefit of the nation. They would be astonished to discover how much their ideals can come together and how similar their plans of action would be.[43]

The last idea is intriguing. Trudeau was proposing a strategic alliance with nationalists. It was not a statement of pure nationalism but it made clear that in his estimation injustice in Quebec had some kind of "national" dimension. Perhaps this was a reference to the different levels of economic well-being of English and French workers there and the overwhelmingly Anglophone ownership of manufacturing and extractive industries. But, clearly, Trudeau—for all his vaunted zeal for consistency—was not beyond improvising a response to the exigencies of the moment. Equally though there was the evident commitment he displayed towards democratic socialism and the CCF. But about his analysis of the economic system there was evident ambivalence. It was as if he had absorbed two competing paradigms and did not quite know how to integrate them. He seemed to be influenced by both Marx and Keynes. While he foresaw a possible structural crisis of capitalism, he was not convinced that such a catastrophe would be for the best. Of one thing, however, he was sure: the postwar course of the Left could no longer be envisaged as one of uncomplicated, linear progress. The workers' cause waxed but it also waned. They were involved in an intense battle against a resolute and powerful enemy. Trudeau doubted that workers and socialists were "being cheered on by the universe."[44] For the first time Trudeau recognized that the class struggle in Canada might not work out as he would have liked. For by the mid-1950s a growing affluence in Canada was taking hold. Disaster and depression were perhaps not in Canada's stars; Keynes would vanquish Marx, and Trudeau was not altogether disappointed although he did not put it in such triumphalist terms. The Keynesian bureaucrats in the federal government were doing their jobs well.

IV

If Trudeau successfully anticipated the triumph of Keynes and the economic ascendancy of the Ottawa mandarinate, predicting the direction of *political* events was more difficult. In his earliest postwar pronunciamentos about the federal political parties, he had been dismissive of all of them, with the possible exception of the CCF—and it was not beyond criticism either. He was genuinely non-partisan in his estimate of both the Liberals and the PCs; that is, he was equally scornful of both of them. If anything his view was that the PCs were the ones most exposed to history's rejection. Basically what Trudeau longed for was new political alternatives. Yet such was his conviction about the contingencies of history, as far as he was concerned, these might even include a revamped PC party. Some improvement and redirection of a party's fortunes were always imaginable. As he would argue later, political parties were tools: they might be used well or poorly and they could be put to different uses. So he welcomed John Diefenbaker's triumphs in 1957 and 1958. The Liberals had been properly punished for their arrogance and anti-democratic tendencies. But Diefenbaker in time failed badly. He turned out to be, in Trudeau's estimation, too impetuous and impatient, not to say incompetent, and little different in policy-orientation from the party he had supplanted. As early as April 1960 Trudeau offered a damning indictment of Diefenbaker's PC party:

> The Conservative Party is becoming the usual grab-bag of loud mouths and flashy upstarts, a pack of lawyers at so much a mile and entrepreneurs at so much a square foot—in short, a traditional party of Canadian politicians.[45]

Nevertheless at the height of the Bomarc crisis in 1962–63 Trudeau commended Diefenbaker for his independent stance towards the Americans.[46] Trudeau's political judgments were invariably made within the framework of the rough legitimacy of the institutional order of liberal democracy in general and, given his immense sense of practicality, there was always the possibility that he would commend a traditional party for a greater evil avoided or a small improvement attained. Overall he disdained the old parties but he did not dismiss them altogether.

Regarding the Liberals he started from the premise that they were the natural governing party. Ever since Laurier's rise to power in 1896 they had been the great, unchallenged paladins of the political order. Consequently whatever malady infected Canada's political culture was inevitably present in them, *in extremis*. Contemporary Liberalism was the perfect instance of a non-ideological party operating in a land of deep, regional, and ethnic cleavages.[47] Largely devoid of ideas and principles—and self-consciously and self-congratulatedly so—the Liberals exhibited little constancy. Their politics was a tangle of interests and tactical calculations, such as winning power and choosing popular leaders. The party was little more than a cadre of power-brokers whose raison d'être was to dispense patronage and the spoils of office and to resist change within a party structure that was hierarchical and leader-centred. None of this hindered its success however. An odour of malignant ethnocentrism hung over its intra-party relations between French and English members. Trudeau noticed that the party invariably included a reform wing but that it was usually without much influence. Even the renowned progressive Kingston Thinkers Conference in 1960, though not unnoticed, went largely unremarked by him.[48]

Also part of Trudeau's basic perspective in the 1950s and early 1960s was a judgment about the role of political parties in a capitalist economy. Party politicians were at heart cat's paws of business and finance. He had dwelt on this in his commentary on the 1953 national election. In an article in *Le Devoir* in September 1954, he put it very succinctly:[49]

> In their historical origins, as much as in the source of their funds, the old parties are devoted to the interests of the possessing classes; their ideology postulates that social progress is indissolubly bound to the privileges of capital and great wealth. . . . It is not that the old parties do nothing for workers but it follows that in the face of an irresolvable conflict of interests, they will side with the protagonists who fill their coffers and so permit them to win the next election.[49]

At the provincial level in Quebec, things might have been different because there the Liberals had been out of power since 1936, apart from the one-term government of Adélard Godbout during the Second World War, and by the 1950s they were perennial also-rans. Yet Trudeau was deeply concerned that Liberal incompetence and moral laxity would maintain Duplessis in power for as long as the Premier lived and his party, the Union Nationale, in office possibly forever.[50] The Quebec Liberal Party was "vacillating," "imprecise," and "contradictory."[51] It was reactionary too and its legislative caucus had been complicit in Duplessis' statutory assaults upon workers and their unions. Writing about the 1956 provincial Liberal convention, Trudeau mused that, as with politics in general in Quebec, democracy had come late to the Liberal Party.[52] Only after 1950 had it come to see itself as a member-based party and only in 1955 had the Quebec Liberal Federation established formal democratic structures. He criticized the banal and anachronistic character of its recent draft statement of principles. He admitted that he had a sneaking regard for reformers within the party who wanted "to infuse democratic blood into the veins of a party which has never been other than a syndicate of interests," but he doubted that they would succeed. Writing in 1958 about the convention that elected Jean Lesage as its new leader, Trudeau observed that the Liberal Party of Quebec had an interest neither in ideology nor in democratic reform but only in selecting a leader.[53] At the party's core existed a secretive elite that financed and controlled everything. This was its "reality." Again, he expressed admiration for "reformers" within the party—especially Georges-Émile Lapalme, who had been the leader since May 1950—but he considered them naive in their belief that talking about reform was equivalent to making it happen.[54] A party must democratize itself from the bottom up, Trudeau attested, and the making of true reform was more than a short-run dander on the eve of a convention. Trudeau's criticism was unrelenting and unforgiving. The provincial Liberals offered little promise of either change or reform, it seemed.

His classic denunciation of their federal namesakes came in two essays, one in 1958, "Some obstacles to democracy in Quebec," and the other in April 1963, "Pearson ou l'abdication de l'esprit." In the first, after a long, somber account of the fierce nationalisms that he believed had warred seemingly forever within the bosom of the Canadian polity—the French stoically defending themselves against the English and the latter wielding the cudgel of their majoritarian power to dominate and assimilate them—Trudeau turned to one instance of an apparently successful collaboration between the two, namely French-Canadian participation in the Liberal Party after Laurier's victory in 1896.

> [The Liberals] deserve credit for preventing the growth in Quebec
> of a federal nationalist party, even at the height of Mercier's and
> later of Bourassa's influence, and even when the Bloc Populaire
> was in full sway. For they learned to cater to French Canada's

intuition that its destinies would be better protected at Ottawa by a more or less independent bloc within the party in power than by a nationalist party, bound, because of its ethnic basis, to remain forever seated on the opposition benches.[55]

But what appeared as an encouraging instance of intra-party ethnic collaboration, on closer examination he found to be deficient. Leadership, Trudeau asserted, included educating the electorate in higher things and especially in the rudiments of democracy. Here both French and English-speaking leaders in the party had failed miserably:

> [French leaders] forgetful of the common weal . . . have always encouraged Quebeckers to continue to use their voting bloc as an instrument of racial defence, or of personal gain.

They had been happy to stigmatize the Conservatives as the party of "the Protestants and imperialists" and the CCF as a band of "atheists and centralizers":

> But the fact remains that throughout most of its existence the federal Liberal Party overwhelmingly has been an English-speaking party. And that majority in my view should bear the blame for serious faults of omission with respect to the backwardness of democracy in Quebec. . . . The shameful incompetence of the average Liberal M.P. from Quebec was a welcome asset to a government that needed little more than a herd of *ânes savants* to file in when the division bells rang. The party strategists had but to find an acceptable stable master—Laurier, Lapointe, St. Laurent—and the trained donkeys sitting in the back benches could be trusted to behave. Even the choice of front-benchers very often smacked of shysterism. Excepting the French-Canadian leader, who was usually a man of quality, many ministers of that ethnic group were chosen not so much for their ability to serve democracy as for their ability to make democracy serve the party;

their main qualification was familiarity with machine politicians and schemers, and until lately they were traditionally put
at the head of patronage departments such as the Post Office and
Public Works. To sum up, English-speaking Canadians have long
behaved in national politics as though they believed that democracy was not for French Canadians.[56]

Five years later there appeared his broadside against Lester
Pearson and the Liberals over the Bomarc missile crisis. Trudeau
was at his scathing best—or worst if one was a Liberal—letting loose
most of the weapons of his considerable rhetorical arsenal: sarcasm,
satire, ridicule, and farce, among others. Generally, though, what
Trudeau expressed was simple, unadorned outrage at their hypocrisy.
He began with a comment by his friend Pierre Vadeboncoeur about
Lester Pearson—a comment that Trudeau, by repeating, helped make
famous—as "the defrocked [priest] of peace." He also put to good use
the comment of a famous English Catholic, a prominent layman of
the time who, opposing the declaration of papal infallibility in 1870,
had proclaimed that just because the Pope had changed his religion
that was no reason for him to change his:

> Don't bother looking for men of that stamp at the heart of the
> Canadian Liberal party. It was sufficient that Pope Pearson—not
> even at the end of a Council but one morning while eating his
> breakfast—decided to embrace a pro-nuclear policy in support of
> which the entire party defrocked itself in turn.[57]

For Trudeau the issue of Canada's acquisition of nuclear weapons was in itself deeply important but it was about something else
as well. It was about the utter lack of principle—literally—and the
rank political opportunism of Lester Pearson and his party in their
complete reversal of their positions on the issue. He reminded his
readers of Pearson's original statement of January 1961 in which
he categorically opposed installing nuclear warheads on missiles
and rejected the placement of any kind of nuclear weapons on

Canadian soil. Indeed, said Trudeau, Pearson was so opposed to Canada joining the nuclear club that he was prepared, he said, to withdraw Canada from the North American Air Defence Command (NORAD), if need be. Such policies, Trudeau pointed out, were subsequently confirmed by the Liberal Party in convention and in public statements and manifestos. But then there had occurred the conflict in Diefenbaker's cabinet between Howard Green, the Minister of External Affairs, and Douglas Harkness, the Minister of Defence, over nuclear defence policy, and the Liberals had been handed a political opportunity. Earlier, Trudeau observed, the Cuban missile crisis in 1962 had begun to sour relations between Canada and the United States with mutterings within NATO over the United States's failure to consult its allies. As Trudeau saw it, it was Diefenbaker's insistence on not being pushed around once more by the Americans that had led to the decision by President Kennedy and his "hipsters," as Trudeau called them, to make an example of him. Hence the unseemly sight of the American government and the American General Lauris Norstad putting public pressure on Diefenbaker's government to install the nuclear warheads.

Amidst the uproar Pearson reversed his field, arguing that public agreements entered into and monies already spent made necessary a change of Liberal position. Trudeau saw this as nothing more than a crude grasping after power:

> This nudge came from the Pentagon and obliged Mr. Pearson to betray at one and the same time the party programme and the ideal he had always espoused. The donors to the party promised to be generous. And the *Gallup* poll showed that a pro-nuclear policy would not offend a majority of the voters. Power offered itself to Mr Pearson; he had nothing to lose except his honour. He lost it. And his entire party lost it with him.[58]

That was the doubly appalling aspect of the crisis. Pearson reversed his field, and his party—like sheep—had fallen in behind him.

Trudeau spared no-one in his roll call of "dishonour": the Young Liberals and such party notables as Jack Pickersgill, Jean Lesage, Paul Gérin-Lajoie, and Walter Gordon, among others.

In a coda, Trudeau offered an intriguing insight. The whole sordid Bomarc affair, he said, had disclosed nothing less than the complete "bankruptcy of ideas" of Canadian politics; the "decadence of Canadian political thought . . . [and its] intellectual deterioration . . . [It was] a system absolutely denuded of principles." This outcome had been building for a long time. Indeed he traced its origins back to the Union government in Upper and Lower Canada between 1840 and 1867, when the principle of the double majority had come to prevail in legislative matters and in the selection of political leaders. What this had produced, according to Trudeau, was extreme political instability, with eighteen government ministries in twenty-seven years. The lesson drawn by the Fathers of Confederation—rightly he believed—was that alternative arrangements were necessary or else "paralysis" was inevitable. This was especially pertinent after the newly enlarged Dominion had come to incorporate even more divergent interests and regions with the inclusion of the Maritimes and the west. So there had arisen the convention that good political practice required the suppression of the ideological content of politics. But now, Trudeau concluded, the Liberals had plunged to new depths, to a politics devoid of morality altogether:

> I well remember the federal Liberals of 1957. They were made up of cynics who thought that they were entitled to Power [sic] and they had come to within an inch of putting Parliament under their control. Now, six years in opposition might well have had the same effect as Purgatory on these Liberals. Alas, the events of the last two months have proven the opposite. I see among their old guard the same mindless cynicism; and among the [Liberal] youth associations I see again the same self-serving passiveness; between the two of them are the people of my generation who are trembling with anticipation because they have caught a

glimpse of the painted face of power. In the name of realism and practicality I have—God forgive me—sometimes betrayed the rebellions of my youth. But I have not yet stooped to trample on democracy. That is why in the election of 8th April my intention is to vote for the New Democratic Party.[59]

Leaving aside any speculation about what Trudeau might have understood by the "rebellions of his youth" (which, unfortunately, he did not disclose), probably what particularly irked him about the Bomarc crisis was that in that strangely amoral culture in which Canadian politics wallowed, against all standards of fairness the Liberals—the consummate amoralists—had now been given a chance to overtake the new party, the NDP, and the suddenly popular Social Crediters. In his ongoing search for new political possibilities, Trudeau had taken notice of the latter's recent electoral success under Réal Caouette and had celebrated this as proof of Quebec's growing maturity as a democratic society.[60] (Earlier, in the 1950s, he had had only disdain for Social Credit as a party of reaction and anti-Semitism.[61]) But now the Liberals' exploitation of the Bomarc crisis had made possible the re-establishment of the bleakly anti-theoretical, accommodationist landscape of Canadian politics and the overturning of the forces of reform.

V

Expecting the Liberals and the PCs to constitute the vanguard of political change was certainly not Trudeau's usual conviction. His politics had mainly presumed the necessity of new formations and initiatives. In the early 1950s, his hopes had rested with the CCF. Now, time and circumstance had brought him to different conclusions. The federal election in 1953, as we saw, persuaded him of the relevance of Keynesianism and led him to doubt the inevitable triumph of the Left. Doubts surfaced too about the prospects for the Left in Quebec but less immediately so. There the dawning of the need of a new strategy emerged out of the failure of the CCF/PSD in the provincial election of 1956. Trudeau now turned to a more flexible, less ideologically pure, and more broadly based formation, the Rassemblement. However several contradictions soon emerged and quickly confounded its activities. Its manifesto was agreeable to socialists and social democrats, but was it broad enough to satisfy Liberals, independents, and nationalists? And could an ostensibly non-party organization successfully integrate the sectional and partisan differences of many different members? In December 1957 André Laurendeau decamped, along with other important nationalists, and some trade unionists too. By early 1958 the whole project was in disarray. The demise of the Rassemblement further alienated Trudeau, not so much from his left-wing convictions but from the established formations of the Left. It led him to critically reflect on the political potentiality of the CCF/PSD and later the NDP and ultimately to a rejection of their usefulness.

His critique started with his belief that it had been the PSD that had been the main culprit in the failure of the Rassemblement. It was bent on dominating the organization for its own ends, he said. It had adopted a "doctrinaire" attitude demanding the inclusion of its leaders and the exclusion of those of other parties. It had repudiated, he said, "any orientation that might lead to the setting up of a left-wing political group, newer and stronger than the CCF."[62] Only slightly less scathing was his criticism of the Liberals who he said had participated in the project only to protect their own political interests.[63] Not yet totally discouraged Trudeau now helped launch another project, the Union des forces démocratiques. He claimed in his *Memoirs* to have personally "founded" the Union.[64] Again his initiative was to be a sort of non-party movement but this time more aspirational than organizational. It would be lighter on ideology and more flexible in strategy. There would be no detailed manifesto. Decidedly, though, the Union's purpose was still to unite the centre-left against Duplessis, perhaps through a new political formation or a new basic program or an electoral pact.[65] The common ideological bond was now to be the advancement of democracy: "Démocratie d'abord," "Democracy First," as Trudeau put it.[66] All that would be required of the Union's members was an acceptance of a simple constitution and, of course, a commitment to the ongoing democratization of Quebec society. The Union would seek public declarations from a number of notables from different parties who in "good faith . . . would undertake . . . not to belong to a party which refused to align itself with a democratic union."[67] It was a convoluted idea. But the Union too proved futile and once more Trudeau blamed the PSD, this time not for joining it and then wanting to dominate it, but for not wanting to join it at all.[68] Probably as important a reason for its failure, though Trudeau did not say so, was the provincial Liberal Party which gave it a cold shoulder and proceeded under its own steam towards the election of June 1960 (in which it was narrowly victorious).

Although Ramsay Cook is one important commentator who sees virtue in these two initiatives, most other commentators have offered far-reaching criticisms.[69] Michael Behiels, John English, and Pierre Vadeboncoeur have poured forth a litany of reasons for the initiatives' failures: naivety, disorganization, fecklessness, elitism, quixoticism, insouciance, dilettantism, and even, oddly, in one critic's estimation, "clear-sightedness."[70] Behiels has provided a deep sociological explanation too.[71] In the 1950s, he says, a central conundrum in Quebec's politics was over who would lead and coordinate the opposition to Duplessis. What set of ideas and policies would provide the impetus to overcome the conservative bastion Duplessis had built? Trudeau and the other Citélibristes provided one possible source but in the end, Behiels contends, they failed because they did not sufficiently recognize the aspirations of the new rising middle class of Francophone technocrats, scientists, teachers, and professionals who sought a more modern and secular Quebec, but a Quebec that would be nationalist as well. In the end this new class placed its support behind the Lesage Liberals with their secular, modernizing policies and their message of neo-nationalism. Trudeau was of course a strong secularizer and modernizer but he was deeply anti-nationalist. As well he might have been the victim of his own residual socialism given that the new class on which he pinned his hopes was not so much the professional, managerial clerisy but the industrial working class. But even here there was a problem, according to Behiels: the working class was not immune to nationalism either.

Regarding the failure of "clear-sightedness," this was the reproach of Pierre Vadeboncoeur who sardonically observed that "those analysts who are too clear-sighted sometimes make the greatest errors."[72] He was referring to Trudeau who in support of the Union and its slogan of "Democracy First" had offered the most sublimely logical and subtle arguments for political party co-operation in support of democracy but, uncharacteristically perhaps, had overlooked certain obvious realities. However, perhaps Thérèse Casgrain provided the most damning indictment, coming as it did from a comrade of early CCF days and a close friend of Trudeau's family: "At that period, Trudeau had the reputation of being rather a dilettante and, despite his first-rate intelligence, lacking in perseverance. . . . While he was president, he took a trip overseas and when he returned the Rassemblement no longer existed."[73] Nevertheless Casgrain's comments were written in 1972 and the suspicion is that she was motivated by resentments over Trudeau's later criticism of the PSD and NDP.[74]

In October 1958 Trudeau had drawn lessons from the demise of the Rassemblement in his long essay, "Un manifeste démocratique," where he also laid out his ideas on a substitute for it, the Union des forces démocratiques.[75] Whatever the explanation of the failures of the two initiatives, for Trudeau there was no going back to the old model. For him there was something structurally inadequate about the Left. Further evidence of new directions in his thinking would appear in 1961 in "The Practice and Theory of Federalism," and several other highly charged articles in *Cité Libre* about the provincial elections of 1960 and 1962 would give further evidence of his political turn.

One of the fundamental premises of "Un manifeste démocratique" was that social democrats had "hardly contributed to fill the ideological vacuum [of the Left] in Quebec."[76] The PSD, he said, had all the surface hallmarks of a successful party, in spite of its policy confusions over bilingualism, federal grants to universities, and a provincial tax system. It had an identifiable set of policies that were more or less coherent though it had displayed a fundamental weakness communicating them to the Quebec public. But there were other problems. It required, Trudeau said, a "terrifying" energy to achieve anything through the party and somehow its paltry electoral appeal had bred a sort of collective neurosis that was the bitter fruit of endless cycles of hope and despair:

> For it does not operate by adding new teams to older ones; instead it operates by constantly burning out one team after another; and among the ruins are to be found men of great value who have often become impossible to use for later efforts. Barrel of the Danaïdes [*Tonneau des Danaïdes*], the Party always seems to lose an equal number of disillusioned members for each new cohort of enthusiastic recruits. A social class, an ethnic group, or a generation which enters is just enough to fill the void left by those who have left.[77]

Those who remained were kept going for a while by the hope of "the next time." As Trudeau put it: "A party which is endlessly rebuilding itself on the basis of neophytes risks becoming doctrinaire."[78] Yet the PSD, though a party with few members and not many more voters, had been the most intransigent of the political groups resisting the broadening-out strategy of the Rassemblement. The intensity of the PSD's convictions, it seemed to Trudeau, was in inverse proportion to its popularity.

In the same essay Trudeau offered another explanation for the demise of the CCF/PSD.[79] This had to do with the realities of the Westminster parliamentary system, built irrevocably he seemed to say, on the basis of two parties—one forming the government and the other the opposition and government-in-waiting. Such were its dualistic imperatives, he said, that any new third party, if it were to break in, must do so quickly and replace one of the major parties. Otherwise it risked becoming permanently irrelevant and an eternal minority with its own inevitable pla-toon of disciples and fanatics, so to speak. Trudeau was aware that such a judgment could also be made of the CCF in the rest of Canada. He was well acquainted with the success of the CCF in Saskatchewan and he celebrated it frequently. But its success there was the exception to the rule. Generally, he thought, the condition of the federal party was parlous—a state of affairs, he claimed, which had been conceded in the decision by the national CCF in April 1958 to found a new party. Indeed, in launching this new departure, Trudeau initially thought the CCF had taken a leaf out of the books of the Rassemblement and the Union des forces démocratiques, in other words it had resolved to become a more inclusive party-movement with a place in its ranks for all liberal-minded Canadians. Yet, as Trudeau looked ahead, even a "new" federal socialist party might be subject to the same strictures of irrelevance and marginality.

The PSD was, unsurprisingly, not impressed by Trudeau's arguments. It continued its opposition towards the new Union movement and remained aggressively uncooperative towards the provincial Liberals. In the end natural causes dealt with Duplessis in September 1959 but for Trudeau the struggle continued. The old despot had expired but his ghost lived on. A victory by the Union Nationale in the next election was still a possibility, so that the con-tinuing disunity of the centre-left remained for Trudeau something close to a scandal. Moral choice, he reasoned, must sometimes be about choosing lesser evils and, in this case, it was crucial that all reformers put aside their partisan loyalties and join an historic effort to end the corruption and autocracy of the old order. As the 1960 election drew near he broached the idea of an explicit elec-toral pact. The PSD might decide not to run candidates at all or it might enter into an agreement of some kind with the Liberals and avoid splitting the reformist vote. In the absence of such co-operation and, if his preferred option of the Union was impossible, Trudeau was increasingly of the view that supporting the Liberals was the only alternative.

In the end the PSD did in fact decide not to run candidates.[80] But surveying its strategic failures over the last four years and especially its refusal to participate in any "degrading contact" with the Liberals, Trudeau's summary judgment was that the PSD was not only "doctrinaire in its political thought [and] intolerant in its democratic action"; it was "fanciful in its general strategy."[81] It sought to have "clean hands" by basically "cutting" them off. Rendered irrelevant through its own failures it had handed the reform mantle to the Liberals.[82] In fact the election was a close run thing, with very close margins of victory in several crucial seats. Trudeau believed he was vindicated in his judgment about the unity of the centre-left and the absurdity of the PSD persisting in its naive, sectarian conceits.[83] Writing in *Cité Libre* in January 1961 he continued his campaign against the PSD and its sectarianism towards the Liberals who for all their "stupidity" and "ideological poverty" must, he felt, be supported, at least for now. Trudeau did not easily forgive the PSD, and he saw little that was different in the New Party. It "[is a] rabble of doctrinaires without roots and of union leaders looking for a political bed [to lie in]."[84]

Approaching the 1962 provincial election, Trudeau continued his acidly frank critique of what had now become the Quebec NDP in his "L'homme de gauche et les élections provinciales."[85] This was the election that for the most part was a referendum on the Liberals' proposal to nationalize the remaining private hydro companies in the province. Such a theme especially stimulated Trudeau's sense of the absurd as he mocked the convoluted logic of NDPers over an issue so central to socialism. NDPers, he said, castigated the Liberals and especially Lévesque and wanted to run a candidate against him in his constituency. Yet at the same time they wanted him to resign from the Liberal Party or be defeated and then lead the NDP—and all this in an election that at its heart was all about nationalization, "the touchstone" of socialism which Lévesque had singlehandedly pressed the Liberals into adopting. The Left in Quebec, Trudeau reasoned, defined itself neither with reference to reality nor even with reference to other Leftists but only with reference to itself. In affirming its purity as "an authentic socialist party," it risked once again dividing the vote and allowing the Union Nationale to sneak back to power. It might easily be concluded, Trudeau asserted, that the Quebec NDP was in fact

> led by agents provocateurs whose secret plan is to sabotage the Left. . . . The truth is however much less Machiavellian. The NDP is motivated on the one hand by intellectuals who have never had to trouble themselves about popular reactions; and on the other hand by union leaders whose terms of reference in political matters are situated outside the province of Quebec. The danger of the domination of the NDP by the Canadian Labour Congress is not that it might make it into a class party but that it will make it into a nothing party. I believe that the leaders of the QFL-CLC are bowing to union considerations rather than political ones when they insist on applying to Quebec political imperatives that the CLC conceived to suit Canadian reality. In other words, the leaders of the QFL find themselves somehow forced, by reason of professional standing, to sell willy-nilly the NDP line. It is moreover why they have sometimes compensated by pushing for lamentably extreme quasi-separatist policies.[86]

Trudeau in effect was repeating the lecture he had given to trade unionists in 1953 about the importance of avoiding a type of socialism in Quebec that was essentially an importation from outside or a response to external pressures. Earlier the CCF, nationally, had imposed an overly centralist and Anglophone view of things. Now the play of forces between the national party and its provincial wing was leading the Quebec NDP to a position that was about as anathema to Trudeau as anything at the time: a two-nations policy and a special constitutional status for the province. He went on: the NDP was continuing the pattern of the former PSD, endlessly driven by the necessity to be the only left-wing party in the province and unremittingly jealous of any other group that was somehow progressive or reformist. It wished to burnish "its revolutionary purity," asserted Trudeau, when all that it had that was pure was its ignorance:

> If our intellectuals had read *even a little bit* of Marx and Lenin, and Mao Zedong they would know that true revolutionaries are willing to undertake quite a few tactical compromises when that is necessary to allow a still embryonic left to come into being. And if our men of action had examined *even a little* the experience of the Labour Party in the United Kingdom and of the CCF in Saskatchewan, they would have seen that these parties were only able to grow because in their earliest years they made all sorts of agreements with liberal parties. Later, when the left has come into being, when it has become substantial, when it has popular roots, then it will be possible for it to develop more independent strategies. But even then, in a parliamentary democratic system, governed by a first-past-the-post voting arrangement, the left should avoid slipping into the absolute. As a French militant once said: "We are of the left but no further than that."[87]

Given that the issue of public ownership was central to the debate taking place at the time about the meaning of socialism, Trudeau's comment on the proposal to nationalize the hydro companies is worth examining. His was a subtle analysis that intimated that he was unimpressed by the policy. In private conversations with René Lévesque he lamented the expenditure involved in nationalizing an industry that already existed. The money could be better spent on other things—education for example.[88] He did see some possible technological merits in the proposal but mainly he treated it with deep suspicion. Whatever validity it might have depended on its being done for the right reasons, reasons that in the present circumstances were largely absent. For Trudeau it was as if the nationalizing of hydro was pursued to affirm the machismo of Quebec's politicians:

The state ownership of electricity is a measure which is not necessary, either economically or politically. Only the technological
advantages impress me but I fear greatly that the nationalist passions aroused by this may prevent us from getting the slightest bit
of profit from those advantages. In the last analysis, if electricity
must be nationalized it's for one reason above all others. For the
last thirty years, the right as much as the left has wanted to see
in that (rightly or wrongly) the symbol of our political manhood;
for the last thirty years almost every idealist that our people has
produced has never stopped beating his chest bawling endlessly
at the "trusts." "Just you wait and see what will happen." I believe
sincerely that if we were to retreat now we would for ever after be
considered impotent.[89]

Perhaps Trudeau had put it more directly—and even more dramatically—earlier in the year:

If . . . Hydro-Quebec were to expropriate the province's hydro-
electric industries for nationalistic reasons rather than economic
reasons, we would already be on the road to fascism. The right
can nationalize; it is the left that socializes and controls for the
common good.[90]

Once again Trudeau revealed his profound doubts about the
liberal-democratic proclivities of Francophones in the province.

Trudeau finished his eve-of-election commentary in 1962 by
making it very clear that he intended to support the Liberals. He
was aware of their limitations and he admitted that they might
not be completely unified since some members of the Liberal government probably harboured a secret hope that Lévesque would
be defeated and banished. But, that said, the Lesage government
in two and a half years had done more to reform certain sectors
than the previous administration had done in sixteen. And for all
the "cowards and flunkeys" in its ranks, the Liberal Party was to

be commended for having allowed a man of the Left, Lévesque, to become a member of cabinet and influential enough to make his personal priority the central theme of its campaign. Trudeau's was a qualified but firm endorsement of the Liberals and a generous declaration of support for Lévesque. He concluded by saying that he had never endorsed a "politics of the worse"—that is, a political strategy that pursued an adverse policy from which society would hopefully recoil towards a more completely ideal condition, one step backward to go two steps forward. Everything must be done to keep the Union Nationale from power. And so he remained disquieted by the ongoing intransigence of the NDP towards an anti-Union Nationale strategy.

In other essays there were two other important "realities" that Trudeau talked about at this time: the party system and the electoral system, something we have already noted. The first was about the two-party dynamic of a Westminster-type system and the necessity that, once new parties had emerged, they must break through quickly and replace one of the established ones. Trudeau did not put an exact figure on the number of years within which this must be attained. If he was thinking of the British Labour Party—as he almost certainly was—and if we measure the length of time that elapsed between the founding of Keir Hardie's Labour Representation Committee in 1900 until Ramsay MacDonald's first Labour government in 1924, the period was twenty-four years. If Saskatchewan was his prototype then it is even shorter, between the founding of the CCF in 1932 and its becoming a major party in 1938, and ultimately triumphing in 1944. However, at the federal level by the mid-1950s, the CCF had been pursuing power largely unsuccessfully for twenty years and similarly so in every other province except Saskatchewan, though with passing successes as the Official Opposition in British Columbia and Ontario. When Trudeau finally cut his ties with the NDP in 1965 it was over thirty years since the founding of the CCF and only in Saskatchewan and British Columbia had it attained major party status. If these were the appropriate metrics, by 1965 the CCF/NDP in general was indeed a slowly moving cause and perhaps a lost one. There were also his comments on the electoral system. Here he expressed a realism derived from a skepticism about the likelihood of politicians ever reforming the traditional Westminster system of first-past-the-post for electing members of parliament. The dominant parties were significantly advantaged by the existing system, while third parties were decidedly disadvantaged. For this reason, making changes—for example in the direction of proportional representation—was unimaginable. Sober realism determined that the probability of established parties' leaders' acting against their self-interest was close to zero. For these reasons too Trudeau concluded that the NDP would find it difficult to move beyond being a minority party.

Beginning, then, in 1956 with his decision to promote the Rassemblement and in particular following the publication of "Un manifeste démocratique" in 1958, Trudeau enucleated his anxieties about the Canadian Left. Left-wing politics for him needed above all to be culturally and regionally relevant. He attached great importance to leaders being subject to the moral discipline of actually winning the support of the electorate and leading a majority party. Leaders were obligated to identify the singular issues of the moment and to demonstrate flexibility over political means. Flexibility was also necessary in the choice of one's partisan political commitment. He iterated the crucial importance of strategic and tactical compromises; and, if it came to it, a willingness to endorse lesser evils, or, something similar. Perhaps something like what Avishai Margalit has called "second best choices" was on Trudeau's mind.[91] Especially he was adamant about the importance of engaging the political world in a manner that was effective. He allowed no room for abstractions that achieved little material consequence; there was no point in pyrrhic victories. Of course there existed no certain means of calculating how everything might possibly work out in the long run. Immediate evils could be more clearly perceived and averted, while distant ideals removed politicians from the here-and-now and were very difficult to achieve. Yet it was not

just a matter of the politician following his nose and simply react-
ing to existing states of affairs. There was instead for Trudeau a sort
of mid-distance, an intermediate horizon of reflection and practice
that permitted leaders to see large, important political possibilities.
These, however, would still call for tough choices. Farther out than
that, politics might indeed establish a world of apparent certainty
and truth but at the cost of becoming entrapped in dogma, honour,
and unreality, the irrelevant world of "perfect little salon leftists," as
Trudeau once put it.[92]

One conclusion that might be drawn from all this is that Trudeau
was whittling away his socialist faith and drawing back from old
political loyalties and, as early as 1962, arcing towards an eventual
union with official Liberalism. But if he had mixed feelings about
Canadian socialism and the CCF/PSD/NDP he felt the same about
Liberalism and the Liberal Party, indeed *in extremis*. Provincially he
favoured Lesage's Liberals in the 1962 election, but only with strong
reservations. Soon he would rail against the strident nationalism of
his administration. And within a year he would make his lacerating
assessment of Lester Pearson and the federal Liberals. Yet he never
quite burned his bridges with the federal Liberals, and he did receive
some modest patronage from them. At the same time he was still
developing deeper affiliations with individuals and organizations
on the Left, some of them connected with the NDP. And there was
his own robust socialist beliefs expressed, for example, in his 1962
article, "Economic Rights." He was on the board of directors of the
Canadian Peace Research Institute after its founding in 1962 and in
October 1963 he agreed to stand for the provisional executive of the
newly founded Exchange for Political Ideas in Canada, in Toronto,
which envisaged itself as a sort of Fabian Society for the times and
which probably had pretensions of forming some sort of coalition
between the NDP and the Liberals.[93] In 1963 in Montreal he began
to participate in Le comité pour une politique fonctionelle and was
on the board of the La Ligue des droits de l'homme, the Quebec
branch of the Canadian Civil Liberties Union. In late 1964 he joined
a federal Justice Department committee on hate literature. He was

still close to NDP supporters like Frank Scott, Eugene Forsey, and Michael Oliver. Oliver, by now the research director of the Royal Commission on Bilingualism and Biculturalism, was instrumental in early 1964 in getting Trudeau to join the advisory committee of the Commission. His task was to research the idea of entrenching a bill of rights in the constitution. Trudeau corresponded with David Lewis, a federal Member of Parliament for the NDP since 1962. He campaigned for Charles Taylor in 1963 and he voted for the NDP in the election of that year. Likely some time in 1964, or earlier, he gave the NDP a $100 donation earmarked for Charles Taylor.[94] If Trudeau was increasingly disenchanted by the NDP—and publicly he was—he did not cut his informal ties with it until the last minute. For all his doubts he was still decidedly a man of the Left—but, as he was wont to say, "no further than that."

VI

Along with the idea of a common good, running like a golden thread through Trudeau's thinking there was his realism, or pragmatism as he alternatively called it. It was more than simply a subconscious disposition or an afterthought on his part; it was something he consciously pursued. To help us understand the overall shape of pragmatism we might recall the example of John Dewey, whose ideas Trudeau invoked in his Harvard essay: knowledge is socially derived and grows out of the social forces of the time; political action must be judged not on the intentions of its practitioners but on their achievements; human thought emerges out of a struggle against the obscurantism and conservatism of the customary and the traditional; common sense is important in making political judgments, as is science because both test the factual truth of things; democracy is the crucial vehicle for organizing the thrilling possibilities that modernity makes possible; and human knowledge is concerned above all with solving problems and liberating humanity. Dewey also argued that truth is contingent and rooted in contexts and is fundamentally subjective; there is no possibility of apprehending an ultimate metaphysical reality.[95]

Realism has been given a more recent rendering by Bernard Williams in his *In the Beginning Was the Deed: Realism and Moralism in Political Argument* (2005).[96] Williams affirms that "political" values emerge from within the activity of politics itself and if there are to be "universal" values these too must be derived from some type of universal political activity. "Political moralism" is his term for political principles that are believed to emanate from "outside" politics or to exist somehow "prior" to it. Williams does not deny that there are some universal political values, but these are few and far between and their validity lies in being part of the lived reality of an actual world-wide political practice. Such are found in humanity's abhorrence of the "negative capacities" of human beings: that is, their tendencies to violent, cruel, and terrorizing behaviour. Initiatives to overcome these realities could be said to constitute a legitimate form of universal politics. However this cannot be good news for a certain kind of liberalism, as Williams calls it, which lays claim to universal truths such as the self-determining person, government based on discussion and deliberation, and the global relevance of human rights. According to Williams these are emanations of local cultures and are specific to Western society.

Comparing Dewey's and Williams's ideas with Trudeau's allows some interesting conclusions. Obvious points are that Trudeau's pragmatism came with principles so that his ethical thinking was a kind of pastiche or amalgam. The more critically minded—Williams perhaps—would argue that his positions were less a synthesis and more a contradiction. One part of Trudeau's thinking, the major part, was pragmatic in taking account of existing political practices and actual circumstances; but there was another part that fell under the rubric of Williams's account of political moralism. Trudeau's moral universe included ideas drawn from an array of thinkers: Laski, Maritain, Mounier, Aristotle, Aquinas, John Stuart Mill, Acton, Montesquieu, and Tocqueville, as well as from documents like the United Nations' Declaration of Human Rights. Some of these gave his thought an "unpragmatic" and "unrealistic" cast, a sense of there being universal truths, in effect a utopianism, sometimes even a sense of ideals transcendentally existing and discerned. Clearly for Trudeau the wise politician should opt neither for pure pragmatism nor pure utopianism. The preferred position was some kind of combination or interfusing of the two.

However, if the mixture was not right, Trudeau might become an idealist too, as there was also the possibility that, going in the other direction, he might become an utter pragmatist. In spite of what he said about the dangers of utopian, dogmatic socialism, he too was capable of taking off in directions that seemed unrelated to context, practice and realities. Indeed we might see Trudeau as living out a constant tension within him between two personalities, his practical self and his utopian self. His involvement in the Rassemblement and the Union des forces démocratiques might be thought to have been instances of his capability of being utopian. Trudeau was capable of understanding all of the realities that constrained political leaders at the time: the first-past-the-post electoral system, Westminster-style two-partyism, the demands of democracy, the contingencies of regional diversity, the predominance of industry and urbanization, and so on. Yet in thinking about how to get rid of Duplessis in the late-1950s he launched forth upon an adventure in which political activists from across the centre-left would suspend their partisanship, their special ideals and their entrenched loyalties and establish something new and untried. Trudeau's error was not just that he advocated a new party but also that what he proposed was of such an unusual character. His proposal might or might not become a permanent party, which was how he imagined the Rassemblement, or it might become one in which its "members" would still retain membership in their existing parties, which was how he conceived of the Rassemblement and the Union. Another possibility was that the "party" was to be united in support of a spacious goal, like democracy, as was the case with the Union. The obvious reality that Trudeau overlooked was that of the "normal" Canadian political party—which he had already decided was, in its typical manifestations, factional, elitist, submissive to wealth and capital, averse to theory, electorally opportunistic, protective of its own power and ideology, and suspicious if not contemptuous of other parties.

Of course what was "realistic" in Trudeau's prescriptions involved a judgment and some kind of interpretive leap. Realism's disciples can sometimes selectively perceive what is "real." In the matter of the Rassemblement and the Union, Trudeau did what he accused the CCF and the NDP of doing: that is, persisting in an impractical course that had little chance of success, all because his position was somehow axiologically true or pristinely principled. In both cases the moral imperative was to get rid of Duplessis. But how to achieve this outcome was the question. In trying to answer it, Trudeau might be said to have misplaced his pragmatism. The final pages of his lengthy 1958 article, "Un manifeste démocratique," explained with exquisite, painstaking logic all the possible objections there could be to a democratic Union. He then answered them all, one by one, with spell-binding aplomb, *to his own satisfaction*. His argument was compellingly brilliant and somehow "true"—and it was indeed an intellectual tour de force—but only within his own mind.

There was, then, always a possibility that with a quixotic, utopian turn—some will call it a swagger—Trudeau might venture forth to argue and agitate and, paradoxically, sometimes to prevail, often against all the odds and in the face of all the sober predictions that "realists" might adduce. In 1980 he defied the "reality" of the combined opposition of eight provincial governments, including a separatist government in Quebec, a majority on the Supreme Court of Canada, and the main opposition party in the House of Commons and continued his long march towards an entrenched charter of rights. Realism would surely have counselled him not to have considered such a project in the first place. Yet he won out. Three years later he pursued, single-handedly, his crusade for peace and nuclear disarmament. The reality he challenged here was the structured, bipolar order of the global system with its nuclear superpowers, among whom were Canada's closest allies. He acted late in his mandate and largely alone. On this occasion he was defeated and his venture looked fanciful and irrelevant. His stance was noble, honourable, and far-seeing—and also inconsequential. Yet at other times in his political career he might be thought to have been inordinately and supinely pragmatic. His willingness to countenance fairly traditional forms of political patronage while he was prime minister would be one such instance, and some have said that his decision to join the Liberals might have been another.

VII

Anyway, to his critics Trudeau's jump to the Liberals was neither the action of an idealist nor that of a *principled* realist. To them he had scraped the bottom of the barrel and become a rank opportunist, an unprincipled power-seeker, and a base pragmatist. However such a view does not make sense of all the available evidence nor of all of the considerations that went into his decision. But it does raise searching questions.

Of course in his apologia in *Cité Libre* in September 1965 he himself saw his decision to join the Liberals as a principled one and founded on a clear sense of personal volition. He was moved, he said, by the evidence—he might surely have called it the "reality"— of a country in crisis, beset by rising nationalism in Quebec and a weak government in Ottawa led by Lester Pearson who believed, as Ramsay Cook has put it, that "everything could be negotiatied."[97] Canada needed reinforcing at the centre. Trudeau also mentioned his lifelong concern for socially progressive policies, the advancement of human rights and the importance of a politics of the Left. Such priorities were indeed consistent with his overall postwar convictions. He said nothing about international matters, although he was in other contexts increasingly resistant to nationalist claims to a provincial jurisdiction in foreign affairs. Yet there was that troubling question, one posed by many people in 1965: if it was to be party politics, why must it be the Liberals? He had after all castigated them and mocked them unforgivingly.

Trudeau parried possible criticism by alleging that the matter was in some senses beyond ethical determination, either because it would take too long for his critics to obtain empirical evidence to make a valid judgment or because it was in fact not a matter of moral judgment at all. In the latter case he invoked an argument about the instrumental nature of the political party. This was a popular form of thinking at the time, especially in revisionist, social democratic circles: means were flexible, variable, and contingent even if the ends of socialism were essential and constant. Trudeau, we saw, employed this argument powerfully in his long essay on a pluralist understanding of socialism in Canada in 1961. Now once more he affirmed that political parties were merely means or tools or instruments to be used for a given end. As such they were to be assessed in terms of whether they were "the most suitable for the chosen goal."[98] Put simply, would they work? The justification of a tool was a technical one, not a moral one. In its literal simplicity Trudeau's idea was at first sight a compelling one. Was the Liberal Party the most effective means to realize the goals of a strong federal government and a liberal and socially progressive society?

But was a political party a dumb tool? Presumably it comes with a complicated identity and it has a history of its performance under stress. It is not that a political party is unchangeable but, like any human institution, it will have an established structure and tendency that limit its capacity to change. Trudeau seemed not to have considered these kinds of questions. Regardless of its past, a political party could be selected and put to work in whatever cause one chose, he seemed to say. In this version the political party existed in some acultural, ahistorical space. Perhaps Trudeau's idea was altogether too simple. He might have been better advised to dispense with the instrumentalist analogy and gone with the argument to which he was, anyway, also partial, about the awfulness and the risk of decisions in real political situations and how historical actors were never given perfect choices to make. Actually he used that argument too.

Trudeau's invoking of the instrumentalist argument is interesting because it was the type of claim that contemporary Canadian social critics like Harold Innis and Marshall McLuhan had taken great pains to challenge. A political party in their view might be better thought of as some kind of communications system or medium, its dominant organizational patterns establishing an internal environment or context for its operations. These patterns in a sense biased its capacity to move in new directions. To employ McLuhan's famous metaphor, all societies and organizations steered towards the future looking in their rear-view mirror. Trudeau developed an avid interest in McLuhan in the 1960s but there was no sign in 1965 that his ideas had deeply penetrated his thinking, especially his idea that the medium determined the message. For Trudeau, the Liberal Party seemed to be some kind of immaculate medium that could be made to carry any message whatsoever, perhaps even the message of social democracy.[99] If, when he articulated such views, Trudeau had recalled his previous comments about the three parties in question—a fourth, Social Credit, he dismissed as irrelevant in the circumstance—he would have remembered that he had established a number of verities about each of them: the feckless PCs, the irrelevant CCF/NDP, and the unscrupulous, elitist Liberals. Choosing any one of them would seem to have been a dubious proposition. It was not as if they were slates that could easily be wiped clean as one would a dirty tool and be used again with perfect effectiveness. Canada's political parties had been defective instruments all along and likely would continue to be. The problem of course for Trudeau was not what he had said about the PCs and the CCF/NDP, because in the end he chose to dismiss them as unsuitable anyway. His dilemma was to square his actions with what he had said about the Liberal Party, since that was the party he joined.

Perhaps in his mind the overriding consideration was indeed about political power and the necessity of responding to contingent circumstances, not necessarily power in some self-aggrandizing, lascivious sense but power employed somehow to attain a larger human good. If the country was in crisis, now was the time for effective action rather than theoretical reflection. The advantage of this line of argument was that it allowed Trudeau to claim that the circumstances of federal politics were now at such a pass that his previous arguments about the Liberals were irrelevant or of less consequence. From this perspective the only party that met the demands of the moment *were* the Liberals. They were, as it were, the only tool left in the tool-box. The PCs were out of power and the NDP were likely never to win it. It was the Liberals who were now in office and in the past they had demonstrated very well how to use and keep power, although mainly for self-serving purposes as Trudeau had argued. So could they be the true reformers and believers in his agenda for the country? In his justificatory statement on September 10, 1965, Trudeau asked another question: was someone disqualified from joining a political party simply because he had in the past been radically critical of it? His answer was of course "no." He had criticized all of them because that was the job of any competent critic. Now, he alleged, his role must be different. The critic now had to get out of the front-row seats and climb onto the stage and become a participant in the performance.

And so, in joining the Liberals, Trudeau seems to have decided the matter by appealing to some implicit principle of the necessity and obligation of action—inaction was apparently not acceptable—and by invoking some principle of the lesser evil or the least offensive alternative under the circumstances or indeed the only alternative in the circumstances. It was a "shabby compromise" but not a "rotten" one.[100] Trudeau's decision was taken not with a sense of overwhelming moral purpose and essential rightness but with a highly fraught and contingent calculatedness, with risk and ambiguity at its core. It was a kind of pragmatism to be sure and it was a straitened and pinched kind. At its best pragmatism for Trudeau was not just about making choices that were contingent and contextually based but ones that were intelligent and principled as well. Yet the decision Trudeau made that September day was more like a leap of faith and a flight into the unknown. Only if it could be imagined that the party he was joining could be wiped clean, or detooled and then re-tooled, could the decision be thought of, in his terms, as one founded on consistent principle and untroubled pragmatic virtue. Trudeau was of course, like everyone else, wholly ignorant

in 1965 of what the future would hold. What the decision did corroborate was his sense of the necessity of making pressing choices
between contingent goods in a context not of one's choosing. It is
possible to disparage the motives of politicians and in this case to
question the seriousness of the crisis that Trudeau was positing.
His decision has been seen by some—Charles Taylor for one—as
a sort of self-deception or as a smokescreen that masked a will to
power. But Trudeau might have been right about the depth of the
national crisis. René Lévesque and nationalism were increasingly
predominant, Quebec was within a decade of electing a separatist
government and at the end of its first term in office the PQ would
hold a referendum on sovereignty-association. Certainly in retrospect we can see that indeed he was a crucial, if not *the* crucial,
participant in overcoming the national crisis that was eventually to
unfold. But he could not have known this at the time. Whichever
way his decision is framed it was at the "messy" end of his spectrum
of pragmatic considerations, in a place where judgment was more
about flying blind. But it was in its way pragmatic and realistic, and,
if we accept that Trudeau was honest in his reasons for making it—
and we think he should be taken at his word—in its awkward fashion, it was a moral one too. He was immersed in the world, with all
its complications and ambiguities, getting his hands dirty, just as
Mounier and Maritain had predicted would happen when a person
involved himself in politics.

10

Afterword

We contemplate our ideas in the sunlight of heaven and apply them in the darkness of earth.
Lord Acton

I

Trudeau's was a sublime intellect. He grasped so much and he spoke so emphatically about what he understood, and he was intellectually ambitious too. He was also a man of praxis, but action had to be undertaken within a horizon of intellectual principle. The world in its reality must be apprehended, but the good society required a belief in some fundamental principles. Governance could not properly proceed without understanding the common good and a federal system required a social contract that must undergird the constitution. According to Trudeau, not everything was negotiable or could be accommodated. Politics entailed compromise but not in all cases. Among Canadian politicians these characteristics made him unique. So strong were his convictions that he usually spoke forcefully about them. He seemed to speak as someone who had received a special revelation denied to his compatriots, especially in Quebec. Consequently he spoke loudly and, in the opinion of some, insensitively. In this respect Trudeau may be said to have favoured reason over passion; he spoke the truth and had small regard for people's feelings. He knew little about the rhetoric of affective communication, we might say. Yet as well as principle, he claimed to know about mere mortals' existence and their sometimes difficult compromises. His understanding of political leadership lay within this polarity.

Holding to principle Trudeau prided himself on his actions being systematically conceived and to an unusual degree he was consistent in his positions. But he was not primarily a philosopher as much as he was a man of action who thought about the moral purposes of actual political engagement. And so, because Trudeau was not primarily a systematic philosopher, then perhaps it is to be expected that he would not have attempted a methodical account of realism. Judgment for him was frequently situational. Apart from his early essay on political violence—and that work he admitted was ultimately unsatisfactory—his realism has to be teased out of the comments that he made about the many disparate situations he confronted. What emerges is a series of at times loosely linked and sometimes discordant claims. For him realism was about the constant calibrating of means to ends because it was the effectiveness of action that justified entering upon it. His ethic was a consequentialist one. Action must have a clear intention; the goal must be achievable and the most effective means must be employed to attain it. In that early essay on political violence he had not only talked of the importance of having perfect control over the means but also the necessity of pursuing ends implacably. Without clear goals and plans of action political engagements were literally pointless, as well as useless. The situations that political leaders confronted were invariably less than ideal so that political choice was frequently ambiguous and about choosing lesser evils. While evil must be recognized for what it was, this did not mean that the politician should avoid making a choice. His hands would be dirty but that was the nature of politics. Yet evil situations could always be made worse. Trudeau's invoking of just war theory in the Korean War is instructive: action should take account of proportionality and extreme actions should be undertaken only in the last resort after all other alternatives had been considered and attempted. But violence and force could not in principle be excluded. The world was an imperfect place and Trudeau was not a pacifist.

There were other parts to his realism. Social life, for Trudeau, was lived within a given economic and cultural reality, and the duty of the statesperson was to be relevant to the lived experience of actual people. Certainly there were themes of progress that hovered around Trudeau's view of history. In spite of his doubts about the resolve of "the people," generally his view was unpessimistic. Democracy was on the march. There was more than a suggestion that industrial, urban society was to be embraced not just because it "existed" but because it was a decided improvement over what had gone before. There *was* a theory of modernization in his world view so that industrial society was to be celebrated because it was more competent technologically and scientifically and because it was somehow more potentially democratic. To that extent he was a Voltairian Enlightenment thinker. Yet his view of history was not straightforward. Modern technology made life more commodious but it also made it more dangerous. Nor was his view of history a determinist one. Humans made history through their actions and their wills, though he was not of the view that they could make it in any way they chose. The structured reality of societies was a kind of given within which human determinations took place. There was no real life outside of the contemporary. Justice in Canada must now be sought within the realities of cities and factories. Citizens had adapted willy-nilly to these realities and the obligation of the political leader was to come to terms with the everyday experiences of citizens and make improvements within these realities. What citizens had decided for themselves established a moral discipline that was laid upon the politician. It was not that every popular prejudice was to be acceded to but a life built on experience had to be respected. To this extent Trudeau could never be a revolutionary, at least under the circumstances of an existing electoral democracy. No doubt for him the circumstances of Russia and China were different and prescribed different methods of change, alternative modernities, as it were. But in Canada political leaders were bound to remonstrate with the electorate and, if need be, change public opinion. There could be no forcing of the issue. Implicit in this was the idea of a dialectical relationship between ideas and realities: the proof of the integrity of an idea was not its abstract and metaphysical symmetry, but its relevance to lived life. That was how ordinary citizens made their judgments and politicians should learn from them.

Trudeau's several comments on the Westminster parliamentary tradition also help explicate his realism. Parliament's two-party character was to be accepted, as was its electoral system; direct democracy was practically impossible and various schemes of proportional representation unlikely to come about. Realism entailed a sense of limits and an avoidance of the perfect and the doctrinaire. Democratic politics was inherently moderate and gradualist. All of this Trudeau freely conceded even as he knew that the political game of liberal democracy under capitalism was unequal and unfair; it was stacked against workers and farmers. He would have been naive in the extreme and in defiance of his own analysis of power in a class-divided society to have actually believed (as Taylor alleges) that politics could be pursued within a "consensus" model in which all interests could be equally accommodated or satisfied, or (as Whitaker claims) that democratic politics rested on an acceptance of "effective demand." Trudeau understood very well the origins of political inequality and the need to move beyond it. But he was restrained by the morality of peaceful change in a democracy.

His realism was principled however. It was a moral realism. Here is a paradox. He was a moralist driven by profoundly held beliefs about justice. Indeed he might in some respects have fallen under Bernard Williams's criticism of being a political moralist who advocated principles from outside the lived experience of a given political tradition. Certainly at the beginning of his encounter with China he held to a universal, personalist, and liberal-democratic solution to China's problems, a view that he later replaced with one that emphasized China's differences from the West and the inapplicability, at least for now, of individual freedom and democracy. His later view that Western values did not apply there represents a powerful instance of the degree to which his mature thought emphasized the role of context in determining political

action and indeed perhaps a sense that cultures might be fundamentally different.

Out of the interplay of pragmatism and principle there emerged
with Trudeau a definition of justice as social democracy. Trudeau
stood on the revisionist side of the debate about public ownership
in the mid-1950s and he took the view that a welfare state, equalization, effective trade unions, public education, and the redistribution of income, along with parliamentary democracy, were for now
the acme of justice when combined with liberal ideas to do with
the rule of law and the rights of individuals and minorities. It is a
fair comment to say that Trudeau remained a socialist of sorts. He
was unimpressed with capitalism and he recognized the limitations
of purely individual immunity rights (while of course supporting
them), favouring as well an account of rights as the empowering of
individuals to live a life of their choosing. Of course it is clear that
Trudeau never challenged the idea of private property as such but at
the same time he clearly rejected the idea that private property was
an absolute. There was much that was wrong with capitalism and
there was much that a social democratic state should do to reform
it. Trudeau's account of "*civisme*" and civic obligation was that the
citizen should participate as much as possible in the discovery of
justice. Society was a lived reality and justice involved the citizen
in acts of co-operation with others. That is, there was a communal
dimension to his thought but in general he was tepid in his commitment to community. He worried about the dominance of the
collective over the free individual. We see this both in his account
of the importance of bills of rights and, particularly, in his account
of nationalism. The human ideal was to live in a world beyond the
domain of the tribe and ghetto in open, flexible, and free dialogical relations with others. What preoccupied Francophone opinion
in Quebec was nationalism and for Trudeau it was *the* collectivism
that must be confronted. It was the reality that must be endlessly
contested and with which there could be no compromise.

There was sufficient communitarianism, however, to lead to
the conclusion that Trudeau's views went beyond atomism and that

he can be seen as expressing a republicanism or "civic humanism" (as Charles Taylor calls it) in his belief in participation, the rule of law, mutual respect, and the value of the person. It can also be held that Trudeau does not quite fall under Taylor's anathema of being an exponent of the so-called primacy-of-rights model. This maintained that the good society was fundamentally about the enjoyment of rights but without any offsetting sense of the individual's duty to belong to society and without a sense as well of what it was about individuals that justified their enjoyment of rights. Here is another paradox in Trudeau. His Catholic background and especially the influence of Maritain and Mounier helped shape in him an ontology of the person. The mystery of the Incarnation was not just that humans were embodied creatures, but that they inhabited bodies created in the image of God, the form of which God Himself had assumed in Jesus Christ. The conscience at the heart of the person meant that God was present in each individual's freedom. And so, in spite of his pragmatism, Trudeau provided a theological account of the value of the person and thus an explanation of what it was about humans in virtue of which they should be ascribed rights. We have already noticed the importance he accorded to belonging to society. However, as time went on Trudeau was increasingly taciturn about discussing these theoretical underpinnings, either because he came less and less convinced of them or because he believed that public discourse about them was improper and indecent. But it is hard to know the solution to this puzzle because Trudeau was indeed very successfully tight-lipped about his own theological beliefs.

What is clear is that a very definite moral foundation lay beneath Trudeau's political views. He had a broad sense of the meaning of justice. The state existed to do more than keep the peace and provide liberal rights, and while the state should be neutral in its relations with different religious groups and denominations and cultivate the rule of law, it must have decided convictions about justice as freedom, material equality and equal opportunity. Social democratic justice was more than procedural in its nature and it entailed more than simply mediating conflict. It postulated an overarching common good and was indeed substantive. This was the distinctiveness of Trudeau. He advanced a pragmatic account of action but he joined to it a strong sense of justice. Because he never offered a systematic treatise on his moral realism we do not know whether he believed there was a formula that specified the relationship between principle and praxis. Likely he believed that there could be no hard and fast rules because context was everything. Even so it seems that now and then he was erratic in how it was he applied his own implicit "formula." Thus we noted his conviction about the importance of the Rassemblement and the Union as means to overcome Duplessis in defiance of the evident reality of an established party system in Quebec. There were also the strange gyrations of his thinking about China in 1961 that seemed to defy every dimension of both prudence and indeed democratic principle. In his account of federalism Trudeau was adamant about the principle of symmetry in the relationship of the provinces to each other, and between themselves and the federal government—a federation required a unifying social contract or moral order undergirding it. In their advocacy of constitutional asymmetry James Tully and Kenneth McRoberts, and Taylor too, would disagree. Against them Trudeau would offer the judgment that they preached too much pragmatism and not enough understanding of principle. But their further retort against him might be that, in the absence of a clear account of the relationship between practice and principle, Trudeau himself was guilty sometimes of pursuing too much principle. An example of this might be his opposition to the Meech Lake Accord and its provisions for a distinct society for Quebec and its opting-out provisions so that he helped defeat a potentially accommodative agreement and risked the breakup of the country, as nearly happened in the subsequent 1995 referendum. Was it possible that, as Kenneth McRoberts put it, Trudeau's emphasis on principle could become a "messianism"? But Trudeau's final point would be that some principles cannot be compromised. He was not beyond arguing that if a truly rights-respecting country was impossible, then its disappearance was not necessarily a loss.

Trudeau's argument against the "utopianism" of the CCF/PSD/NDP is intriguing. His "utopians" were actually prosaic and decidedly democratic socialists like Charles Taylor himself, and Robert Cliche, David Lewis, and Tommy Douglas. Nevertheless he considered them, it seems, irredeemably impractical and irrelevant to the course of contemporary Canadian politics and doomed to fashion a party with a never-ending minority status. Power for good required majorities: this was what Trudeau believed. Who was right? Was it Trudeau who thought the CCF/NDP would never become a majority phenomenon in his lifetime or Taylor who believed the NDP needed more time to succeed? Trudeau surely must have known that the NDP might need a little longer to develop as a national party. But was it true that the crisis he identified could not wait? Here is where judgment is important and where the indeterminacy of history becomes all too evident. The curvature of time is difficult to plot, and within its uncertainties it is hard to know the present and predict the future. But one must act, was Trudeau's position. For him the national crisis trumped all other considerations and it was immediate. The NDP was flawed because of its two-nations policy. But it was its minority status that especially irked him. And so it was the Liberal Party that would save the nation.

Trudeau's engagement with Marxism allows us some final thoughts. We have already touched on elements of Whitaker's critique but we might recall his view that Trudeau espoused a superstructural idealism combined with a cynical acceptance of capitalism and a strong state. A later devotee of what is called the liberal-order school of Marxism, Christo Aivalis, has offered a similar view.[1] His claim is that Trudeau was motivated by a fundamental liberalism that undercut the class appeal of a working-class politics, favouring instead workers being integrated into the overarching citizenship of a liberal order. Trudeau, he says, is best understood "as a consistent liberal defender of the rights of property;"[2] for him "liberal economic theory provided his only analytical horizon."[3] It is true that, although greatly influenced by Marxism and considered by some Marxists as sympathetic to their cause, Trudeau departed from many of the assumptions of Marxism and indeed he may be said to have challenged them, although not necessarily in the cause of legitimizing capitalism but in order to vindicate an alternative social democratic approach. He did not believe in the primacy of the class struggle over other struggles; he did not hold that the working class was a universal class and he certainly did not believe that there was a predetermined end or telos to history in which a state of perfect communism would emerge. But Marxism does not exhaust the meaning of socialism. To be sure, his social democracy did have liberal elements. He saw merit in the evolved tradition of English-speaking, liberal democracy with its rule of law and universal adult suffrage and for him there could be no absolute dismissal of Canadian political and constitutional developments from the Constitution Act of 1791 to the BNA Act in 1867 to the present—its parliamentarism, its far-sighted division of powers, and its polymorphous pluralism, for example.

But the evidence offered here, I believe, makes a convincing case for viewing him as being something other than a liberal. As a liberal he would have held atomist beliefs that humans were self-sufficient and devoid of a duty to belong to society, and it would have rendered him a devotee of classical market theory and laissez-faire, which were never his perspectives. He was in fact a social democrat who registered a sense of the inadequacies of capitalism and who sought regulation and planning, wealth redistribution, and cultural freedom and material sufficiency for all. He valued both freedom and equality but he believed that a levelling equality was a threat to freedom. It must then be equality of opportunity but within a framework of a social wage and self-fulfilment for all. Trudeau was well aware that actual politics in the aftermath of the neo-liberal reaction of the early 1950s made necessary an accommodation of some sort with capitalism. But this did not necessarily make him a believer in capitalism. He was, to repeat, a pragmatist. So his view was that for now there must be a strategic compromise with the existing economic order but, of course, the future was an open possibility. And for all the ambiguity of their relation to his overall thought there were his consistently anti-imperialist and indeed anti-capitalist views on the Third World. Most important for him was the moral question of what to do in the here-and-now when history did not provide perfect circumstances but when there was nevertheless laid on politicians the burden of action. In so many ways Trudeau was an existentialist.

Trudeau offered a social democratic vision distinguishable from both liberalism and Marxism and, although hedged around by the compromises of time and place, it had and continues to have a compelling moral logic. Perhaps this was what Whitaker meant when he mentioned Trudeau's superstructural idealism. But was his position one of a cynical acceptance of capitalism? His views were hardly cynical but certainly realistic, yet they also postulated the imperative of ongoing progressive reform. Whitaker wrote in the aftermath of the War Measures Act crisis, at a time when it was plausible for activists on the Left to argue that Trudeau was a natural authoritarian. Perhaps, however, this view has been diminished by his subsequent achievement of an entrenched Charter of Rights. Certainly Trudeau, like Laski and Maritain, believed that in an emergency there needed to be strong action by a democratic state to deal with terrorism; and, contrary to the authoritarian view of him, the intellectual pedigree of his theory of the state derived from the participatory, pluralistic, and consensual theories on sovereignty of Proudhon, Mounier, Maritain, McIlwain, and Laski and their opposition to the hierarchical, absolutist statism of Hobbes and Hegel. In this regard Trudeau might be thought to have been influenced by a view of sovereignty that saw it as something "negotiated" constantly between government and the people, a view of sovereignty to which in the contemporary context James Tully especially subscribes.

Trudeau did not intend to be a liberal but a social democrat when he entered federal politics in 1965. Perhaps there is little difference between the two when they are measured against the backdrop of the world-historical vision of Marxism with societies rising and falling so convulsively and so totally. Trudeau thought there was a difference. Canadian social democracy is a syncretic idea and it has absorbed several of the ideals of liberalism, particularly its accounts of individual rights and the democratic state. It is not surprising that two of the strongest advocates of individual rights in the Canadian tradition have been two socialists, J.S. Woodsworth and Frank Scott. (Especially Trudeau admired Scott.) When Trudeau joined the Liberal Party he did so as a social democrat. There must have been a sense somewhere in his mind that the Liberal Party was not utterly antithetical to such a perspective. As he viewed the political scene in the late summer of 1965, if he remained true to his convictions and if he were to have some power to change the party he was about to join, he would turn it into a social-democratic formation that would be different from the reactive centrism and fitful progressivism of Mackenzie King and St. Laurent and the overly accommodative reformism of Lester Pearson. The Liberals under Trudeau would become a consistent party of the Left. But as he himself might have said: "We are of the left but no further than that." Official Liberalism would finally believe in something, but it would be pragmatic too.

In office as prime minister in 1969 Trudeau published a number of position papers, one of which was *The Constitution and the People of Canada: An Approach to the Objectives of Confederation, the Rights of the People and the Institutions of Government*. It proposed an entrenched charter of rights that would bind both federal and provincial levels of government, a new amending formula, expanded bilingualism, and a provincial role in the appointment of senators to a reformed upper house, part of whose responsibilities would be to approve the appointment of justices to the Supreme Court, which, the paper suggested, should be entrenched in the constitution. Most of these proposals had been advanced by Trudeau since 1950. But there was more. As he had stated as early as his time in the PCO, it was also important to put into the constitution a statement about the objectives of Confederation and the "common values" of Canadians, that chimerical idea of a social contract and a common good that, he thought, should have been established as early as 1760.[4] But it was never too late and what he now proposed was that the precepts of social democracy should be enshrined in the fundamental law of the land: individual fulfilment and opportunity, government as "a vehicle by which [Canadians] can contribute to the well-being of other Canadians," democratic and other human rights, and "power to redistribute income and to maintain reasonable levels of livelihood for individual Canadians."[5] In the wider world security was to be an important goal but peace and improved standards of living for all humanity were as well.[6] In effect not only would social democracy become the lingua franca of the Liberal Party but it would become the very moral vocabulary of Canada itself. Trudeau was never less than supremely ambitious for himself and his party, and now for his country. Canada was to become a social democracy. And, of course, in an often overlooked section of the 1982 Constitution Act, Section 36, there was a provision to reduce the disparity of opportunities and to establish essential public services of reasonable quality all across the country. In short an entrenched scheme of equalization for all Canadians.

Notes

Introduction

1. This was the conclusion of an informal reader survey conducted by the Winnipeg-based history magazine, *The Beaver*, in July, 2007.

2. Quoted in Robert Bothwell, *Canada and Quebec: One Country, Two Histories* (Vancouver: UBC Press, 1995), 179–80.

3. Trudeau frequently referred to *The Federalist*, particularly Paper no. 10 by James Madison.

4. Quoted in Bothwell, *Canada and Quebec*, 180.

5. Trudeau, *Memoirs* (Toronto: McClelland and Stewart, 1993), 47.

6. Michael Oakeshott, *Rationalism in Politics and Other Essays* (London: Methuen, 1962), 195–96.

7. Ed Broadbent, *The Liberal Rip-off: Trudeauism versus the Politics of Equality* (Toronto: New Press, 1970).

8. Oakeshott, *Rationalism*, 195.

9. Leszek Kołakowski, *Main Currents of Marxism: Its Origins, Growth and Dissolution*, vol. 1: *The Founders* (Oxford: Oxford University Press, 1978), v.

Chapter 1

1. John English, *Citizen of the World: The Life of Pierre Elliott Trudeau* (Toronto: Knopf, 2006); Max and Monique Nemni, *Young Trudeau: Son of Quebec, Father of Canada, 1919–1944* (Toronto: McClelland and Stewart, 2006).

2. Richard Gwyn, *The Northern Magus: Pierre Trudeau and Canadians* (Toronto: McClelland and Stewart, 1978); Michel Vastel, *The Outsider: The Life of Pierre Elliott Trudeau* (Toronto: Macmillan, 1990); Stephen Clarkson and Christina McCall, *Trudeau and Our Times: The Magnificent Obsession* (Toronto: McClelland and Stewart, 1990) and Christina McCall and Stephen Clarkson, *Trudeau and Our Times: The Heroic Delusion* (Toronto: McClelland and Stewart, 1994).

3. George Radwanski, *Trudeau* (Toronto: Macmillan, 1978).

4. TP 34.3. Trudeau Papers (TP), MG 26, Series 02, Library and Archives Canada.

5. TP 9.7.

6. In the view of Gérard Pelletier Trudeau did not think highly of his journalistic and media work, often having to be cajoled into doing it. Gérard Pelletier, *Years of Impatience, 1950–1960* (Toronto: Methuen, 1984), 187–88.

7. Trudeau believed that the Jesuits in Quebec regularly spread the rumour that he had a "Protestant tendency." See Pierre Elliott Trudeau, *Les cheminements de la politique* (Montreal: Éditions du jour, 1970), 73.

8. Norman DePoe, CBC TV, May 16, 1967.

9. Ron Graham, "The Unending Spiritual Search," in *The Hidden Pierre Elliott Trudeau: The Faith Behind the Politics*, ed. John English, Richard Gwyn and P. Whitney Lackenbauer (Ottawa: Novalis, 2004), 103; Nancy Southam, ed., *Pierre: Colleagues and Friends Talk about the Trudeau They Knew* (Toronto: McClelland and Stewart, 2005), 28.

10. This was the view of Father Jacques Cousineau in his four-part review in the Jesuit journal, *Relations*, of *La grève de l'amiante* in late 1956 and early 1957.

11. Michael W. Higgins, "Defined by Spirituality," in *The Hidden Pierre Elliot Trudeau*, ed. English et al., 29–30.

12. Ibid., 30.

13. B.W. Powe, *Mystic Trudeau: The Fire and the Rose* (Toronto: Thomas Allen, 2007), 29.

14. Higgins, "Defined by Spirituality," 26.

15. The original quotation was by Kenneth McNaught in 1966: "His political fate will likely be the political fate of Canada." Kenneth McNaught, "The National Outlook of English-Speaking Canadians," in *Nationalism in Canada*, ed. Peter Russell (Toronto: McGraw-Hill, 1966), 70.

16. Radwanski, *Trudeau*, 36. Trudeau said something similar earlier in 1967: "I have never been able to accept discipline except that which I imposed upon myself—and there was a time when I used to impose it a lot. For, in the art of living, as of loving, as of governing and they are all one, I could never admit that anyone else could claim to know better than myself what was good for me"; Trudeau, "Avant-propos," *Le fédéralisme et la société française* (Montréal: Éditions HMH, 1967), vii.

17. Gérard Pelletier, ed., *Against the Current: Selected Writings 1939–1996* (Toronto: McClelland and Stewart, 1996), ix.

18. Radwanski, *Trudeau*, 36–37.

19. Ibid., 63.

20. Trudeau, *Memoirs*, 21.

21. Ibid., 21–25.

22. Ibid., 32.

23. Ibid., 34.

24. Ibid., 40.

25. Ron Graham, ed., *The Essential Trudeau* (Toronto: McClelland and Stewart, 1998), 5.

26. Trudeau, *Memoirs*, 46.

27. Ibid., 46.

28. Ibid., 46–47. In his notes on Williams's lectures Trudeau also recorded the uses he had made of the works of other legal realists: Axel Hagerstrom, A. Vilhelm Lundstedt, and Hans Kelsen. Trudeau also became familiar with the ideas of Roscoe Pound (TP 8.25).

29. Trudeau, *Memoirs*, 47.

30. Of the first generation of biographers Michel Vastel's was the only one that really picked up on Trudeau's early fascination with politics and political ideas, and extreme nationalist ones at that. Later Esther Delisle also noticed his youthful nationalism and clericalism.

31. English, *Citizen*, 56, 66.

32. Ibid., 100.

33. Jacques Monet, "The Man's Formation in Faith," in *The Hidden Pierre Elliott Trudeau*, ed. English et al., 87–94.

34. English, *Citizen*, 30.

35. Nemni and Nemni, *Young Trudeau*, 52–54; English, *Citizen*, 223.

36. TP 8.27.

37. Quoted in Nemni and Nemni, *Young Trudeau*, 80.

38. English, *Citizen*, 36.

39. Ibid., 36–38.

40. Ibid., 68.

41. Nemni and Nemni, *Young Trudeau*, 211.

42. Ibid., 227–32; English, Citizen, 75–76, 90–97.

43. Nemni and Nemni, *Young Trudeau*, 220.

44. Quoted in Nemni and Nemni, *Young Trudeau*, 236.

45. Pierre Elliott Trudeau, "La nouvelle trahison des clercs," 162–64.

46. I have followed here William Johnson's English translation in the Nemnis' *Young Trudeau*. Trudeau's speech at Outremont is discussed extensively by them between pages 263–68.

47. Quoted, ibid., 267–68.

48. Quoted in English, *Citizen*, 113.

49. Esther Delisle, *Myths, Memory and Lies: Quebec's Intelligentsia and the Fascist Temptation 1939–1960* (Westmount, QC: Robert Davies Multimedia, 1998), 210.

50. English, *Citizen*, 127.

51. Trudeau, *Memoirs*, 37.

Chapter 2

1. The original quotation is from an interview of Lévesque by Peter Desbarats and is reported in Pelletier, *Impatience*, 27.

2. Interview with David Frost, 1983.

3. Donald Brittain, *The Champions* (National Film Board, 1986).

4. Trudeau talked informatively of "truth in politics" in a speech in April 1968. See Pierre Elliott Trudeau, "Of Truth and Freedom in Politics: French-Canadians and the Federal Challenge," in *Canadian Federalism: Myth or Reality*, ed. J. Peter Meekison (Toronto: Methuen, 1968), 396–406.

5. Michael Zantovsky, *Havel: A Life* (New York: Grove, 2014), back cover.

6. Bob Rae, "Trudeau: Hedgehog or Fox?," in *Trudeau's Shadow: The Life and Legacy of Pierre Elliott Trudeau*, ed. Andrew Cohen and J.L. Granatstein (Toronto: Random House, 1998), 287.

7. English, *Citizen*, 469.

8. John English, *Just Watch Me: The Life of Pierre Elliott Trudeau, 1968–2000*, vol. 2 (Toronto: Knopf Canada, 2009), 105.

9. Ramsay Cook, *The Teeth of Time: Remembering Pierre Elliott Trudeau* (Montreal and Kingston: McGill-Queen's University Press, 2006), 46.

10. Graham, "The Unending Spiritual Search," 102.

11. Interview with Ramsay Cook, Winnipeg, October 20, 2009.

12. Interview with Otto Lang, Winnipeg, December 9, 2008.

13. In an essay at Harvard he stated his preference for Plato's *Republic* over Aristotle's *Politics*: "the former has all the freshness, the candor, and the mysticism of a poem." Pierre Elliott Trudeau, "A Theory of Political Violence," TP 7.23, 30.

14. Max and Monique Nemni argue that Plato was much on Trudeau's mind during the period of his involvement with the "revolutionary cell" in 1942 (Nemni and Nemni, *Young Trudeau*, 221–25).

15. Trudeau, "Avant-propos," *Le fédéralisme*, v, viii.

16. Trudeau, *Les cheminements*, 103–9.

17. Trudeau, "La nouvelle trahison des clercs," 176.

18. Denis Smith, *Bleeding Hearts, Bleeding Country* (Edmonton, Alberta: Hurtig, 1971), passim; Abraham Rotstein, *The Precarious Homestead: Essays on Economics, Technology and Nationalism* (Toronto: New Press, 1973), 73–77, 107–11, 118–24; Abraham Rotstein, ed., *Power Corrupted: The October Crisis and the Repression of Quebec* (Toronto: New Press, 1971), passim.

19. Consider for example the dedication by Michel Vastel in his biography of Trudeau, *The Outsider: The Life of Pierre*

Elliott Trudeau (Toronto: Macmillan, 1990): "To Geneviève, Anne, Violaine, and Marie, who willingly shared a whole summer of my life with 'him.'" What begins in insult cannot surely end in limpid, judicious insight.

20. English, *Citizen*, 208; Nemni and Nemni, *Trudeau Transformed*, 52.

21. Marcel Rioux, *Quebec in Question* (Toronto: James Lorimer, 1978), 10.

22. Ibid., 103.

23. Ibid., 104.

24. Ibid., 102–3.

25. Ibid., 158.

26. Ibid., 197.

27. It is a view well expressed, too, by Guy Laforest in his book, *Trudeau and the End of a Canadian Dream* (Kingston and Montreal: McGill-Queen's University Press, 1995).

28. Kenneth McRoberts, *Misconceiving Canada: The Struggle for National Unity* (Don Mills, ON: Oxford University Press, 1997), 62.

29. Ibid., xii.

30. Ibid., 70.

31. Claude Couture, *Paddling with the Current: Pierre Elliott Trudeau, Étienne Parent, Liberalism and Nationalism in Canada* (Edmonton: University of Alberta Press, 1998).

32. Ibid., 104.

33. Ronald Rudin, *Making History in Twentieth-Century Quebec* (Toronto: University of Toronto Press, 1997), 182–87.

34. Couture, *Paddling*, xv, 32, 46–50, 110.

35. Ibid., 22–23.

36. Ibid., 33.

37. Ibid., 21.

38. Ibid., 91–100.

39. James Tully, *Strange Multiplicity; Constitutionalism in an Age of Diversity* (Cambridge: Cambridge University Press, 1995), passim.

40. Reg Whitaker, "Reason, Passion and Interest: Pierre Trudeau's Eternal Liberal Triangle," *A Sovereign Idea: Essays on Canada as a Democratic Community* (Montreal and Kingston: McGill-Queen's University Press, 1992), 132–62.

41. Ibid., 149.

42. Letter from Leo Huberman to Trudeau, October 11, 1961, TP 21.3.

43. "The Universalist Liberalism of Pierre Trudeau," in *Freedom, Equality and Community: The Political Philosophy of Six Influential Canadians*, ed. James Bickerton, Stephen Brooks, Alain-G. Gagnon (Montreal and Kingston, McGill-Queen's University Press, 2006).

44. Ibid., 122–23.

45. Ibid., 123.

46. Ibid.

47. Ibid., 145.

48. Ibid., 124–25, 139–40.

49. John Hellman, interview with the author, Montreal, May 14, 2011.

50. Taylor talked about his childhood on CBC Radio *Ideas*, April 11, 2011.

51. McCall and Clarkson, *The Heroic Delusion*, 74.

52. Ibid.

53. Duncan Thompson's *Pessimism of the Intellect: A History of the New Left Review* (London: Merlin, 2006) is helpful here.

54. "Marchand, Pelletier, Trudeau et la 8 novembre," *Cité Libre* 15, no. 80 (1965).

55. Taylor on CBC Radio, *Ideas*, April 13, 2011.

56. Pelletier, *Le temps*, 231–34.

57. Charles Taylor, *Montreal Star*, November 6, 1965. Taylor's campaign literature was categorical in its criticism of the two old parties: "Our country is drifting, divided, threatened. Our old political parties cannot meet the challenge. They struggle furiously with each other for power, but when they get it they just stumble from crisis to crisis. The mess in Ottawa proves it." TP, 34.3.

58. Taylor received 14,929 votes to Trudeau's 28,064.

59. Charles Taylor, *The Pattern of Politics* (Toronto: McClelland and Stewart, 1970).

60. Ibid., 1–49.

61. Ibid., 3.

62. Ibid., 15–96.

63. Charles Taylor, "Tories in Britain," *Canadian Commentator*, November 1959, 3; "British Socialism at the Crossroads," *Saturday Night*, October 1, 1960, 19.

64. Taylor, *The Pattern*, 57.

65. Ibid., 70–96, 151.

66. Ibid., 97–127.

67. Ibid., 5–10, 97–127.

68. Ibid., 112–13.

69. Ibid., 128–45.

70. Ibid., 97–127, 146–60.

71. Ibid., 139.

72. Charles Taylor, "Can Canada Survive the Charter?" *Alberta Law Review*, XXX (1992), 427–47.

73. Ibid., 442.

74. Charles Taylor, "Atomism," *Philosophy and the Human Sciences* (Cambridge: Cambridge University Press, 1985), 192.

75. Ibid.

76. Taylor, "Can Canada Survive the Charter?," 443.

77. Charles Taylor, *Modern Social Imaginaries* (Durham and London: Duke University Press, 2004), 190–92.

78. Charles Taylor, "Marxism and Socialist Humanism," in *Out of Apathy; Voices of the New Left Thirty Years On*, ed. Robin Archer et al. (London: Verso, 1989), 59–78.

79. Ibid., 64–65.

Chapter 3

1. Nemni and Nemni, *Trudeau Transformed*, 258.

2. Powe, *Mystic Trudeau*, 130.

3. Letter from the Secretary of the Archbishop, TP 7.6.

4. Thomas A. McGraw, *Prophet of Innovation: Joseph Schumpeter and Creative Destruction* (Cambridge, MA and London: Belknap, 2007), 306.

5. Ibid., 228.

6. Pierre Elliott Trudeau, Lecture notes, TP 7.18

7. Ibid.

8. McGraw, *Prophet of Innovation*, 220–21.

9. D.E. Moggridge, *Maynard Keynes: An Economist's Biography* (London and New York: Routledge, 1992), 593. Robert Skidelsky described Hansen as "the most notable Keynesian convert of the 1930s"; Robert Skidelsky, *John Maynard Keynes; Fighting for Britain 1937–1946* (London: Macmillan, 2000), 109.

10. Copies of Lange's and Hayek's books are in Trudeau's library at his former home at 1418 Pine Avenue, Montreal, which I visited on May 12, 2011.

11. Trudeau, Lecture notes, TP 7.15.

12. Nemni and Nemni, *Trudeau Transformed*, 22.

13. Trudeau, Lecture Notes, TP 7.18.

14. Ibid.

15. Ibid.

16. Ibid.

17. Ibid.

18. Pierre Elliott Trudeau, book review of *The New Belief in the Common Man*, TP 7.24.

19. Trudeau, Lecture Notes, TP 7.21.

20. McIlwain employed the distinction between ancient and modern constitutionalisms in his *Constitutionalism: Ancient and Modern* (Ithaca, New York: Cornell University Press, 1940 and 1947).

21. Trudeau's notes on McIlwains's lectures are to be found at Trudeau, Lecture Notes, TP 7.17.

22. Ibid.

23. Ibid.

24. Of course technically this was not Rousseau's view but McIlwain's interpretation has been quite widely accepted and maybe it is an inevitable consequence of Rousseau's thinking.

25. Trudeau, Lecture Notes, TP 7.17.

26. Ibid.

27. Ibid., 7.21.

28. Ibid.

29. Pierre Elliott Trudeau, "A Theory of Political Violence," TP 7.23.

30. Ibid., 36.

31. Isaac Kramnick and Barry Sheerman, *Harold Laski: A Life on the Left* (New York: Penguin, 1993), 234, 572.

32. Péguy was lionized by many groups in France including the French Right but also the Left.

33. John Dewey, "Force and Coercion" *International Journal of Ethics* 26, no. 3 (1916): 367.

34. Trudeau, "Political Violence," 31.

35. Ibid., 9.

36. Ibid., 41.

37. Ibid., 38.

38. Ibid., 48.

39. Ibid., 48–50.

40. Ibid., 50–52.

41. Ibid., 54–55.

42. Nemni and Nemni, *Young Trudeau*, 183–84, 193–200.

43. Nemni and Nemni, *Trudeau Transformed*, 61–65; English, *Citizen*, 147. Before he went to Harvard and Paris Trudeau applied for a bursary offered by the Quebec government. He was successful in getting one for his stay in Paris but the government insisted he could not hold this with the one he had been awarded by the French government. He turned down the Quebec bursary. Neither bursary was large enough to pay for all his expenses studying in Europe; see TP 7.3; 8.3, 4.

44. Quoted in Clarkson and McCall, *The Magnificent Obsession*, 56.

45. Trudeau, *Memoirs*, 40.

46. R. William Rauch, *Politics and Belief in Contemporary France: Emmanuel Mounier and Christian Democracy, 1932–1950* (The Hague: Martinus Nijhoff, 1972), 227, 256.

47. Pierre Elliott Trudeau, "Journal personnel thérapie, fév.–juin 1947," TP 39.10, x.

48. Monet, "The Man's Formation in Faith," 93.

49. John Hellman, interview with the author, Montreal, May 14, 2011.

50. TP 8.24.

51. It was John Hellman who first mentioned Trudeau's familiarity with *L'affrontement chrétien*. By chance Hellman had met Trudeau when he was prime minister at a hot-dog stand in Saint-Sauveur and he mentioned having read the work. Email to the author, August 31, 2010.

52. Monet, "The Man's Formation in Faith," 91–92. Pelletier called Mounier "one of the people I most admired in the whole world." *Impatience*, 104.

53. E. Martin Meunier and Jean-Phillipe Warren, *Sortir de la "grande noirceur": l'horizon "personnaliste" de la révolution tranquille* (Sillery, QC: Éditions de Septentrion, 2002), 108.

54. Trudeau's Papers contain a receipt for a subscription to *Esprit* and in his famous memo to Jules Léger in the Prime Minister's Office in 1950 Trudeau recommended that he read an article in the review; TP 26.15; Nemni and Nemni, *Trudeau Transformed*, 209; English, *Citizen*, 229.

55. Monet, "The Man's Formation in Faith," 94.

56. Pierre-E.T., "In Memoriam," *Cité Libre* 17 (June 1957). The Nemnis mainly dismiss Mounier's ideas and diminish their influence on Trudeau. They see Mounier as an adept of Soviet Communism, an opponent of the United States, and a voice for an unacceptable "communitarian personalism." They imply that these were positions that Trudeau could never have embraced. Of course these were not the only aspects of Mounier's thought that might have affected Trudeau. And anyway it is quite possible to see Trudeau as having been anti-American and pro-Soviet at certain times. And was Trudeau not marked by his having given a communitarian dimension to his individualism? See Nemni and Nemni, *Trudeau Transformed*, 222–34.

57. Pelletier, *Impatience*, 13–18.

58. Gérard Pelletier mentions the following as constituting the group that got the review going: Alec Leduc, Gary Cormier, Réginald Boisvert, Pauline Lamy, Jean-Paul Geofroy, Renée Desmarais, Pierre Juneau, and Fernande Martin. Soon after, Charles Lussier and Pierre Vadeboncoeur were added to the editorial cohort. See Pelletier, ibid., 101–8.

59. Meunier and Warren, *Sortir de la "grande noirceur,"* 17, 130–31.

60. Nemni and Nemni, *Trudeau Transformed*, 82–84, 142.

61. Michael Gauvreau, *The Catholic Origins of Quebec's Quiet Revolution, 1931–1970* (Montreal and Kingston: McGill-Queen's University Press, 2005), 40, 379.

62. Pelletier, *Impatience*, 113. Eleven pages later Pelletier claimed that it was not so much his personal intervention that had gotten Trudeau included but a realization by the group of how useful Trudeau's knowledge of politics and economics might be.

63. Michael Kelly, *Pioneer of the Catholic Revival: The Ideas and Influence of Emmanuel Mounier* (London: Sheed and Ward, 1979), 64, 74–75.

64. Wojtyła's impressive book on sexuality, *Love and Responsibility* (New York: Farrar, Strauss, Giroux, 1981) placed personalism at the centre of his argument. It also showed the effects of phenomenology and, inevitably, Thomism too.

65. Thomas D. Williams and Jan Olof Bengtsson, "Personalism," http://plato.stanford.edu/entries/personalism

66. Ibid.

67. Part of Trudeau's education in personalism came through reading Nicolas Berdyaev (1874–1948), particularly his

book *De l'esclavage et de la liberté de l'homme* (*Slavery and Freedom*). (See Nemni and Nemni, *Trudeau Transformed*, 70–72.) Of a Russian aristocratic background, Berdyaev was radically inclined in his youth and flirted with Marxism. In the end he was not supportive of the Bolshevik revolution and became suspect in the eyes of the Soviet authorities and interrogated. In 1922 he was allowed to leave the Soviet Union and eventually he settled in Paris. Part of Maritain's circle, along with Gabriel Marcel and Étienne Gilson, he knew Mounier too and he contributed an article to the first edition of *Esprit* in 1932. Berdyaev wrote extensively about personalism. For him the ultimate subject matter was "personality" and the freedom and conscience of the individual. His philosophy was anti-metaphysical and anti-ontological. What were ultimately important were the concrete, particular person and his subjectivity, spirituality, and creativity. Such possibilities had been placed in humans by God. God required humans to exercise freedom and govern themselves according to their conscience. He believed that God was especially revealed in the concrete life of the suffering, pitying Christ, the "God-man." Another important theme in his work was his critique of "objectivization," which he saw in humans' tendency to enslave and to alienate themselves within collectivism, totalitarianism, utopianism, and abstract thought in general, and in nationalism. He was a socialist, however, though he favoured a type that prescribed pluralism, decentralization, co-operativism, and federalism. His existentialism was of a Christian kind with an overlay of a Russian Orthodox background. But in both cases his views were heterodox. A useful introduction to Berdyaev is Donald A. Lowrie, *Rebellious Prophet: A Life of Nicolai Berdyaev* (New York: Harper and Brothers, 1960).

68. Hellman, *Mounier*, 49–50.

69. Ibid., 80.

70. Ibid., 83.

71. Kelly, *Pioneer*, 48.

72. Hellman, *Mounier*, 12.

73. Trudeau read Bergson's 1932 work, *Les deux sources de la morale et de la religion*, though later, during the war. Almost certainly he read Bergson before he read Mounier.

74. Hellman, *Mounier*, 44.

75. Ibid., 54, 76, 78–82, 168. See also Kelly, *Pioneer*, 34–38; Rauch, *Politics and Belief*, 185.

76. Hellman, *Mounier*, 116.

77. Ibid., 80, 87, 103–4.

78. Kelly, *Pioneer*, 31, 41.

79. This was indeed the subject of a whole book by R. William Rauch.

80. Hellman, *Mounier*, 110–21.

81. Ibid., 120.

82. Ibid., 73, 76, 83–84, 86, 108–10, 115–16, 140–44.

83. Ibid., 108–10.

84. Ibid., 143.

85. Nevertheless, Mounier's position here and on Nazism in general have drawn other conclusions. See Kelly, *Pioneer*, 81–84.

86. Hellman, *Mounier*, 170–87.

87. Julian Jackson, *France: The Dark Years 1940–1944* (Oxford: Oxford University Press, 2001), 388.

88. Emmanuel Mounier, *L'affrontement chrétien* (Paris: Éditions parole et silence, 2006), 27–28. An English translation by Katherine Watson appeared under the title *The Spoil of the Violent* (London: Harvill, 1955).

89. Mounier, *Spoil of the Violent*, 31.

90. Mounier, *L'affrontement*, 60.

91. Mounier, *Spoil of the Violent*, 35–36.

92. Ibid., 19–20.

93. Ibid., 31.

94. Michael Gauvreau argues that Trudeau and other Citélibristes espoused a masculine Christianity that emphasized energetic, vitalist action. This led, he says, to *Cité Libre* depending too much on men rather than women as writers and editors. See Gauvreau, *Catholic Origins*, 46, 50, 355.

95. Mounier, *Spoil of the Violent*, 77–78

96. Hellman, *Mounier*, 222–24.

97. Ibid., 236–37.

98. Ibid., 211.

99. Rauch, *Politics and Belief*, 255.

100. Emmanuel Mounier, *Le personnalisme* (Paris: Presses universitaires de France, 1950), 111–12.

100. Ibid., 35–42.

102. Ibid., 10–11.

103. Ibid., 105–14.

104. Ibid., 113.

105. Ibid., 126.

106. Ibid., 77–78.

107. Trudeau, *Conversation with Canadians* (Toronto: University of Toronto Press, 1972), 87. This statement almost by itself discounts the Nemnis' claim that personalism à la Mounier was not influential in Trudeau's political thought. See Nemni and Nemni, *Trudeau Transformed*, 230.

108. Trudeau, *Memoirs*, 40.

109. English, *Citizen*, 36, 54.

110. Nemni and Nemni, *Young Trudeau*, 239–44.

111. Ibid., 201

112. Robert A. Ventresca, *Soldier of Christ: The Life of Pope Pius XII* (Cambridge, MA: Harvard University Press, 2013), 227.

113. Hellman, *Mounier*, 196.

114. Ibid., 60–61.

115. Jacques Maritain, *The Rights of Man and Natural Law* (London: Geoffrey Bles, 1944), 16.

116. Hellman, *Mounier*, 99.

117. Jacques Maritain, *True Humanism* (London: Geoffrey Bles, 1938), 240–48.

118. Ibid., 70.

119. Ibid., 110, 131.

120. Ibid., 113.

121. Maritain, *Rights of Man*, 2.

122. Ibid., 12.

123. Maritain, *True Humanism*, 176.

124. Ibid., 71.

125. Ibid., 78

126. Maritain, *Rights of Man*, 25

127. Ibid.

128. Maritain, *True Humanism*, 132.

129. Ibid., 212.

130. Maritain, *Rights of Man*, 47.

131. Maritain, *True Humanism*, 108.

132. Maritain, *Rights of Man*, 54.

133. Ibid., 56.

134. Ibid., 50.

135. English, *Citizen*, 144.

136. Nemni and Nemni, *Trudeau Transformed*.

137. TP., 8.24–28.

138. F.M. Barnard, *Pluralism, Socialism and Political Legitimacy: Reflections on Opening Up Communism* (Cambridge: Cambridge University Press, 1991), 47.

139. Harold J. Laski, *Studies in the Problem of Sovereignty* (New Haven: Yale University Press, 1917).

140. Barnard, *Pluralism*, 49–50.

141. Harold J. Laski, *Faith, Reason and Civilisation: An Essay in Historical Analysis* (London: Gollancz, 1944), 57.

142. Isaac Kramnick and Barry Sheerman, *Harold Laski: A Life on the Left* (New York: Penguin, 1993), 562.

143. Harold J. Laski, *A Grammar of Politics* (London: Allen and Unwin, 1925), 181.

144. Ibid., 31, 247. See also 36, 95, 171–72.

145. Ibid., 89, 105–6, 272.

146. Ibid., 62, 241–94.

147. Ibid., 218–40.

148. Ibid., 248–52.

149. TP 7.24. The Nemnis offer a tendentious reading of Trudeau's connection to Laski's work, *A Grammar of Politics*. They seem to feel that Trudeau's reading of it brought him into contact with Marxist ideas. This was, they say, because of the underlinings he made in his own copy of *A Grammar* and Laski's remarks about the Marxist view of the state and capitalism. The latter were contained in the new introductory chapter, "The Crisis in the Theory of the State," that he added to a new edition of the work in 1938. However *A Grammar* went through five editions, four in Laski's lifetime. It was mainly in the fourth edition in 1938 that Laski gave expression to a much more Marxist line although he had added a short preface in a similar vein to the third edition in 1934. When Trudeau reviewed the book at Harvard his notes reveal that it was the second edition published in 1931 that he used. This edition was the American one published by Yale University Press. However the Nemnis claim that the version Trudeau read at Harvard was the 1937 edition. Do they mean the 1938 edition? In a sense it does not matter which edition he read because, apart from the inclusion of the introductory essay in 1938, the rest of the text in all subsequent editions was unaltered from the original version of 1925 so that what Trudeau wrote about the book in his review in 1944–45 was completely dominated by the subject matter of the first edition in which themes of socialist pluralism predominated and coexisted with his new appreciation of the state. But it was not quite a Marxist perspective. See Nemni, *Trudeau Transformed*, 45–46.

150. Pierre Elliott Trudeau, "A Grammar of Politics," TP 7.24.

151. Ibid.

152. TP 39.8.

153. Ibid.

154. Ibid.

155. Ibid., 8.28.

156. Ibid.

157. Ibid.

158. TP 8.28.

159. Ibid.

160. The Nemnis make clear that Trudeau wrote the section about Laski and Blum but not the part about Mounier which was written by Pelletier. See Nemni and Nemni, *Trudeau Transformed*, 222.

161. "Faites vos jeux," *Cité Libre*, 1, no. 1 (1950): 38.

162. Jacques Maritain, *Man and the State* (London: Hollis and Carter, 1954), 69.

Chapter 4

1. Trudeau was well aware that French Canada and Quebec were not identical. A crucial part of his political thinking was based on the distinction between the two. But in the interests of simplicity he frequently used the terms interchangeably.

2. Pierre Elliott Trudeau, "La politique canadienne." This lecture was
given as part of a program sponsored
by L'association des étudiants pour les
relations culturelles avec l'Amérique
latine. See TP 8.7.

3. English, *Citizen*, 193.

4. Trudeau would seem to have attended
lectures at the Institut des études politiques in Paris, some of which were
given by Siegfried. See TP 8.13.

5. André Siegfried, *The Race Question in
Canada*, ed. Frank H. Underhill (Toronto:
McClelland and Stewart, 1966), 116.

6. Nemni and Nemni, *Trudeau
Transformed*, 62–63.

7. Trudeau, "La politique," 7.

8. Ibid., 15–16.

9. Pierre Elliott Trudeau, "Notes de voyage, à propos de condition humaine,"
TP 11.21.

10. Trudeau, "La politique," 16.

11. Ibid., 16–17.

12. Pierre Elliott Trudeau, "La promesse
du Québec," TP 8.19, 1–12.

13. Ibid., 1–2.

14. Ibid., 3.

15. Ibid., 4.

16. Ibid.

17. Ibid.

18. Ibid., 5.

19. Ibid., 6.

20. Ibid., 7.

21. Ibid., 8.

22. Ibid.

23. Ibid., 10–11.

24. Ibid., 11.

25. Laski, *A Grammar*, 89–91, 227–29,
272–79.

26. Trudeau, "La promesse," 11–12.

27. Ibid., 12.

28. Pierre Elliott Trudeau, "Lettre de
Londres: réflexions sur une démocratie
et sa variante," *Notre Temps*, February
14, 1948.

29. Ibid.

30. Trudeau, "La nouvelle trahison," 172.

31. Pierre Elliott Trudeau, "La province
de Québec au moment de la grève," in *La
grève de l'amiante* (Montréal: Les éditions
Cité libre, 1956), 54–57. Also there was his
"Considérations sur les mesures à prendre
en vue de prévenir le massacre," Radio-
Canada, January 27, 1953, TP 25.5, 3–4.

32. Ramsay Cook, *The Maple Leaf
Forever: Essays on Nationalism and
Politics in Canada* (Toronto: Macmillan
of Canada, 1971), 100.

33. The phrase "merciless conquerors"
is Rudin's: see his *Making History in
Twentieth-Century Quebec* (Toronto:
University of Toronto Press, 1997), 23.

34. Ibid., 20–128.

35. Ibid., 129–70.

36. Ibid., 171–218.

37. Ibid., 95, 130–31.

38. Fernand Ouellet, "The Quiet
Revolution: A Turning Point," in *Towards
a Just Society: the Trudeau Years*, ed.
Thomas S. Axworthy and Pierre Elliott
Trudeau (Toronto: Viking, 1990), 17–33.

39. Trudeau, "La province," 38. Behiels
considers that the sociologist Maurice
Tremblay had an influence on Trudeau's
historiography as early as 1952. See his
Prelude, 117.

40. Trudeau, "La province," 78.

41. Ibid., passim.

42. Trudeau, "Politique fonctionelle,"
Cité Libre 1, no. 1 (1950): 21.

43. Ibid.

44. Trudeau, "Politique fonctionelle II," *Cité Libre* 1, no. 2 (1951): 24.

45. Trudeau, "Politique fonctionelle," 23.

46. Trudeau, "Réflexions sur la politique au Canada français," *Cité Libre* 2, no. 3 (1952): 53–70.

47. Ibid., 53.

48. Ibid., 56.

49. Trudeau, "Un manifeste démocratique," *Cité Libre* 2, no. 22 (1958): 2.

50. Ibid., 19.

51. Trudeau, "Obstacles à la démocratie," *Rapport de la conférence de l'institut canadien de affaires publiques,* 1954, TP 24.14, 38; Trudeau, "Un manifeste démocratique"; Trudeau, "Biculturalism and Democracy," *McGill Daily*, March 10, 1958; Trudeau, "Democracy in French Canada," University of British Columbia, July 1962; TP 29. 23, 21–22).

52. Trudeau, "Obstacles," 38.

53. Trudeau held that, in spite of their antagonism towards the French, English Canadians had a more progressive civic culture. In a radio broadcast in January 1953, having just mentioned how they had always had more "healthy" or "sound" (*sains*) political reflexes, he went on: "But this superiority of the Anglo-Saxons is not something that has happened by chance; it comes from an ongoing civic education which begins in the schools and is perpetuated throughout the rest of life thanks to those among them who think, write, and discuss things. What is called their political 'flair' is in reality nothing more than a popularized and internalized version of principles that have been raised to the level of a veritable science." Trudeau, "Considérations," 3.

54. Trudeau, "Democracy in French Canada," 26. See also Trudeau, "Some Obstacles," 106, 116.

55. Trudeau, "Some Obstacles," 108. See also Trudeau, "La province," 57–58.

56. Trudeau, "Obstacles à la démocratie," 39; Trudeau, "Democracy in French Canada," 21.

57. Whatever the benefits of the English legal tradition, Trudeau did not believe that it had a proper appreciation of minority rights: "Although English public law developed civil and individual rights to a very high degree, it never developed the idea of minority rights. This only began in Canada as a compromise with the French-Canadian minority policy, which has not gone very far yet. Historically, however, it is a fact that the idea of minority rights was never given any legal substance in English public law"; Trudeau, "Democracy in French Canada," 27. Note his later comment as well: "Indeed the English, who gave so much attention and political ingenuity to developing among themselves the cult of civil liberties, never held to the idea of protecting the rights of minorities"; Trudeau, "La nouvelle trahison," 171.

58. Trudeau, "La nouvelle trahison," 171–72. See also Trudeau, "Democracy in French Canada" 28; Trudeau, "Federalism, Nationalism and Reason," *Federalism*, 200–1. Ramsay Cook tells an interesting story: "When I translated this for the Forum in 1962 . . . the wife of a prominent Poly sci prof at U of T asked me if PET was a separatist since he hated the English so much." Correspondence with the author, July 2010.

59. Trudeau, "La province," 25.

60. In an essay in *Cité Libre*, he talked about conducting "a psychoanalysis of our religious and cultural infantilism"; Pierre Elliott Trudeau, "Politique fonctionelle," *Cité Libre* 1, no. 1 (1950): 24.

61. Trudeau, "Épilogue," *La grève*, 379–80.

62. Trudeau, "La province," 88–89.

63. Trudeau, "La province," and "Épilogue," passim.

64. Trudeau, "Les octrois fédéraux aux universités," 96.

65. "La province," 10–11.

66. Ibid., 21.

67. Ibid., 52–53.

68. Ibid., 19.

69. "Whisky blanc" was a home-brew favoured by working people in Quebec.

70. "La province," 70–72.

71. Ibid., 72–73.

72. Ibid., 76. Trudeau's analysis here offered an intriguing instance of how he saw intercultural transfers taking place within a federation like Canada's and so provides a sense of the ways ostensibly benevolent English ideas might have been transmitted.

73. Trudeau, "Un manifeste démocratique," *Cité Libre* 9, no. 22 (1958): 13.

74. There are similarities here between Trudeau's idea of the universal inclusiveness of all legitimate interests and Bernard Crick's definition of "politics" in *In Defence of Politics* (London: Wiedenfeld and Nicolson, 1992). Crick saw politics as mainly about the aggregating of interests.

75. See Williams, *In the Beginning*, 2.

76. Trudeau, "Réflexions," 54–55.

77. Trudeau, "Un manifeste démocratique," 22, 28.

78. Trudeau, "De la notion d'opposition politique," *Cité Libre* 11, no. 27 (1960): 13.

79. Trudeau, "Note sur la conjoncture politique," *Cité Libre* 13, no. 49 (1962): 2.

80. Harold Laski, *The Rise of European Liberalism: An Essay in Interpretation* (London: Allen and Unwin, 1936), 242.

81. Trudeau, "Note sur la conjoncture politique," 23.

82. Trudeau, "Réflexions," 55.

83. There is a comment in 1948–49 when he said that: "It would be wise not to tie one's fate uniquely to the workers' unions or to agricultural cooperatives but rather to seek to conceive a policy for the whole nation, and not for this or that of its elements." "Notes de voyage, à propos de condition humaine," TP 11.21.

84. Trudeau, "Épilogue," 404.

85. Trudeau, "Réflexions," 65–66.

86. Trudeau, "Causerie" 1–6.

87. He reiterated this view on the inadequacy of democratic elections by themselves in "Un manifeste démocratique," *Cité Libre* 9, no. 22 (1958): 18–19.

88. This would seem a fairly strong indication that Trudeau was going to vote for the PSD which would seem to contradict John English's claim that it is not known how he voted in the 1956 election. See English, *Citizen*, 307. In the constituency of Montreal-Outremont Trudeau would have had available to him a PSD candidate, Michel Forest, who ended up finishing fourth with 726 votes, even behind the Labour Progressive candidate. Trudeau's dilemma might have been that the Liberal candidate and eventual landslide victor was Georges-Émile Lapalme, the Liberal leader, for whom Trudeau had some regard.

89. Trudeau, "Some Obstacles," *Federalism*, 114–15.

90. Ibid., 114.

91. Trudeau, "La nouvelle trahison," 174.

92. Trudeau was fond of applying to Quebec nationalists Othello's famous reflection about being "one that lov'd

not wisely but too well." See Trudeau, "La province," 13, and "La nouvelle trahison," 173.

93. Trudeau, "Federalism, Nationalism and Reason," 197.

94. Trudeau, "Democracy in French Canada," 22.

95. Trudeau, "Note sur la conjuncture politique," *Cité Libre* 13, no. 49 (1962): 1–4.

96. Ibid., 2–3.

97. Ibid., 3–4.

98. Trudeau, "La nouvelle trahison," 187–89.

99. Williams, talking about John Rawls, offered a contrast between a pluralism founded on a sense of fairness and one founded on prudence, self-interest, and mutual advantage. See Williams, *In the Beginning*, 2.

100. Trudeau, "La nouvelle trahison," 189.

101. E.L. Allen, *Christian Humanism: A Guide to the Thought of Jacques Maritain* (London: Hodder and Stoughton, n.d.), 41.

102. Trudeau, "Le Québec et le problème constitutionnel," *Le féderalisme*, 55.

103. *Mémoire de la Fédération des Unions Industrielles du Québec à la Commission Royale d'Enquête sur les problèmes constitutionnels*, Montreal, 1954, 34.

104. Trudeau, "La province," 15, 57; "Socialism in Quebec," (December 30, 1953) TP 26.21; "L'évolution de la pensée politique au Québec," (March 4, 1957 TP 27.3).

105. André Laurendeau dramatically posed the issue of the "negro king" in July 1958 in his criticism of the Anglophone business elite in Quebec and its cavalier, manipulative treatment of the province's Francophone political leaders. It was like the British in Africa, he said, who did not interfere with the politics of the local tribe as long as their economic interests were secure. There is another sense of the black king, one which emphasized more the agency of the local head of state in a neo-colonial context. The local "king" saw his role as actively facilitating foreign economic interests in looting the country. This last theory owed much to the Marxist, psychoanalytic, and identity theories of Fanon, Aimé Césaire, and Léopold Senghor. Trudeau used both senses. He was friendly with Senghor and he read Fanon.

106. Trudeau, "La province," 88–89.

107. *Mémoire de la Fédération des Unions Industrielles du Québec*, 7.

Chapter 5

1. Higgins, "Defined by Spirituality," in *The Hidden Pierre Elliott Trudeau*, 28–29.

2. Allan MacEachen, "Reflections on Faith and Politics," ibid., 154, 159.

3. English, *Citizen*, 368.

4. John Godfrey, "'There is Always a Moment,'" in *The Hidden Pierre Elliott Trudeau*, 175.

5. Southam, ed., *Pierre*, 259.

6. Trudeau, *Conversation with Canadians*, 9–10.

7. Trudeau, "La promesse du Québec," TP 8.19, 4-5.

8. Roger Rolland and Pierre Elliott Trudeau, "Ce que nous dit le lecteur...," *Le Canada,* May 1, 1947.

9. Guy Jasmin to Roger Rolland, June 7, 1947, TP 22.2.

10. Roger Rolland and Pierre Elliott Trudeau to Guy Jasmin, May 16, 1947, TP 22.2, 2.

11. Ibid., 3.

12. Michael Schuck, *That They Be One: The Social Teaching of the Papal Encyclicals 1740–1989* (Washington: Georgetown University Press, 1991), 145.

13. Trudeau, "Journal personnel thérapie, fév.–juin 1947"; TP 39.10.

14. Quoted in English, *Citizen*, 159.

15. Trudeau, "Journal personnel thérapie" TP 39.10.

16. Ibid.

17. Ibid.

18. Trudeau, "Á propos de missions," TP 18.

19. Trudeau, "Citadelles d'orthodoxie," November 15, 1947, *Notre Temps*.

20. Nemni and Nemni, *Trudeau Transformed*, 95–96.

21. Trudeau, "Notes de voyage, à propos de condition humaine," TP 11.21; Pierre-E. Trudeau, "Où il n'est pas question d'amour," *Le Devoir*, July 23, 1949. See also Nemni and Nemni, *Trudeau Transformed*, 159–60.

22. Jacques Hébert and Pierre Elliott Trudeau, *Deux innocents en Chine rouge*, ed. Alexandre Trudeau (Montréal: Les éditions de l'homme, 2007), 220.

23. This is an insight from the Nemnis and I have used their translation of Trudeau's words. See Nemni and Nemni, *Trudeau Transformed*, 224.

24. Trudeau, "Notes de voyage."

25. Trudeau, untitled notebook, TP 11.21.

26. Trudeau, "Notes de voyage."

27. Quoted in Nemni and Nemni, *Trudeau Transformed*, 159.

28. Trudeau, "Réflexions sur l'Orient," TP 11.21.

29. The article is to be found in TP 11.15.

30. Pope John Paul II, in his letter, *Sollicitudo rei socialis*, called on the Church to sell its superfluous ornaments and expensive furnishings in light of the poverty of much of the world. See Schuck, *That They Be One*, 151.

31. Roberto Perin in "Elaborating a Public Culture: The Catholic Church in Nineteenth-Century Quebec," in Marguerite Van Die ed., *Religion and Public Life in Canada: Historical and Comparative Perspectives* (Toronto: University of Toronto Press, 2001), drew attention to the significant ways Ignace Bourget, Bishop of Montreal from 1840 to 1876, transformed the popular religiosity of his diocese. His ultramontanism and fondness for Rome led him to reject local practices in favour of a liturgy and architecture that was lavish, sensual, theatrical, and neo-Baroque.

32. Gauvreau, *Catholic Origins*, 355.

33. Quoted in Nemni and Nemni, *Trudeau Transformed*, 180.

34. Trudeau, "Politique fonctionelle," 24.

35. Trudeau, "Politique fonctionelle ll," 28–29.

36. Trudeau, "Réflexions," in 1952, and "L'élection fédérale," in 1953.

37. Trudeau, "Matériaux pour servir à une enquête sur le cléricalisme," *Cité Libre* 3, no. 7 (1953): 34.

38. Trudeau, "A propos d'un reportage sur l'U.R.S.S.," TP 12.14.

39. Nemni and Nemni, *Trudeau Transformed*, 274.

40. Trudeau, "Matériaux," 29–37.

41. Ibid., 33.

42. Ibid., 29.

43. Ibid.

44. Congar was a Dominican who supported the postwar reform movement. His theology was questioned

by conservatives but he was elevated to become a cardinal under Pope John Paul II.

45. Trudeau, "Matériaux," 35.

46. Ibid.

47. In emphasizing the importance of founding policy on actual social conditions Trudeau's position is close to a theme in later papal social thought in which the movement of the Holy Spirit is seen as taking place within history; that is within real social contexts and dominant social formations, what is called a "signs of the times" perspective. It was a perspective favoured by one of Trudeau's theological mentors, Marie-Dominique Chenu. See Schuck, *That They Be One*, 135, 157, 161.

48. Trudeau, *La grève*, 20–21.

49. Quoted by Pierre Elliott Trudeau, "Le père Cousineau, s.j. et 'La grève de l'amiante,'" *Cité Libre* 10, no. 23 (1959): 38.

50. Trudeau, *Les cheminements*, 22.

51. Ibid., 34.

52. Ibid., 23.

53. See Maritain, *Man and the State*, 72–88.

54. Ibid., 80.

55. In *Secularism and Freedom of Conscience* (Cambridge, MA: Harvard University Press, 2011), Jocelyn Maclure and Charles Taylor argue for what they call a liberal, pluralist account of secularity against a "republican" one associated with the French idea of "*laïcité*." They emphasize the importance of equal respect and freedom of conscience and religion. Consequently the state must be neutral in religious matters. But, against the totalizing claims of the republican view that would permit no religious symbols at all in the public sphere, they hold that there should be "reasonable accommodations" for such personal practices as a worker in a public hospital or daycare wearing a hijab. Especially because of Trudeau's regard for personalism he would likely have agreed with their idea.

56. Trudeau took issue with André Dagenais after he accused him of all the sins that supposedly flowed from his having quoted Rousseau about "man being born free." Said Trudeau: "this is like accusing my priest of pederasty because like André Gide he said that God is everywhere." Gide had been an early defender of homosexuals. Trudeau's comment is witty but it exploits a popular disdain for homosexuals at the time. Trudeau sometimes poured scorn on his critics by associating them indirectly with unpopular groups. He did it in the early 1960s when he accused nationalists of having a "wigwam" complex. Richer was an Ottawa lawyer who had founded *Notre Temps* in 1945. He was a conservative nationalist and in the mid-1950s his review was supported financially by the Catholic Church. See Xavier Gélinas, *La droite intellectuelle québecoise et la Révolution tranquille* (Lévis: Les presses de l'Université Laval, 2007), 75–76.

57. Trudeau, *Les cheminements*, 86.

58. Ibid., 72–73.

59. Ibid., 87–88.

60. A recent addition to the debate is Larry Siedentop, *Inventing the Individual: The Origins of Western Liberalism* (Cambridge, MA and London: Belknap, 2014).

61. Pierre Elliott-Trudeau [sic], "Pearson ou l'abdication de l'esprit," *Cité Libre* 14, no. 56 (1963): 7.

62. Discussing Lord Acton's views of the ideal relation of the church and the modern state, Gertrude Himmelfarb provides an analysis that also sums

up well Trudeau's view of the issue: "Because Catholics could not safely look to the State for favours, their only protection lay in liberty and independence. And to have a free Church there had to be a free nation, for an absolutist State would not tolerate a genuinely independent Church." Gertrude Himmelfarb, *Lord Acton: A Study in Conscience and Politics* (Chicago: The University of Chicago Press, 1952), 44.

63. Ibid.

64. English, *Just Watch Me*, 531. Trudeau's views on abortion are not completely transparent. When he was Minister of Justice he introduced changes to the Criminal Code that permitted therapeutic abortions under certain strict conditions. Deborah Coyne who was Trudeau's lover in the late 1980s and early 1990s, with whom he had a daughter, tells an interesting story about how he responded to the news of her pregnancy: "He was happy for me but, ever the pragmatist, asked if I wanted to keep the baby, making it clear that he would support whatever decision I made." Deborah Coyne, *Unscripted: A Life Devoted to Building a Better Canada* (Kindle Edition, 2013). But it is not clear what "keeping the baby" meant.

65. Schuck, *That They Be One*, 60, 129; Richard L. Camp, *The Papal Ideology of Social Reform: A Study in Historical Development* (Leiden: E.J. Brill, 1969), 29.

66. Trudeau, "Les séparatistes: des contre-révolutionnaires," *Fédéralisme*, 220.

67. G.H. Sabine, *A History of Political Theory* (London: Harrap, 1951), 223.

68. English, *Citizen*, 360.

69. André Burelle, *Pierre Elliott Trudeau: L'intellectuel et la politique* (Montreal: Éditions Fides, 2005) 13–93.

70. TP 9.17.

Chapter 6

1. Pierre Elliott Trudeau to Gérard Filion, July 2, 1949, TP 22.6.

2. English, *Citizen*, 261.

3. TP 28.13, 28.18.

4. English, *Citizen*, 261, 275–76. See Trudeau's remarkable letter on this idea in Pelletier, *Impatience*, 131–33.

5. Nemni and Nemni, *Trudeau Transformed*, 326–27.

6. Trudeau, "Réflexions," 68.

7. Trudeau, "Socialism in Québec," December 30, 1953, TP 26.21.

8. M.J. Coldwell succeeded Woodsworth as CCF federal leader in 1942.

9. Trudeau, "Pour la conference Migneault," February 2, 1954, TP 26.7.

10. Gilles Duguay, "La peur conduit au fascisme, le fascisme à la révolution," *Le Devoir*, February 6, 1954.

11. Thérèse Casgrain, *A Woman in a Man's World* (Toronto: McClelland and Stewart, 1972), 138.

12. Pierre Elliott Trudeau, "Le père Cousineau, s. j. et 'La grève de l'amiante,'" *Cité Libre* 10, no. 23 (1959): 43.

13. The open-endedness and indeterminacy of Trudeau's formulation of the identity of the Rassemblement is reminiscent of Emmanuel Mounier's and *Esprit*'s approach to politics and political organization in the 1930s and 1940s.

14. "Déclaration de principes du Rassemblement," TP 27.1.

15. Nemni and Nemni, *Trudeau Transformed*, 380.

16. "Déclaration de principes du Rassemblement," TP 27.1; Nemni, *Trudeau Transformed*, 378.

17. Trudeau, "Un manifeste démocratique," 21.

18. Pierre Elliott Trudeau, "Fluctuations économiques et méthodes de stabilisation," *Cité Libre* 4, no. 9 (1954): 31–37.

19. *Mémoire de la Fédération des Unions Industrielles du Québec.*

20. Trudeau, *Les cheminements*, 27.

21. Ibid., 125.

22. Ibid., 21.

23. Ibid., 40.

24. Ibid., 28.

25. Ibid., 22.

26. Ibid., 45.

27. Ibid., 135.

28. Ibid., 55.

29. CBC interview, May 16, 1967.

30. Trudeau, *Les cheminements*, 65.

31. Ibid., 95.

32. Nemni and Nemni, *Trudeau Transformed*, 67.

33. Trudeau, *Les cheminements*, 119.

34. Ibid., 23.

35. Ibid., 35.

36. Ibid., 40. The Arab Spring of 2010 prompted an interest in mass civil disobedience as a method of undermining tyrants and dictators. One sixteenth-century exponent of this view was Étienne de la Boétie with his tract *Discours sur la servitude voluntaire*. Certainly Trudeau did not believe that violence was necessary for political change under democratic conditions but tyrants certainly should be physically resisted. According to de la Boétie even with tyrants non-violent mass resistance was an effective alternative. When the people withdraw consent all sorts of beneficial things can occur.

37. Trudeau, *Les cheminements*, 113.

38. Ibid., 45.

39. Ibid., 46.

40. Ibid., 45–49, 77–78

41. Ibid., 35–36.

42. Ibid., 41–42.

43. Ibid., 120.

44. Ibid., 141.

45. Ibid., 142.

46. Ibid., 140–41.

47. Ibid.

48. Trudeau, "The Practice and Theory of Federalism," *Federalism*, 133.

49. Pierre Elliott Trudeau, "Economic Rights," TP 32.11, 1.

50. Ibid.

51. Ibid., 1–2.

52. Ibid., 3.

53. Laski talked of "the transvaluation of all values and the birth of a new civilization" in his book *Reflections on the Revolution of Our Time* (1943). See also Kramnick and Sheermen, *Harold Laski*, 468.

54. Trudeau, "Economic Rights," TP 32.11, 3–4.

55. Trudeau, "Economic Rights," *McGill Law Review* 8, no. 2 (1962): 121

56. Ibid.

57. The copy of *The Affluent Society* in Trudeau's library indicates that it was acquired in 1959.

58. Denis Smith, *Gentle Patriot: A Political Biography of Walter Gordon* (Edmonton: Hurtig, 1973), 48.

59. Ibid., 42.

60. Trudeau, "A propos de 'domination économique,'" *Cité Libre* no. 20 (1958): 7–16. If the quotation marks around the phrase "domination économique" might be thought to indicate uncertainty on Trudeau's part about the appropriateness

of the term, it should be noted that he also published an abbreviated version of the original article in which the quotation marks did not appear: "De la domination économique dans les relations internationales," TP 26.19.

61. This is the sense of his article in January 1960 in *Cité Libre*, "Propos sur le développement économique du Québec," in which Trudeau criticized Quebec's culture of resistance to foreign investment and how this had discouraged the development of entrepreneurialism and technology. Quebec had failed to take advantage of what foreign investment it had received and had developed the worst of all possible worlds in which it resisted regulating the economy and engendered a world of "peripheral" capitalism in which free enterprise was absolute and private property was regarded almost as a holy thing.

62. Trudeau, "A propos," 11.

63. Trudeau, "The Practice and Theory of Federalism," 124–50.

64. Ibid., 128.

65. The juxtaposition of "principle" and "application" appeared as early as 1949 in his "Notes de voyage."

66. Trudeau, "The Practice and Theory of Federalism," 147–48.

67. Ibid., 124.

68. Ibid., 125.

69. Ibid., 127.

70. Trudeau did make referrence to the work on stages of development by W.W. Rostow, the well-known American economist, *Stages of Economic Growth* (1960).

71. Trudeau, "The Practice and Theory of Federalism," 126.

72. Ibid., 128–29.

73. Ibid., 130.

74. Ibid., 127–28.

75. McCall and Clarkson, *The Heroic Delusion*, 11.

76. Ibid., 79.

77. Ibid., 79–81, 86–88. Stephen Clarkson's sense of Trudeau as an incorrigible liberal is revealed in a later reference to "his defiant nineteenth-century liberalism." (See English et al., *The Hidden Pierre Elliott Trudeau*, 39.) This is not an accurate account of Trudeau.

78. Albert Breton, email to author, February 21, 2010.

79. Albert Breton, email to author, April 4, 2013

80. Albert Breton, "The Economics of Nationalism," *Journal of Political Economy* 72, no. 4 (August 1964): 376–86.

81. Albert Breton, email to author, April 4, 2013.

Chapter 7

1. Sandra Djwa, *The Politics of the Imagination: A Life of F.R. Scott* (Toronto: McClelland and Stewart, 1987), 322; and English, *Citizen*, 333.

2. Trudeau, "Au sommet des Caucases," September 18, 1952, Radio-Canada, TP 12.16.

3. Trudeau, "J'ai fait mes Pâques à Moscou," September 4, 1952, Radio-Canada, TP 12.16.

4. Trudeau, letter from Shanghai, March 20, 1949, TP 11.22.

5. Trudeau, "Vietnam," TP 13.5.

6. Trudeau, "Notes de voyage."

7. Ibid.

8. The Nemnis are especially good at unravelling Trudeau's exaggerations about his activities in Jerusalem during the war in 1948. See Nemni and Nemni, *Trudeau Transformed*, 131–35.

9. Trudeau, letter to his mother of February 11, 1949, TP 11.22.

10. Ibid.

11. Hébert and Trudeau, *Deux innocents*, 134.

12. Leslie Paul Thiele, *Friedrich Nietzsche and the Politics of the Soul: A Study of Heroic Individualism* (Princeton, NJ: Princeton University Press, 1990), 3.

13. My account of Trudeau's world trek is mainly based on several notebooks and essays that Trudeau kept, two of which he entitled: "Notes de voyage, à propos de condition humaine" and "Réflexions sur l'Orient." They can be found at TP 11.21.

14. From Trudeau's Papers the sponsoring organization was the PMID, which the Nemnis represent as the World Federation of Democratic Youth (Nemni and Nemni, *Trudeau Transformed*, 127).

15. Anne Applebaum, *Iron Curtain: The Crushing of Eastern Europe 1944–1956* (Toronto: McClelland and Stewart, 2012), 219–20.

16. Pablo Picasso, the Spanish painter, who was a member of the French Communist Party after 1945, was perhaps the most famous of the intellectuals involved in such organizations. See Gertje R. Utley, *Picasso: The Communist Years* (New Haven and London: Yale University Press, 2000).

17. In his work in the PCO Trudeau was involved in a committee dealing with the Schuman Plan for greater European unity (TP 9.10).

18. Pierre Elliott Trudeau, letter to his mother of February 11, 1949, TP 11.22.

19. Nemni and Nemni, *Trudeau Transformed*, 143.

20. Pierre-E. Trudeau, "Où il n'est pas question d'amour," July 23, 1949, *Le Devoir*.

21. Ibid.

22. Pierre Elliott-Trudeau, "Évitez d'être Anglais," February 1, 1952, *Le Devoir*; "Les Anglais auraient tort de s'obstiner," February 2, 1962, *Le Devoir*; "Le Soudan aux Soudanais," 5 February 1952, *Le Devoir*.

23. Trudeau, "Réflexions sur l'Orient," TP 11.21.

24. Edward W. Said, *Orientalism* (New York: Pantheon, 1978), 118–20

25. Ibid., 86.

26. Ibid., 95.

27. See Esther Delisle, *The Traitor and the Jew: Anti-Semitism and Extremist Right-Wing Nationalism in French Canada from 1929 to 1939* (Toronto: Robert Davies Publishing, 1993) and Mordecai Richler, *Oh Canada! Oh Quebec* (Toronto: McClelland and Stewart, 1992).

28. Trudeau, "J'ai fait mes Pâques à Moscou," September 4, 1952, Radio-Canada, TP 12.16, 3.

29. Ibid.

30. Ibid.

31. Hébert and Trudeau, *Deux innocents*, 47. Charles Chiniquy was a nineteenth-century French-Canadian priest who, while serving the Catholic Church in the United States, converted to Protestantism and set out on a crusade to proselytize Catholics. He believed in a general Jesuit conspiracy to control political affairs and accused the order of being behind the assassination of Abraham Lincoln.

32. Ibid.

33. Pierre Elliott Trudeau, "Notes de voyage à propos de condition humaine," TP 11.21

34. Trudeau, "Réflexions sur l'Orient," TP 11.21.

35. Ibid.

36. Quoted in Nemni and Nemni, *Trudeau Transformed*, 126.

37. Ibid., 127.

38. This can be found in TP 11.21.

39. Ibid.

40. In the interwar period Jews in Poland were mainly an urban people. According to the census of 1931 they constituted just over 30 percent of the population of Warsaw. Estimating their knowledge of Polish is difficult however. In Warsaw just under 89 percent of Jews indicated that Yiddish was their mother tongue in the 1931 census and only 18,000 indicated Polish. Of course the latter figure does not include those who could understand and speak Polish (Ezra Mendelsohn, *The Jews of East Central Europe between the World Wars* [Bloomington: Indiana University Press, 1983], 24, 31). Anecdotally the conclusion would be that urban Jews probably spoke Polish extensively. Celia S. Heller points out the lack of firm statistical evidence but she concludes as follows about the 1931 census: "We would venture to guess that there was a substantially larger proportion of Jews in Poland whose chief language of communication was Polish"; Celia S. Heller, *On the Edge of Destruction; Jews of Poland between the Two World Wars* (New York: Columbia University Press, 1977), 68. Older Jews, like Trudeau's well-educated Jewish citizen from Warsaw who had been educated before the coming of the independent Polish state and the Polanization of public education after the First World War would have been less likely to have learned Polish.

41. Rita Dhamoon, *Identity/Difference Politics: How Difference Is Produced, and Why It Matters* (Vancouver and Toronto: UBC Press, 2009), 25.

42. Edward Said, *Orientalism* (New York: Pantheon, 1978), 229.

43. William Stueck, *Rethinking the Korean War* (Princeton and Oxford: Princeton University Press, 2002), 78–82.

44. Nemni and Nemni, *Trudeau Transformed*, 209.

45. Pierre Elliott Trudeau to Jules Léger, August 31, 1950, TP 10.11.

46. Pierre Elliott Trudeau to D.V. LePan, April 28, 1951, ibid.

47. Ibid.

48. Ibid.

49. Pierre Elliott Trudeau, "Positions sur la présente guerre," *Cité Libre* 1, no. 3 (1951): 2

50. Ibid., 2–3.

51. David Rees, *Korea: The Limited War* (London: Macmillan and Co Ltd, 1964), 169–72.

52. Trudeau, "Positions sur la présente guerre," 4.

53. Ibid., 7.

54. Trudeau's idea of a world of competing socialisms that would lead to an anti-Stalinism of the sort expressed by Tito in Yugoslavia was also embraced by Aneurin Bevan in Britain. See Michael Foot, *Aneurin Bevan: 1945–1960* (London: Davis-Paynter, 1973), 305–7.

55. Trudeau, "Positions sur la présente guerre," 9.

56. Nemni and Nemni, *Trudeau Transformed*, 262–65.

57. In the Canadian context the Cominform strategy was channelled through the Canadian Peace Congress established in May 1949 whose first chairman was James Endicott, a China hand. See Norman Penner, *Canadian Communism: The Stalin Years and Beyond* (Toronto: Methuen, 1988), 226.

58. Pierre Elliott Trudeau, "L'auberge de la grande URSS," *Le Devoir*, June 14, 1952.

59. David Somerville, *Trudeau Revealed by his Actions and Words* (Richmond Hill, ON: BMG, 1978), 53.

60. Trudeau, "L'auberge."

61. Nemni and Nemni, *Trudeau Transformed*, 262–65.

62. Joan Robinson, *Conference Sketch Book: Moscow, April 1952* (Cambridge: W. Heffer and Sons, n.d.), 5. One of the better known incidents about Trudeau's time in the Soviet Union was his throwing snowballs at a statue of Stalin. Later, a well-known conservative commentator, Peter Worthington, sought to discredit Trudeau by alleging that there could not have been snow in Moscow in April so the story was untrue. Joan Robinson's testimony is definitive. In her memoir she says nothing about Trudeau. But she does mention snow in Moscow: "We arrived at 5.30, just before the dawn, in an iron frost and woke at ten or so to see brilliant sunshine on the snow. It *never* snows so late in Moscow, we are told. What luck—to have the illusion that we are here in the winter. It snows on and off for the next few days." Ibid., 17.

63. Pierre Elliott Trudeau, "La conférence commence . . .," *Le Devoir*, June 19, 1952.

64. Pierre Elliott Trudeau, "Les conclusions de la conférence," ibid., June 20, 1952.

65. Trudeau, "Au Sommet des Caucases," 6. Tamerlane was the fourteenth-century Tartar warrior-king who established a dynasty in that part of central Asia.

66. Trudeau, ibid., 2.

67. English, *Citizen*, 266–67.

68. Trudeau, "Aux prises avec le politbureau," script of broadcast on Radio-Canada, 25 September 1952, TP 12.16, 7.

69. English, *Citizen*, 272.

70. Trudeau, "Au sommet des Caucases," 1.

71. Ibid., 8–9.

72. Pierre Elliott Trudeau, "Staline est-il poète?," Radio-Canada, September 11, 1952, TP 12.16, 4.

73. Pierre Elliott Trudeau, "Est-ce pour ça qu'on a fait trois révolutions?," *Le Devoir*, June 21, 1952.

74. Trudeau, "Un peuple sympathique; mais conventionelle jusqu'à la nausée," *Le Devoir*, June 17, 1952.

75. "A likeable people but conventional to the point of nausea," "Is it for this that three revolutions were made," "Is Stalin a poet?" and "Battling the Politbureau."

76. Trudeau, "Un peuple sympathique."

77. Trudeau, "Est-ce pour ça."

78. Trudeau, "Staline est-il poète?," 6.

79. The phrase is William Ryan's from his review of Simon Sebag Montefiore's *One Night in Winter* in *The Spectator*, London, October 5, 2013.

80. Trudeau, "Aux prises," 2

81. A.A. Léopold Braün, "Commentaire circonstancié sur les articles de M. Pierre Elliott-Trudeau: 'Je reviens de Moscou,'" *Nos Cours* 14, no. 8 (1952): 15–28.

82. Ibid., 16.

83. Ibid., 28.

84. Ibid., 17.

85. TP 12.14.

86. English, *Citizen*, 357–58.

87. Trudeau, "Voyage en Chine," TP 24.7, 3–4.

88. Nemni and Nemni, *Trudeau Transformed*, 286.

89. Ibid., 302–4.

90. Radio-Canada, October 31, 1952, TP 25.2.

91. "Note sur une guerre momentanément évitée," *Cité Libre* 8, no. 16 (1957): 1.

92. Trudeau, "La guerre! La guerre!," *Cité Libre* 12, no. 42 (1961): 1–3.

93. John English says that Trudeau wrote the chapters on Shanghai and the conclusion, while the Nemnis say that he wrote the sections on economics and politics, and the prologue and epilogue. However it is unlikely that Trudeau would have allowed his name to stand as a co-author with Hébert if he disagreed with him in any substantial way about anything they wrote together. See English, *Citizen*, 350 and Nemni and Nemni, *Trudeau Transformed*, 414–15. There is an independent check on what Trudeau believed and this is his own unpublished essay entitled "China's Economic Planning in Action" (TP 25.26). In it he expressed many of the themes of the book, (indeed he even cribbed his own words in some places): Chinese technical and organizational proficiency, the successful mobilizing force of the Chinese Communist Party, the inapplicability of Western standards of political morality when faced with the extreme natural and demographic circumstances of China, the improvements in productivity in China under Mao, and the eventual Third World triumph of China's version of economic planning.

94. Hébert and Trudeau, *Deux innocents*, 100–1

95. Ibid., 92.

96. In their well-regarded biography of Mao, Jung Chang and Jon Halliday deem *Deux innocents* "a starry-eyed book." See their *Mao: The Unknown Story* (New York: Alfred A. Knopf, 2005), 460.

97. Hébert and Trudeau, *Deux innocents*, 111.

98. Ibid.

99. Ibid., 112.

100. Ibid.

101. Ibid., 123.

102. Ibid., 197–98.

103. Ibid., 198–99.

104. Ibid., 205.

105. Ibid., 101–2.

106. Ibid., 232.

107. Ibid., 226.

108. Trudeau, "The Practice and Theory of Federalism," 126.

109. Hébert and Trudeau, *Deux innocents*, 134. The words are almost certainly Trudeau's because they appear almost word for word in his diary of his China trip, "Voyage en Chine," TP 24.7, 31.

110. Yang Jisheng, *Tombstone: The Great Chinese Famine, 1958–1962* (New York: Farrar, Straus and Giroux, 2012), 484–85.

111. Frank Dikötter, *Mao's Great Famine: The History of China's Most Devastating Catastrophe* (New York: Walker, 2010), 78.

112. Yang, *Tombstone*, 77.

113. Ibid., x.

114. Ibid., x–xi.

115. Ibid., xii.

116. James C. Scott, "Tyranny of the Ladle," *London Review of Books* 21, December 6, 2012, 21–27.

117. Yang, *Tombstone*, 128.

118. Dikötter, *Mao's Great Famine*, xi.

119. Yang, *Tombstone*, 14–15.

120. Dikötter, *Mao's Great Famine*, 110–13.

121. Yang, *Tombstone*, 17.

122. Hébert and Trudeau, *Deux innocents*, 168.

123. Ibid., 199.

124. Trudeau, "Les séparatistes: des contre-révolutionnaires," 224. John English quotes this remarkable theoretical trope but does not draw any great significance from it while the Nemnis mention it not at all.

Chapter 8

1. R.M. Dawson, *The Government of Canada* (Toronto: The University of Toronto Press, 1956), 126.

2. A copy of Wheare's book, bought in Oxford in 1947, remains in Trudeau's library.

3. Allen Mills, "Of Charters, Rights and Freedoms: The Social Thought of F.R. Scott, 1930–1985," *Journal of Canadian Studies* 32, no. 1 (Spring 1997): 44–62.

4. Trudeau, "Memo to R.G. Robertson re office of Lieutenant Governor," TP 9.18.

5. Trudeau, "Notes on the Compact Theory," TP 10.15, 3.

6. Ibid., passim.

7. Trudeau, "La promesse du Québec," 7.

8. K.C. Wheare, *Federal Government* (London: Oxford University Press, 1953), 21.

9. Nemni and Nemni, *Trudeau Transformed*, 287.

10. Ramsay Cook's *Provincial Autonomy, Minority Rights and the Compact Theory, 1867–1921* (Ottawa: Queen's Printer, 1969) is a useful work on the subject.

11. Trudeau, "Notes on the Compact Theory," TP 10.15, 3.

12. Ibid., 4.

13. Trudeau, "The Practice and Theory of Federalism," 132.

14. Trudeau, "Federalism Revisited," December 1949, TP 9.9.

15. Ibid.

16. Trudeau, "Theory and Practice of Federal–Provincial Co-operation," June 1950, TP 10.6.

17. Nemni and Nemni, *Trudeau Transformed*, 200–6.

18. Trudeau, "Theory and Practice of Federal–Provincial Co-operation."

19. Ibid.

20. *Mémoire de la Fédération des Unions Industrielles du Québec à la Commission Royale d'Enquête sur les problèmes constitutionnels*, second edition, (Montreal: 1955), 6.

21. Ibid., 7

22. Ibid., 34

23. Trudeau, "De libro, tributo . . . et quibusdam aliis," *Le fédéralisme*, 76.

24. Trudeau, "The Practice and Theory of Federalism," 144.

25. Trudeau, "Theory and Practice of Federal–Provincial Co-operation."

26. "Mémoire," 46.

27. See his argument in "The Practice and Theory of Federalism," 150.

28. Trudeau, "Les octrois fédéraux aux universités," 82.

29. Ibid., 83.

30. Ronald L. Watts defines the federal spending power as "the power of Parliament to make payments to people, institutions or provincial governments for purposes on which Parliament does not necessarily have the power to legislate, for example, in areas of provincial legislative jurisdiction." Ronald L. Watts, *The Spending Power in Federal Systems: A Comparative Study* (Kingston: Institute of Governmental Relations, 1999), 1.

31. Peter C. Hogg, *Constitutional Law of Canada*, second edition (Toronto: Carswell, 1985), 124–25.

32. Trudeau, "The Practice and Theory of Federalism," 137.

33. Watts, *The Spending Power*, 2. What Trudeau proposed in 1969 in *Federal–Provincial Grants and the Spending Power of Parliament* was that in the case of unconditional grants to the provinces to support their programmes and public services the federal spending power should be unrestricted but that conditional grants in areas of provincial jurisdiction should meet two conditions: 1) a broad national consensus in support of the shared-cost programme in question measured by provincial legislative support by Senate regions; and 2) that the citizens of any dissenting, non-participating province should not be subject to any fiscal penalty so that there should be paid to such citizens a direct grant from the federal government in the amount of the average per capita amount paid to participating provinces. All of this was to be entrenched in the constitution.

34. Trudeau, "La nouvelle trahison," 166.

35. The phrase about Napoleon is found in Alfred Cobban, *Dictatorship: Its History and Theory* (New York: Haskell, 1939), 79.

36. Acton's phrase is quoted in Himmelfarb, *Lord Acton*, 72; Delos's argument can be found in *La problème de civilisation: la nation* (Montreal: Éditions de l'Arbre, 1944), volume II, *Le nationalisme et l'ordre de droit*, 150–60.

37. Kedourie may have been the exception. He argued in favour of an Oakeshottian skepticism regarding modern political idioms. For him politics was best left to the experienced; nationalism's deficiencies were because it had been mainly an initiative of young radicals.

38. Julien Benda, *The Treason of the Intellectuals* (New York: Norton, 1969), 27.

39. Ibid., 22.

40. Ibid., 83.

41. Ibid., 183.

42. Delos did not go completely unnoticed in English-speaking North America. A young and largely unknown German immigrant, Hannah Arendt, wrote a review of *La problème de civilisation: la nation* in *The Review of Politics* in January 1946. See her, *Essays in Understanding 1930–1954* (New York: Harcourt Brace, 1994), 206–11.

43. Trudeau, "La nouvelle trahison," 169.

44. Joseph T. Delos, "The Theory of the Institution: The Realist Solution of the Problem of Moral Personality and Law with an Objective Foundation," in Albert Broderick, ed., *The French Institutionalists: Maurice Hauriou, Georges Renard, Joseph T. Delos* (Cambridge, MA: Harvard University Press, 1970), 224–25.

45. Georges Renard, "The Interior Life of the Institution: Intimacy, Authority, Objectivity," in *The French Institutionalists*, 191–213.

46. Albert Broderick, "Preface," in *The French Institutionalists*, xiii.

47. Joseph T. Delos, "The Evolution of the Institutional Conception of Positive Law: A Backward Glance," in *The French Institutionalists*, 37.

48. Joseph T. Delos, *La problème*, vol. II, 168.

49. Joseph T. Delos, "The Theory of the Institution," in Broderick, ed., 240.

50. Delos, *La problème*, vol. I, *Sociologie de la nation*, 169, 174.

51. Delos, *La problème*, vol. II, 154, 167.

52. Joseph T. Delos, "The Rights of the Human Person vis-à-vis of the State and the Race," in Joseph.T. Delos et al., eds, *Race: Nation: Person: Social Aspects of the Race Problem* (Freeport, NY: Books for Libraries Press, 1944), 44.

53. Trudeau, "La nouvelle trahison," 190.

54. Barry Callaghan, *Raise You Five: Essays and Encounters* (Toronto: McArthur, 2005), 294.

55. John Emerich Edward Dalberg-Acton, "Freedom in Antiquity," *The History of Freedom and Other Essays*, ed., John Neville Figgis (London: Macmillan, 1907), 3.

56. Acton, "May's Democracy in Europe," ibid., 93.

57. Acton, "Freedom in Antiquity," ibid., 19.

58. Timothy Lang, "Lord Acton and 'the Insanity of Nationality,'" *Project Muse*, http://muse.jhu.edu, 2002, 129–49.

59. Acton, "Nationality," *The History of Freedom*, 292.

60. Ibid., 298.

61. Trudeau, "Federalism, Nationalism and Reason," 188.

62. Trudeau, "La nouvelle trahison," 165.

63. Ibid.

64. Ibid., 162.

65. Trudeau, "Federalism, Nationalism and Reason," 184.

66. Ibid., 184–85

67. Trudeau, "La nouvelle trahison," 170.

68. Hubert Aquin was one noted nationalist in Quebec who sought to discredit Trudeau's account. Aquin has Trudeau basically saying that nationalism and technology had caused all wars. This was in spite of Trudeau's explicit point that nationalism was not behind all wars and that technology's role had been to increase war's destructiveness. He also has Trudeau basically believing in pacifism such was his detestation of war. See Hubert Aquin, "The Cultural Fatigue of French Canada," in Anthony Purdy, ed., *Writing Quebec: Selected Essays by Hubert Aquin* (Edmonton: University of Alberta Press, 1988), 19–48.

69. Trudeau, "La nouvelle trahison," 166–67.

70. Ibid., 186.

71. Trudeau, "Federalism, Nationalism and Reason," 186–87.

72. Benedict Anderson, *Imagined Communities: Reflections on the Origin and Spread of Nationalism* (London: Verso, 2006), 141.

73. Trudeau, "La nouvelle trahison," 178.

74. Ibid., 179.

75. Ibid., 177.

76. Trudeau, "Les séparatistes: des contre-révolutionnaires," 226–27.

77. Trudeau, "La nouvelle trahison," 161.

78. Ibid., 186.

79. Trudeau, "Les séparatistes: des contre-révolutionnaires," 226.

80. Ibid., 186–87.

81. Ibid., 187.

82. Ibid.

83. Trudeau, "Is a Federal State Viable if Composed of Two Equal 'Nations.'" This was a presentation, as was his "Concepts of Federalism"—the latter the basis of his future article "Federalism, Nationalism and Reason"—to the meeting of the Canadian Political Science Association and the Association of Canadian Law Teachers in Charlottetown in June 1964. See TP 31.4.

84. The typescript of the full presentation made in Charlottetown included a final paragraph in which Trudeau talked

once more of a "functional" approach to Canadian politics that would seek a more dispassionate analysis of the costs and benefits of staying together and particularly what "values or benefits Canadians in general . . . wish to see guaranteed as of right to every citizen." A functional approach, Trudeau thought, might produce a "less passionate people's consensus." He ended the original draft by extolling the virtues of an entrenched bill of rights.

85. Trudeau, "Federalism, Nationalism and Reason," 192.

86. Ibid., 203

87. Ibid., 202–3.

88. What is interesting about Trudeau's social thought is the degree to which he failed to apply utilitarian principles and criteria.

89. Quoted in Powe, *Mystic Trudeau*, 38.

90. Trudeau, "Justice in our Time; Remarks on Aboriginal and Treaty Rights," in *Ethical Issues: Perspectives for Canadians*, ed. Eldon Soifer (Peterborough, ON: Broadview, 1992), 296. Trudeau gave the speech in Vancouver in August 1969.

91. Ibid.

92. Trudeau, "Le Québec et le problème constitutionnel," 38.

93. Ibid., 17.

94. Ibid., 37.

95. Charles Taylor, interview with Evan Solomon, CBC TV, "Power and Politics," October 2, 2013.

96. English argues that a French journalist, Claude Julien, was especially influential in this regard. See English, *Citizen*, 404.

97. Trudeau, "Le Québec et le problème constitutionnel," 36.

98. Ibid., 18.

99. Ibid., 38.

100. See Ernest Gellner, *Nations and Nationalism* (Ithaca and London: Cornell University Press, 1983) and *Conditions of Liberty: Civil Society and its Rivals* (London: Hamish Hamilton, 1994), and Will Kymlicka, *Multicultural Citizenship: A Liberal Theory of Minority Rights* (Oxford: Clarendon Press, 1995).

101. Trudeau, "Le Québec et le problème constitutionnel," 51–52.

102. Ibid., 48–50.

103. Ibid., 50.

104. Judy La Marsh has a good chapter on this in her *Memoirs of a Bird in a Gilded Cage* (Toronto: McClelland and Stewart, 1968), 77–99.

105. Government of Canada, *Federal–Provincial Grants and the Spending Power of Parliament* (Ottawa: Government of Canada, 1969), 32.

106. See Eric Hobsbawm, *Nations and Nationalism since 1780: Programme, Myth, Reality* (Cambridge: Cambridge University Press, 1990).

107. Conor Cruise O'Brien used the phrase in *The Siege: The Saga of Israel and Zionism* (New York: Simon and Schuster, 1986).

Chapter 9

1. Gérard Pelletier, *Le temps des choix: 1960–1968* (Montréal: Les éditions internationales Alain Sanké, 1986), 218.

2. Cook, *Teeth of Time*, 29.

3. Pelletier, *Le temps*, 201–26; Vastel, *The Outsider*, 105–9; Peter Stursberg, *Lester Pearson and the Dream of Unity* (Toronto: Doubleday Canada, 1976), 253–59.

4. Pelletier, *Le temps*, 212.

5. Brittain, "The Champions"; John Yorston, "Trudeau Choice in Mt. Royal," *Montreal Star*, October 8, 1965.

6. Pierre Trudeau and Gérard Pelletier, "Pelletier et Trudeau s'expliquent," *Cité Libre* 15, no. 80 (1965): 3–6. Marchand believed it was better not to answer the critics but Trudeau and Pelletier thought otherwise.

7. Pelletier, *Le temps*, 219.

8. Trudeau was fond of the quotation because he also used it at the beginning of *Les cheminements de la politique*. It is found at paragraph 347 of *The Republic*. F.M. Cornford translated the original Greek as follows: "And the heaviest penalty for declining to rule is to be ruled by someone inferior to yourself." My colleague, Robert Gold, offered the following literal translation: "The greatest part of the penalty is to be ruled by a more knavish individual, if he [the good man] himself is unwilling to rule."

9. The words they used were *insignifiants*, *racaille*, and *combinards*. The last two can mean "rabble" and "tricksters."

10. What they failed to notice was that in that case almost anyone would be an improvement.

11. Trudeau and Pelletier, "Pelletier et Trudeau," 3.

12. Benda, *The Treason of the Intellectuals*, 44.

13. Trudeau, "La nouvelle trahison," 184.

14. Trudeau, *The Essential Trudeau*, 2–3.

15. John Stuart Mill, *The Subjection of Women* (London: Longman, Green, Reader and Dyer, 1869), 54.

16. Trudeau and Pelletier, "Pelletier et Trudeau," 3.

17. Ibid., 3–4.

18. Ibid., 4.

19. Ibid., 5.

20. Trudeau, *Memoirs*, 72–77.

21. Ibid., 76. Marchand too would not have stood for the Liberals in such circumstances.

22. Ibid., 70.

23. Trudeau, *Memoirs*, 77. The article to which Trudeau alluded was likely "Some Obstacles to Democracy in Quebec," written in 1958, where he referred to "the shameful incompetence of the average MP from Quebec," and the caucus in general as "trained donkeys." See Trudeau, "Some Obstacles," *Federalism*, 120

24. A later instructive version is found in Pierre Elliott Trudeau, "Causerie aux jeunes C.C.F.," March 6, 1953, TP 26.1.

25. Many of these ideas are to be found in his earliest contributions to *Cité Libre*: "Politique fonctionelle," and "Politique fonctionelle II."

26. Trudeau, "A Democratic Manifesto," October 1958, TP 28.11.

27. Trudeau, "Réflexions," 68–69.

28. European opinion too in the early years after the war was doubtful about the inevitability of prosperity and democracy. See Tony Judt, *Postwar: A History of Europe since 1945* (New York: Penguin, 2005), 236.

29. See Laski, *European Liberalism*, 247–48.

30. Trudeau, "Notes de voyage, à propos de condition humaine," TP 11.21; "Évitez d'être Anglais, *Le Devoir*, February 1, 1952.

31. Trudeau, *Conversation with Canadians*, 14.

32. Trudeau's essay on "Quebec and the Constitutional Problem" in 1965 has extensive commentary about technology.

33. Trudeau, "The Practice and Theory of Federalism," 145.

34. Pelletier, *Impatience*, passim.

35. Trudeau, "L'élection fédérale du 10 août 1953: prodromes et conjectures," *Cité Libre* 3, no. 8 (1953): 1–9.

36. Ibid., 1–2.

37. Trudeau, "Épilogue," *La grève*, 393.

38. This was not just a convoluted evaluation of the Conscription Crisis but a rather uncritical one too because as late as 1962 Trudeau saw it as a sign of English-Canadian perfidy and anti-democracy.

39. Trudeau, "L'élection fédérale," 3.

40. Ibid., 4.

41. Ibid., 8.

42. Ibid., 7–8.

43. Ibid., 9–10.

44. The quotation is by Bernard Williams and is used by Tony Judt in his "What is living and dead in social democracy?," *New York Review of Books* 56, no. 20, December 17, 2009, 92.

45. Trudeau, "Diefenbaker monte en ballon," *Cité Libre* 11, no. 26 (1960), 15.

46. Trudeau, "Pearson ou l'abdication de l'esprit," *Cité Libre* 14, no. 56 (1963), 9.

47. The analysis here is based on the following sources, all of them by Trudeau: "L'élection fédérale du 10 août 1953: prodromes et conjectures," *Cité Libre* 3, no. 8 (1953); "Pour la conférence Migneault," February 2, 1954, TP 27.7; "Sur la politique" September 1954, TP 22.9, 1–10; "Some obstacles," *Federalism*, 114–23; "À l'ouest rien de nouveau," *Cité Libre* 12, no. 34 (1961); "Note sur la conjuncture politique"; "Pearson."

48. "The new Liberal platform" was the subject of the first meeting between Ramsay Cook and Trudeau at a wedding in Ottawa in April 1961. Trudeau, he says "thought the new program represented signs that the Liberals were returning to reform." Cook, *Teeth of Time*, 14.

49. Trudeau, "Sur la politique: lettre à un ouvrier, à une dame et à un curé," TP 22.9.

50. Here the composite is derived from the following sources: "Réflexions," 67–68; "Sur la politique"; "Le congrès de la Fédération Libérale provincial," 1956, TP 22.34; "Causerie prononcée à Radio Canada," 15 June 1956, TP 25.14, 1–6; "Notes sur le Congrès libéral provincial" *Vrai*, June 14, 1958, 12; "Un manifeste démocratique," *Cité Libre* 9, no. 22 (1958), 1–31; "Notes sur l'élection provinciale," *Cité Libre*, 11, no. 28 (1960), 12–13.

51. Trudeau, "Un manifeste démocratique," 5–8.

52. Trudeau, "Le congrès," 1–7.

53. Trudeau, "Notes sur le Congrès," 12.

54. See also Dale C. Thomson, *Jean Lesage and the Quiet Revolution* (Toronto: Macmillan, 1984), 72.

55. Trudeau, "Some obstacles," *Federalism*, 119.

56. Ibid., 119–29.

57. Trudeau, "Pearson," 7.

58. Ibid., 10.

59. Ibid., 12.

60. See Trudeau, "Note sur la conjoncture politique," *Cité Libre* 13, no. 49 (1962): 2–4.

61. Trudeau, "Réflexions," 69–70; "Un manifeste démocratique," *Cité Libre* 9, no. 22 (1958): 10–12.

62. Trudeau, "The Practice and Theory of Federalism," 129. See also Trudeau, "Un manifeste démocratique," passim.

63. Trudeau, "Un manifeste démocratique," 28–29.

64. Trudeau, *Memoirs*, 70.

65. Trudeau, "Un manifeste démocratique," 2.

66. Ibid.

67. Trudeau, "Un manifeste démocratique," 29.

68. Trudeau, *Memoirs*, 70.

69. Cook has expressed his views in "Approaches to Politics after Forty Years," and "Introduction" to *Approaches to Politics* (Don Mills, ON: Oxford University Press, 2010).

70. Behiels, *Prelude*, 254–56, 269–75; English, *Citizen*, 312–15, 321–23, 330–31, 340–41.

71. Behiels, *Prelude*, 268–70.

72. Quoted in English, *Citizen*, 331.

73. Casgrain, *A Woman*, 139. Grace Trudeau, Trudeau's mother, accompanied Casgrain on a trip to Asia in the mid-1950s.

74. Nemni and Nemni, *Trudeau Transformed*, 385.

75. Trudeau, "Un manifeste démocratique," 1–31.

76. Ibid., 9.

77. Ibid., 8–9. The daughters of Danaïdes murdered their husbands and were punished in Hades. They were forced to carry water from the Styx in leaky jars. Trudeau was obviously making a point about futility.

78. Ibid., 9.

79. Ibid., 23–24.

80. In the 1960 provincial election only one Social Democrat ran, in Abitibi East.

81. Trudeau, "Notes sur l'élection provinciale," *Cité Libre* 11, no. 28 (1960): 13.

82. Ibid., 12.

83. Trudeau, "L'élection du 22 juin 1960," *Cité Libre* 11, no. 29 (1960): 3–8. Trudeau's estimate was that if the votes given to the PSD and other fringe parties in 1956 were to have gone to them again in 1960 the Liberals would have had five fewer seats and the Union Nationale would have won the election. Of course that assumed that everything else would have held constant. See ibid., 4.

84. "La Restauration," *Cité Libre* 11, no. 33 (1961): 1–3.

85. Pierre Elliott Trudeau, "L'homme de gauche et les élections provinciales," *Cité Libre* 13, no. 51 (1962): 3–5.

86. Ibid., 4.

87. Ibid.

88. English, *Citizen*, 378.

89. Trudeau, "L'homme de gauche et les élections provinciales," 5.

90. Trudeau, "La nouvelle trahison," 178.

91. Avishai Margalit, *On Compromise and Rotten Compromises* (Princeton and Oxford: Princeton University Press, 2010), 5.

92. Trudeau, "L'homme de gauche," 4.

93. TP 31.1.

94. In Trudeau's papers there is a receipt for the contribution. Apparently the NDP thought it was for the purchase of a membership in the party and Trudeau duly received a membership card dated 1965. Helpfully Trudeau made clear for future historians that there had been a mistake. On the envelope, in Trudeau's handwriting, is an explanation: he had made the contribution of behalf of "Chuck" Taylor and someone had sent him a membership card without him asking for it. See TP 28.27.

95. I have relied on two collections of Dewey's writings, *Liberalism and*

Social Action and *The Political Writings,* ed. Debra Morris and Ian Shapiro (Indianapolis and Cambridge: Hackett, 1993).

96. See especially Bernard Williams, *In the Beginning Was the Deed: Realism and Moralism in Political Argument* (Princeton and Oxford: Princeton University Press, 2005), 1–28, 52–74.

97. Ramsay Cook, correspondence with the author, August 24, 2014.

98. Trudeau and Pelletier, "Pelletier et Trudeau s'expliquent," 3. This instrumentalist way of thinking might be thought to detract from what Charles Taylor calls the "republican" model of politics. For Taylor political participation is part of the intrinsically fulfilling dimension of politics and not just a means to an end.

99. Interestingly the main argument of Trudeau in *La grève de l'amiante* was a McLuhanesque insight about how economic and technological realities determine the consciousness of the people who live under them. Urban, industrial Quebec produced in its citizens a social democratic consciousness. That is, new media give forth new cognitions. Trudeau's claim was that Quebecers had learned to adapt to a new techno-economic environment in spite of the "rear-view mirror" mentality of the Church and nationalist intellectuals and organizations. As McLuhan once put it, humans always live ahead of their thinking. Of course for McLuhan the transition in Quebec was about a move from a preliterate, organic, and oral culture to one that was literate, individualistic, print-based, and mechanical. In Trudeau's Papers there is a marked copy of a brief that McLuhan had submitted to the Bilingualism and Biculturalism Commission in 1963 in which he talked about the role of media in the transformation of Quebec; M. McLuhan, "The Effects of the Influences of Centralism and Decentralism in Canadian Society," TP 28.24.

100. The distinction again is Avishai Margalit's.

Chapter 10

1. Christo Aivalis, "In the Name of Liberalism: Pierre Trudeau, Organized Labour, and the Canadian Social Democratic Left, 1949–1959," *The Canadian Historical Review* 94, June 2, 2013, 263–88.

2. Ibid., 265.

3. Ibid., 269.

4. Trudeau, *The Constitution and the People of Canada: An Approach to the Objectives of Confederation, the Rights of the People and the Institutions of Government* (Ottawa: Government of Canada, 1969), 4, 10.

5. Ibid., 6, 10.

6. Ibid., 12–14.

Index